ADDITIONAL PRAISE FOR *THE ZERO MARGINAL COST SOCIETY*

"An amazing work. . . . This insightful, surprising, and practical book helps us understand how the emerging Internet of Things is driving extreme productivity, the rush to a near zero marginal cost society, and the rise of a new economic paradigm. Rifkin solves the puzzle of what companies, nonprofit organizations, and governments need to do to reposition themselves on the new Collaborative Commons. The book is a must read for every citizen and decision maker."

—*Jerry Wind, the Wharton School*

"Free-market traditionalists have trouble recognizing that the future of governance and economics lies with the Commons—a world of collaboration, sharing, ecological concern and human connection. Jeremy Rifkin deftly describes the powerful forces that are driving this new paradigm and transforming our personal lives and the economy. A highly readable account of the next big turn of the wheel."

—*David Bollier, author of* Think Like a Commoner: A Short Introduction to the Life of the Commons

"Brilliantly tackled. . . . Rifkin describes how the dramatic lowering of transaction, communication, and coordination costs allow the global scaling of small group dynamics, fundamentally changing the choices that humanity can make for its social organization. Read it, rejoice, and take action to build the new world in which the market and the state are not destroying the Commons, but aligned with it."

—*Michel Bauwens, founder of P2P Foundation*

"Jeremy Rifkin has always been ahead of the curve. In *The Zero Marginal Cost Society*, Rifkin takes us on a journey to the future, beyond consumerism to 'prosumers' who produce what they consume and share what they have on a Collaborative Commons, a contemporary expression of Gandhi's 'Swadeshi.' His down to earth vision of democratizing innovation and creativity on a global scale, for the well-being of all, is inspiring and, equally important, doable."

—*Vandana Shiva, environmental activist and recipient of the Right Livelihood Award*

"If you want to understand why we are in the midst of a massive paradigm shift from an age of top-down, centralized institutions to a world of distributed and collaborative power, I would highly recommend reading Jeremy Rifkin's new book. He clearly joins the dots on how the likes of 3D printing, crowdfunding, and online education platforms are all connected and describes the disruptions that lie just around the corner for most sectors."

—*Rachel Botsman, author of* What's Mine is Yours:
How Collaborative Consumption Is Changing The Way We Live

"Jeremy Rifkin understands that it's people and communities who are at the heart of the new economic paradigm. People all over the world are building the collaborative economy and Rifkin's thoughtful analysis further illustrates that this is an idea whose time has come."

—*Natalie Foster, executive director of peers.org*

THE
ZERO MARGINAL
COST SOCIETY

THE
ZERO MARGINAL
COST SOCIETY

THE INTERNET OF THINGS,
THE COLLABORATIVE COMMONS,
AND THE ECLIPSE OF CAPITALISM

JEREMY RIFKIN

 St. Martin's Griffin ☭ New York

www.stmartins.com

Designed by Letra Libre, Inc.

The Library of Congress has cataloged the hardcover edition as follows:

Rifkin, Jeremy.
    The zero marginal cost society : the internet of things, the collaborative commons, and the eclipse of capitalism / Jeremy Rifkin.
        p.   cm.
    ISBN 978-1-137-27846-3 (hardcover)
    1. Capitalism. 2. Cost. 3. Cooperation. I. Title.
    HB501.R555   2014
    330.12'6—dc23

                                                              2013033940

ISBN 978-1-137-28011-4 (trade paperback)

Our books may be purchased in bulk for promotional, educational, or business use. Please contact your local bookseller or the Macmillan Corporate and Premium Sales Department at 1-800-221-7945, extension 5442, or by e-mail at MacmillanSpecialMarkets@macmillan.com.

First published by Palgrave Macmillan, a division of St. Martin's Press LLC

First St. Martin's Griffin Edition: July 2015

D   10   9   8

CONTENTS

ACKNOWLEDGMENTS

I would like to thank Lisa Mankowsky and Shawn Moorhead for the extraordinary work they did in overseeing and editing *The Zero Marginal Cost Society*. Virtually every book is a collaborative effort. An author's effectiveness depends, to a great extent, on the individuals who work with him in the preparation of a manuscript. Mr. Moorhead and Ms. Mankowsky are a dream team. Mr. Moorhead paid particular attention to ensuring the proper integration of themes and conceptual details throughout the book. Ms. Mankowsky focused on ensuring a smooth editorial flow throughout the narrative and consistency in the presentation. Their dedication to the project, keen editorial advice, and wise counsel were instrumental in shaping the final content. Their contributions can be found on every page of the final book.

I would also like to thank Christian Pollard, who not only assisted in the editorial preparation of the book, but who also developed an elegant marketing and outreach campaign for its publication.

We had the opportunity of working with some very talented interns during the two-year preparation of *The Zero Marginal Cost Society*. Their contributions added significantly to the value of the final work. Thanks to Dan Michell, Alexandra Martin, Jared Madden, Elizabeth Ortega, James Partlow, Shuyang "Cherry" Yu, James Najarian, Daniel McGowan, Gannon McHenry, Kevin Gardner, Justin Green, and Stan Kozlowski.

I'd also like to thank my editor, Emily Carleton, at Palgrave Macmillan, for her enthusiasm for the project and her many insightful editorial suggestions along the way that helped hone the manuscript. Thanks to my publisher, Karen Wolny, for her unflagging support throughout the process.

Finally, as always, I'd like to thank my wife, Carol Grunewald, for the many fruitful conversations during the preparation of the book that helped shape my thinking and tighten the arguments in the text. Quite frankly, Carol is the best editor and wordsmith I've ever known.

Writing this book was a pleasure and a true labor of love. I hope readers will enjoy the book as much as I enjoyed writing it.

CHAPTER ONE
THE GREAT PARADIGM SHIFT FROM MARKET CAPITALISM TO THE COLLABORATIVE COMMONS

apitalism is giving birth to a progeny. It is called the sharing economy on the Collaborative Commons. This is the first new economic system to enter onto the world stage since the advent of capitalism and socialism in the early nineteenth century, making it a remarkable historical event. The Collaborative Commons is already changing the way we organize economic life, offering the possibility of dramatically narrowing the income divide, democratizing the global economy, and creating a more ecologically sustainable society.

Like every parent-child relationship, the two economic systems generally cooperate but occasionally are at odds. And while the capitalist parent will need to nurture its child and allow it to mature, the child will also transform the parent in this unfolding relationship. We are already witnessing the emergence of a hybrid economy, part capitalist market and part sharing economy on the Collaborative Commons.

To the extent that capitalism can create new business models and practices that will support the development of the sharing economy, it will
prosper along with its offspring.

What is becoming increasingly clear is that the capitalist system
that provided both a compelling narrative of human nature and the
overarching organizational framework for the day-to-day commercial,
social, and political life of society—spanning more than ten generations—has peaked and begun its slow decline. Although the indicators
of the great transformation to a new economic system are still soft
and largely anecdotal, the Collaborative Commons is ascendant, and
by 2050, it will likely settle in as the primary arbiter of economic life
in most of the world. An increasingly streamlined and savvy capitalist system will continue to thrive and find sufficient vulnerabilities to
exploit, primarily as an aggregator of network services and solutions,
allowing it to flourish as a powerful partner in the new economic era;
but it will no longer reign. We are entering a world partially beyond
markets where we are learning how to live together in an increasingly
interdependent global Collaborative Commons.

I understand that this seems utterly incredible to most people,
so conditioned have we become to the belief that capitalism is as
indispensable to our well-being as the air we breathe. But despite
the best efforts of philosophers and economists over the centuries to
attribute their operating assumptions to the same laws that govern
nature, economic paradigms are just human constructs, not natural
phenomena.

As economic paradigms go, capitalism has had a good run. Although its timeline has been relatively short compared to other economic paradigms in history, it's fair to say that its impact on the
human journey, both positive and negative, has been more dramatic
and far-reaching than perhaps any other economic era in history, save
for the shift from foraging/hunting to an agricultural way of life.

Ironically, capitalism's decline is not coming at the hands of hos-
tile forces. There are no hordes at the front gates ready to tear down
the walls of the capitalist edifice. Quite the contrary. What's under-
mining the capitalist system is the dramatic success of the very operating assumptions that govern it. At the heart of capitalism there lies
a contradiction in the driving mechanism that has propelled it ever
upward to commanding heights, but now is speeding it to its death.

THE ECLIPSE OF CAPITALISM

Capitalism's raison d'être is to bring every aspect of human life into the economic arena, where it is transformed into a commodity to be exchanged as property in the marketplace. Very little of the human endeavor has been spared this transformation. The food we eat, the water we drink, the artifacts we make and use, the social relationships we engage in, the ideas we bring forth, the time we expend, and even the DNA that determines so much of who we are have all been thrown into the capitalist cauldron, where they are reorganized, assigned a price, and delivered to the market. Through most of history, markets were occasional meeting places where goods were exchanged. Today, virtually every aspect of our daily lives is connected in some way to commercial exchanges. The market defines us.

But here lies the contradiction. Capitalism's operating logic is designed to fail by succeeding. Let me explain.

In his magnum opus, *The Wealth of Nations*, Adam Smith, the father of modern capitalism, posits that the market operates in much the same way as the laws governing gravity, as discovered by Isaac Newton. Just as in nature, where for every action there is an equal and opposite reaction, so too do supply and demand balance each other in the self-regulating marketplace. If consumer demand for goods and services goes up, sellers will raise their prices accordingly. If the sellers' prices become too high, demand will drop, forcing sellers to lower the prices.

The French Enlightenment philosopher Jean-Baptiste Say, another early architect of classical economic theory, added a second assumption, again borrowing a metaphor from Newtonian physics. Say reasoned that economic activity was self-perpetuating, and that as in Newton's first law, once economic forces are set in motion, they remain in motion unless acted upon by outside forces. He argued that "a product is no sooner created, than it, from that instant, affords a market for other products to the full extent of its own value. . . . The creation of one product immediately opens a vent for other products."[1] A later generation of neoclassical economists refined Say's Law by asserting that new technologies increase productivity, allowing the seller to produce more goods at a cheaper cost per unit. The increased supply of cheaper goods then creates its own demand and, in the process, forces competitors to invent their own technologies to increase productivity in order to sell their goods even more cheaply and win back or draw in new customers (or both). The entire process operates like a perpetual-motion machine. Cheaper prices, resulting from new technology and increased productivity, mean more money left over for consumers to spend elsewhere, which spurs a fresh round of competition among sellers.

There is a caveat, however. These operating principles assume a competitive market. If one or a few sellers are able to outgrow and eliminate their competition and establish a monopoly or oligopoly in the market—especially if their goods and services are essential—they can keep prices artificially high, knowing that buyers will have little alternative. In this situation, the monopolist has scant need or inclination to bring on new labor-saving technologies to advance productivity, reduce prices, and remain competitive. We've seen this happen repeatedly throughout history, if only for short periods of time.

In the long run, however, new players invariably come along and introduce breakthroughs in technology that increase productivity and lower prices for similar or alternative goods and services, and break the monopolistic hold on the market.

Yet suppose we carry these guiding assumptions of capitalist economic theory to their logical conclusion. Imagine a scenario in which the operating logic of the capitalist system succeeds beyond anyone's wildest expectations and the competitive process leads to "extreme productivity" and what economists call the "optimum general welfare"— an endgame in which intense competition forces the introduction of ever-leaner technology, boosting productivity to the optimum point in which each additional unit introduced for sale approaches "near zero" marginal cost. In other words, the cost of actually producing each additional unit—if fixed costs are not counted—becomes essentially zero, making the product nearly free. If that were to happen, profit, the life-blood of capitalism, would dry up.

In a market-exchange economy, profit is made at the margins. For example, as an author, I sell my intellectual work product to a publisher in return for an advance and future royalties on my book. The book then goes through several hands on the way to the end buyer, including an outside copyeditor, compositor, printer, as well as wholesalers, distributors, and retailers. Each party in this process is marking up the transaction costs to include a profit margin large enough to justify their participation.

But what if the marginal cost of producing and distributing a book plummeted to near zero? In fact, it's already happening. A growing number of authors are writing books and making them available at a very small price, or even for free, on the Internet—bypassing publishers, editors, printers, wholesalers, distributors, and retailers. The cost of marketing and distributing each copy is nearly free. The only cost is the amount of time consumed by creating the product and the cost of computing and connecting online. An e-book can be produced and distributed at near zero marginal cost.

The near zero marginal cost phenomenon has already wreaked havoc on the publishing, communications, and entertainment industries as more and more information is being made available nearly free to billions of people. Today, more than one-third of the human race is producing its own information on relatively cheap cellphones and computers and sharing it via video, audio, and text at near zero marginal cost in a collaborative networked world. And now the zero marginal cost revolution is beginning to affect other commercial sectors, including renewable energy, 3D printing in manufacturing, and online higher education. There are already millions of "prosumers"—consumers who have become their own producers—generating their own green electricity at near zero marginal cost around the world. It's estimated that around 100,000 hobbyists are manufacturing their own goods using 3D printing at nearly zero marginal cost.[2] Meanwhile, six million students are currently enrolled in free Massive Open Online Courses (MOOCs) that operate at near zero marginal cost and are taught by some of the most distinguished professors in the world, and receiving college credits. In all three instances, while the up-front costs are still relatively high, these sectors are riding exponential growth curves, not unlike the exponential curve that reduced the marginal cost of computing to near zero over the past several decades. Within the next two to three decades, prosumers in vast continental and global networks will be producing and sharing green energy as well as physical goods and services, and learning in online virtual classrooms at near zero marginal cost, bringing the economy into an era of nearly free goods and services.

Many of the leading players in the near zero marginal cost revolution argue that while nearly free goods and services will become far more prevalent, they will also open up new possibilities for creating other goods and services at sufficient profit margins to maintain growth and even allow the capitalistic system to flourish. Chris Anderson, the former editor of *Wired* magazine, reminds us that giveaway products have long been used to draw potential customers into purchasing other goods, citing the example of Gillette, the first mass producer of disposable razors. Gillette gave away the razors to hook consumers into buying the blades that fit the devices.[3]

Similarly, today's performing artists often allow their music to be shared freely online by millions of people with the hope of developing loyal fans who will pay to attend their live concerts. *The New York Times* and *The Economist* provide some free online articles to millions of people in anticipation that a percentage of the readers will choose to pay for more detailed reporting by subscribing. "Free," in this sense, is a marketing device to build a customer base for paid purchases.

These aspirations are shortsighted, and perhaps even naïve. As more and more of the goods and services that make up the economic life of society edge toward near zero marginal cost and become almost free, the capitalist market will continue to shrink into more narrow niches where profit-making enterprises survive only at the edges of the economy, relying on a diminishing consumer base for very specialized products and services.

The reluctance to come to grips with near zero marginal cost is understandable. Many, though not all, of the old guard in the commercial arena can't imagine how economic life would proceed in a world where most goods and services are nearly free, profit is defunct, property is meaningless, and the market is superfluous. What then?

Some are just beginning to ask that question. They might find some solace in the fact that several of the great architects of modern economic thinking glimpsed the problem long ago. John Maynard Keynes, Robert Heilbroner, and Wassily Leontief, to name a few, pondered the critical contradiction that drove capitalism forward. They wondered whether, in the distant future, new technologies might so boost productivity and lower prices as to create the coming state of affairs.

Oskar Lange, a University of Chicago professor of the early twentieth century, captured a sense of the conundrum underlying a mature capitalism in which the search for new technological innovations to advance productivity and cheapen prices put the system at war with itself. Writing in 1936, in the throes of the Great Depression, he asked whether the institution of private ownership of the means of production would continue indefinitely to foster economic progress, or whether at a certain stage of technological development the very success of the system would become a shackle to its further advance.[4]

Lange noted that when an entrepreneur introduces technological innovations that allow him to lower the price of goods and services, he gains a temporary advantage over competitors strapped with antiquated means of production, resulting in the devaluation of the older investments they are locked into. This forces them to respond by introducing their own technological innovations, again increasing productivity and cheapening prices and so on.

But in mature industries where a handful of enterprises have succeeded in capturing much of the market and forced a monopoly or oligopoly, they would have every interest in blocking further economic progress in order to protect the value of the capital already invested in outmoded technology. Lange observes that "when the maintenance of the value of the capital already invested becomes the chief concern of the entrepreneurs, further economic progress has to stop, or, at least, to slow down considerably. . . . This result will be even more accentuated when a part of the industries enjoy a monopoly position."[5]

Powerful industry leaders often strive to restrict entry of new enterprises and innovations. But slowing down or stopping new, more productive technologies to protect prior capital investments creates a positive-feedback loop by preventing capital from investing in profitable new opportunities. If capital can't migrate to new profitable investments, the economy goes into a protracted stall.

Lange described the struggle that pits capitalist against capitalist in stark terms. He writes:

> The stability of the capitalist system is shaken by the alternation of attempts to stop economic progress in order to protect old investments and tremendous collapses when those attempts fail.[6]

Attempts to block economic progress invariably fail because new entrepreneurs are continually roaming the edges of the system in search of innovations that increase productivity and reduce costs, allowing them to win over consumers with cheaper prices than those of their competitors. The race Lange outlines is relentless over the long run, with productivity continually pushing costs and prices down, forcing profit margins to shrink.

While most economists today would look at an era of nearly free goods and services with a sense of foreboding, a few earlier economists expressed a guarded enthusiasm over the prospect. Keynes, the venerable twentieth-century economist whose economic theories still hold considerable weight, penned a small essay in 1930 entitled "Economic Possibilities for Our Grandchildren," which appeared as millions of Americans were beginning to sense that the sudden economic downturn of 1929 was in fact the beginning of a long plunge to the bottom.

Keynes observed that new technologies were advancing productivity and reducing the cost of goods and services at an unprecedented rate. They were also dramatically reducing the amount of human labor needed to produce goods and services. Keynes even introduced a new term, which, he told his readers, they "will hear a great deal in the years to come—namely, *technological unemployment*. This means unemployment due to our discovery of means of economising the use of labour outrunning the pace at which we can find new uses for labour." Keynes hastened to add that technological unemployment, while vexing in the short run, is a great boon in the long run because it means *"that mankind is solving its economic problem."*[7]

Keynes believed that "a point may soon be reached, much sooner perhaps than we are all of us aware of, when these [economic] needs are satisfied in the sense that we prefer to devote our further energies to non-economic purposes."[8] He looked expectantly to a future in which machines would produce an abundance of nearly free goods and services, liberating the human race from toil and hardships and freeing the human mind from a preoccupation with strictly pecuniary interests to focus more on the "arts for life" and the quest for transcendence.

Both Lange and Keynes foresaw, back in the 1930s, the schizophrenia that lies at the nucleus of the capitalist system: the inherent entrepreneurial dynamism of competitive markets that drives productivity up and marginal costs down. Economists have long understood that the most efficient economy is one in which consumers pay only for the marginal cost of the goods they purchase. But if consumers pay only for the marginal cost and those costs continue to race toward zero, businesses would not be able to ensure a return on their investment and sufficient profit to satisfy their shareholders. That being the case, market leaders would attempt to gain market dominance to ensure a monopoly hold so they could impose prices higher than the marginal cost of the products they're selling, thus preventing the invisible hand from hurrying the market along to the most efficient economy of near zero marginal cost and the prospect of nearly free goods and services. This catch-22 is the inherent contradiction that underlies capitalist theory and practice.

Eighty years after Lange and Keynes made their observations, contemporary economists are once again peering into the contradictory workings of the capitalist system, unsure of how to make the market economy function without self-destructing in the wake of new technologies that are speeding society into a near zero marginal cost era.

Lawrence Summers, U.S. secretary of the treasury during President Bill Clinton's administration and former president of Harvard University, and J. Bradford DeLong, a professor of economics at the University of California, Berkeley, revisited the capitalist dilemma in a joint paper delivered at the Federal Reserve Bank of Kansas City's symposium, "Economic Policy for the Information Economy," in August 2001. This time, there was much more at stake as the new information technologies and the incipient Internet communication revolution were threatening to take the capitalist system to a near zero marginal cost reality in the coming decades.

Summers and DeLong's concerns focused on the emerging data-processing and communication technologies. They wrote that these "seismic innovations" were forcing a wholesale reconfiguration of commercial life, with potential impacts whose expanse rivaled the advent of electricity. The technological changes afoot, according to Summers and DeLong, were likely to dramatically push down marginal costs, which became the departure point for their discussion. They accepted that "the most basic condition for economic efficiency . . . [is] that price equal marginal cost."[9] They further conceded that "with information goods, the social and marginal cost of distribution is close to zero."[10] Now the paradox: Summers and DeLong argued that

> if information goods are to be distributed at their marginal cost of production—zero—they cannot be created and produced by entrepreneurial firms that use revenues obtained from sales to consumers to cover their [fixed set-up] costs. If information goods are to be created and produced . . . [companies] must be able to anticipate selling their products at a profit to someone.[11]

Summers and DeLong opposed government subsidies to cover the upfront costs, arguing that the shortcomings of "administrative bureaucracy," "group-think," and "red-tape" "destroy the entrepreneurial energy of the market."[12]

In lieu of government intervention, the two distinguished economists reluctantly suggested that perhaps the best way to protect innovation in an economy where "goods are produced under conditions of substantial increasing returns to scale" was to favor short-term natural monopolies.[13] Summers and DeLong made the point that "temporary monopoly power and profits are the reward needed to spur private enterprise to engage in such innovation."[14] They both realized the bind this put private enterprise in, admitting that "natural monopoly does not meet the most basic conditions for economic efficiency: that price equal marginal cost."[15] Indeed, the modus operandi of a monopoly, as every economist knows, is to hold back would-be competitors from introducing new innovations that increase productivity, reduce marginal costs, and lower the price to customers. Nonetheless, Summers and DeLong concluded that in the "new economy" this might be the only way forward. In an incredible admission, the two acknowledged that "the right way to think about this complex set of issues is not clear, but it is clear that the competitive paradigm cannot be fully appropriate . . . but we do not yet know what the right replacement paradigm will be."[16]

Summers and DeLong found themselves hopelessly trapped. Although economists and entrepreneurs never intended for the capitalist system to self-destruct (they expected it to reign forever), a careful look at its operating logic reveals the inevitability of a future of near zero marginal cost. A near zero marginal cost society is the optimally efficient state for promoting the general welfare and represents the ultimate triumph of capitalism. Its moment of triumph, however, also marks its inescapable passage from the world stage. While capitalism is far from putting itself out of business, it's apparent that as it brings us ever closer to a near zero marginal cost society, its once unchallenged prowess is diminishing, making way for an entirely new way of organizing economic life in an age characterized by abundance rather than scarcity.

CHANGING THE ECONOMIC PARADIGM

The most intriguing passage in Summers and DeLong's paper on the contradictions and challenges facing capitalist theory and practice in the unfolding Information Age is their comment that they "do not yet know what the right replacement paradigm will be." The fact that they were even alluding to the likelihood of a new replacement paradigm is suggestive of the anomalies that are building up and casting a dark shadow on the long-term viability of the existing economic regime.

We are, it appears, in the early stages of a game-changing transformation in economic paradigms. A new economic model is emerging in the twilight of the capitalist era that is better suited to organize a society in which more and more goods and services are nearly free.

The term *paradigm shift* has been thrown around so much in recent years, in reference to virtually any kind of change, that it might be helpful to revisit the words of Thomas Kuhn, whose book *The Structure of Scientific Revolutions* made the word *paradigm* part of the general discourse. Kuhn described a paradigm as a system of beliefs and assumptions that operate together to establish an integrated and unified worldview that is so convincing and compelling that it is regarded as tantamount to reality itself. He used the term to refer to standard and nearly universally accepted models in science, like Newtonian physics and Darwinian evolution.[17]

A paradigm's narrative power rests on its all-encompassing description of reality. Once accepted, it becomes difficult, if not impossible, to question its central assumptions, which appear to reflect the natural order of things. Alternative explanations of the world are rarely entertained, as they fly in the face of what is accepted as unambiguous truth. But this unquestioning acceptance, and refusal to envision alternative explanations, leads to a festering of inconsistencies that pile up until a tipping point is reached where the existing paradigm is torn apart and replaced with a new explanatory paradigm better able to marshal the anomalies, insights, and new developments into a comprehensive new narrative.

The capitalist paradigm, long accepted as the best mechanism for promoting the efficient organization of economic activity, is now under siege on two fronts.

On the first front, a new generation of interdisciplinary scholarship that has brought together previously distinct fields—including the ecological sciences, chemistry, biology, engineering, architecture, urban planning, and information technology—is challenging standard economic theory (which is wedded to the metaphors of Newtonian physics) with a new theoretical economics grounded in the laws of thermodynamics. Standard capitalist theory is virtually silent on the indissoluble relationship between economic activity and the ecological constraints imposed by the laws of energy. In classical and neoclassical economic theory, the dynamics that govern Earth's biosphere are mere externalities to economic activity—small, adjustable factors of little real consequence to the working of the capitalist system as a whole.

Conventional economists fail to recognize that the laws of thermodynamics govern all economic activity. The first and second laws of thermodynamics state that "the total energy content of the universe is constant and the total entropy is continually increasing."[18] The first law, the conservation law, posits that energy can neither be created nor destroyed—that the amount of energy in the universe has remained the same since the beginning of time and will be until the end of time. While the energy remains fixed, it is continually changing form, but only in one direction, from available to unavailable. This is where the second law of thermodynamics comes into play. According to the second law, energy always flows from hot to cold, concentrated to dispersed, ordered to disordered. For example, if a chunk of coal is burned, the sum total of the energy remains constant, but is dispersed into the atmosphere in the form of carbon dioxide, sulfur dioxide, and other gases. While no energy is lost, the dispersed energy is no longer capable of performing useful work. Physicists refer to the no-longer-useable energy as entropy.

All economic activity comes from harnessing available energy in nature—in material, liquid, or gaseous form—and converting it into goods and services. At every step in the production, storage, and distribution process, energy is used to transform nature's resources into finished goods and services. Whatever energy is embedded in the product or service is at the expense of energy used and lost—the entropic bill—in moving the economic activity along the value chain. Eventually, the goods we produce are consumed, discarded, and recycled back into nature, again, with an increase in entropy. Engineers and chemists point out that in regard to economic activity there is never a net energy gain but always a loss in available energy in the process of converting nature's resources into economic value. The only question is: When does the bill come due?

The entropic bill for the Industrial Age has arrived. The accumulation in carbon dioxide emissions in the atmosphere from burning massive amounts of carbon energy has given rise to climate change and the wholesale destruction of the Earth's biosphere, throwing the existing economic model into question. The field of economics, by and large, has yet to confront the fact that economic activity is conditioned by the laws of thermodynamics. The profession's glaring misunderstanding of its own subject is what's forcing a rethinking of the paradigm by academics coming from other disciplines across the natural and social sciences. I dealt with this in more detail in my previous book, *The Third Industrial Revolution*, in a chapter entitled "Retiring Adam Smith."

On a second front, a powerful new technology platform is developing out of the bowels of the Second Industrial Revolution, speeding the central contradiction of capitalist ideology to the end game mentioned above. The coming together of the Communications Internet with a digitalized renewable Energy Internet and automated Transportation and Logistics Internet in a seamless twenty-first-century intelligent infrastructure—the Internet of Things (IoT)—is giving rise to a Third Industrial Revolution. The IoT is already boosting productivity to the point where the marginal cost of producing many goods and services is nearly zero, making them practically free and shareable on the emerging Collaborative Commons. The result is corporate profits are beginning to dry up, property rights are weakening, and an economy based on scarcity is slowly giving way to an economy of abundance.

THE INTERNET OF THINGS

The Internet of Things will connect every thing with everyone in an integrated global network. People, machines, natural resources, production lines, logistics networks, consumption habits, recycling flows, and virtually every other aspect of economic and social life will be linked via sensors and software to the IoT platform, continually feeding Big Data to every node—businesses, homes, vehicles—moment to moment, in real time. Big Data, in turn, will be processed with advanced analytics, transformed into predictive algorithms, and programmed into automated systems to improve thermodynamic efficiencies, dramatically increase productivity, and reduce the marginal cost of producing and delivering a full range of goods and services to near zero across the entire economy.

The Internet of Things European Research Cluster, a body set up by the European Commission, the executive body of the European Union, to help facilitate the transition into the new era of "ubiquitous computing," has mapped out some of the myriad ways the Internet of Things is already being deployed to connect the planet in a distributed global network.

The IoT is being introduced across industrial and commercial sectors. Companies are installing sensors all along the commercial corridor to monitor and track the flow of goods and services. For example, UPS uses Big Data to keep up to the moment with its 60,000 vehicles in the United States. The logistics giant embeds sensors in their vehicles to monitor individual parts for signs of potential malfunction or fatigue so they can replace them before a costly breakdown on the road occurs.[19]

Sensors record and communicate the availability of raw resources, inform the front office on current inventories in the warehouses, and troubleshoot dysfunctions on the production lines. Other sensors report on the moment to moment changes in the use of electricity by appliances in businesses and households, and their impact on the price of electricity on the transmission grid. Electricity consumers can program their appliances to reduce their power consumption or switch off during peak periods of electricity use on the power lines to prevent a dramatic spike in the electricity price or even a brownout across the grid and receive a credit on their next month's electricity bill.

Sensors in retail outlets keep the sales and marketing departments apprised of which items are being looked at, handled, put back on shelves, or purchased to gauge consumer behavior. Other sensors track the whereabouts of products shipped to retailers and consumers and keep tabs on the amount of waste being recycled and processed for reuse. The Big Data is analyzed 24/7 to recalibrate supply chain inventories, production and distribution processes, and to initiate new business practices to increase thermodynamic efficiencies and productivity across the value chain.

The IoT is also beginning to be used to create smart cities. Sensors measure vibrations and material conditions in buildings, bridges, roads, and other infrastructure to assess the structural health of the built environment and when to make needed repairs. Other sensors track noise pollution from neighborhood to neighborhood, monitor traffic congestion on streets, and pedestrian density on sidewalks to optimize driving and walking routes. Sensors placed along street curbs inform drivers of the availability of parking spaces. Smart roads and intelligent highways keep drivers up to date on accidents and traffic delays. Insurance companies are beginning to experiment with placing sensors in vehicles to provide data on the time of day they are being used, the locations they are in, and the distances traveled over a given period of time to predict risk and determine insurance rates.[20] Sensors embedded in public lighting allow them to brighten and dim in response to the ambient lighting in the surrounding environment. Sensors are even being placed in garbage cans to ascertain the amount of rubbish in order to optimize waste collection.

The Internet of Things is quickly being applied in the natural environment to better steward the Earth's ecosystems. Sensors are being used in forests to alert firefighters of dangerous conditions that could precipitate fires. Scientists are installing sensors across cities, suburbs, and rural communities to measure pollution levels and warn the public of toxic conditions so they can minimize exposure by remaining indoors. In 2013, sensors placed atop the U.S. Embassy in Beijing reported hour to hour changes in carbon emissions across the Chinese capital. The data was instantaneously posted on the Internet, warning inhabitants of dangerous pollution levels. The information pushed the Chinese government into implementing drastic measures to reduce carbon emissions in nearby coal-powered plants and even restrict automobile traffic and production in energy-intensive factories in the region to protect public health.

Sensors are being placed in soil to detect subtle changes in vibrations and earth density to provide an early warning system for avalanches, sink holes, volcanic eruptions, and earthquakes. IBM is placing sensors in the air and in the ground in Rio de Janeiro to predict heavy rains and mudslides up to two days in advance to enable city authorities to evacuate local populations.[21]

Researchers are implanting sensors in wild animals and placing sensors along migratory trails to assess environmental and behavioral changes that might affect their well-being so that preventative actions can be taken to restore ecosystem dynamics. Sensors are also being installed in rivers, lakes, and oceans to detect changes in the quality of water and measure the impact on flora and fauna in these ecosystems for potential remediation. In a pilot program in Dubuque, Iowa, digital water meters and accompanying software have been installed in homes to monitor water use patterns to inform homeowners of likely leaks as well as ways to reduce water consumption.[22]

The IoT is also transforming the way we produce and deliver food. Farmers are using sensors to monitor weather conditions, changes in soil moisture, the spread of pollen, and other factors that affect yields, and automated response mechanisms are being installed to ensure proper growing conditions. Sensors are being attached to vegetable and fruit cartons in transit to both track their whereabouts and sniff the produce to warn of imminent spoilage so shipments can be re-routed to closer vendors.[23]

Physicians are even attaching or implanting sensors inside human bodies to monitor bodily functions including heart rate, pulse, body temperature, and skin coloration to notify doctors of vital changes that might require proactive attention. General Electric (GE) is working with computer vision software that "can analyze facial expressions for signs of severe pain, the onset of delirium or other hints of distress" to alert nurses.[24] In the near future, body sensors will be linked to one's electronic health records, allowing the IoT to quickly diagnose the patient's likely physical state to assist emergency medical personnel and expedite treatment.

Arguably, the IoT's most dramatic impact thus far has been in security systems. Homes, offices, factories, stores, and even public gathering places have been outfitted with cameras and sensors to detect criminal activity. The IoT alerts security services and police for a quick response and provides a data trail for apprehending perpetrators.

The IoT embeds the built environment and the natural environment in a coherent operating network, allowing every human being and every thing to communicate with one another in searching out synergies and facilitating interconnections in ways that optimize the thermodynamic efficiencies of society while ensuring the well-being of the Earth as a whole. If the technology platforms of the First and Second Industrial Revolutions aided in the severing and enclosing of the Earth's myriad ecological interdependencies for market exchange and personal gain, the IoT platform of the Third Industrial Revolution reverses the process. What makes the IoT a disruptive technology in the way we organize economic life is that it helps humanity reintegrate itself into the complex choreography of the biosphere, and by doing so, dramatically increases productivity without compromising the ecological relationships that govern the planet. Using less of the Earth's resources more efficiently and productively in a circular economy and making the transition from carbon-based fuels to renewable energies are defining features of the emerging economic paradigm. In the new era, we each become a node in the nervous system of the biosphere.

While the IoT offers the prospect of a sweeping transformation in the way humanity lives on earth, putting us on a course toward a more sustainable and abundant future, it also raises disturbing issues regarding data security and personal privacy, which will be addressed at length in chapter 5 and in other chapters throughout the book.

Some of the leading information technology companies in the world are already at work on the build-out of the Internet of Things. General Electric's "Industrial Internet," Cisco's "Internet of Everything," IBM's "Smarter Planet," and Siemens's "Sustainable Cities" are among the many initiatives currently underway to bring online an intelligent Third Industrial Revolution infrastructure that can connect neighborhoods, cities, regions, and continents in what industry observers call a global neural network. The network is designed to be open, distributed, and collaborative, allowing anyone, anywhere, and at any time the opportunity to access it and use Big Data to create new applications for managing their daily lives at near zero marginal cost.

Early on, the global companies championing the IoT were some-what unsure of what exactly constituted the core operating mechanism of the platform. In 2012, Cisco invited me to Berlin to discuss the Third Industrial Revolution with chief information officers from their client companies. The following year, Siemens extended an invitation for me to meet with their CEO Peter Loescher, as well as the Siemens global board of directors and 20 of their key global division leaders. The IoT was very much on the minds of executives in both companies.

At the Cisco conference, I began by asking what was common to every infrastructure system in history. Infrastructure requires three elements, each of which interacts with the other to enable the system to operate as a whole: a communication medium, a power source, and a transportation mechanism. In this sense, infrastructure can be thought of as a prosthetic extension, a way to enlarge the social organism. Absent a way to communicate, an energy source, and a form of mobility, society would cease to function.

As previously discussed, the IoT is made up of a Communications Internet, an Energy Internet, and a Transportation Internet that work together in a single operating system, continuously finding ways to increase the production and distribution of goods and services, and the recycling of waste. Each of these three Internets enables the others. Without communication, we can't manage economic activity. Without energy, we can't generate information or power transport. Without transportation and logistics, we can't move economic activity across the value chain. Together, these three operating systems compose the physiology of the new economic organism.

The three interoperable Internets of the IoT require a transformation in the functions of every enterprise. In specific regard to Cisco, I expressed my doubts about the viability of chief information officers (CIO) in an evolving IoT economy and suggested that in the future, IT, energy services, and transportation and logistics would be integrated into a single function under the supervision of a chief productivity officer (CPO). The CPO would combine IT expertise, energy expertise, and transportation and logistics expertise with the aim of using the IoT to optimize the thermodynamic efficiencies and productivity of the company's operations.

While Cisco is primarily an IT company, Siemens is more diverse and houses an IT division, energy division, logistics division, and infrastructure division among others. When I met with the Siemens corporate leadership, it was clear that the divisions were still operating more or less independently, each selling their own products and services. The company's rebranding as a solution provider to help create smart and sustainable cities is forcing these traditionally siloed units to begin a conversation on how they might each add value to the other in advancing the new vision of an IoT world. The concept of the three Internets operating in a single IoT system to increase the thermodynamic efficiencies and productivity of cities, regions, and countries suddenly began to make sense. The devil is in the details: how best to create a new business model that would mesh Siemens's powerful divisions into an overarching solution provider that could help governing jurisdictions build out an Internet of Things technology platform and successfully make the change into a "smart" and "sustainable" society.

The question of rethinking business practices is beginning to loom large with the sudden evolution of the IoT platform. My own social enterprise, the TIR Consulting Group, is made up of many of the world's leading architectural firms, energy companies, construction companies, power and utility companies, IT and electronics companies, and logistics and transport companies. Since 2009, we have been working with cities, regions, and countries to establish Third Industrial Revolution Master Plans for introducing IoT infrastructure. I would be remiss if I didn't acknowledge that we find ourselves in uncharted territory and are on a steep learning curve to figure out how to best build out the new smart society. But this much we know. The core of the IoT operating system is the coming together of the Communications Internet, Energy Internet, and Transportation Internet in a cohesive operating platform. If each remains siloed from the others, it will be impossible to erect the IoT and pursue the vision of a smart society and sustainable world. (We will continue to come back to the three Internets that make up the driving mechanism of the IoT throughout the book.)

THE RISE OF THE COLLABORATIVE COMMONS

Lost in all of the excitement over the prospect of the Internet of Things is that connecting everyone and everything in a global network driven by extreme productivity moves us ever faster toward an era of nearly free goods and services and, with it, the shrinking of capitalism in the next half century and the rise of a Collaborative Commons as the dominant model for organizing economic life.

We are so used to thinking of the capitalist market and government as the only two means of organizing economic life that we overlook the other organizing model in our midst that we depend on daily to deliver a range of goods and services that neither market nor government provides. The Commons predates both the capitalist market and representative government and is the oldest form of institutionalized, self-managed activity in the world.

The contemporary Commons is where billions of people engage in the deeply social aspects of life. It is made up of literally millions of self-managed, mostly democratically run organizations, including charities, religious bodies, arts and cultural groups, educational foundations, amateur sports clubs, producer and consumer cooperatives, credit unions, health-care organizations, advocacy groups, condominium associations, and a near endless list of other formal and informal institutions that generate the social capital of society.

The traditional democratically managed commons is still found in scattered communities on every continent. Local rural communities pool their common resources—land, water, forests, fish and game, pastures, etc.—and agree to use them collectively. Decisions regarding the expropriation, cultivation, distribution, and recycling of resources are made democratically by the members of the Commons. In addition, sanctions and punishments for violating the norms and protocols are built into the governing codes, making the Commons a self-managing economic enterprise. The Commons has proven to be a relatively successful governing model in subsistence-based agricultural communities where production and consumption are primarily for use rather than exchange. They are the early archetypes of today's circular economy.

The success of the Commons is all the more impressive given the political circumstances that gave rise to them. For the most part, commons management emerged in feudal societies where powerful overlords pauperized local populations and forced them to pay tribute by either working the manorial fields or handing over part of their production in the form of a tax. Coming together in a sharing economy became the only viable way to ensure the meager largesse they were left with would be optimized. The takeaway lesson is that a democratic form of self-management and governance designed to pool and share "commons" resources proved to be a resilient economic model for surviving a despotic feudal system that kept people locked in bondage.

The great Enclosure Movements across Europe that led to the downfall of feudal society, the rise of the modern market economy, and eventually the capitalist system, put an end to rural commons but not the sharing spirit that animated them. Peasant farmers took their lessons learned to the new urban landscapes where they faced an equally imposing foe in the form of factory overlords of the industrial revolution. Urban workers and an emerging middle class, like their peasant serf forbearers, pooled their common resources—this time in the form of wages and labor skills—and created new kinds of self-governing Commons. Charitable societies, schools, hospitals, trade unions, cooperatives, and popular cultural institutions of all kinds began to take root and flourish, creating the foundation for what came to be known as the civil society in the nineteenth century. These new Commons institutions were lubricated by social capital and driven by the democratic spirit. They came to play a key role in improving the welfare of millions of urban dwellers.

In the twentieth century, civil society became institutionalized in the form of tax-exempt organizations and was partially rebranded as the nonprofit sector. Today, we use the terms *civil society* and *nonprofit sector* interchangeably, depending on whether we are referring to their purely social function or their institutional classification. Now, a new generation is beginning to move beyond these older distinctions, preferring to use the term *social Commons*.

In the long passage from the feudal commons to the social Commons, successive generations have effectively honed the principles of democratic self-governance to a fine art. Currently, the social Commons is growing faster than the market economy in many countries around the world. Still, because what the social Commons creates is largely of social value, not pecuniary value, it is often dismissed by economists. Nonetheless, the social economy is an impressive force. According to a survey of 40 nations conducted by the Johns Hopkins University Center for Civil Society Studies, the nonprofit Commons accounts for $2.2 trillion in operating expenditures. In eight countries surveyed—the United States, Canada, Japan, France, Belgium,

Australia, the Czech Republic, and New Zealand—the nonprofit sector makes up, on average, 5 percent of the GDP.[25] Its portion of the GDP in these countries exceeds the GDP of all utilities, is equal to the GDP of the construction industry, and is nearly equal to the GDP of banks, insurance companies, and financial services.[26]

The social Commons is where we generate the good will that allows a society to cohere as a cultural entity. Markets and governments are an extension of a people's social identity. Without the continuous replenishment of social capital, there would be insufficient trust to enable markets and governments to function, yet we pejoratively categorize the social Commons as "the third sector" as if it were less important than markets or governments.

However, were we to wake up one day to find that all of our civil society organizations had vanished overnight, society would quickly wither and die. Without places of worship, schools, hospitals, community support groups, advocacy organizations, sports and recreation facilities, and arts and other cultural institutions, we would lose our sense of purpose and identity and the social ties that unite us as an extended human family.

While the capitalist market is based on self-interest and driven by material gain, the social Commons is motivated by collaborative interests and driven by a deep desire to connect with others and share. If the former promotes property rights, caveat emptor, and the search for autonomy, the latter advances open-source innovation, transparency, and the search for community.

What makes the Commons more relevant today than at any other time in its long history is that we are now erecting a high-tech global technology platform whose defining characteristics potentially optimize the very values and operational principles that animate this age-old institution.

The IoT is the technological "soul mate" of an emerging Collaborative Commons. The new infrastructure is configured to be distributed in nature in order to facilitate collaboration and the search for synergies, making it an ideal technological framework for advancing the social economy. The operating logic of the IoT is to optimize lateral peer production, universal access, and inclusion, the same sensibilities that are critical to the nurturing and creation of social capital in the civil society. The very purpose of the new technology platform is to encourage a sharing culture, which is what the Commons is all about. It is these design features of the IoT that bring the social Commons out of the shadows, giving it a high-tech platform to become the dominant economic paradigm of the twenty-first century.

The IoT enables billions of people to engage in peer-to-peer social networks and cocreate the many new economic opportunities and practices that constitute life on the emerging Collaborative Commons. The platform turns everyone into a prosumer and every activity into a collaboration. The IoT potentially connects every human being in a global community, allowing social capital to flourish on an unprecedented scale, making a sharing economy possible. Without the IoT platform, the Collaborative Commons would be neither feasible nor realizable.

The adjective *collaborative* didn't even exist until well into the twentieth century. A check of Google Ngram Viewer's word tracker is a powerful sign of the changes afoot. The Ngram Viewer allows a researcher to search five million books published between 1500 and 2008—now digitized—to see when a particular word was first used and to track the increase or decrease of its use over time. The word *collaborative* was first used, very spottily, in the 1940s and 1950s; then usage shot straight up from the late 1960s to today, paralleling the emergence of the computer and Internet technology as peer-to-peer interactive communications media.[27]

The Collaborative Commons is already profoundly impacting economic life. Markets are beginning to give way to networks, ownership is becoming less important than access, the pursuit of self-interest is being tempered by the pull of collaborative interests, and the traditional dream of rags to riches is being supplanted by a new dream of a sustainable quality of life.

In the coming era, both capitalism and socialism will lose their once-dominant hold over society, as a new generation increasingly identifies with Collaboratism. The young collaboratists are borrowing the principle virtues of both the capitalists and socialists, while eliminating the centralizing nature of both the free market and the bureaucratic state.

The distributed and interconnected nature of the Internet of Things deepens individual entrepreneurial engagement in direct proportion to the diversity and strength of one's collaborative relationships in the social economy. That's because the democratization of communication, energy, and transportation allows billions of people to be individually "empowered." But that empowerment is only achievable by one's participation in peer-to-peer networks that are underwritten by social capital. A new generation is coming of age that is more entrepreneurially self-directed by means of being more socially embedded. It's no surprise that the best and brightest of the Millennial Generation think of themselves as "social entrepreneurs." For them, being both entrepreneurial and social is no longer an oxymoron, but rather a tautology.

Hundreds of millions of people are already transferring bits and pieces of their economic life from capitalist markets to the global Collaborative Commons. Prosumers are not only producing and sharing their own information, entertainment, green energy, 3D-printed goods, and massive open online courses on the Collaborative Commons at near zero marginal cost. They are also sharing cars, homes, and even clothes with one another via social media sites, rentals, redistribution clubs, and cooperatives, at low or near zero marginal cost. An increasing number of people are collaborating in "patient-driven" health-care networks to improve diagnoses and find new treatments and cures for diseases, again at near zero marginal cost. And young social entrepreneurs are establishing ecologically sensitive businesses, crowdfunding new enterprises, and even creating alternative social currencies in the new economy. The result is that "exchange value" in the marketplace is increasingly being replaced by "shareable value" on the Collaborative Commons. When prosumers share their goods and services on a Collaborative Commons, the rule book that governs a market-exchange economy becomes far less relevant to the life of society.

The current debate among economists, business leaders, and public officials on what appears to be a new type of long-term economic stagnation emerging around the world is an indicator of the great transformation taking place as the economy shifts from exchange value in the marketplace to sharable value on the Collaborative Commons.

Global GDP has been growing at a declining rate in the aftermath of the Great Recession. While economists point to the high cost of energy, demographics, slower growth in the labor force, consumer and government debt, an increase in the share of global income going to the very wealthy, and consumer risk aversion to spending, among other causes, there may be a more far-reaching underlying factor, although still nascent, that might explain at least some of the slowing of GDP. As the marginal cost of producing goods and services moves toward near zero in sector after sector, profits are narrowing and GDP is beginning to wane. And, with more goods and services becoming nearly free, fewer purchases are being made in the marketplace, again reducing GDP. Even those items still being purchased in the exchange economy are becoming fewer in number as more people redistribute and recycle previously purchased goods in the sharable economy, extending their usable lifecycle, with a concomitant loss of GDP. A growing legion of consumers are also opting for access over ownership of goods, preferring to pay only for the limited time they use a car, bicycle, toy, tool, or other item, which translates to less GDP. Meanwhile, as automation, robotics, and Artificial Intelligence (AI) replace tens of millions of workers, consumer purchasing power in the marketplace continues to contract, further reducing GDP. Concurrently, as the number of prosumers proliferates, more economic activity is migrating from the exchange economy in the marketplace to the sharable economy on the Collaborative Commons, again shrinking the growth of GDP.

The point is, while economic stagnation may be occurring for many other reasons, a more crucial change is just beginning to unfold which could account for part of the sluggishness: the slow demise of the capitalist system and the rise of a Collaborative Commons in which economic welfare is measured less by the accumulation of market capital and more by the aggregation of social capital. The steady decline of GDP in the coming years and decades is going to be increasingly attributable to the changeover to a vibrant new economic paradigm that measures economic value in totally new ways.

Nowhere is the change more apparent than in the growing global debate about how best to judge economic success. The conventional GDP metrics for measuring economic performance in the capitalist marketplace focus exclusively on itemizing the sum total of goods and services produced each year with no attempt to differentiate between negative and positive economic growth. An increase in expenditures for cleaning up toxic waste dumps, police protection and the expansion of prison facilities, military appropriations, and the like are all included in gross domestic product.

Today, the transformation of economic life from finance capital and the exchange of goods and services in markets to social capital and the sharing of goods and services in the Collaborative Commons is reshaping society's thinking about how to evaluate economic performance. The European Union, the United Nations, the Organization for Economic Co-operation and Development (OECD), and a number of industrialized and developing countries have introduced new metrics for determining economic progress, emphasizing "quality of life" indicators rather than merely the quantity of economic output. Social priorities, including educational attainment of the population, availability of health-care services, infant mortality and life expectancy, the extent of environmental stewardship and sustainable development, protection of human rights, the degree of democratic participation in society, levels of volunteerism, the amount of leisure time available to the citizenry, the percentage of the population below the poverty level, and the equitable distribution of wealth, are among the many new categories used by governments to evaluate the general economic welfare of society. The GDP metric will likely decline in significance as an indicator of economic performance along with the diminution of the market exchange economy in the coming decades. By midcentury, quality of life indices on the Collaborative Commons are likely to be the litmus test for measuring the economic well-being of every nation.

In the unfolding struggle between the exchange economy and the sharing economy, economists' last fallback position is that if everything were nearly free, there would be no incentive to innovate and bring new goods and services to the fore because inventors and entrepreneurs would have no way to recoup their up-front costs. Yet millions of prosumers are freely collaborating in social Commons, creating new IT and software, new forms of entertainment, new learning tools, new media outlets, new green energies, new 3D-printed manufactured products, new peer-to-peer health-research initiatives, and new nonprofit social entrepreneurial business ventures, using open-source legal agreements freed up from intellectual property restraints. The upshot is a surge in creativity that is at least equal to the great innovative thrusts experienced by the capitalist market economy in the twentieth century.

The democratization of innovation and creativity on the emerging Collaborative Commons is spawning a new kind of incentive, based less on the expectation of financial reward and more on the desire to advance the social well-being of humanity. And it's succeeding.

While the capitalist market is not likely to disappear, it will no longer exclusively define the economic agenda for civilization. There will still be goods and services whose marginal costs are high enough to warrant their exchange in markets and sufficient profit to ensure a return on investment. But in a world in which more things are potentially nearly free, social capital is going to play a far more significant role than financial capital, and economic life is increasingly going to take place on a Collaborative Commons.

The purpose of this book is not merely to present a laundry list of collaborative initiatives—there are hundreds of articles and dozens of books on the budding collaborative world. Rather, we will examine how this change in human behavior is making obsolete the core values upon which we live and the institutions we created in the capitalist era, and explore the new values and institutions that will propel the coming collaborative era.

Until now, the many books and articles devoted to the growing collaborative culture have assumed that the new ways of organizing commerce, while disruptive, would not ultimately threaten the overarching assumptions upon which market capitalism—and its foe, state socialism—are based. The prevailing sentiment, even among many of the most ardent proselytizers of the new model, is that a collaborative future will greatly expand human participation and creativity across society and flatten the way we organize institutional life in virtually every field, but ultimately be absorbable into a more humane and efficient capitalist market.

A quick glance at the current configuration of global capitalism certainly suggests its staying power. The global Fortune 500 companies continue to consolidate control over the commercial affairs of the planet, with 2011 revenues exceeding one-third of the GDP of the world.[28] Given the enormous power and reach of the capitalist system, it's difficult to imagine a world in which capitalism plays a much diminished role.

Part of the reason we have such a difficult time contemplating life after capitalism is the failure to understand the pivotal role that new communication technologies, energy sources, and transportation modalities play in reorienting the temporal-spatial dynamic, allowing larger numbers of people to come together and cohere in more complex, interdependent social organizations. The accompanying technology platforms constitute the infrastructure but also dictate the way the economy is organized and managed. In the nineteenth century, steam-powered printing and the telegraph became the communication media for linking and managing a complex coal-powered rail and factory system, connecting densely populated urban areas across national markets. In the twentieth century, the telephone, and later, radio and television, became the communication media for managing and marketing a more geographically dispersed oil, auto, and suburban era and a mass consumer society. In the twenty-first century, the Internet is becoming the communication medium for managing distributed renewable energies and automated logistics and transport in an increasingly interconnected global Commons.

The technology platforms of the First and Second Industrial Revolutions were designed to be centralized with top-down command and control. That's because fossil fuels are only found in certain places and require centralized management to move them from underground to the final end users. The centralized energies, in turn, require centralized, vertically integrated forms of communication in order to manage the momentous speed-up in commercial transactions made possible by the new sources of power.

The enormous capital cost in establishing centralized communication/energy/transportation matrices meant that the new industrial and commercial enterprises embedded in and dependent on these technology platforms had to create their own giant, vertically integrated operations across the value chain. This was the only way to ensure sufficient economies of scale to guarantee a return on the investment. The high up-front cost of establishing vertically integrated enterprises in the First and Second Industrial Revolutions required large amounts of investment capital.

Still, the investment of huge amounts of capital paid off. Bringing the entire value chain under one roof allowed businesses to cut out some of the costly middle men, significantly reducing their marginal costs and the price of their goods and services sold in the market. But the irony is that the same vertical integration allowed a few market leaders to emerge in each industry and monopolize their respective fields, often preventing startup companies from introducing even newer technologies to reduce marginal cost and the price of goods and services, and by so doing, gain a foothold and sufficient market share to effectively compete.

The emergence of the IoT infrastructure of the Third Industrial Revolution, with its open architecture and distributed features, allows social enterprises on the Collaborative Commons to break the monopoly hold of giant, vertically integrated companies operating in capitalist markets by enabling peer production in laterally scaled continental and global networks at near zero marginal cost.

To begin with, the IoT technology platform relies on renewable energies that are found everywhere in some frequency or proportion. Moreover, while the harvesting technologies are getting ever cheaper and will be as inexpensive as cell phones and computers in the coming decade, the sun off your roof, the wind off the side of your building, the garbage converted to biomass in your kitchen are nearly free— after the fixed investment in the harvesting technology is paid back— just like the information we now generate and share on the Internet is nearly free. However, these distributed renewable energies have to be organized collaboratively and shared peer-to-peer across communities and regions to create sufficient lateral economies of scale to bring their marginal cost to zero for everyone in society. The IoT, because it is a distributed, collaborative, and peer-to-peer technology platform, is the only mechanism agile enough to manage renewable energies that are similarly constituted and organized.

The fixed costs of bringing online a distributed IoT infrastructure, while considerable, are far less than those required to build out and maintain the more centralized technology platforms of the First and Second Industrial Revolutions. While fixed costs are less, the Internet of Things also brings down the marginal cost of communication, energy, and transportation in the production and distribution of goods and services. By eliminating virtually all of the remaining middlemen who mark up the transaction costs at every stage of the value chain, small- and medium-sized enterprises—especially cooperatives and other nonprofit businesses—and billions of prosumers can share their goods and services directly with one another on the Collaborative Commons—at near zero marginal cost. The reduction in both fixed and marginal costs dramatically reduces the entry costs of creating new businesses in distributed peer-to-peer networks. The low entry costs encourage more people to become potential entrepreneurs and collaborators, creating and sharing information, energy, and goods and services on the Commons.

The changes brought on by the establishment of an IoT infrastructure and Collaborative Commons go far beyond the narrow confines of commerce. Every communication/energy/transportation matrix is accompanied by a set of broad prescriptions about how society and economic life are to be organized that mirror the possibilities and potentials unleashed by the new enabling technologies. Those prescriptions become canonized in an overarching belief system designed to suggest that the society's new economic paradigm is merely a reflection of the natural order and therefore the only legitimate way to conduct social life. I know of no single instance in history in which a society's view of the natural order was at odds with the way it orchestrated its particular relationship with the environment. By constructing a view of nature that replicated its own way of acting on the world, every society could take comfort in knowing that the way it was organized conformed to the natural order of things. Once this unconscious process of mass self-justification became firmly entrenched in the public mind, any criticism of the way the economy and society was organized came to be seen as heresy or idiocy since it was at odds with the rules governing nature and the cosmos. The cosmologies that governed each economic paradigm were ultimately a more reliable guarantor of social stability than all the armies in history in defending the status quo.

That's why paradigm shifts are so disruptive and painful: they bring into question the operating assumptions that underlie the existing economic and social models as well as the belief system that accompanies them and the worldview that legitimizes them.

In order to fully appreciate the immense economic, social, political, and psychological changes that will likely come with the transition from a capitalist market to a Collaborative Commons, it is helpful to place this turning point in the human journey within the context of the equally disruptive changes that accompanied the shift from the feudal to the market economy in the late medieval era and, again, from the market economy to the capitalist economy in the modern era. Understanding, in each instance, how the changeover to a new communication/energy/transportation matrix triggered a transformation into a new economic paradigm, fundamentally altering the worldview

of much of human society, will help us better grasp the evolutionary mechanisms that guide the economic journey and that have led us
to the present. This understanding gives us the historical perspective
to wrestle with the tumultuous changes occurring across the global
economy today as the paradigm shifts again, this time from capitalist
markets to Collaborative Commons.

PART I
THE UNTOLD HISTORY
OF CAPITALISM

CHAPTER TWO
THE EUROPEAN ENCLOSURES AND THE BIRTH OF THE MARKET ECONOMY

The feudal economy in Europe can best be characterized as a subsistence communication/energy complex. The labor power of serfs, oxen, and horses made up the bulk of the energy matrix. The woodlands of Europe produced abundant thermal energy for heating and small-scale metallurgy. With the exception of the clergy and a small number of landowners who presided over the manorial lands, the population was illiterate, and economic life was yoked to the temporal and spatial restraints of oral culture. With the old Roman roads abandoned and in disrepair, commerce and trade virtually disappeared between the seventh and twelfth centuries, returning economic life back to thousands of isolated localities whose primitive existence relied almost entirely on subsistence agriculture.[1] Virtually all economic production was for immediate use and only the most meager surpluses were traded in local fairs to supplement the daily life of manorial estates and small villages scattered across the European countryside.

THE FEUDAL COMMONS

In England, as elsewhere in Europe, agricultural life was organized around the commons. Feudal landlords leased their land to peasant farmers under various tenancy arrangements. While freeholders were guaranteed tenancy from generation to generation and could not be dislodged from their ancestral homes, leaseholders were less fortunate and were only guaranteed limited occupancy that rarely exceeded three lifetimes, after which the landlords could either impose new leasing arrangements or withdraw the leases. Customary tenants had virtually no tenancy rights and occupied land at the sole discretion of the landlord.

The tenancy arrangements required that the peasants either turn over a percentage of their harvest to the landlord or work his fields as well as their own throughout the year. In the late medieval period, with the limited introduction of a money economy, tenants were required to pay rent or taxes to the landlord as a condition of their lease.

Feudal agriculture was communally structured. Peasants combined their individual plots into open fields and common pastures and farmed them collectively. The commons became the first primitive exercise in democratic decision making in Europe. Peasant councils were responsible for overseeing economic activity, including planting and harvesting, crop rotation, the use of forest and water resources, and the number of animals that could graze on the common pastures.

The feudal notion of property relations was completely different from ours today. We think of property as an exclusive personal possession that can be held or exchanged in the marketplace. By contrast, in the feudal economy, all earthly things made up God's creation and were his exclusively to dispose of. God's creation, in turn, was conceived of as a "Great Chain of Being," a rigidly constructed hierarchy of responsibilities that ascended upward from the lowest creatures to the angels in heaven. Each creature on the rungs of the spiritual ladder was expected to serve those above and below in a tightly prescribed set of obligations to ensure the proper functioning of the creation as a whole. Within this theological framework, property was conceptualized as a series of trusts administered pyramidally from the celestial throne down to the peasants working the communal fields. In this schema, property was never exclusively owned, but rather divvied up into spheres of responsibility conforming to a fixed code of proprietary obligations. For example, when the king granted land to a lord or vassal, "his rights over the land remained, except for the particular interest he had parted with." The Harvard historian Richard Schlatter explains that "no one could be said to own the land; everyone from the king down through the tenants and sub-tenants to the peasants who tilled it had a certain dominion over it, but no one had an absolute lordship over it."[2]

The feudal economy persisted, relatively unmodified, for more than 700 years. In the 1500s, however, new economic forces began to chip away at the feudal order, beginning in Tudor England and later spreading to other parts of Europe. Communally held land was enclosed and transformed into private property and exchanged in the marketplace, in some instances by license of the king or by acts of parliament and, at other times, by joint agreement of the village commons.[3]

The Enclosure Movement, viewed by many historians as "the revolution of the rich against the poor," was carried out in England between the sixteenth and early nineteenth centuries, fundamentally altering the economic and political landscape. Millions of peasants were uprooted from their ancestral lands and forced to act as free agents whose labor power would henceforth be available for hire in the budding medieval marketplace.[4]

The first wave of English enclosures was sparked by two related phenomena that acted synergistically to undermine the feudal order. In the early stages, rising demand for food, occasioned by a burgeoning urban population, triggered an inflationary spiral, placing increasing hardships on feudal landlords whose land rents were fixed at preinflationary rates. At the same time, an incipient textile industry was forcing up the price of wool, making it more financially lucrative for landlords to enclose communal land and switch over to raising sheep.[5]

Hundreds of thousands of displaced farm families watched helplessly as sheep grazed on the grassland that just a few years earlier had been tilled for oats and rye to feed their own children. Everywhere people were reduced to starvation while sheep were fattened and fleeced to rush wool to the new textile factories going up in England and on the continent.

Sir Thomas More captured the bitter spirit of the times in *Utopia*, a scathing attack on the greed of the landlord class:

Your sheep, that were wont to be so meek and tame and so small
eaters, now, and I hear say, become so great devourers and so wild,
that they eat up and swallow down the very men themselves. They
consume, destroy, and devour whole fields, houses and cities.[6]

A second wave of enclosures occurred roughly between 1760 and
the 1840s.[7] The First Industrial Revolution was beginning to spread
across England and the rest of Europe. The new economy brought
with it an ever-expanding urban population requiring more food. The
high prices spurred landlords to enclose their remaining lands, com-
pleting a long transition that took Europe from a subsistence-based
rural economy to a modern market-directed agricultural economy.

The great enclosures and the market economy that ensued changed
the very nature of property relations, from conditional rights to exclusive ownership. After centuries in which people belonged to the land,
the land now belonged to individual people in the form of real estate
that was negotiable and exchangeable in the open marketplace. One's
ancestral home metamorphosed into a commercial resource that could
be used both as a source of capital and credit in the pursuit of commercial gain. One's labor similarly became a form of exclusive property
that could be freely bought and sold in the marketplace in a new world
governed by contractual relationships rather than communal obligations and social status.

The enclosure of the English countryside gave rise not only to the
modern notion of private property relations operating in markets, but
also to a legal system to oversee it. In the feudal economy, the very
limited economic exchange rarely extended beyond close family relations and kinship communities. Lacking an enforceable common law
and statutes to accompany it, people were reluctant to sell and buy
property outside their immediate social sphere. In tightly knit kinship communities, one's word guaranteed the trustworthiness of the
exchange between neighbors.

It is generally acknowledged that a private-property regime makes
modern markets viable. But, it's also important to realize that an
anonymous market where strangers are exchanging goods and services would not be possible without an enforceable legal code. A fully
functioning private-property regime operating in markets requires a
legal system backed up by police enforcement and courts to ensure

that sellers and buyers uphold their contractual obligations. The English legal code, which matured alongside the transition from proprietary obligations on the feudal commons to property rights in the modern marketplace, was instrumental in ensuring the passage from the old order to the new era.

Most historians note the importance of the growing wool market and the development of a legally enforceable private-property regime in the passage from feudal life to the modern market economy. There were, however, other economic forces at work. Anthropologists point to a slew of new agricultural technologies, like the heavy-wheeled plow in northern Europe, the replacement of oxen by horses, and the changeover from two-field to three-field rotation that greatly increased agricultural productivity in the thirteenth and fourteenth centuries, leading to a dramatic growth in human population—interrupted only temporarily by the plague—and the advent of urban life. Historical accounts of the period also focus on the new innovations in metallurgy and a spate of new mechanical inventions like the cam, spring and treadle, sophisticated cranks, connecting rods, and governors that helped spur the changeover from reciprocating to continuous rotary motion.[8]

All these developments were significant, but secondary to a more fundamental change that gave rise to what a handful of historians have dubbed the soft proto-industrial revolution of the medieval era.

THE RISE OF THE MARKET ECONOMY

It was the coming together of the print revolution and water and wind power in the late Middle Ages that ushered in the transformation from the feudal to the market economy, altering the economic paradigm and social construction of Europe. What many historians and economic theorists often miss is that the capitalist economy emerged out of the soft proto-industrial market economy that existed in much of Europe (and later America), and not out of the earlier feudal economy. In fairness to Adam Smith and Karl Marx, each at least touched on water and wind power in their writings. Smith referred to the new sources of power generation as an example of the division of labor, and Marx contrasted the intermittence of water and wind power to the reliable continuity of steam power, which assured a dependable and perpetual production cycle. Marx, like other intellectuals of the period, also failed to differentiate the feudal economy from the medieval one that grew out of it, famously and mistakenly remarking that "the hand-mill gives you society with the feudal lord; the steam-mill, society with the industrial capitalist."[9] In fact, wind energy helped fundamentally alter power relations away from the feudal lord and toward the townsmen and the rising burgher class of the medieval era.

Marx also alluded to the importance of the printing press, but only as a means of reawakening scientific interests and pursuits:

> *Gunpowder, the compass, and the printing press* were the 3 great inventions which ushered in bourgeois society. Gunpowder blew up the knightly class, the compass discovered the world market and founded the colonies, and the printing press was the instrument of Protestantism and the regeneration of science in general; the most powerful lever for creating the intellectual prerequisites.[10]

Neither Smith nor Marx seemed to understand, however, that the print revolution and water and wind power were indispensable to each other and that together they created a general-purpose technology platform for an economic paradigm shift that changed the European social and political landscape.

The water mill was known in antiquity and experimented with in Rome. Yet the technology never developed sufficiently to challenge human slavery as a power source. New technological innovations, beginning in the tenth and eleventh centuries in Europe, catapulted water power to the center of economic life. By the late eleventh century, there were more than 5,600 water mills operating in 34 counties in England, according to the census. France boasted 20,000 water mills at the time, for an average of one mill for every 250 people.[11] The economic impact was dramatic. A typical water mill generated two to three horsepower for approximately half the time the mill was operating. A water mill could replace the labor of 10 to 20 people. In France alone, the hydraulic energy generated by water mills equaled the power generated by one-quarter of the adult population of the kingdom—a staggering increase in power capacity.[12]

Most of the early water mills were financed by the manorial lords and installed on the rivers and streams that coursed through their lands. The emerging towns and cities of Europe erected their own water mills, providing a competing source of power to the lord.

Where water was either lacking, too intermittent, or on the property of the lords, towns and cities turned to wind power. The first European windmill was erected in Yorkshire, England, in 1185.[13] Windmills quickly spread across the plains of northern Europe. Because wind is everywhere, not bound to royal lands, and free, the power source could be erected anywhere. Towns and cities rushed headlong into the new energy regime, with a source of power at hand that allowed them to even the playing field with local lords. Mindful that wind brought them a new democratic source of power, the burghers of the cities referred to this new invention as the "commoners' mill."[14]

While water mills and windmills were used in milling grains, tanning, laundering, operating bellows for blast furnaces, creating pigments for paint, crushing olives, and a host of other economic activities, the water mill's most important use was in the fulling industry. Fulling is the first step in turning wool into cloth. As the wool leaves the loom, it has to be scoured of impurities, cleaned, and thickened by beating it in water. This was traditionally done by men trampling the cloth in a trough. The water mill transformed the process of fulling. Human feet were replaced by wooden hammers, which were raised and dropped by a mechanism powered by the water mill. A series of wood hammers could replace an entire group of fullers and be operated by a single person.

The dramatic productivity gains brought on by the fulling mill made it economical and highly profitable to switch land use from growing food for subsistence to raising sheep for export and exchange in markets. It is no wonder that the fulling mills were sometimes referred to as "an industrial revolution of the thirteenth century."[15] The historian E. M. Carus-Wilson says of the fulling mill that it was a "revolution which brought . . . opportunity and prosperity to the country as a whole, and which was destined to alter the face of medieval England."[16] In this regard, notes Carus-Wilson, the mechanization of fulling "was as decisive an event as the mechanization of spinning and weaving in the eighteenth century."[17]

In the 1790s, on the eve of the introduction of steam power and the First Industrial Revolution, there were more than half a million water mills operating in Europe with the equivalent of 2,250,000 horsepower. Although fewer in number, the thousands of windmills up and running at the time were generating even more power than the water mills. The average windmill could produce upward of 30 horsepower.[18]

Although the new energy sources were bitterly fought over by the feudal aristocracy and an incipient burgher class in the towns and cities, these widely distributed and abundantly available sources of power ultimately favored the interests of the latter. For the first time, the power of urban craftsmen and merchants began to match and even exceed the power of the feudal lords, giving the burghers the edge they needed to shift the economic paradigm away from a feudal economy, which was organized around proprietary obligations, to a market economy, which was structured around property rights. The medieval historian Lynn White summed up the economic significance wrought by the introduction of water and wind power and the spate of new technologies that accompanied the new sources of power:

> By the latter part of the fifteenth century, Europe was equipped not only with sources of power far more diversified than those known to any previous culture, but also with an arsenal of technical means for grasping, guiding, and utilizing such energies which was immeasurably more varied and skillful than any people of the past had possessed, or than was known to any contemporary society of the Old World or the New. The expansion of Europe from 1492 onward was based in great measure upon Europe's high consumption of energy, with consequent productivity, economic weight and military might.[19]

The shift from a subsistence economy to a market economy, and from production for use to production for exchange, was a watershed event in the human journey. But it would not have been possible without an accompanying communication revolution to manage the increased flow of economic activity generated by these new sources of power. That revolution came in the form of the printing press, invented by the German Johannes Gutenberg in 1436.

The effect of the new printing press on day-to-day life was immediate, with consequences every bit as significant as the introduction of the Internet today. The sheer volume of printed material being distributed was striking:

> A man born in 1453, the year of the fall of Constantinople, could look back from his fiftieth year on a lifetime in which about eight million books had been printed, more perhaps than all the scribes of Europe had produced since Constantine founded his city in AD 330.[20]

We take print for granted today. It's so much a part of our daily existence that we rarely stop to consider how growing up on the printed word affects the very way our minds are organized. While medieval script was idiosyncratic and varied with the subjective contribution of each scribe's input, print removed the subjective element, replacing it with a more rational, calculating, and analytical approach to knowledge. And unlike oral communication, which depended on memory and therefore formulaic responses, print stored memory and systematized the retrieval of information—in the form of tables of contents, indexes, footnotes, and bibliographies—allowing the mind to deepen and expand vocabulary and develop a far more nuanced language that could be tailored to the specific moment or experience.

Print had a profound impact on the way human beings conducted business. Print introduced charts, lists, and graphs that offered a more objective and accurate account of the world than someone's personal assessment. Print not only standardized maps, but made them cheap and reproducible in large numbers, making land travel and navigation more predictable and accessible for commercial trade.

Print also enabled commercial contracts, a key element in advancing long-distance trade and extending market exchange over a wider terrain. We forget that in the feudal economy, where economic interaction relied on the spoken word, economic activity was largely constrained by walking distance and shouting distance. In an oral culture, one's "word" sufficed to settle economic arrangements. Even today, accountants use the word *audit* to describe financial probes, a throwback to the preprint days of feudal economic life when auditors spoke the financial information out loud to one another as a way of verifying the authenticity of the transaction. Print opened the way to modern bookkeeping. Standardized bills of lading, schedules, invoices, checks, and promissory notes could be delivered over distances and stored over time, providing a versatile and expansive management tool that could keep pace with the speed, reach, and scope of commercial life unleashed by the new power sources of water and wind. With print, commercial "trust" was sealed in written accounts accompanied by personal signatures.

The convergence of print and renewable energies had the effect of democratizing both literacy and power, posing a formidable challenge to the hierarchical organization of feudal life. The synergies created by the print revolution and wind and water power, along with steady improvements in road and river transport, sped up exchange and de-creased transaction costs, making possible trade in larger regional markets.

The new communication/energy/transportation matrix not only shortened distances and quickened time, bringing diverse people to-gether in joint economic pursuits after centuries of isolation, but in so doing, also encouraged a new openness to others and the beginning of a more cosmopolitan frame of mind. Centuries of provincialism and xenophobia that had stultified life began to melt away and a new sense of possibility seized the human imagination. This period saw the flow-ering of what historians call the Northern Renaissance—an awaken-ing of the arts, literature, scientific experimentation, and exploration of new worlds.

By the late medieval era, more than a thousand towns had sprung up across Europe, each bustling with economic activity. Aside from providing granaries, lodging, and shops, these urban centers became the gathering place for craftsmen of all stripes and shades. These new urban jurisdictions were often called free cities, as they were deemed independent of the reach of local lords. For example, it was custom-ary practice that if a serf were to escape the feudal commons and take refuge in a nearby town for a year and a day, he would be deemed free, having safely left one jurisdiction and taken up residence in another.[21]

The craftsmen in the new towns organized themselves into guilds by trade—metalworkers, weavers and dyers, armorers, masons, broi-ders and glaziers, scriveners, hatters, and upholsterers—in order to establish quality standards for their goods, set fixed prices for their products, and determine how much to produce. The guilds were half-way houses to fully functioning markets. The guilds charged what they called a just price for their goods, rather than the market price, preferring to maintain a customary way of life rather than making a profit. The guilds steered clear of free-labor markets and competitive prices—the critical features of a market economy—and put store in maintaining the status quo.[22]

The breaking up of the feudal commons and the sudden availability of cheap wage labor, combined with the new productivity potential unleashed by the convergence of the printing press and water and wind power, were enough to push the guild system to the side in the seventeenth century. Merchants began to bypass the guilds, dispensing work to the cheaper labor force in the rural countryside—called the putting-out system—steadily eroding the once entrenched control the guilds exercised over commercial life. The putting-out system paved the way to a fully operational market economy.[23]

While merchants were struggling with the craft guilds, a new force of small-manufacturing entrepreneurs, many of whom were harvesting the new water and wind energies to power their minifactories, were battling the guilds on the other end in an effort to open up domestic markets for their cheaper goods.

The new manufacturers found common cause with merchants in pushing for the liberalization of national markets, and they jointly championed domestic free trade, the elimination of restrictions on labor mobility, the legal enforcement of commercial contracts, and improvements in transport to enlarge markets. They parted company, however, on the question of exports for foreign trade. The merchants aligned with the monarchies in pursuit of colonial policies that favored foreign over domestic trade. The mercantilist's rationale was to heavily regulate domestic production to secure high-quality goods at cheap prices for sale abroad at inflated prices, to be paid in precious metals. The overseas colonies, in turn, were prevented from producing finished goods and restricted to producing cheap raw materials for export back to the host countries, and then forced to buy the finished manufactured goods from the home country at a higher price.

Mercantilist policies favored merchant exporters but hurt domestic manufacturers in the host countries as well as in the colonies. Moreover, restricting the volume of domestic products that could be produced for the home market in order to keep export prices artificially high worked not only to the disadvantage of the domestic manufacturers, but also the rising middle class and urban working poor, who had to contend with higher prices for domestic goods.

Opposition to mercantilist policies in Europe and the colonies continued to mount, leading the 13 American colonies to break with England in 1776, followed by the French Revolution, which initiated the overthrow of that nation's monarchy in 1789. These two great defining moments in political history were as much about the struggle to secure private property through free trade in open markets as they were about securing political freedom and democratic representation. Any doubt on that score was quickly put to rest as the first modern nation-states deliberated the question of who should be extended the right to vote. The United States, Britain, France, and most other nation-states in the eighteenth and nineteenth centuries believed that the central mission of government was to protect private property and a market economy. With that rationale in mind, the right to vote was extended only to men of property, aligning the new nation-state with a market economy based on the free exchange of private property.

CHAPTER THREE
THE COURTSHIP OF CAPITALISM AND VERTICAL INTEGRATION

I t is not uncommon to suppose that the free exchange of property in markets and capitalism are one and the same. They are not. While capitalism operates through the free market, free markets don't require capitalism.

THE BIRTH OF CAPITALISM

The soft proto-industrial revolution of the late medieval era gave rise to the free market, but capitalism, as we conceive of it now, didn't emerge until the late eighteenth century with the introduction of steam power. The earliest manufacturers headed small, family-owned enterprises that generally employed relatives, augmented by a few itinerant laborers. These entrepreneurs operated in markets but capitalism was not yet a part of the equation. The changeover to capitalism first began in the textile trade. Recall from chapter 2 that merchants, anxious to bypass the guilds, began putting-out work (an early form of subcontracting) to cheaper labor in the countryside. While guild craftsmen in urban centers were sufficiently well-off to afford their own looms, rural labor was destitute and unable to purchase looms of their own. Merchants supplied the looms—usually leasing them out in return for a fee. The fees were often so high that the rural workforce was barely able to earn enough to pay for their leases, leaving them little for their own survival.[1] By transferring ownership of the workers' tools to the merchants, a pattern was set that would change the course of economic history.

In the late sixteenth century, a new generation of small manufacturers began to bring together workers under one roof to take advantage of the economies of scale in harnessing water mills and windmills to the production process. These small manufacturers also owned the machinery used by the workers. The result is that craftsmen, who had previously owned their own equipment, were stripped of the tools of their trade and turned into wage laborers working for a new type of master—the capitalist.

The textile trade fell into the hands of the capitalists and soon other trades followed. The historian Maurice Dobb makes the point that

> the subordination of production to capital, and the appearance of this class relationship between capitalist and producer is, therefore, to be regarded as the crucial watershed between the old mode of production and the new.[2]

The concentration of ownership of the means of production by the capitalists and the subjugation of labor to capital would come to define the class struggle by the late eighteenth century. Adam Smith penetrated to the very core of the contradiction that would plague capitalism until the end of its reign. Smith saw a correlation between the enclosure of land and the enclosure of the tools of craftsmen. In both cases, millions of people were separated from control over the means of their economic survival. In the first instance, the serfs and peasant farmers were expelled from their ancestral lands and, in the second instance, craftsmen were separated from the tools of their trade. Their new status was euphemistically referred to as free labor, but in reality, that freedom came at a cost—as Smith understood. He wrote:

> In that early and rude state of society which precedes both the accumulation of stock and the appropriation of land . . . the whole produce of labour belongs to the labourer. . . . [However] as soon as stock has accumulated in the hands of particular persons, some of them will naturally employ it in setting to work industrious people,

whom they will supply with materials and subsistence, in order to make a profit by the sale of their work, or by what their labour adds to the value of the materials.[3]

If this doesn't seem fair, Smith argued that

something must be given for the profits of the undertaker of the work, who hazards his stock in this adventure. The value which the workmen add to the materials, therefore, resolves itself in this case into two parts, of which the one pays their wages, the other the profits of their employer upon the whole stock of materials and wages which he advanced.[4]

The transformation of land from commons to real estate followed a similar logic. Smith assumed that "as soon as the land of any country has all become private property, the landlords, like all other men, love to reap where they never sowed, and demand a rent even for its natural produce."[5]

Smith then summed up the operating logic that drives the entire capitalist system with the succinct observation that

the whole of what is annually either collected or produced by the labour of every society, or, what comes to the same thing, the whole price of it, is in this manner originally distributed among some of its different members. Wages, profit, and rent, are the three original sources of all revenue, as well as of all exchangeable value. All other revenue is ultimately derived from some one or other of these.[6]

Most classical and neoclassical economists believe that profits are the just reward for capitalists who risk their capital. Socialist economists, however, might agree with the young Karl Marx, who argued that the part of the worker's contribution that is subtracted from his wages and kept as profit—surplus value—is an unjust appropriation and that a more equitable arrangement would be to socialize production and let the workers enjoy the full benefit of their labor contribution.

Capitalism played little role in the soft proto-industrial revolution of the medieval era. As previously discussed, small manufacturers did begin to appear near the end of the era and some began to organize production under a single roof to better economize investment in water and wind power, but for the most part, these precursors to full-fledged capitalist enterprises were still quite small and the financing owners used came from family coffers.

What we call capitalism today emerged alongside the shift to a new communication/energy/transportation matrix in the last decade of the eighteenth century and the first few decades of the nineteenth.

A COAL-POWERED STEAM INFRASTRUCTURE

In 1769, James Watt invented and patented the modern steam engine powered by coal.[7] The cotton industry became the first to deploy the new technology. The productivity gains were dramatic. Between 1787 and 1840, British cotton production "jumped from 22 million to 366 million pounds" while the cost of production plunged. By 1850, coal-powered steam engines could be found across Europe and America. Still, as late as 1848—the year of the great European revolutions—hydraulic power "accounted for two and a half times more power than steam engines" in France. Hydraulic energy continued to be used in more French factories than coal-fired steam technology. For example, of the 784 firms in the French steel industry, 672 were still using water mills for their energy.[8]

The energy mix quickly changed in the second half of the nineteenth century. Steam power rose from 4 million horsepower in 1850 to about 18.5 million horsepower in 1870.[9]

Steam power made its quickest inroads in countries with large coal reserves. England was the first European country to make the shift from water and wind to coal, followed by Germany. The United States, with its abundance of coal deposits, quickly caught up to its European neighbors. By the outbreak of World War I, these three countries dominated the First Industrial Revolution.

Coal-powered steam technology ushered in a new communication/energy/transportation matrix—steam printing and the steam locomotive—which provided a general-purpose megatechnology platform for the First Industrial Revolution.

The coal-powered steam locomotive transformed the nature of commerce by shrinking space and shortening transaction times. By the 1830s, locomotives were traveling at speeds in excess of 60 miles per hour. It's difficult for us in the twenty-first century to imagine the impact of a machine that could carry passengers and freight at such speeds.

By 1845, 48 million Britons were traveling the rails annually.[10] In the 1850s alone, more than 21,000 miles of railroad tracks were laid down in the United States, connecting much of the country east of the Mississippi River.[11] To get a feel for how the train compressed our sense of time and space, consider the fact that a journey from New York to Chicago by stagecoach would have taken three weeks or more in 1847. By 1857, that same trip by rail would have taken 72 hours.[12]

Besides its speed, the steam locomotive provided a dependable form of transportation that, unlike roads and water, was not affected by changes in the weather. They could make several trips back and forth in the time it took a barge to make one trip and could carry three times the amount of freight as barges at the same price. The combination of speed and reliability allowed for a vast expansion of commerce and trade across a wide continental terrain at greatly reduced costs.

Railroad construction was spotty in America in the first half of the nineteenth century. The railroad boom began in earnest in the late 1840s. By 1859, overall capital investment in private railroad corporations in the United States topped $1 billion, a staggering figure by the standards of the day. The funds capitalized the completion of 30 large railroads.[13] This capital investment ran apace until the depression of the 1870s. By that time, 70,000 miles of track were laid down, connecting much of the continental United States. By 1900, locomotives were running over 200,000 miles of track, connecting large cities, small towns, and even rural hamlets across the breadth of America.[14]

Financing for a transport infrastructure on this scale required a whole new type of business model—the modern stock-holding corporation. While stock-holding enterprises were not unknown previously, they were few in number and generally limited to short-term trading expeditions. Both the British East India and Dutch East India companies were state-chartered stock-holding enterprises.[15] The sale of railroad securities turned the small provincial New York Stock Exchange into a financial powerhouse. Although few Americans are aware of the fact, much of the stock in U.S. railroads were purchased by British, and to a lesser extent, French and German, investors.

The railroads became, in effect, the first modern capitalist business corporations. They created a new business model that separated ownership from management and control. Henceforth, giant business enterprises would be run entirely by paid professional managers whose primary responsibility would be to ensure a return on investment to their shareholders. Capitalism is a unique and peculiar form of enterprise in which the workforce is stripped of its ownership of the tools it uses to create the products, and the investors who own the enterprises are stripped of their power to control and manage their businesses.

The high capital cost of establishing a rail infrastructure made necessary a business model that could organize around vertical integration, bringing upstream suppliers and downstream customers together under one roof. The major railroads bought mining properties to secure a guaranteed supply of coal for their locomotives. The Pennsylvania Railroad even financed the Pennsylvania Steelworks Company to ensure a steady supply of steel to make its rails. The Canadian Pacific Railroad built and managed hotels near its rail stations to accommodate its passengers.[16]

Managing large, vertically integrated enterprises, in turn, was most efficiently carried out by centralized, top-down command and control mechanisms. The railroad companies were the first to understand the operating requisites that came with the new communication/energy/transportation matrix. Laying down and maintaining thousands of miles of track, monitoring rail traffic across vast regions of the country, repairing and manufacturing thousands of pieces of equipment, coordinating the shipment and delivery of freight, managing passenger schedules, assuring on-time performance, and overseeing the work of thousands of employees was a momentous task. Moreover, a lapse or breakdown of any part of the system could—and often did—have a cascading effect, jeopardizing the entire operation.

Running these mammoth enterprises required the successful rationalization of every aspect of the company's business operations. Max Weber, the great nineteenth-century sociologist, provided a good description of what is entailed in the rationalization of business. To begin with, the modern business corporation is arranged pyramidically, with all decision making automatically flowing from the top down. Formal rules and procedures dictating the flow of activity, the definition of tasks, how work is to be carried out, and how performance is to be judged at every stage of operations and every level of engagement are meticulously planned, leaving little room for improvisation. The tasks are broken down by division of labor and each worker is given precise instructions on how he or she is to perform their work. Promotions in the company are based on merit and calculable objective criteria.

The business historian Alfred Chandler described how the railroads adopted the rationalizing process into their management structure. He observed that railroads

> were the first to require a large number of salaried managers; the first to have a central office operated by middle managers and commanded by top managers who reported to a board of directors. They were the first American business enterprise to build a large internal organizational structure with carefully defined lines of responsibility, authority, and communication between the central office, departmental headquarters, and field units; and they were the first to develop financial and statistical flows to control and evaluate the work of many managers.[17]

Weber and other thinkers took it for granted that a mature capitalism required vertically integrated companies to create economies of scale and highly rationalized corporate bureaucracies—with centralized management and top-down command and control mechanisms—to organize commercial life.[18] The ideal capitalist enterprise, according to Weber, is a bureaucratic organization that rationalizes every aspect of commercial life under a single roof. The marshaling of investment capital through the sale of stock, the mobilization of free labor, the setting up of mass-production processes, and competitive exchanges in the market, buttressed by formalistic legal codes, are all subject to calculability and rational bureaucratic management designed to facilitate the centralization of decision-making power in a hierarchical command structure. Weber was right, but left unsaid was that the same centralized hierarchical command and control mechanisms were equally required under a socialist economic system.

Managing the acceleration and expansion of commerce and trade across national markets would have been impossible without an accompanying communications revolution. In 1814, Friedrich Koenig's steam-powered printing machine began producing newspaper pages at

The Times of London at lightning speed—the new presses could print a thousand copies of the paper per hour compared to a mere 250 copies with the older manual presses.[19] By 1832, printing machines at the newspaper had more than doubled the run per hour.[20]

Fast, cheap, steam-powered print encouraged a drive for mass literacy across Europe and America. Public school systems were established and compulsory education was mandated in the newly industrialized cities to prepare the future workforce with the communication skills they would need to attend to the more complex business operations that accompanied the First Industrial Revolution.

In the ensuing decades, a succession of advances in steam-powered printing, including papermaking machines, stereotypes, and rotary printers, significantly reduced labor costs while increasing production, allowing the steam-printing revolution to keep pace with the productivity gains in coal-powered rail transport.

When national postal services switched from stagecoaches to rail, cheap and fast print combined with cheap and fast transport to quicken commercial transactions. Time-sensitive contracts, bills, shipping orders, newspapers, advertising, instruction manuals, books, catalogs, and the like could be sped along by rail, connecting businesses across the supply chain as well as sellers and consumers in hours or days, rather than weeks or even months, greatly accelerating the pace of commerce.

The new print communications revolution didn't come cheap. Like the railroads, the capital investment costs of bringing steam-powered printing to the market were significant. The first steam-powered presses were complex and could cost up to £500 or more per unit (equivalent to $26,500 in today's economy).[21] The cost of steam-powered printing continued to rise as new, more expensive presses came online. By 1846, the Hoe double-cylinder rotary press was churning out 12,000 sheets per hour, and by 1865, the roll-fed rotary press was producing 12,000 newspapers per hour. The startup cost of funding a newspaper had also increased dramatically to $100,000, or about $2.38 million in 2005 dollars.[22]

In America, giant printing companies sprung up in Chicago in the aftermath of the great fire of 1871. R. R. Donnelley & Sons, Rand McNally, and M. A. Donohue and Company were among the industry leaders. Their printing plants could take advantage of economies of scale by handling much of the print material for the entire country in a central location. These companies were surrounded by type foundries and printing press manufacturers, creating an integrated industrial complex near the Chicago rail yards—the central rail connection for the country—ensuring the quick postal delivery of textbooks, magazines, and catalogs across the country.[23]

The cost of building and running those enormous facilities was beyond the reach of most family-owned businesses. R. R. Donnelly, realizing early on that if it was to gain dominance in the industry it would need to raise large sums of finance capital, made the decision to incorporate as a public company in 1890.[24]

By 1900, these highly centralized print operations were churning out millions of catalogs for mass mail-order companies like Montgomery Ward and Sears, Roebuck and Company. Montgomery Ward's 540-page catalog listed more than 24,000 items, including groceries, drugs, jewelry, handbags, shoes, men's clothing, stoves, furniture, buggies, sporting goods, and musical instruments. Sears even sold prefabricated homes through the mail. The homes were shipped by train in pieces in crates and assembled on-site.[25] Sears bungalows can still be seen in the Washington, D.C., area, where my wife and I live.

Millions of Americans in smaller towns and rural areas purchased virtually all their business equipment, home furnishings, and personal attire by catalogs printed in the great Chicago printing houses. The items were then transported by rail and delivered, via the U.S. Postal Service, directly to their businesses and homes. Sears's mail-order revenue in 1905 was a whopping $2,868,000, the equivalent of $75,473,680 in 2013 dollars.[26]

The convergence of coal-powered steam printing and coal-powered steam rail transport created an infrastructure for the First Industrial Revolution. The communications part of the infrastructure was augmented with the build-out of a nationwide telegraph network in the 1860s, allowing businesses instantaneous communication across their supply chains and distribution channels.

The coming together of steam-powered printing, the telegraph, and the steam-powered locomotive dramatically increased the speed and dependability with which economic resources could be marshaled, transported, processed, transformed into products, and distributed to customers. Chandler observes that "cheap power and heat and quick and reliable transportation and communication" were the key factors in the rapid spread of centralized factories in the 1840s and 1850s.[27]

The newfound speed and volume of economic activity made possible by the new communication/energy/transportation matrix required a complete rethinking of the business model across every other industry. Previously, production and distribution of manufactured goods were kept separate. Manufacturers relied on independent wholesalers, distributors, and retailers, scattered across the country, to move their goods to market. These antiquated distribution channels proved to be too slow and unreliable and far too provincial to handle the onslaught of mass-produced products flooding out of factories operating the first automated continuous-process machinery. In addition, many of the new manufactured products, like the Singer sewing machine and the McCormick reaper, required skilled personnel who could demonstrate them to customers. An increasing number of mass-produced goods also required specialized after-sale servicing, which necessitated maintaining an ongoing relationship with customers. The traditional distribution system was simply incapable of accommodating the new commercial practices.

The solution was to bring production and distribution all together, in house, under centralized management. The vertically integrated business enterprise took off in the last quarter of the nineteenth century and became the dominant business model during the whole of the twentieth century.

The great value of vertically integrated companies is that by eliminating many of the middle men across the value chain, these new mega-enterprises were able to significantly reduce their transaction costs while dramatically increasing productivity. In a nutshell, vertically integrated companies introduced vast new efficiencies whose economies of scale lowered their marginal costs, enabling them to sell ever larger volumes of cheap mass-produced goods to an eager public. Cheaper products stimulated mass consumer demand, which in turn spawned new business opportunities and the hiring of workers, improving the standard of living for millions of people in the industrializing economies.

The new business model spread quickly as firms saw the great advantage of bringing together production and distribution under one roof and extending their business operations across an entire continent. Diamond Match Company, W. Duke and Sons Tobacco, Pillsbury, H.

J. Heinz, Procter & Gamble, Eastman Kodak, and I. M. Singer and Company were among the hundreds of companies to adopt the vertically integrated business model to achieve efficient economies of scale.

Virtually all the entrepreneurs who prospered during the takeoff stage of the First Industrial Revolution in the second half of the nineteenth century succeeded in large part because they were able to raise sufficient financial capital by incorporating and becoming a publicly traded shareholding company. The capital allowed them to capture vertically scaled market opportunities and become the standard bearers of their respective industries.

THE SECOND INDUSTRIAL REVOLUTION

At the very time the First Industrial Revolution was peaking in the last two decades of the nineteenth century, a Second Industrial Revolution was being born in America and Europe. The discovery of oil, the invention of the internal combustion engine, and the introduction of the telephone gave rise to a new communication/energy/transportation complex that would dominate the twentieth century.

The most important thing to understand about oil is that it requires more finance capital to marshal than any other single resource in the global economy. Moreover, recouping the investment across the many steps involved in getting the oil and the products derived from it to end users can only be obtained by organizing the entire process— discovery, drilling, transporting, refining, and marketing—under the aegis of vertically integrated companies operated by highly centralized management.

Discovering and bringing online new oil fields today is time consuming and costly, and, more often than not, unsuccessful. The activation index, which measures the total investment needed to access new oil discoveries, is enough to leave the faint-hearted out of the game. It is not unusual for the leading energy companies to invest several billion dollars in new oil projects. When Iraq decided it wanted to triple its oil production in the first decade of the twenty-first century, the cost of financing the investment was calculated at nearly $30 billion.[28] The total cost of capital investment in worldwide exploration and production of oil and natural gas was nearly $2.4 trillion between 2000 and 2011.[29]

Oil exploration requires sophisticated satellite data analyses and a knowledge of geology, geophysics, and geochemistry. The most advanced computers and software are needed to collect and interpret three-dimensional reflection seismic data and create three-dimensional images of the Earth's interior. Drilling wells to depths of 20,000 feet or more requires expensive and complex high-tech oil equipment. Erecting massive oil-drilling platforms on the ocean floor is a major engineering feat. Laying out pipelines, often across hundreds and even thousands of miles of difficult and inaccessible terrain, is equally challenging.

The refining process is also difficult. The geologist Robert Anderson describes the complex set of operations. Organic chemists have to break down the crude oil hydrocarbon complex and reconstruct it into a slew of products that range from gasoline to polyurethane. The particular properties of crude oil vary considerably from one oil region to another, which requires building customized refineries to process particular feedstocks.

The marketing of oil is no less complicated. Petroleum product sales vary considerably from season to season. Gasoline prices are higher in the summer months; heating oil is more expensive in the winter months. Energy companies must therefore rely on meteorological forecasts and economic growth projections and scenarios, and even factor in potential political events that could be either disruptive or opportunistic, in determining future oil needs—at least six months in advance—to ensure that the correct crudes are channeled to the appropriate refineries to be ready for the coming seasons.

Further complicating the process, Anderson explains, is that the marketing departments of energy companies are subdivided into industrial, wholesale, and retail units, and further divided by specialty products including asphalt, aviation fuel, natural gas, liquids for chemicals, agricultural fertilizers and pesticides, and coke for the metal and rubber industries. Fifty percent of the petroleum sold in the United States is refined into gasoline for transport.[30]

Even at the very beginning of the oil age, some entrepreneurs understood that the complex, multilayered process required to bring oil to end users could only be made financially lucrative by consolidating control over the entire operation. Only then could companies employ the rationalizing practices of centralized management and reap the optimum profit.

John D. Rockefeller founded the Standard Oil Company in 1868 with just that end in mind. Rockefeller bought up oil wells and refineries around the country and secured special arrangements with the railroads to ensure that his oil shipments had favored status. At the dawn of the automobile era in the opening decade of the twentieth century, Standard Oil became the first company to set up gasoline stations across the United States, creating a complex, vertically integrated business operation that combined production and distribution from the wellhead to the end user. By 1910 Rockefeller controlled most of the oil business in the United States. Competitors and the public cried foul, and the federal government brought suit against his company under the Sherman Antitrust Act. In 1911, the Supreme Court ordered the breakup of the Standard Oil Company. The government effort to curtail big oil was short-lived. By the 1930s, 26 oil companies, including Standard Oil of New Jersey, Standard Oil of Indiana, Texaco, Gulf Oil, Sinclair, Phillips 66, Union 76, and Sunoco, owned two-thirds of the capital structure of the industry, 60 percent of the drilling, 90 percent of the pipelines, 70 percent of the refining stations, and 80 percent of the marketing.[31]

The concentration of the oil industry today, while less pronounced, is still formidable. In the United States, five companies—Chevron, BP, Royal Dutch Shell, ExxonMobil, and Conoco Philips—control 34 percent of domestic oil exploration and production.[32]

Around the same time Rockefeller was busy consolidating control over the new energy source of the Second Industrial Revolution, Alexander Graham Bell was experimenting with electricity. In 1876 Bell invented the telephone, a device that would become a critical factor in managing the new and more expansive oil, auto, and suburban economy and the mass consumer culture of the twentieth century.

Bell's ambition was to create a national long-distance network that could connect every telephone into a single system. He reasoned that telecommunications required the ultimate vertically integrated company to be effective—that is, a single system, centrally controlled and under one roof. In 1885, Bell created the American Telephone and Telegraph Company subsidiary to connect all of the local Bell

Telephone companies, and in 1899 he transferred the assets of Bell to the subsidiary—making AT&T synonymous with phone service.[33] A phone service connecting every community in the country would promote a continental communications network to manage and service an integrated national economy.

AT&T enjoyed a head start on any potential competitors because of Bell's ownership of the patents on the telephone. After the patents expired in the early 1890s, competitors swarmed into the market. By 1900 some 3,000 telephone companies were doing business in the United States.[34] Despite the robust competition, a number of observers, including elected officials, both in Washington, D.C., and the state houses, were worried over AT&T's aggressive policy of eliminating its competition. Theodore Newton Vail, AT&T's president, made clear his intention of controlling the national telephone service and even created a new corporate advertising slogan of "One Policy, One System, Universal Service." He openly taunted the feds by exclaiming that "effective, aggressive competition, and regulation and control are inconsistent with each other, and cannot be had at the same time."[35]

Concerned that AT&T was quickly devouring its competitors—even acquiring a controlling interest in Western Union—in the first decade of the twentieth century, the federal government began considering taking action to break up the giant.[36]

While fearful that AT&T was becoming a monopoly, federal officials were also beginning to realize that universal phone service was so important in the life of every American and the well-being of American society that it was more akin to a right than a privilege. Government regulators came to believe that the telephone industry would function more effectively as a single unified entity and thus avoid "duplicative," "destructive," and "wasteful" practices. In 1921 the Senate Commerce Committee went on record to state that "telephoning is a natural monopoly."[37] The committee argued that because of the enormous amount of capital required to install a nationwide infrastructure for communications and to achieve economies of scale, it would be difficult, if not impossible, to imagine competing infrastructures across the country. Economists began to talk about phone service as a public good.

Vail sensed a gaping contradiction in the federal government's approach to the telephone industry and seized on it to strike a deal with Washington. Realizing that the federal government might take action against AT&T, Vail reversed his earlier stance, which called for a deregulated competitive market, and called instead for government regulation, hoping it would make his own company the "natural monopoly" the government was looking for. Writing of the daring new counterintuitive strategy, Harvard business professor Richard H. K. Vietor observed:

> Vail chose at this time to put AT&T squarely behind government regulation, as the quid pro quo for avoiding competition. This was the only politically acceptable way for AT&T to monopolize telephony. . . . It seemed a necessary trade-off for the attainment of universal service.[38]

The maneuver ultimately paid off, but it took a world war for Vail to achieve his dream. In 1918, the U.S. government nationalized the telecommunications industry for national security purposes and put it under the stewardship of Albert S. Burleson, the postmaster general and a long-standing advocate of nationalization of the telephone and telegraph industries. Burleson immediately appointed Vail to manage the telephone industry as part of the war effort. Vail turned around and quickly accepted the terms of a contract written up by his own company, AT&T, laying out the conditions of the government's new ownership. It was as sweet an arrangement as ever would be made between the federal government and a private company. Among other things:

> The federal government . . . agreed to pay to AT&T 4.5 percent of the gross operating revenues of the telephone companies as a service fee; to make provisions for depreciation and obsolescence at the high rate of 5.72 percent per plant; to make provision for the amortization of the intangible capital; to disburse all interest and dividend requirements; and in addition, to keep the properties in as good a condition as before.[39]

As soon as the ink was dry on the contract, AT&T applied for significant rate increases for service connection charges and received them. Then, using its new position as a government-owned entity, it began making similar demands on the states. Within five and half months of being "taken over" by the federal government, the company had secured a 20 percent increase in its long-distance rates, a far greater return than it had enjoyed when still wrestling in the competitive free-enterprise marketplace. Even when AT&T was put back in private hands after the war, the rates established by the federal government during its short tenure in government trusteeship remained in effect.

Gerald Brock, professor of telecommunication and of public policy and public administration at George Washington University, summed up what AT&T gained in the process of embracing federal and state government regulation in establishing a national telecommunications infrastructure:

> The acceptance of regulation was a risk-reducing decision. It substituted a limited but guaranteed return on capital and management freedom for the uncertainty of the marketplace. It gave the Bell system a powerful weapon to exclude competitors and justification for seeking a monopoly, as well as reducing the chances of outright nationalization or serious antitrust action.[40]

AT&T remained a virtual monopoly until the 1980s, when, as with Standard Oil, the federal government stepped in and broke it up. By 2011, however, AT&T had climbed back to dominance with a 39.5 percent share of the telecommunications market in the United States. Verizon, AT&T's main competitor, enjoys 24.7 percent of the market, and together the two companies control 64.2 percent of the telecommunications market in the United States, making them a near oligopoly.[41]

The telephone provided an agile communications medium for managing far more dispersed economic activity across an urban/suburban landscape. The shift in transport from coal-powered locomotives traveling between fixed points to oil-powered cars, buses, and trucks traveling radially expanded the geographic range of economic activity. The telephone, unlike print and the telegraph, could be everywhere at every moment, coordinating the more voluminous economic activity made possible in the auto era. With the telephone, businesses could supervise new and larger vertically integrated operations with even tighter centralized control in "real time." The efficiency and productivity gains brought on by the new communications medium were spectacular.

The telephone, of course, required electricity. In 1896, there were about 2,500 electric light companies and nearly 200 municipal power plants operating throughout the United States and an additional 7,500 isolated power plants, with a total capital investment of $500 million—a massive financial outlay.[42] Besides producing power for telephone communications, the power plants produced electricity for lighting and to run machinery in the factories and appliances in the home.

The new electrical lighting lit up commercial businesses, allowing for an extension of working hours into the evening, which fed additional economic growth. By 1910, one out of every ten homes in the United States had electricity, and by 1929, most urban homes were connected to the electricity grid.[43]

Factories were slower to adopt electricity. In 1900, only 5 percent of factories were using electricity.[44] That changed quickly with the introduction of the automobile and mass-production assembly lines. Henry Ford was among the first to see the potential of electricity in ramping up automobile production. He would later muse that his ambitious goal of producing an affordable Model T for every working family would have been unrealizable were it not for the electrification of factories and the introduction of electrical motors. He wrote:

> The provision of a whole new system of electric generation emancipated industry from the leather belt and line shaft, for it eventually became possible to provide each tool with its own electric motor. . . .
> The motor enabled machinery to be arranged according to the sequence of the work, and that alone has probably doubled the efficiency of industry. . . . Without high speed tools . . . there could be nothing of what we call modern industry.[45]

The changeover from steam power to electrification of factories led to a whopping 300 percent increase in productivity in the first half of the twentieth century.[46]

The electrification of automobile factories unleashed the power of mass production and put millions of people behind the wheel of a car.

By 1916, 3.4 million registered autos were on U.S. roads. Fourteen years later, there were 23 million registered cars in the United States.[47] The automobile became the key "engine" of economic growth for the whole of the Second Industrial Revolution.

Other critical industries became part of a giant business complex, later referred to as the "Auto Age." Automobiles consumed "20 percent of the steel, 12 percent of the aluminum, 10 percent of the copper, 51 percent of the lead, 95 percent of the nickel, 35 percent of the zinc, and 60 percent of the rubber used in the U.S." by 1933.[48] One enthusiast, writing in 1932, marveled at the automobile's impact on the economy, noting that "as a consumer of raw material, the automobile has no equal in the history of the world."[49]

The mass production of automobiles kicked the oil industry into overdrive. New oil fields were opening up weekly in America and gasoline stations became an omnipresent part of the American landscape. By the late 1930s, oil had surpassed coal as the primary energy source in America. Texas oil wells became synonymous with American power around the world as the United States became the leading oil-producing country. The British statesmen Ernest Bevin once quipped that "the kingdom of heaven may run on righteousness, but the kingdom of earth runs on oil."[50]

Like the laying down of tracks for rail transport, building roads and mass producing automobiles were expensive undertakings. While road systems were financed by the government in America and everywhere else, the automobile industry—at least in the United States—was financed wholly by private capital. At first, dozens of small car companies came on the scene. Before long, however, the sheer costs involved in creating the large, vertically integrated enterprises necessary for the mass production and distribution of autos narrowed the field to half a dozen automobile giants led by the Big Three—Ford, General Motors, and Chrysler—which remain market leaders to this day.

And, like the railroads, the auto industry realized early on that effective supervision of the many diverse activities that come together in the production and sale of automobiles needed rationalized central management and top-down bureaucratic control to succeed. Nor could the scale of operations be financed by a single individual or family. Every major automobile manufacturer in the United States eventually became a publicly traded corporation.

Putting the economy on wheels also radically changed the spatial orientation of society. Steam-powered printing and coal-powered rail transport encouraged urbanization. Print communication and freight traveling by rail to fixed endpoint destinations largely defined where commercial and residential life clustered. Smaller cities grew into bigger metropolises and new towns were spawned along rail links. Businesses dependent on print communications and freight by rail naturally chose to locate close to the communication/energy/transportation hubs.

The coming of the automobile and the construction of a national road system that could carry passengers and freight into rural areas outside the reach of railroad connectivity spawned suburban development in the first half of the twentieth century. The construction of the interstate highway system from the 1950s to the 1980s—the biggest and most costly public works project in history—led to a frenzy of suburban commercial and residential development along the interstate exits. Factories began to relocate away from dense urban centers—which had high real estate and labor costs—to rural areas, transferring deliveries from rail to trucking. The workforce followed. Sixty-five million homes, most in new suburban developments, were built in the United States since 1945, and 48,000 strip malls and shopping centers have been erected as the nation's population scattered into thousands of suburban enclaves.[51] The dispersal of commercial and residential housing was accompanied by the spread of electrical infrastructure and telephone wires and, later, radio and television transmission into new suburban communities.

The dramatic growth of the suburbs and the increasingly complex logistics that came with organizing and integrating economic activity across tens of thousands of communities led to even more centralized command and control in the hands of fewer industry leaders in each sector as they struggled to capture ever larger vertically integrated economies of scale. By the time the Second Industrial Revolution peaked and crashed in July 2008, when the price of crude oil hit a record $147 a barrel on world markets, the concentration of economic power in the hands of a small number of corporate players in each industry had similarly peaked. Three energy companies—ExxonMobil, Chevron, and Conoco Phillips—are among the four largest U.S. companies and control much of the domestic oil market.

I already mentioned that AT&T and Verizon together control a 64 percent share of the telecommunication industry. In a study published in 2010, the federal government found that in most states one electricity company controlled 25 to 50 percent of ownership; overall, just 38 companies—5 percent of the 699 companies identified—control 40 percent of the nation's electricity generation.[52] Four automobile companies—General Motors, Ford, Chrysler, and Toyota—control 60 percent of the automobile market.[53] Five media companies—News Corp., Google, Garnett, Yahoo, and Viacom—control 54 percent of the U.S. media market.[54] In the arcade, food, and entertainment industry, CEC (Chuck E. Cheese's) Entertainment, Dave & Busters, Sega Entertainment, and Namco Bandai Holdings control 96 percent of the market share. In the household appliances manufacturing industry, the top four companies—Whirlpool, AB Electrolux, General Electric, and LG Electronics—control 90 percent of the market.[55] Similar concentration patterns can be found across every other major sector of the U.S. economy.

Today, in the sunset of the fossil fuel era, the oil industry remains the most concentrated industry in the world, followed closely by the telecommunications and the electrical power generation and distribution industry. Virtually all the other industries that depend on the fossil fuel/telecommunications matrix require, by necessity, huge capital expenditures to establish sufficient vertical integration and accompanying economies of scale to recoup their investments and are therefore forced to manage their own far-flung activities using highly rationalizing command-and-control processes.

Three of the four largest shareholding companies in the world today are oil companies—Royal Dutch Shell, ExxonMobil, and BP. Underneath the oil giants are ten banks—JPMorgan Chase, Goldman Sachs, BOA Merrill Lynch, Morgan Stanley, Citigroup, Deutsche Bank, Credit Suisse, Barclays Capital, UBS, and Wells Fargo Securities—that control nearly 60 percent of the worldwide investment banking market.[56] And, as mentioned in chapter 1, beneath the financial investors are 500 globally traded companies—with combined revenue of $22.5 trillion, which is equal to one-third of the world's $62 trillion GDP—that are inextricably connected to and dependent on fossil fuel energy, global telecommunications, and the world's electricity grid for their very existence.[57] In no other period of history have so few institutions wielded so much economic power over the lives of so many people.

This unprecedented—and unimaginable—concentration of economic power was not just happenstance or a byproduct of man's insatiable avarice. Nor can it be rationalized away by simply blaming deregulation or finding fault with political ineptitude or, worse still, political collusion and enablement—although these were all contributing factors to its growth. Rather, on a more fundamental level, it flowed inexorably from the communication/energy/transportation matrices that were the foundation of the First and Second Industrial Revolutions.

Like it or not, giant, vertically integrated corporate enterprises were the most efficient means of organizing the production and distribution of mass produced goods and services. Bringing together supply chains, production processes, and distribution channels in vertically integrated companies under centralized management dramatically reduced transaction costs, increased efficiencies and productivity, lowered the marginal cost of production and distribution, and, for the most part, lowered the price of goods and services to consumers, allowing the economy to flourish. While those at the top of the corporate pyramid disproportionately benefited from the increasing returns on investment, it's only fair to acknowledge that the lives of millions of consumers also improved appreciably in industrialized nations.

CHAPTER FOUR
HUMAN NATURE THROUGH A CAPITALIST LENS

W hat's most remarkable about the concentration of economic power in the hands of a few corporate players in each industry is how little public angst it has generated—at least in the United States—over the course of the nineteenth and twentieth centuries. While the labor unions' struggles against corporate power were bitterly fought, they never attracted a majority of the workforce to their cause. Although there have also been occasional populist uprisings challenging the unbridled corporate control exercised over the economic life of society—the most recent being the Occupy Movement, with its rallying cry of the 99 percent versus the 1 percent—such outbursts have generally been few and far between and led to only mild regulatory reforms that did little to curb the concentration of power.

To some extent, the criticism was muted because these large, vertically integrated corporate enterprises succeeded in bringing ever-cheaper products and services to the market, spawned millions of jobs, and improved the standard of living of working people throughout the industrial world.

There is, however, an additional and more subtle factor at play that has proven to be every bit as effective in dampening potential public opposition. The First and Second Industrial Revolutions brought with them an all-encompassing world view that legitimized the economic system by suggesting that its workings are a reflection of the way nature itself is organized and, therefore, unimpeachable.

RETHINKING SALVATION

The practice of legitimizing economic paradigms by creating grand cosmological narratives to accompany them is an age-old practice. Contemporary historians point to St. Thomas Aquinas's description of creation as a Great Chain of Being during the feudal era as a good example of the process of framing a cosmology that legitimizes the existing social order. Aquinas argued that the proper workings of nature depend on a labyrinth of obligations among God's creatures. While each creature differs in intellect and capabilities, the diversity and inequality is essential to the orderly functioning of the overall system. If all creatures were equal, St. Thomas reasoned, than they could not act for the advantage of others. By making each creature different, God established a hierarchy of obligations in nature that, if faithfully carried out, allowed the Creation to flourish.

St. Thomas's description of God's creation bears a striking resemblance to the way feudal society was set up: everyone's individual survival depended on them faithfully performing their duties within a rigidly defined social hierarchy. Serfs, knights, lords, and the pope were all unequal in degree and kind but obligated to serve others by the feudal bonds of fealty. The performance of their duties according to their place on the hierarchy paid homage to the perfection of God's creation.

The late historian Robert Hoyt of the University of Minnesota summed up the mirror relationship between the organization of feudal society and the Great Chain of Being:

> The basic idea that the created universe was a hierarchy, in which all created beings were assigned a proper rank and station, was congenial with the feudal notion of status within the feudal hierarchy, where every member had his proper rank with its attendant rights and duties.[1]

The cosmology of the Protestant Reformation that accompanied the soft proto-industrial revolution of the late medieval era performed a similar legitimizing role. Martin Luther launched a frontal attack on the church's notion of the Great Chain of Being, arguing that it legitimized the corrupt hierarchal rule of the pope and the papal administration over the lives of the faithful. The Protestant theologian replaced the church's feudal cosmology with a worldview centered on the personal relationship of each believer with Christ. The democratization of worship fit well with the new communication/energy/transportation matrix that was empowering the new burgher class.

Luther accused the pope of being the Antichrist and warned that the Catholic church was neither God's chosen emissary on Earth nor the anointed intermediary by which the faithful could communicate with the Lord. Nor could church leaders legitimately claim the power to intercede with God on behalf of their parishioners and assure salvation in the next world.

Instead, Luther called for the priesthood of all believers. He argued that each man and woman stands alone before God. Armed with the Bible, every Christian had a personal responsibility to interpret the word of God, without relying on church authority to decipher the meaning of the text and assume the role of gatekeeper to heaven. Luther's admonition spawned the first mass-literacy campaign in world history, as converts to Protestantism quickly learned to read in order to interpret God's word in the Bible.

Luther also changed the rules for salvation. The church had long taught that performing good works along with receiving the church's sacraments would help secure a place in heaven for believers. Luther, by contrast, argued that one can't win a place in heaven by racking up good works on Earth. Rather, according to Luther, one's ultimate fate is sealed at the very get-go, that every individual is either elected to salvation or damned at birth by God. But then the question is: How does one live with the terrible anxiety of not knowing what awaits him? Luther's answer was that accepting one's calling in life and performing one's role fully and without a lapse might be a sign that one had been elected to salvation.

John Calvin went a step further, calling on his followers to continuously work at improving their lot in life as a sign of possible election. By contending that each individual was duty-bound to improve his or her calling, Protestant theologians unwittingly lent theological support to the new spirit of entrepreneurialism. Implicit was the assumption that bettering one's economic lot was a reflection of one's proper relationship with God and the natural order.

Although neither Luther nor Calvin had any intention of despiritualizing the faithful and creating *homo economicus*, eventually the idea of improving one's calling became indistinguishable from improving one's economic fortunes. The new emphasis on diligence, hard work, and frugality metamorphosed over the course of the sixteenth and seventeenth centuries into the more economically laden term of being "more productive." Self-worth became less about being of good character in the eyes of God and more about being productive in the new market exchange economy.

In time, the idea of each person standing alone with their Lord began to take a back seat to the notion of each person standing alone in the marketplace. Self-worth was now to be measured by self-interest, which, in turn, was measured by the accumulation of property and wealth by cunning dealings in the new market economy. Max Weber referred to this process that created the new man and woman of the market as "the Protestant [work] ethic."[2]

The new commercial zeal spilled over, bringing increasing numbers of Catholics and others into the market fold. Where previously one's place on the rungs of the Great Chain of Being that made up God's creation had defined one's life journey in the feudal era, the new autonomous individual of the soft market economy came to define his journey by the amassing of private property in the marketplace.

THE ENLIGHTENMENT VIEW OF HUMAN NATURE

By the end of the soft market era in the late eighteenth century, a new cosmology had begun to emerge that would give the new man and woman of the market an overarching narrative powerful enough to push the Christian cosmology nearer to the sideline of history.

John Locke, the great Enlightenment philosopher, led the charge, presenting a spirited defense of private property, arguing that its pursuit was a more accurate reflection of man's "inherent nature" than communal management of the feudal commons. Locke argued that each person creates his own property by adding his labor to the raw material of nature, transforming it into things of value. Although

Locke acknowledged that in the primal state of nature all the Earth was held in common by human beings and our fellow creatures, he explained in *Two Treatises of Government* that each individual also "has a *property* in his own *person*: [and] this no body has any right to but himself."[3] Locke made the case that private property is a natural right, and therefore, any repudiation of it would be tantamount to rejecting the natural order of things and denying the laws of nature.

Locke reasoned that

> whatsoever then he removes out of the state that nature hath provided, and left it in, he hath mixed his *labour* with, and joined to it something that is his own, and thereby makes it his *property*. It being by him removed from the common state nature hath placed it in, it hath by this *labour* something annexed to it, that excludes the common right of other men: for his *labour* being the unquestionable property of the labourer, no man but he can have a right to what is once joined to, at least where there is enough, and as good, left in common for others.[4]

Locke then used his theory of the natural right to private property to tear apart the feudal property regime based on proprietary obligations on the commons.

> He, who appropriates land to himself by his labour, does not lessen, but increases the common stock of mankind: for the provisions serving to the support of human life, produced by one acre of inclosed and cultivated land, are . . . ten times more than those which are yielded by an acre of land of an equal richness lying waste in common. And therefore he that incloses land, and has a greater plenty of the conveniences of life from ten acres, than he could have from an hundred left to nature, may truly be said to give ninety acres to mankind.[5]

In this brief essay, Locke articulated the emerging cosmological narrative that would accompany the modern market economy. The natural order of things was no longer to be found in Christianity's Great Chain of Being but, rather, in the natural right to create private property by the sweat of one's own brow.

Adam Smith followed on the heels of Locke. In a final rebuff to the communal life exercised on the feudal commons, he declared that market behavior represents people's true nature. Smith wrote that

every individual is continually exerting himself to find out the most advantageous employment for whatever capital he can command. It is his own advantage, indeed, and not that of society, which he has in view. But the study of his own advantage naturally, or rather necessarily, leads him to prefer that employment which is most advantageous to the society.[6]

The social critic R. H. Tawney would later write of the momentous change that took European society from a feudal to a market economy and from a theocratic to an economic worldview. He observed that after the fall of the Christian-centered universe, what was left "was private rights and private interests, the material of a society rather than a society itself." Private property exchanged in the market economy was henceforth "taken for granted as the fundamentals upon which social organization was to be based, and about which no further argument was admissible."[7] Max Weber was even more harsh, arguing that the replacement of spiritual values with economic ones in the changeover from a Christian-centered universe to a materialist one represented "the disenchantment of the world."[8]

In fairness, it should be noted that despite the terrible toll in human suffering brought on by the enclosure of the commons and the letting loose of millions of peasants from their ancestral land to make their own way in a new urban world not yet ready to absorb their labor, the shift to a market economy did eventually improve the lot of the average person in ways that would be unfathomable to families living on the feudal commons.

The shift from a purely market-exchange economy in the late medieval era to a capitalist economy by the mid-nineteenth century posed serious problems in regard to the notion of property. Recall Locke's natural right theory that what a person adds to nature by his own labor belongs to him alone in the form of private property. Locke's theory fit well in the simple market-exchange economy of the late medieval era in which virtually everything sold and bought in the marketplace was the product of an individual or family's own labor.

The coming of capitalism, however, fundamentally changed the economic model. As mentioned, craftsmen were stripped of their tools by capitalists and turned into free laborers, reclaiming only a portion of the labor they expended in the form of a wage. The remainder of the labor value in the product went to the company in the form of profit. Ownership was also transformed. The new owners were shareholder investors whose own labor never went into the product at all and who had little to no say over the management of the company, but who still received dividends from the profit appropriated from the workers' surplus labor. The dilemma is transparent. Were the workers being deprived of their natural right to full ownership and disposition of the products they created with their own labor? Feeble attempts were made to justify the appropriation of the workers' surplus labor value by arguing that capital is stored-up labor and that therefore investors are, in a more indirect sense, "adding" their past labor to the process. Such justification appeared to be a thin reed and didn't hold up. Richard Schlatter keenly observed that

> the classical school, beginning with the assumption that labour was
> the creator of property, was unable to construct an economic theory
> which was both consistent and did not lead to the conclusion that
> the man who profited without working was necessarily robbing the
> workman.[9]

Socialist militants, whose collective voice was gaining strength across Europe by the 1840s, picked up on the contradiction, which threatened to sever classical economic theory from capitalism. The socialists castigated capitalism as an outlier, while praising the claims of classical economic theory that every individual has a natural right to own the full fruits of his or her own labor.

Determined to avoid the break between classical economic theory and a budding capitalism, the economists chose to abandon Locke's natural rights theory of private property to the socialists and scurried to find a new theory to fill the void. They found their answer in David Hume and Jeremy Bentham's theory of utilitarian value. Hume argued that property is a human convention born out of common interest that leads each man "in concurrence with others, into a general plan or system of actions, which tends to public utility."[10] In other words, the laws of property are codes that human beings agree to follow because it is in their common interest.

Hume made it plain that he was sympathetic to the notion that what a man makes out of nature is his own. He argued, however, that private property rights should be encouraged not because they were based in natural rights but because they were "*useful* habits" and that property should be freely exchanged in the marketplace because it was "so *beneficial* to human society."[11]

By contending that the general welfare of society, defined as the pursuit of pleasure over pain, was the basis of all property arrangements, the utilitarians could justify championing both the private property of the laborer and the property rights embedded in capital, arguing that both forms of property advanced the general welfare and are therefore useful. In both instances, it is utility alone that justifies the practice.

Bentham was a bit more willing to take on the natural rights theory of property head on, arguing that there is no such thing as natural property. Bentham explained that

> rights are, then, the fruits of the law, and of the law alone. There are no rights without law—no rights contrary to the law—no rights anterior to law . . . property and law are born and must die together.[12]

Utilitarian doctrine gave capitalists the lifeline they needed to justify their growing role as the dominant force in the new industrial economy. Still, the natural rights theory of property continued to hold sway, especially among the throngs of workers streaming into the factories and front offices of the industrial economy and the small craftsmen and business owners who would continue to play a critical, if not diminished, role in the era of big capital.

The utility doctrine, although ostensibly grounded in social convention rather than natural law, got an unintentional boost from Charles Darwin. In his second book, *The Descent of Man*, Darwin argued that human beings' evolved mental faculties spawned the development of conscience, which predisposed them to increasingly adhere to the utilitarian principle of championing the greatest good for the greatest number. Darwin's musings armed the economists with some reassuring "natural support" for their utilitarianism.

However, Darwin wasn't happy with the purloining of his theory of evolution. After all, he had argued that our species' utilitarian nature was of a higher order—one that promoted empathic extension and cooperation among people—and was understandably upset to see his insights reduced to a more strictly economic agenda of legitimizing a collective material self-interest. In his last writings, Darwin challenged John Stuart Mill and other popular utilitarian economists, arguing that "impulses do not by any means always arise from . . . anticipated pleasure."[13] To make his point, he used the example of a person rushing to save a stranger in a fire despite the personal risk and without any expectation of a reward. Darwin argued that the motivation to come to another's rescue derived from a deeper human impulse than pleasure—what he called the social instinct.[14]

The misuse of Darwin's theory to jack up the utility theory of property had some measurable effect. However, far more egregious and impactful was the wholesale expropriation of Darwin's theory of natural selection by the sociologist and philosopher Herbert Spencer to advance what would later be called Social Darwinism—an ideologically inspired movement designed to justify the worst excesses of a rampant capitalism in the latter part of the nineteenth century. Spencer seized on Darwin's description of natural selection to justify his own theory of economic evolution. Spencer wrote that "this survival of the fittest, which I have here sought to express in mechanical terms, is that which Mr. Darwin has called 'natural selection, or the preservation of favored races in the struggle for life.'"[15] While Darwin is widely credited with coining the term *survival of the fittest*, it was actually conceived by Spencer after reading Darwin's work. However, Darwin unfortunately inserted Spencer's narrative into the fifth edition of *The Origin of Species*, which was published in 1869. Darwin wrote, "this preservation, during the battle for life, of varieties which possess any advantage in structure, constitution, or instinct, I have called Natural Selection; and Mr. Herbert Spencer has well expressed the same idea by the Survival of the Fittest."[16] Darwin meant the term as a metaphor for "better designed for immediate, local environment."[17] Spencer, however, used the term to mean in the best physical shape.

In Spencer's hands, *survival of the fittest* came to mean that only the fittest organisms will survive. Spencer hammered the term into the public discourse, unabashedly aligning himself with Darwin, despite the fact that his own views of evolution were far more Lamarckian.

Darwin later went to great lengths to distance himself from the term *survival of the fittest*, even apologizing for using it, but to no avail.[18] The term stuck in the public consciousness and came to define Darwin's theory in the minds of successive generations.

Spencer argued that all the structures in the universe develop from a simple, undifferentiated state to an ever more complex and differentiated state, characterized by greater integration of the various parts. This process applied equally to the stars in the galaxies and the biological evolution here on earth, as well as to human social organization.

Spencer viewed competition among firms in the marketplace as the expression of society's natural evolutionary development and believed that competition should be allowed to play out without government interference—assuring that only the most complex and vertically integrated companies would survive and flourish.

Spencer's views helped legitimize the business interests of the day. By finding a rationale in nature for companies' pursuing ever larger, vertically integrated enterprises, controlled by even more rationalized, centralized management, Spencer and the free-market economists who followed him successfully tempered any serious public opposition to the existing economic arrangements.

WHERE SPENCER AND HIS COMPATRIOTS erred was in believing that the increasing complexity of society invariably required vertically integrated businesses and more centralized command and control in the hands of fewer institutions and individuals. Complexity is not always synonymous with vertical integration and centralization. In the case of the First and Second Industrial Revolutions, the nature of the communication/energy/transportation matrices favored vertical integration of economic activity to reduce marginal cost and create sufficient economies of scale to recoup investments and make a profit. This proved to be equally true, I might add, under both capitalist and socialist regimes, as we saw in both the Soviet Union and China and even in the mixed social market economies in Europe. We shouldn't confuse ownership of the means of production with the organization of the mode of production. Both capitalist and socialist regimes organize production in integrated, vertically scaled enterprises because of the increased efficiencies, despite their different patterns of ownership and distribution of earnings.

But how do we go about organizing an economy where the entry costs in establishing a communication/energy/transportation matrix are substantially lower and paid for in large part by hundreds of millions of individuals in peer-to-peer networks, and where the marginal costs of generating, storing, and sharing communications, energy, and a growing number of products and services are heading to nearly zero?

A new communication/energy/transportation matrix is emerging, and with it a new "smart" public infrastructure. The Internet of Things (IoT) will connect everyone and everything in a new economic paradigm that is far more complex than the First and Second Industrial Revolutions, but one whose architecture is distributed rather than centralized. Even more important, the new economy will optimize the general welfare by way of laterally integrated networks on the Collaborative Commons, rather than vertically integrated businesses in the capitalist market.

The effect of all this is that the corporate monopolies of the twentieth century are now coming up against a disruptive threat of incalculable proportions brought on by the emerging IoT infrastructure. New types of social enterprises can plug and play into the IoT and take advantage of its open, distributed, and collaborative architecture to create peer-to-peer lateral economies of scale that eliminate virtually all of the remaining middlemen. The compression dramatically increases efficiencies and productivity while reducing marginal costs to near zero, enabling the production and distribution of nearly free goods and services.

Although the vertically integrated monopolies that ruled over the Second Industrial Revolution of the twentieth century are struggling to hold off the assault, their efforts are proving futile. The giant monopolies that presided over the music industry, the publishing industry, the print and electronic media, and large parts of the entertainment industry, have already experienced, firsthand, the "shock and awe" of peer production in laterally integrated economies of scale networks that push marginal costs to near zero. As the IoT infrastructure matures, we can expect a routing of many of the corporate giants in fields ranging from energy and power generation to communications, manufacturing, and services.

These far reaching economic changes are beginning to affect an even more profound change in human consciousness itself. The new economic paradigm is being accompanied by a sweeping rethink of human nature that is fundamentally altering the way we perceive our relationship to the Earth. Thomas Paine, the great American revolutionary, once remarked that "every age and generation must be as free to act for itself."[19] A new generation is nurturing an embryonic near zero marginal cost society, changing its worldview, and bringing new meaning to the human journey.

PART II
THE NEAR ZERO MARGINAL COST SOCIETY

CHAPTER FIVE
EXTREME PRODUCTIVITY, THE INTERNET OF THINGS, AND FREE ENERGY

f I had told you 25 years ago that, in a quarter century's time, one-third of the human race would be communicating with one another in huge global networks of hundreds of millions of people—exchanging audio, video, and text—and that the combined knowledge of the world would be accessible from a cellphone, that any single individual could post a new idea, introduce a product, or pass a thought to a billion people simultaneously, and that the cost of doing so would be nearly free, you would have shaken your head in disbelief. All are now reality.

But what if I were to say to you that 25 years from now, the bulk of the energy you use to heat your home and run your appliances, power your business, drive your vehicle, and operate every part of the global economy will likewise be nearly free? That's already the case for several million early adopters who have transformed their homes and businesses into micropower plants to harvest renewable energy on site. Even before any of the fixed costs for installation of solar and wind are paid back—often in as little as two to eight years—the marginal cost of the harvested energy is nearly free.[1] Unlike fossil fuels and uranium for nuclear power, in which the commodity itself always costs something, the sun collected on your rooftop, the wind traveling up the side of your building, the heat coming up from the ground under your office, and the garbage anaerobically decomposing into biomass energy in your kitchen are all nearly free.

And what if nearly free information were to begin managing nearly free green energy, creating an intelligent communication/energy matrix and infrastructure that would allow any business in the world to connect, share energy across a continental Energy Internet, and produce and sell goods at a fraction of the price charged by today's global manufacturing giants? That too is beginning to evolve on a small scale as hundreds of start-up businesses establish 3D printing operations, infofacturing products at near zero marginal cost, powering their Fab Labs with their own green energy, marketing their goods for nearly free on hundreds of global websites, and delivering their products in electric and fuel-cell vehicles powered by their own green energy. (We will discuss the up-front fixed capital costs of establishing the collaborative infrastructure shortly.)

And what if millions of students around the world who had never before had access to a college education were suddenly able to take courses taught by the most distinguished scholars on the planet and receive credit for their work, all for free? That's now happening.

And finally, what if the marginal cost of human labor in the production and distribution of goods and services were to plummet to near zero as intelligent technology substitutes for workers across every industry and professional and technical field, allowing businesses to conduct much of the commercial activity of civilization more intelligently, efficiently, and cheaply than with conventional workforces? That too is occuring as tens of millions of workers have already been replaced by intelligent technology in industries and professional bodies around the world. What would the human race do, and more importantly, how would it define its future on Earth, if mass and professional labor were to disappear from economic life over the course of the next two generations? That question is now being seriously raised for the first time in intellectual circles and public policy debates.

EXTREME PRODUCTIVITY

Getting to near zero marginal cost and nearly free goods and services is a function of advances in productivity. Productivity is "a measure of productive efficiency calculated as the ratio of what is produced to what is required to produce it."[2] If the cost of producing an additional good or service is nearly zero, that would be the optimum level of productivity.

Here again, we come face-to-face with the ultimate contradiction at the heart of capitalism. The driving force of the system is greater productivity, brought on by increasing thermodynamic efficiencies. The process is unsparing as competitors race to introduce new, more productive technologies that will lower their production costs and the price of their products and services to lure in buyers. The race continues to pick up momentum until it approaches the finish line, where the optimum efficiency is reached and productivity peaks. That finish line is where the marginal cost of producing each additional unit is nearly zero. When that finish line is crossed, goods and services become nearly free, profits dry up, the exchange of property in markets shuts down, and the capitalist system dies.

Until very recently, economists were content to measure productivity by two factors: machine capital and labor performance. But when Robert Solow—who won the Nobel Prize in economics in 1987 for his growth theory—tracked the Industrial Age, he found that machine capital and labor performance only accounted for approximately 14 percent of all of the economic growth, raising the question of what was responsible for the other 86 percent. This mystery led economist Moses Abramovitz, former president of the American Economic Association, to admit what other economists were afraid to acknowledge— that the other 86 percent is a "measure of our ignorance."[3]

Over the past 25 years, a number of analysts, including physicist Reiner Kümmel of the University of Würzburg, Germany, and economist Robert Ayres at INSEAD business school in Fontainebleau, France, have gone back and retraced the economic growth of the industrial period using a three-factor analysis of machine capital, labor performance, and thermodynamic efficiency of energy use. They found that it is "the increasing thermodynamic efficiency with which energy and raw materials are converted into useful work" that accounts for most of the rest of the gains in productivity and growth in industrial economies. In other words, "energy" is the missing factor.[4]

A deeper look into the First and Second Industrial Revolutions reveals that the leaps in productivity and growth were made possible by the communication/energy/transportation matrix and accompanying infrastructure that composed the general-purpose technology platform that firms connected to. For example, Henry Ford could not have enjoyed the dramatic advances in efficiency and productivity brought on by electrical power tools on the factory floor without an electricity grid. Nor could businesses reap the efficiencies and productivity gains of large, vertically integrated operations without the telegraph and, later, the telephone providing them with instant communication, both upstream to suppliers and downstream to distributors, as well as instant access to chains of command in their internal and external operations. Nor could businesses significantly reduce their logistics costs without a fully built-out road system across national markets. Likewise, the electricity grid, telecommunications networks, and cars and trucks running on a national road system were all powered by fossil fuel energy, which required a vertically integrated energy infrastructure to move the resource from the wellhead to the refineries and gasoline stations.

This is what President Barack Obama was trying to get at in his now-famous utterance during the 2012 presidential election campaign: "You didn't build that." While the Republican Party opportunistically took the quote out of context, what Obama meant was that successful businesses require infrastructure—electricity transmission lines, oil and gas pipelines, communication networks, roads, schools, etc.—if they are to be productive.[5] No business in an integrated market economy can succeed without an infrastructure. Infrastructures are public goods and require government enablement as well as market facilitation. Common sense, yes, but it was lost in the fury that followed President Obama's remarks, in a country where the prevailing myth is that all economic success is a result of entrepreneurial acumen alone and that government involvement is always a deterrent to growth.

Public infrastructure is, for the most part, paid for or subsidized by taxes and overseen and regulated by the government, be it on the local, state, or national level. The general-purpose technology infra-structure of the Second Industrial Revolution provided the productive potential for a dramatic increase in growth in the twentieth century. Between 1900 and 1929, the United States built out an incipient Sec-ond Industrial Revolution infrastructure—the electricity grid, tele-communications network, road system, oil and gas pipelines, water and sewer systems, and public school systems. The Depression and World War II slowed the effort, but after the war the laying down of the interstate highway system and the completion of a nationwide electricity grid and telecommunications network provided a mature, fully integrated infrastructure. The Second Industrial Revolution in-frastructure advanced productivity across every industry, from auto-mobile production to suburban commercial and residential building developments along the interstate highway exits.

During the period from 1900 to 1980 in the United States, aggre-gate energy efficiency—the ratio of useful to potential physical work that can be extracted from materials—steadily rose along with the development of the nation's infrastructure, from 2.48 percent to 12.3 percent. The aggregate energy efficiency leveled off in the late 1990s at around 13 percent with the completion of the Second Industrial Revolution infrastructure.[6] Despite a significant increase in efficiency, which gave the United States extraordinary productivity and growth, nearly 87 percent of the energy we used in the Second Industrial Rev-olution was wasted during transmission.[7]

Even if we were to upgrade the Second Industrial Revolution in-frastructure, it's unlikely to have any measurable effect on efficiency, productivity, and growth. Fossil fuel energies have matured and are becoming more expensive to bring to market. And the technologies designed and engineered to run on these energies, like the internal-combustion engine and the centralized electricity grid, have exhausted their productivity, with little potential left to exploit.

Needless to say, 100 percent thermodynamic efficiency is impos-sible. New studies, however, including one conducted by my global consulting group, show that with the shift to a Third Industrial Rev-olution infrastructure, it is conceivable to increase aggregate energy efficiency to 40 percent or more in the next 40 years, amounting to a dramatic increase in productivity beyond what the economy experi-enced in the twentieth century.[8]

THE INTERNET OF THINGS

The enormous leap in productivity is possible because the emerging Internet of Things is the first smart-infrastructure revolution in history: one that will connect every machine, business, residence, and vehicle in an intelligent network comprised of a Communications Internet, Energy Internet, and Transportation Internet, all embedded in a single operating system. In the United States alone, 37 million digital smart meters are now providing real-time information on electricity use.[9] Within ten years, every building in America and Europe, as well as other countries around the world, will be equipped with smart meters. And every device—thermostats, assembly lines, warehouse equipment, TVs, washing machines, and computers—will have sensors connected to the smart meter and the Internet of Things platform. In 2007, there were 10 million sensors connecting every type of human contrivance to the Internet of Things. In 2013, that number was set to exceed 3.5 billion, and even more impressive, by 2030 it is projected that 100 trillion sensors will connect to the IoT.[10] Other sensing devices, including aerial sensory technologies, software logs, radio frequency identification readers, and wireless sensor networks, will assist in collecting Big Data on a wide range of subjects from the changing price of electricity on the grid, to logistics traffic across supply chains, production flows on the assembly line, services in the back and front office, as well as up-to-the-moment tracking of consumer activities.[11] As mentioned in chapter 1, the intelligent infrastructure, in turn, will feed a continuous stream of Big Data to every business connected to the network, which they can then process with advanced analytics to create predictive algorithms and automated systems to improve their thermodynamic efficiency, dramatically increase their productivity, and reduce their marginal costs across the value chain to near zero.

Cisco systems forecasts that by 2022, the Internet of Everything will generate $14.4 trillion in cost savings and revenue.[12] A General Electric study published in November 2012 concludes that the efficiency gains and productivity advances made possible by a smart industrial Internet could resound across virtually every economic sector by 2025, impacting "approximately one half of the global economy." It's when we look at each industry, however, that we begin to understand the productive potential of establishing the first intelligent infrastructure in history. For example, in just the aviation industry alone, a mere 1 percent improvement in fuel efficiency, brought about by using Big Data analytics to more successfully route traffic, monitor equipment, and make repairs, would generate savings of $30 billion over 15 years.[13]

The health-care field is still another poignant example of the productive potential that comes with being embedded in an Internet of Things. Health care accounted for 10 percent of global GDP, or $7.1 trillion in 2011, and 10 percent of the expenditures in the sector "are wasted from inefficiencies in the system," amounting to at least $731 billion per year. Moreover, according to the GE study, 59 percent of the health-care inefficiencies, or $429 billion, could be directly impacted by the deployment of an industrial Internet. Big Data feedback, advanced analytics, predictive algorithms, and automation systems could cut the cost in the global health-care sector by 25 percent according to the GE study, for a savings of $100 billion per year. Just a 1 percent reduction in cost would result in a savings of $4.2 billion per year, or $63 billion over a 15-year period.[14] Push these gains in efficiency from 1 percent, to 2 percent, to 5 percent, to 10 percent, in the aviation and health-care sectors and across every other sector, and the magnitude of the economic change becomes readily apparent.

The term *Internet of Things* was coined by Kevin Ashton, one of the founders of the MIT Auto ID Center, back in 1995. In the years that followed, the IoT languished, in part, because the cost of sensors and actuators embedded in "things" was still relatively expensive. In an 18 month period between 2012 and 2013, however, the cost of radio-frequency identification (RFID) chips, which are used to monitor and track things, plummeted by 40 percent. These tags now cost less than ten cents each.[15] Moreover, the tags don't require a power source because they are able to transmit their data using the energy from the radio signals that are probing them. The price of micro-electromechanical systems (MEMS), including gyroscopes, accelerometers, and pressure sensors, has also dropped by 80 to 90 percent in the past five years.[16]

The other obstacle that slowed the deployment of the IoT has been the Internet protocol, IPv4, which allows only 4.3 billion unique addresses on the Internet (every device on the Internet must be assigned an Internet protocol address). With most of the IP addresses already gobbled up by the more than 2 billion people now connected to the Internet, few addresses remain available to connect millions and eventually trillions of things to the Internet. Now, a new Internet protocol version, IPv6, has been developed by the Internet Engineering Task Force; it will expand the number of available addresses to a staggering 340 trillion trillion trillion—more than enough to accommodate the projected 2 trillion devices expected to be connected to the Internet in the next ten years.[17]

Nick Valéry, a columnist at *The Economist*, breaks down these incomprehensibly large numbers, making sense of them for the average individual. To reach the threshold of 2 trillion devices connected to the Internet in less than ten years, each person would only need to have "1,000 of their possessions talking to the Internet."[18] In developed economies, most people have approximately 1,000 to 5,000 possessions.[19] That might seem like an inordinately high number, but when we start to look around the house, garage, automobile, and office, and count up all the things from electric toothbrushes to books to garage openers to electronic pass cards to buildings, it's surprising how many devices we have. Many of these devices will be tagged over the next decade or so, using the Intenet to connect our things to other things.

Valérey is quick to point out a number of big unresolved issues that are beginning to dog the widespread rollout of the IoT, potentially impeding its rapid deployment and public acceptance. He writes:

> The questions then become: Who assigns the identifier? Where and how is the information in the database made accessible? How are the details, in both the chip and the database, secured? What is the legal framework for holding those in charge accountable?

Valéry warns that

> glossing over such matters could seriously compromise any personal or corporate information associated with devices connected to the internet. Should that happen through ignorance or carelessness, the internet of things could be hobbled before it gets out of the gate.[20]

Connecting everyone and everything in a neural network brings the human race out of the age of privacy, a defining characteristic of modernity, and into the era of transparency. While privacy has long been considered a fundamental right, it has never been an inherent right. Indeed, for all of human history, until the modern era, life was lived more or less publicly, as befits the most social species on Earth. As late as the sixteenth century, if an individual was to wander alone aimlessly for long periods of time in daylight, or hide away at night, he or she was likely to be regarded as possessed. In virtually every society that we know of before the modern era, people bathed together in public, often urinated and defecated in public, ate at communal tables, frequently engaged in sexual intimacy in public, and slept huddled together en masse.

It wasn't until the early capitalist era that people began to retreat behind locked doors. The bourgeois life was a private affair. Although people took on a public persona, much of their daily lives were pursued in cloistered spaces. At home, life was further isolated into separate rooms, each with their own function—parlors, music rooms, libraries, etc. Individuals even began to sleep alone in separate beds and bedrooms for the very first time.

The enclosure and privatization of human life went hand-in-hand with the enclosure and privatization of the commons. In the new world of private property relations, where everything was reduced to "mine" versus "thine," the notion of the autonomous agent, surrounded by his or her possessions and fenced off from the rest of the world, took on a life of its own. The right to privacy came to be the right to exclude. The notion that every man's home is his castle accompanied the privatization of life. Successive generations came to think of privacy as an inherent human quality endowed by nature rather than a mere social convention fitting a particular moment in the human journey.

Today, the evolving Internet of Things is ripping away the layers of enclosure that made privacy sacrosanct and a right regarded as important as the right to life, liberty, and the pursuit of happiness. For a younger generation growing up in a globally connected world where every moment of their lives are eagerly posted and shared with the world via Facebook, Twitter, YouTube, Instagram, and countless other social media sites, privacy has lost much of its appeal. For them, freedom is not bound up in self-contained autonomy and exclusion, but rather, in enjoying access to others and inclusion in a global virtual public square. The moniker of the younger generation is transparency, its modus operandi is collaboration, and its self-expression is exercised by way of peer production in laterally scaled networks.

Whether future generations living in an increasingly interconnected world—where everyone and everything is embedded in the Internet of Things—will care much about privacy is an open question.

Still, in the long passage from the capitalist era to the Collaborative Age, privacy issues will continue to be a pivotal concern, determining, to a great extent, both the speed of the transition and the pathways taken into the next period of history.

The central question is: When every human being and every thing is connected, what boundaries need to be established to ensure that an individual's right to privacy will be protected? The problem is that third parties with access to the flow of data across the IoT, and armed with sophisticated software skills, can penetrate every layer of the global nervous system in search of new ways to exploit the medium for their own ends. Cyber thieves can steal personal identities for commercial gain, social media sites can sell data to advertisers and marketers to enhance their profits, and political operatives can pass on vital information to foreign governments. How then do we ensure an open, transparent flow of data that can benefit everyone while guaranteeing that information concerning every aspect of one's life is not used without their permission and against their wishes in ways that compromise and harm their well-being?

The European Commission has begun to address these issues. In 2012, the Commission held an intensive three month consultation, bringing together more than 600 leaders from business associations, civil society organizations, and academia, in search of a policy approach that will "foster a dynamic development of the Internet of Things in the digital single market while ensuring appropriate protection and trust of EU citizens."[21]

The Commission established a broad principle to guide all future developments of the Internet of Things:

In general, we consider that privacy & data protection and information security are complimentary requirements for IoT services. In particular, information security is regarded as preserving the confidentiality, integrity and availability (CIA) of information. We also consider that information security is perceived as a basic requirement in the provision of IoT services for the industry, both with a view to ensure information security for the organization itself, but also for the benefit of citizens.[22]

To advance these protections and safeguards, the Commission proposed that mechanisms be put in place

> to ensure that no unwanted processing of personal data takes place and that individuals are informed of the processing, its purposes, the identity of the processor and how to exercise their rights. At the same time processors need to comply with the data protection principles.[23]

The Commission further proposed specific technical means to safeguard user privacy, including technology to secure data protection. The Commission concluded with a declaration that "it should be ensured, that individuals remain in control of their personal data and that IoT systems provide sufficient transparency to enable individuals to effectively exercise their data subject rights."[24]

No one is naïve regarding the difficulty of turning theory to practice when it comes to securing everyone's right to control and dispose of their own data in an era that thrives on transparency, collaboration, and inclusivity. Yet there is a clear understanding that if the proper balance is not struck between transparency and the right to privacy, the evolution of the Internet of Things is likely to be slowed, or worse, irretrievably compromised and lost, thwarting the prospects of a Collaborative Age. (These questions of privacy, security, access, and governance will be examined at length throughout the book.)

Although the specter of connecting everyone and everything in a global neural network is a bit scary, it's also exciting and liberating at the same time, opening up new possibilities for living together on Earth, which we can only barely envision at the outset of this new saga in the human story.

The business community is quickly marshaling its resources, determined to wrest value from a technological revolution whose effects are likely to match and even exceed the advent of electricity at the dawn of the Second Industrial Revolution. In 2013 *The Economist*'s intelligence unit published the first global business index on the "quiet revolution" that's beginning to change society. *The Economist* surveyed business leaders across the world, concentrating on the key industries of financial services, manufacturing, health care, pharmaceuticals, biotechnology, IT and technology, energy and natural resources, and construction and real estate.

The report started off by observing that the rapid drop in technology costs and new developments in complimentary fields including mobile communication and cloud computing, along with an increase in government support, is pushing the IoT to the center stage of the global economy. Thirty-eight percent of the corporate leaders surveyed forecast that the IoT would have a "major impact in most markets and most industries" within the next three years, and an additional 40 percent of respondents said it would have "some impact on a few markets or industries." Only 15 percent of corporate executives felt that the IoT would have only "a big impact for only a small number of global players."[25] Already, more that 75 percent of global companies are exploring or using the IoT in their businesses to some extent and two in five CEOs, CFOs, and other C-suite level respondents say they have "a formal meeting or conversation about the IoT at least once a month."[26]

Equally interesting, 30 percent of the corporate leaders interviewed said that the IoT will "unlock new revenue opportunities for existing products/services." Twenty-nine percent said the IoT "will inspire new working practices or business processes." Twenty-three percent of those surveyed said the IoT "will change our existing business model or business strategy." Finally, 23 percent of respondents said that the IoT "will spark a new wave of innovation." Most telling, more than 60 percent of executives "agree that companies that are slow to integrate the IoT will fall behind the competition."[27]

The central message in *The Economist* survey is that most corporate leaders are convinced that the potential productivity gains of using the Internet of Things across the value chain are so compelling and disruptive to the old ways of doing business that they have no choice but to try to get ahead of the game by embedding their business operations in the IoT platform.

However, the IoT is a double-edged sword. The pressure to increase thermodynamic efficiency and productivity and to reduce marginal costs will be irresistible. Companies that don't forge ahead by taking advantage of the productivity potential will be left behind. Yet the unrelenting forward thrust in productivity let loose by an intelligent force operating at every link and node across the entire Third Industrial Revolution infrastructure is going to take the marginal cost of generating green electricity and producing and delivering an array of goods and services to near zero within a 25-year span. The evolution of the Internet of Things will likely follow roughly the same time line that occurred from the takeoff stage of the World Wide Web in 1990 to now, when an exponential curve resulted in the plummeting costs of producing and sending information.

EXPONENTIAL CURVES

Admittedly, such claims appear overstated until we take a closer look at the meaning of the word *exponential*. I remember when I was a kid—around 13 years old—a friend offered me an interesting hypothetical choice. He asked whether I would accept $1 million up front or, instead, one dollar the first day and a doubling of that amount every day for one month. I initially said "you have to be kidding . . . anyone in their right mind would take the million." He said, "hold on, do the math." So I took out a paper and pencil and began doubling the dollar. After 31 days of doubling, I was at over one billion dollars. That's one thousand millions. I was blown away.

Exponential growth is deceptive; it creeps up on you. On day 15, the doubling process had only reached $16,384, leaving me confident that I had struck the right deal going for one million cash in hand. The next six days of doubling was a shocker. With just six more doublings, the figure had already topped $1 million. The next ten days knocked my socks off. By the thirty-first day of the month, the doubling of that dollar had topped $1 billion. I had just been introduced to exponential growth.

Most of us have a difficult time grasping exponential growth because we are so used to thinking in linear terms. The concept itself received very little attention in the public mind until Gordon Moore, cofounder of Intel, the world's largest semiconductor chip maker, noted a curious phenomenon, which he described in a now-famous paper published in 1965. Moore observed that the number of components in an integrated circuit had been doubling every year since its invention in 1958:

The complexity for minimum component costs has increased at a rate of roughly a factor of two per year. Certainly over the short term this rate can be expected to continue, if not to increase.[28]

Moore slightly modified his earlier projection in 1975 saying that the doubling is occurring every two years. That doubling process continued for another 37 years, although recently, scientists have begun to predict a slowing in the number of transistors that can be put on a computer chip. The physicist Michio Kaku says we're already beginning to see a slowdown and that Moore's Law, at least in regard to chips, will peter out in another ten years using conventional silicon technology. Anticipating the slowdown, Intel is introducing its 3D processors, confident it can keep the doubling in place a bit longer.

Kaku points out that there is an upper limit on how much computing power can be squeezed out of silicon. He adds, however, that newer technologies like 3D chips, optical chips, parallel processing, and eventually molecular computing and even quantum computing will likely ensure an exponential growth curve in computing power well into the future.[29]

Moore's Law has since been observed in a wide range of information technologies. Hard-disc storage capacity is experiencing a similar exponential growth curve. Network capacity—the amount of data going through an optical fiber—has achieved an even steeper exponential curve: the amount of data transmitted on an optical network is doubling every nine months or so.[30]

It's the exponential factor that allowed computing costs to plummet for more than 50 years. When the first giant mainframe computers were being developed, the cost of computing was huge and out of commercial reach. The conventional wisdom was that, at best, only the military and a few research institutions could ever cover the costs. What experts failed to take into account was exponential growth in capacity and the falling costs of production. The invention of the integrated circuit (the microchip) changed the equation. Where 50 years ago a computer might cost millions of dollars, today hundreds of millions of people are equipped with relatively cheap smartphones with thousands of times more computing capacity than the most powerful mainframe computers of the 1960s.[31] In the year 2000, one gigabyte of hard-drive space cost in the neighborhood of 44 dollars. By 2012, the cost had plunged to seven cents. In 2000, it cost $193 per giga-byte to stream video. Ten years later, that cost had dropped to three cents.[32]

To appreciate the significance of the exponential curve in com-puting power and cost reduction, consider this: the first commercially successful mass-produced business computer, the IBM 1401, often re-ferred to as the Model T of the computer industry, debuted in 1959. The machine was five feet high and three feet wide and came with 4,096 characters of memory. It could perform 193,000 additions of eight-digit numbers in 60 seconds. The cost to rent IBM's computer was $30,000 per year.[33] In 2012, the Raspberry Pi, the world's cheap-est computer, went on sale for 25 dollars.[34] The Raspberry Pi Founda-tion is being swamped with orders from buyers in developing countries as well as in first-world markets.

Today's cell phones weigh a few ounces, can fit into a coat pocket, and cost a few hundred dollars. Sometimes they are even given away for free if the customer buys the carrier's service plan. Yet they have thousands of times as much memory as the original Cray-1A computer of the late 1970s, which cost close to $9 million and weighed over 12,000 pounds.[35] The marginal cost of computing power is heading to zero.

The exponential curve in generating information has fundamen-tally altered the way we live. As mentioned earlier, much of the human race is connecting with one another on the Internet and sharing in-formation, entertainment, news, and knowledge for nearly free. They have already passed into the zero marginal cost society.

The exponential curve has migrated from the world of computing to become a standard for measuring economic success across a range of technologies, becoming a new benchmark for commercial perfor-mance and returns on investment.

FREE ENERGY

Nowhere is exponentiality more discussed today than in the renewable-energy industry. Many of the key players have come over from the in-formation technology and Internet sectors to apply experience they garnered there to the new energy paradigm. They correctly sense two uncanny parallels.

First, the harvesting power of renewable energy technology is experiencing its own exponential growth curve in solar and wind, with geothermal, biomass, and hydro expected to follow. Like the computer industry, the renewable energy industry has had to reckon with initially high capital costs in the research, development, and market deployment of each new generation of the technology. Companies are also forced to stay two to three generations ahead of their competitors in anticipating when to bring new innovations online, or risk being crushed by the force of the exponential curve. A number of market leaders have gone belly-up in recent years because they were tied into old technologies and were swept away by the speed of innovation. Industry analysts forecast that the harvesting technology for solar and small wind power will be as cheap as cell phones and laptops within 15 years.

Second, like the Communications Internet where the up-front costs of establishing the infrastructure were considerable, but the marginal cost of producing and distributing information is negligible, the up-front costs of establishing an Energy Internet are likewise significant, but the marginal cost of producing each unit of solar and wind power is nearly zero. Renewable energy, like information, is nearly free after accounting for the fixed costs of research, development, and deployment.

Internet technology and renewable energies are beginning to merge to create an Energy Internet that will change the way power is generated and distributed in society. In the coming era, hundreds of millions of people will produce their own renewable energy in their homes, offices, and factories and share green electricity with each other on an Energy Internet, just as we now generate and share information online. When Internet communications manage green energy, every human being on Earth becomes his or her own source of power, both literally and figuratively. The creation of a renewable-energy regime, loaded by buildings, partially stored in the form of hydrogen, distributed via a green electricity Internet, and connected to plug-in, zero-emission transport, establishes the five pillar mechanism that will allow billions of people to share energy at near zero marginal cost in an IoT world.

The scientific community is abuzz over the exponential curves in renewable-energy generation. *Scientific American* published an article in 2011 asking whether Moore's Law applies to solar energy, and if so, might we already be on the course of a paradigm shift in energy similar to what has occurred in computing. The answer is an unqualified yes.

The impact on society is all the more pronounced when we consider the vast potential of solar as a future energy source. The sun beams 470 exajoules of energy to Earth every 88 minutes—equaling the amount of energy human beings use in a year. If we could grab hold of one-tenth of 1 percent of the sun's energy that reaches Earth, it would give us six times the energy we now use across the global economy.[36]

Despite the fact that the sun is clearly the universal energy source from which all our fossil fuel and other energies are derived, it makes up less than 0.2 percent of the current energy mix primarily because, up until recently, it has been expensive to capture and distribute—this is no longer the case.

Richard Swanson, the founder of SunPower Corporation, observed the same doubling phenomena in solar that Moore did in computer chips. Swanson's law holds that the price of solar photovoltaic (PV) cells tends to drop by 20 percent for every doubling of industry capacity. Crystalline silicon photovoltaic cell prices have fallen dramatically, from $60 a watt in 1976 to $0.66 a watt in 2013.[37]

Solar cells are capturing more solar energy that strikes them while reducing the cost of harvesting the energy. Solar efficiencies for triple junction solar cells in the laboratory have reached 41 percent. Thin film has hit 20 percent efficiency in the laboratory.[38]

If this trend continues at the current pace—and most studies actually show an acceleration in exponentiality—solar energy will be as cheap as the current average retail price of electricity today by 2020 and half the price of coal electricity today by 2030.[39]

The German power market is just beginning to experience the commercial impact of near zero marginal cost renewable energy. In 2013, Germany was already generating 23 percent of its electricity by renewable energy and is expected to generate 35 percent of its electricity from renewables by 2020.[40] The problem is that during certain times of day, the surge of solar and wind power flooding into the grid is exceeding the demand for electricity, resulting in negative prices. Nor is Germany alone. Negative prices for electricity are popping up in places as diverse as Sicily and Texas.[41]

This is a wholly new reality in the electricity market and a harbinger of the future as renewable energy comes to make up an increasing percentage of electricity generation. Negative prices are disrupting the entire energy industry. Utilities are having to push back on investing in "backup" gas and coal fired power plants because they can no longer guarantee a reliable return on their investments. In Germany, a gas- or coal-fired power plant that might cost $1 billion to build, but that will no longer run at full capacity because of the onslaught of renewable energies into the grid, can only pay for itself on days when there is no wind or heavy cloud cover. This extends the time it takes to pay off building new coal- and gas-fired plants, making the investments unfeasable. As a result, renewable energy is already beginning to push fossil-fuel-powered plants off the grid, even at this early stage of the Third Industrial Revolution.[42]

Global energy companies are being pummeled by the exponentiality of renewable energy. BP released a global energy study in 2011, reporting that solar generating capacity grew by 73.3 percent in 2011, producing 63.4 gigawatts, or ten times greater than its level just five years earlier.[43] Installed solar capacity has been doubling every two years for the past 20 years with no end in sight.[44]

Even in the United States, where the transition to new green energies has been tepid compared to Europe, the power sector is reeling. David Crane, president and CEO of NGR Energy, noted in November 2011 that "in the last two years, the delivered cost of energy from PV was cut in half. NGR expects the cost to fall in half again in the next two years, which would make solar power less expensive than retail electricity in roughly 20 states," all of which will revolutionize the energy industry.[45]

Like solar radiation, wind is ubiquitous and blows everywhere in the world—although its strength and frequency varies. A Stanford University study on global wind capacity concluded that if 20 percent of the world's available wind was harvested, it would generate seven times more electricity than we currently use to run the entire global economy.[46] Wind capacity has been growing exponentially since the early 1990s and has already reached parity with conventionally generated electricity from fossil fuels and nuclear power in many regions of the world. In the past quarter century, wind turbine productivity increased 100-fold and the average capacity per turbine grew by more than 1,000 percent. Increased performance and productivity has significantly reduced the cost of production, installation, and maintenance, leading to a growth rate of more than 30 percent per year between 1998 and 2007, or a doubling of capacity every two and a half years.[47]

Naysayers argue that subsidies for green energy, in the form of feed-in tariffs, artificially prop up the growth curve. The reality is that they merely speed up adoption and scale, encourage competition, and spur innovation, which further increases the efficiency of renewable energy harvesting technologies and lowers the cost of production and installation. In country after country, solar and wind energy are nearing parity with conventional fossil fuel and nuclear power, allowing the government to begin phasing out tariffs. Meanwhile, the older fossil fuel energies and nuclear power, although mature and well past their prime, continue to be subsidized at levels that far exceed the subsidies extended to renewable energy.

A study prepared by the Energy Watch Group predicts four different future market-share scenarios of new wind- and solar-power-plant installations, estimating 50 percent market share by 2033, with a more optimistic estimate of reaching the same goal as early as 2017.[48] While solar and wind are on a seemingly irreversible exponential path to near zero marginal costs, geothermal energy, biomass, and wave and tidal power are likely to reach their own exponential takeoff stage within the next decade, bringing the full sweep of renewable energies into an exponential curve in the first half of the twenty-first century.

Still, the powers that be continually lowball their projections of renewable energy's future share of the global energy market, in part because, like the IT and telecommunications industry in the 1970s, they aren't anticipating the transformative nature of exponential curves, even when faced with the cumulative doubling evidence of several decades.

Ray Kurzweil, the MIT inventor and entrepreneur who is now head of engineering at Google and has spent a lifetime watching the powerful disruptive impact of exponential growth on the IT industry, did the math just on solar alone. Based on the past 20 years of doubling, Kurzweil concluded that "after we double eight more times and we're meeting all of the world's energy needs through solar, we'll be using one part in 10,000 of the sunlight that falls on earth."[49] Eight more doublings will take just 16 years, putting us into the solar age by 2028.

Kurzweil may be a bit optimistic. My own read is that we'll reach nearly 80 percent renewable energy generation well before 2040, barring unforeseen circumstances.

GETTING CLOSER TO NEAR ZERO

Skeptics legitimately argue that nothing we exchange is ever really free. Even after the IoT is fully paid for and plugged in, there will always be some costs in generating and distributing information and energy. For that reason, we always use the term *near zero* when referring to the marginal cost of delivering information, green energy, and goods and services.

Although the marginal costs of delivering information are already tiny, there is a considerable effort afoot to reduce them even further, to get as close as possible to zero marginal cost. It is estimated that the Internet service providers (ISPs) that connect users to the Internet enjoyed revenues of $196 billion in 2011.[50] All in all, an amazingly low cost for connecting nearly 40 percent of the human race and the entire global economy.[51] Besides paying for service providers, everyone using the Internet pays for the electricity used to send and access information. It is estimated that the online delivery of a one-megabyte file costs only $0.001.[52] However, the megabytes add up. The Internet uses up to 1.5 percent of the world's electricity, costing $8.5 billion—again a small cost for enjoying global communication.[53] That's equivalent to the price of building four to five new gambling casinos in Las Vegas. Still, with ever-increasing interconnectivity and more powerful computing devices, electricity use is escalating. Google, for example, uses enough energy to power 200,000 homes.[54]

Much of the electricity generated is consumed by servers and data centers around the world. In 2011 in the United States alone, the electricity used to run servers and data centers cost approximately $7.5 billion.[55] The number of federal data centers grew from 432 in 1998 to 2,094 in 2010.[56] By 2011 there were more than 509,000 data centers on Earth taking up 285 million square feet of space, or the equivalent of 5,955 football fields.[57] Because most of the electrical power drawn by IT equipment in these data centers is converted to heat energy, even more power is needed to cool the facilities. Often between 25 and 50 percent of the power is used for cooling the equipment.[58]

A large amount of electricity is also wasted just to keep the servers idling and ready in case a surge in activity slows down or crashes the system. The consulting firm McKinsey found that, on average, data centers are using only 6 to 12 percent of their electricity to power their servers during computation—the rest is used to keep them up and ready.[59] New power-management applications are being put in place to lower the power mode when idle or to run at lower frequencies and voltages. Slowing down the actual computation also saves electricity. Another approach to what the industry calls energy-adaptive computing is to reduce energy requirements by minimizing overdesign and waste in the way IT equipment itself is built and operated.[60]

Cutting energy costs at data centers will ultimately come from powering the facilities with renewable energy. Although the up-front fixed cost of powering data centers with renewable energy will be significant, the payback time will continue to narrow as the costs of constructing positive power facilities continue to fall. And once the facilities and harvesting technologies are up and running, the marginal cost of generating solar and wind power and other renewable energies will be nearly zero, making the electricity almost free. This reality has not been lost on the big players in the data-storage arena.

Apple announced in 2012 that its huge new data center in North Carolina will be powered by a massive 20-megawatt solar-power facility and include a five-megawatt fuel-storage system powered by biogas to store intermittent solar power to ensure a reliable 24/7 supply of electricity.[61] McGraw-Hill's data center in East Windsor, New Jersey, will be powered by a 14-megawatt solar array. Other companies are planning to construct similar data-center facilities that will run on renewable energy.[62]

Apple's data center is also installing a free cooling system in which cool nighttime outside air is incorporated into a heat exchange to provide cold water for the data center cooling system.[63] Providing data centers with onsite renewable energy whose marginal cost is nearly free is going to dramatically reduce the cost of electricity in the powering of a global Internet of Things, getting us ever closer to nearly free electricity in organizing economic activity.

Reducing the cost of electricity in the management of data centers goes hand in hand with cutting the cost of storing data, an ever larger part of the data-management process. And the sheer volume of data is mushrooming faster than the capacity of hard drives to save it.

Researchers are just beginning to experiment with a new way of storing data that could eventually drop the marginal cost to near zero. In January 2013 scientists at the European Bioinformatics Institute in Cambridge, England, announced a revolutionary new method of storing massive electronic data by embedding it in synthetic DNA. Two researchers, Nick Goldman and Ewan Birney, converted text from five computer files—which included an MP3 recording of Martin Luther King Jr.'s "I Have a Dream" speech, a paper by James Watson and Francis Crick describing the structure of DNA, and all of Shakespeare's sonnets and plays—and converted the ones and zeros of digital information into the letters that make up the alphabet of the DNA code. The code was then used to create strands of synthetic DNA. Machines read the DNA molecules and returned the encoded information.[64]

This innovative method opens up the possibility of virtually unlimited information storage. Harvard researcher George Church notes that the information currently stored in all the disk drives in the world could fit in a tiny bit of DNA the size of the palm of one's hand. Researchers add that DNA information can be preserved for centuries, as long as it is kept in a dark, cool environment.[65]

At this early stage of development, the cost of reading the code is high and the time it takes to decode information is substantial. Researchers, however, are reasonably confident that an exponential rate of change in bioinformatics will drive the marginal cost to near zero over the next several decades.

A NEAR ZERO MARGINAL COST communication/energy/transportation infrastructure for the Collaborative Age is now within sight. The technology needed to make it happen is already being deployed. At present, it's all about scaling up and building out. When we compare the increasing expenses of maintaining an old Second Industrial Revolution matrix of centralized telecommunications, fossil fuel energy generation, and internal combustion engine transport, whose costs are rising with each passing day, with a Third Industrial Revolution communication/energy/transportation grid whose costs are dramatically shrinking, it's clear that the future lies with the latter. Internet communication is already being generated and shared at near zero marginal cost and so too is solar and wind power for millions of early adopters, and in the near future, automated transportation and logistics will also head toward zero marginal cost.

The stalwart supporters of fossil fuels argue that tar sands and shale gas are readily available, making it unnecessary to scale up renewable energies, at least in the short term. But it's only because crude oil reserves are dwindling, forcing a rise in price on global markets, that these other more costly fossil fuels are even being introduced. Extracting oil from sand and rock is an expensive undertaking when compared to the cost of drilling a hole and letting crude oil gush up from under the ground. Tar sands are not even commercially viable when crude oil prices dip below $80-per barrel, and recall that just a few years ago, $80-per-barrel oil was considered prohibitively expensive. As for shale gas, while prices are currently low, troubling new reports from the field suggest that the promise of shale gas independence has been overhyped by the financial markets and the energy industry. Industry analysts are voicing growing concern that the shale gas rush, like the gold rushes of the nineteenth century, is already creating a dangerous bubble, with potentially damaging consequences for the American economy because too much investment has moved too quickly into shale gas fields.[66]

Andy Hall, an oil trader known in the sector as "God," owing to his remarkably accurate trend forecasts on oil futures, shook up the industry in May 2013 with his declaration that shale gas will only "temporarily" boost energy production. Hall informed investors in his $4.5 billion Astenbeck hedge fund that, although shale gas gushes at first, production rapidly declines because each well only taps a single pool of oil in a large reservoir. The quick exhaustion of existing shale gas reservoirs requires producers to continuously find new shale gas deposits and dig new wells, which jack up the cost of production. The result, says Hall, is that it is "impossible to maintain production . . . without constant new wells being drilled [which would] require high oil prices." Hall believes that shale gas euphoria will be a short-lived phenomenon.[67] The International Energy Agency (IEA) agrees. In its annual 2013 World Energy Outlook report, the IEA forecast that "light tight oil," a popular term for shale gas, will peak around 2020 and then plateau, with production falling by the mid-2020s. The U.S. shale gas outlook is even more bearish. The U.S. Energy Department's Energy Information Administration expects higher shale gas levels to continue only to the late teens (another five years or so) and then slow.[68]

What hasn't yet sunk in is that fossil fuel energies are never going to approach zero marginal cost, or even come close. Renewable energies, however, are already at near zero marginal cost for millions of early adopters. Scaling them so that everyone on Earth can produce green energy and share it across the Internet of Things, again, at near zero marginal cost, is the next great task for a civilization transitioning from a capitalist market to a Collaborative Commons.

CHAPTER SIX

3D PRINTING

FROM MASS PRODUCTION TO
PRODUCTION BY THE MASSES

The distributed, collaborative, and laterally scaled nature of the Internet of Things will fundamentally change the way we manufacture, market, and deliver goods in the coming era. Recall that the communication/energy/transportation matrices of the First and Second Industrial Revolutions were extremely capital intensive and required vertical integration to achieve economies of scale and centralized management to ensure profit margins and secure sufficient returns on investment. Manufacturing facilities have even supersized over the past half century of the Second Industrial Revolution. In China and throughout the developing world, giant factories are churning out products at speeds and in volumes that would have been unheard of half a century ago.

MICRO INFOFACTURING

The long-dominant manufacturing mode of the Second Industrial Revolution is likely going to give way, however, at least in part, over the coming three decades. A new Third Industrial Revolution manufacturing model has seized the public stage and is growing exponentially along with the other components of the IoT infrastructure. Hundreds of companies are now producing physical products the way software produces information in the form of video, audio, and text. It's called

3D printing and it is the "manufacturing" model that accompanies an IoT economy.

Software—often open source—directs molten plastic, molten metal, or other feedstocks inside a printer, to build up a physical product layer by layer, creating a fully formed object, even with moveable parts, which then pops out of the printer. Like the replicator in the *Star Trek* television series, the printer can be programmed to produce an infinite variety of products. Printers are already producing products from jewelry and airplane parts to human prostheses. And cheap printers are being purchased by hobbyists interested in printing out their own parts and products. The consumer is beginning to give way to the prosumer as increasing numbers of people become both the producer and consumer of their own products.

Three-dimensional printing differs from conventional centralized manufacturing in several important ways:

First, there is little human involvement aside from creating the software. The software does all the work, which is why it's more appropriate to think of the process as "infofacture" rather than "manufacture."

Second, the early practitioners of 3D printing have made strides to ensure that the software used to program and print physical products remains open source, allowing prosumers to share new ideas with one another in do-it-yourself (DIY) hobbyist networks. The open design concept conceives of the production of goods as a dynamic process in which thousands—even millions—of players learn from one another by making things together. The elimination of intellectual-property protection also significantly reduces the cost of printing products, giving the 3D printing enterprise an edge over traditional manufacturing enterprises, which must factor in the cost of myriad patents. The open-source production model has encouraged exponential growth.

The steep growth curve was helped along by the plunging costs of 3D printers. In 2002 Stratasys put the first "low-cost" printer onto the market. The price tag was $30,000.[1] Today, "high-quality" 3D printers can be purchased for as little as $1,500.[2] It's a similar cost curve reduction to that of computers, cell phones, and wind-harnessing and solar technologies. In the next three decades, industry analysts expect that 3D printers will be equipped to produce far more sophisticated and complex products at ever-cheaper prices—taking the infofacturing process to near zero marginal cost.

Third, the production process is organized completely differently than the manufacturing process of the First and Second Industrial Revolutions. Traditional factory manufacturing is a subtractive process. Raw materials are cut down and winnowed and then assembled to manufacture the final product. In the process, a significant amount of the material is wasted and never finds its way into the end product. Three-dimensional printing, by contrast, is additive infofacturing. The software is directing the molten material to add layer upon layer, creating the product as a whole piece. Additive infofacturing uses one-tenth of the material of subtractive manufacturing, giving the 3D printer a substantial leg up in efficiency and productivity. In 2011, additive manufacturing enjoyed a blistering 29.4 percent growth, besting the 26.4 percent collective historical growth of the industry in just one year.[3]

Fourth, 3D printers can print their own spare parts without having to invest in expensive retooling and the time delays that go with it. With 3D printers, products can also be customized to create a single product or small batches designed to order, at minimum cost. Centralized factories, with their capital-intensive economies of scale and expensive fixed-production lines designed for mass production, lack the agility to compete with a 3D production process that can create a single customized product at virtually the same unit cost as it can producing 100,000 copies of the same item.

Fifth, the 3D printing movement is deeply committed to sustainable production. Emphasis is on durability and recyclability and using nonpolluting materials. William McDonough and Michael Braungart's vision of "upcycling"—adding value to the product at every stage of its lifecycle—is built into the ecology of production.[4]

Sixth, because the IoT is distributed, collaborative, and laterally scaled, 3D printers can set up shop and connect anywhere there is a Third Industrial Revolution (TIR) infrastructure and enjoy thermodynamic efficiencies far beyond those of centralized factories, with productivity gains in excess of what was achievable in either the First or Second Industrial Revolution.

For example, a local 3D printer can power his or her infofactory with green electricity harvested from renewable energy onsite or generated by local producer cooperatives. Small- and medium-sized enterprises in Europe and elsewhere are already beginning to collaborate in regional green-electricity cooperatives to take advantage of lateral scaling. With the cost of centralized fossil fuels and nuclear power constantly increasing, the advantage skews to small- and medium-sized enterprises that can power their factories with renewable energies whose marginal cost is nearly free.

Marketing costs also plummet in an IoT economy. The high cost of centralized communications in both the First and Second Industrial Revolutions—in the form of magazines, newspapers, radio, and television—meant that only the bigger manufacturing firms with integrated national operations could afford advertising across national and global markets, greatly limiting the market reach of smaller manufacturing enterprises.

In the Third Industrial Revolution, a small 3D printing operation anywhere in the world can advertise infofactured products on the growing number of global Internet marketing sites at nearly zero marginal cost. Etsy is among the new distributed marketing websites that are bringing together suppliers and users on a global playing field at low marginal cost. Etsy is an eight-year-old company started by a young American social entrepreneur named Rob Kalin. Currently 900,000 small producers of goods advertise at no cost on the Etsy website. Nearly 60 million consumers per month from around the world browse the website, often interacting personally with suppliers.[5] When a purchase is made, Etsy receives only a tiny commission from the producers. This form of laterally scaled marketing puts the small enterprise on a level playing field with the big boys, allowing them to reach a worldwide user market at a fraction of the cost.

Seventh, plugging into an IoT infrastructure at the local level gives the small infofacturers one final, critical advantage over the vertically integrated, centralized enterprises of the nineteenth and twentieth centuries: they can power their vehicles with renewable energy whose marginal cost is nearly free, significantly reducing their logistics costs along the supply chain and in the delivery of their finished products to users.

A 3D PRINTING PROCESS EMBEDDED in an Internet of Things infrastructure means that virtually anyone in the world can become a prosumer, producing his or her own products for use or sharing, employing open-source software. The production process itself uses one-tenth of the material of conventional manufacturing and requires very little human labor in the making of the product. The energy used in the production is generated from renewable energy harvested on-site or locally, at near zero marginal cost. The product is marketed on global marketing websites, again at near zero marginal cost. Lastly, the product is delivered to users in e-mobility transport powered by locally generated renewable energy, again at near zero marginal cost.

The ability to produce, market, and distribute physical goods anywhere there is an IoT infrastructure to plug into is going to dramatically affect the spatial organization of society. The First Industrial Revolution favored the development of dense urban centers. Factories and logistics networks had to cluster in and around cities where there were major rail links that could bring in energy and materials from suppliers upstream and package and deliver finished products to wholesalers and retailers downstream. The workforce had to live within walking distance of their factories and offices or have access to commuter trains and trolleys. In the Second Industrial Revolution, production migrated from dense urban centers to suburban industrial parks, accessible from the exits of the nationwide interstate highway system. Truck transport overtook rail, and workers traveled longer distances to work by automobile.

Three-dimensional printing is both local and global; it is also highly mobile, allowing infofacturers to be anywhere and quickly move to wherever there is an IoT infrastructure to connect to. More and more prosumers will make and use simple products at home. Small- and medium-sized 3D businesses, infofacturing more sophisticated products, will likely cluster in local technology parks to establish an optimum lateral scale. Homes and workplaces will no longer be separated by lengthy commutes. It is even conceivable that today's overcrowded road systems will be less traveled and that the expense of building new roads will diminish as workers become owners and consumers become producers. Smaller urban centers of 150,000 to 250,000 people, surrounded by a rewilding of green space, might slowly replace dense urban cores and suburban sprawl in a more distributed and collaborative economic era.

DEMOCRATIZING THE REPLICATOR

The new 3D printing revolution is an example of "extreme productivity." It is not fully here yet, but as it kicks in, it will eventually and inevitably reduce marginal costs to near zero, eliminate profit, and make property exchange in markets unnecessary for many (though not all) products.

The democratization of manufacturing means that anyone and eventually everyone can access the means of production, making the question of who should own and control the means of production irrelevant, and capitalism along with it.

Three-dimensional printing, like so many inventions, was inspired by science-fiction writers. A generation of geeks sat enthralled in front of their TV screens, watching episodes of *Star Trek*. In long journeys through the universe, the crew needed to be able to repair and replace parts of the spaceship and keep stocked with everything from machine parts to pharmaceutical products. The replicator was programmed to rearrange subatomic particles that are ubiquitous in the universe into objects, including food and water. The deeper significance of the replicator is that it does away with scarcity itself—a theme we will come back to in part V.

The 3D printing revolution began in the 1980s. The early printers were very expensive and used primarily to create prototypes. Architects and automobile and airplane manufacturers were among the first to take up the new replicating technology.[6]

This innovation moved from prototyping to customizing products when computer hackers and hobbyists began to migrate into the field. (The term *hacker* has both positive and negative connotations. While some characterize hackers as criminals, illegally accessing proprietary and classified information, others regard hackers as clever programmers whose contributions benefit the general public. Here and throughout the book the term *hacker* is being used in the latter sense.)[7] The hackers immediately realized the potential of conceiving of "atoms as the new bits." These pioneers envisioned bringing the open-source format from the IT and computing arena into the production of "things." Open-source hardware became the rallying cry of a disparate group of inventors and enthusiasts loosely identifying themselves as part of the Makers Movement. The players collaborated with one another on the

Internet, exchanging innovative ideas and learning from each other as they advanced the 3D printing process.[8]

Open-source 3D printing reached a new phase when Adrian Bowyer and a team at the University of Bath in the United Kingdom invented the RepRap, the first open-source 3D printer that could be made with readily available tools and that could replicate itself—that is, it was a machine that could make its own parts. The RepRap can already fabricate 48 percent of its own components and is on its way to becoming a totally self-replicating machine.[9]

MakerBot Industries, financed by Bowyer, was one of the first enterprises to emerge out of the Makers Movement, with the market introduction of its 3D printer, called Cupcake, in 2009. A succession of more versatile, easier-to-use, and less costly 3D printers followed, with names like Thing-O-Matic in 2010 and the Replicator in 2012. MakerBot Industries makes freely available the specifications for assembling the machine to anyone who would like to make their own, while also selling it to those customers who prefer the convenience of purchase.

Two other trailblazers, Zach "Hoken" Smith and Bre Pettis, created a website called Thingiverse—owned by MakerBot Industries—in 2008. The site is the meeting place for the 3D printing community. The website holds open-source, user-created digital design files licensed under both the General Public Licenses (GPL) and Creative Commons Licenses. (These licenses will be discussed in greater detail in Part III.) The DIY community relies heavily on the website as a library of sorts for uploading and sharing open-source designs and for engaging in new 3D printed collaborations.

The Makers Movement took a big step toward the democratization of digitally produced things with the introduction of the Fab Lab in 2005. The Fab Lab, a fabrication laboratory, is the brainchild of the MIT physicist and professor Neil Gershenfeld. The idea came out of a popular course at MIT called "How to Make (Almost) Anything."

The Fab Lab was born at the MIT Center for Bits and Atoms that grew out of the MIT Media Lab with the mission of providing a laboratory to which anyone could come and use the tools to create their own 3D-printed projects. Gershenfeld's Fab Foundation charter emphasizes the organization's commitment to open-access, peer-to-peer learning. The labs are outfitted with various types of flexible manufacturing equipment, which includes laser cutters, routers, 3D printers, mini mills, and the accompanying open-source software. Setting up the fully equipped lab costs around $50,000.[10] There are now over 70 Fab Labs, most in urban areas in highly industrialized countries, but many, surprisingly enough, are in developing countries where access to the fabricating tools and equipment creates a beachhead for establishing a 3D printing community.[11] In remote areas of the world, unconnected to the global supply chain, being able to fabricate even simple tools and objects can greatly improve economic welfare. The great majority of Fab Labs are community-led projects managed by universities and nonprofit associations, although a few commercial retailers are beginning to explore the idea of attaching Fab Labs to their stores—so that a hobbyist can buy the supplies he or she needs and then use the Fab Lab to create the product.[12] The idea, says Gershenfeld, is to provide the tools and materials anyone would need to build whatever they can envision. His ultimate goal "is to create a *Star Trek*-style replicator in 20 years."[13]

The Fab Lab is "the people's R&D laboratory" of the Third Industrial Revolution. It takes R&D and new innovations out of the elite laboratories of world-class universities and global companies and distributes it to neighborhoods and communities where it becomes a collaborative pursuit and a powerful expression of peer-to-peer lateral power at work.

The democratization of production fundamentally disrupts the centralized manufacturing practices of the vertically integrated Second Industrial Revolution. The radical implications of installing Fab Labs all over the world so that everyone can be a prosumer has not gone unnoticed. Again, science-fiction writers were among the first to imagine the repercussions.

In *Printcrime*, published in 2006, Cory Doctorow described a future society in which 3D printers could print copies of physical goods. In Doctorow's dystopian society, a powerful authoritarian government makes the 3D printing of physical copies of goods illegal. Doctorow's protagonist, an early prosumer, is imprisoned for ten years for 3D printing. After serving his prison sentence, the hero realizes that an overthrow of the existing order is best accomplished not by just printing a few products, but rather by printing printers. He proclaims, "I'm going to print more printers. Lots more printers. One for everyone.

That's worth going to jail for. That's worth anything."[14] Fab Labs are
the new high-tech arsenals where DIY hackers are arming themselves
with the tools to eclipse the existing economic order.

Hackers are just beginning to turn their attention to 3D printing
of some of the many components that make up the IoT infrastructure.
Renewable energy harvesting technologies are at the top of the list.
Xerox is developing a special silver ink that could be substituted for
the silicon that is currently used as the semiconductor within photovoltaic (PV) solar cells. The silver ink melts at a lower temperature
than plastic, which could allow users to print integrated circuits into
plastic, fabric, and film. DIY printing of paper-thin PV solar strips
could allow anyone to produce their own solar harvesting technology
at an ever-diminishing cost, bringing solar energy a step closer to near
zero marginal cost. Xerox's silver ink process is still experimental, but
it is indicative of the new infofacturing possibilities opened up by 3D
printing.[15]

Making 3D printing a truly local, self-sufficient process requires
that the feedstock used to create the filament is abundant and locally available. Staples, the office supply company, has introduced a
3D printer, manufactured by Mcor Technologies, in its store in Al-
mere, the Netherlands, that uses cheap paper as feedstock. The process, called selective deposition lamination (SDL), prints out hard 3D
objects in full color with the consistency of wood. The 3D printers
are used to infofacture craft products, architectural designs, and even
surgical models for facial reconstruction. The paper feedstock costs a
mere 5 percent of previous feedstocks.[16]

Other feedstocks being introduced are even cheaper, reducing the
cost of materials to near zero. Markus Kayser, a graduate student at
the Royal College of Art in London, has invented a Solar Sinter 3D
printer that prints glass objects from sun and sand. The Solar Sinter,
which was successfully tested in the Sahara Desert in 2011, is powered
by two PV panels. It is also equipped with a large lens that focuses the
sun's rays to heat sand to a melting point. The software then directs
melted sand to form each layer, creating a fully formed glass object.[17]

Filabot is a nifty new device the size of a shoe box that grinds and
melts old household items made out of plastic: buckets, DVDs, bottles,
water pipes, sunglasses, milk jugs, and the like. The ground plastic is
then fed into a hopper and into a barrel where it is melted down by

a heating coil. The molten plastic then travels through nozzles and is sent through sizing rollers to create plastic filaments which are stored on a spool for printing. An assembled Filabot costs $649.[18]

A Dutch student, Dirk Vander Kooij, reprogrammed an industrial robot to print customized furniture in a continuous line using plastic material from old refrigerators. The robot can print out a chair in multiple colors and designs in less than three hours. His 3D printer can turn out 4,000 customized chairs a year.[19] Other printers of furniture are using recycled glass, wood, fabrics, ceramics, and even stainless steel as feedstock, demonstrating the versatility in recycled feedstocks that can be employed in the new infofacturing process.

If infofacturers are going to print furniture, why not print the building the furniture will be housed in? Engineers, architects, and designers are scrambling to bring 3D-printed buildings to market. While the technology is still in the R&D stage, it is already clear that 3D printing of buildings will reinvent construction in the coming decades.

Dr. Behrokh Khoshnevis is a professor of industrial and systems engineering and director of the Center for Rapid Automated Fabrication Technologies at the University of Southern California. With support and financing from the U.S. Department of Defense, the National Science Foundation, and the National Aeronautics and Space Administration (NASA), Khoshnevis is experimenting with a 3D printing process called "contour crafting" to print buildings. He has created a form-free composite-fiber concrete that can be extruded and that is strong enough to allow a printed wall to support itself during construction. His team has already successfully constructed a wall that is five feet long, three feet high, and six inches thick using a 3D printer. Equally important, the viscous material does not clog the machine's nozzle with sand and particles during the infusion process.

Admitting that this is only the first step, Khoshnevis nonetheless gushed that the printed wall is "the most historic wall since the Great Wall of China." He added that after 20,000 years of human construction, "the process of constructing buildings is about to be revolutionized."[20]

Khoshnevis says that the giant printers will cost a few hundred thousand dollars each—a small price for construction equipment. A new home could be potentially printed at a cost far below standard construction because of the cheap composite materials being used and the additive infofacturing process, which uses far fewer materials and human labor. He believes that 3D-printed building construction will be the dominant industry standard by 2025 around the world.

Khoshnevis is not alone. The MIT research lab is using 3D printing to explore ways to create the frame of a house in one day with virtually no human labor. That same frame would take an entire construction crew a month to put up.[21]

Janjaap Ruijssenaars, a Dutch architect, is collaborating with Enrico Dini, chairman of Monolite, a U.K.-based 3D printing company. The two Europeans have announced that they will print out six-by-nine-foot frames made of sand and inorganic binder and then fill the frames with fiber-reinforced concrete. They hope to have a two-story building up in 2014.[22]

Dini and Foster + Partners, one of the world's largest architectural firms, have teamed up with the European Space Agency to explore the possibility of using 3D printing to construct a permanent base on the moon. The buildings would be printed using lunar soil as the feedstock. The goal is to construct lunar habitats with locally sustainable materials found on the moon in order to avoid the logistical cost of shipping in materials from Earth. Xavier De Kestelier of Foster + Partners says that "as a practice, we are used to designing for extreme climates on Earth and exploiting the environmental benefits of using local, sustainable materials—our lunar habitation follows a similar logic."[23]

The plan is to use Dini's D-Shape printer to pour out the lunar buildings, each of which would take about a week to construct. The buildings are hollow, closed-cell structures that look a little like a bird skeleton. The catenary dome and cellular walls are designed to withstand micrometeoroids and space radiation. The building's base and inflatable dome would be delivered by spacecraft from Earth. Foster explains that the layers of lunar soil, called regolith, would be printed out by the D-Shape printer and built up around the frame. Foster architects have already used simulated material to construct a 1.5-ton prototype building block. The first lunar building would be printed at the moon's south pole, which is exposed to ample sunlight.[24]

While the 3D printing of buildings is in the very early stages of development, it is projected to grow exponentially in the coming two decades as the production process becomes increasingly efficient and cheaper. Unlike conventional construction techniques, where the cost of designing architectural blueprints is high, construction materials are expensive, labor costs are steep, and the time necessary to erect the structures is lengthy, 3D printing is not affected by these factors.

Three-dimensional printing can use the cheapest building materials on Earth—sand and rock, as well as virtually any kind of discarded waste materials, all from locally available sources—thereby avoiding the high cost of traditional building materials and the equally high logistical costs of delivering them on-site. The additive process of building up a structure layer by layer provides a further savings on the materials used in construction. The open-source programs are virtually free, in contrast to the considerable time and expense involved in having an architect draw up blueprints. The building frame is erected with very little human labor compared to traditional construction and can be put up in a fraction of the time. Lastly, the marginal cost of generating electricity to power the 3D printer could approach zero by relying on locally harvested renewable energy, making it conceivable that, at least in the not-too-distant future, a small building could cost little more than what it takes to round up the rocks, sand, recyclable material, and other feedstock nearby.

Whether on the moon or here on Earth, human beings will need transport to get around. The first 3D-printed automobile, the Urbee, is already being field tested. The Urbee was developed by KOR Eco-Logic, a company based in Winnipeg, Canada. The automobile is a two-passenger hybrid-electric vehicle (the name Urbee is short for *urban electric*), which is designed to run on solar and wind power that can be harvested in a one-car garage each day. The car can reach speeds of 40 miles per hour.[25] If long driving distances are necessary, the user can switch over to the car's ethanol-powered backup engine.[26] Granted, the Urbee is just the first working prototype of the new TIR-era automobile, but like the introduction of Henry Ford's first mass-produced, gas-powered internal-combustion engine automobile, the nature of the vehicle's construction and power source is highly suggestive of the kind of future it portends for the economy and society.

Ford's automobile required the construction of huge centralized factories to accommodate the delivery and storage of materials that went into the car's assembly. Tooling the assembly line was highly capital intensive and required long runs of the exact same mass-produced vehicles to ensure a proper return on investment. Most people are aware of Ford's flip response when a customer asked him which color he could choose for the automobile. Ford replied, "Any colour that he wants so long as it is black."[27]

The subtractive manufacturing process on the Ford assembly line was highly wasteful, since bulk materials had to be cut and shaved before the final assembly of the automobile. The car itself was made up of hundreds of parts requiring both time and labor to assemble. It then had to be shipped across the country to dealers, again resulting in additional logistical costs. And even though Ford was able to use the new efficiencies made possible by the Second Industrial Revolution to create vertically integrated operations and achieve sufficient economies of scale to provide a relatively cheap vehicle that put millions of people behind the wheel, the marginal cost of producing and using each vehicle never got close to zero—especially when you factor in the price of gasoline.

A 3D-printed automobile is produced with a very different logic. The automobile can be made from nearly free feedstock available locally, eliminating the high cost of rare materials and the costs of shipping them to the factory and storing them on-site. Most of the parts in the car are made with 3D-printed plastic, with the exception of the base chassis and engine.[28] The rest of the car is produced in layers, which are "added" one onto another in a continuous flow rather than being assembled together from individual parts, meaning less material, less time, and less labor are used. A six-foot-high 3D printer poured out Urbee's shell in only ten pieces, with no wasted material.[29]

Three-dimensional printing does not require huge capital investments to tool the factory floor and long lead times to change production models. Simply by changing the open-source software, each vehicle can be poured and printed to the customized specifications of a single user or batch of users at little additional cost.

Because the 3D printing factory can be located anywhere where it can plug into an IoT infrastructure, it can deliver vehicles locally or regionally for less expense than shipping vehicles across countries from centralized factories.

Finally, the cost of driving a 3D-printed car, using locally harvested renewable energy, is nearly free. The fuel cost for the Urbee is only $0.02 per mile—or one-third the cost of driving a Toyota Prius.[30]

A MAKERS INFRASTRUCTURE

Until now, the Makers Movement has been more about hackers, hobbyists, and social entrepreneurs playing with new ways to print out specific objects for personal and general use. The movement has been driven by four principles: the open-source sharing of new inventions, the promotion of a collaborative learning culture, a belief in community self-sufficiency, and a commitment to sustainable production practices. But underneath the surface, an even more radical agenda is beginning to unfold, albeit undeveloped and still largely unconscious. If we were to put all the disparate pieces of the 3D printing culture together, what we begin to see is a powerful new narrative arising that could change the way civilization is organized in the twenty-first century.

Think about it. The DIY culture is growing around the world, empowered by the idea of using bits to arrange atoms. Like the early software hackers of a generation ago, who were motivated to create their own software to share new information, DIY players are passionate about creating their own software to print and share things. Many of the things that 3D hobbyists are creating, if put together, make up the essential nodes of a do-it-yourself TIR infrastructure.

The really revolutionary aspect of 3D printing, which will take it from a hobbyist subculture to a new economic paradigm, is the impending "Makers Infrastructure." This development will spawn new business practices whose efficiencies and productivity take us to near zero marginal costs in the production and distribution of goods and services—easing us out of the capitalist period and into the collaboratist era.

Among the first to glimpse the historical significance of a "Makers Infrastructure" were the local grassroots activists who constituted the Appropriate Technology Movement. The movement began in the 1970s and was inspired by the writing of Mahatma Gandhi, and later E. F. Schumacher, Ivan Illich, and—if it's not too presumptuous—a book I authored called *Entropy: A New World View*. A new generation of DIY hobbyists, most of whom were veterans of the peace and civil rights movements, loosely affiliated themselves under the appropriate technology banner. Some preached a "back to the land" ethos and migrated to rural areas. Others remained in the poor, urban neighborhoods of major cities, often squatting and occupying abandoned neighborhood buildings. Their self-proclaimed mission was to create "appropriate technologies," meaning tools and machines that could be made from locally available resources, that were scaled to steward rather than exploit their ecological surroundings, and that could be shared in a collaborative culture. Their rallying cry was "think globally and act locally," by which they meant to take care of the planet by living in a sustainable way in one's local community.

The movement, which started in the industrialized countries of the global North, soon became an even more powerful force in the developing countries in the global South, as the world's poor struggled to create their own self-sufficient communities at the margins of a global capitalist economy.

Particularly noticeable, at least in hindsight, is that a decade after the Appropriate Technology Movement emerged, a distinctly different movement of young tech-hobbyists came on the scene. These were the geeks and nerds of IT culture who shared a love of computer programming and a passion for sharing software in collaborative learning communities. They made up the Free Software Movement, whose aim was to create a global Collaborative Commons (that movement will be considered in greater detail in Part III). Their slogan was "information wants to be free," coined by Stewart Brand, one of the few who bridged the Appropriate Technology Movement and hacker culture. (*The Whole Earth Catalog*, which Brand edited, helped elevate the Appropriate Technology Movement from a niche subculture to a broader cultural phenomenon.) What's often lost in Brand's remarks on the software revolution is the rest of the utterance, which he delivered at the first hackers conference in 1984:

> On the one hand information wants to be expensive, because it's so valuable. The right information in the right place just changes your life. On the other hand, information wants to be free, because the cost of getting it out is getting lower and lower all the time. So you have these two fighting against each other.[31]

Brand saw early on the coming contradiction between intellectual-property rights and open-source access. That contradiction would eventually frame the battle between capitalists and collaboratists as the marginal costs of sharing information approached zero.

The Appropriate Technology Movement was decidedly low-tech, interested in both rediscovering and upgrading effective traditional technologies that had been abandoned or forgotten in the rush into the Industrial Age and developing newer technologies—especially renewable energies. They favored the simple over the complex and technology that could be replicated from scratch using local resources and know-how, so as to stay true to the principle of local self-reliance.

The hackers were of a different ilk. They were the young, often brilliant engineers and scientists at the leading edge of the IT revolution—the very epitome of high-tech culture. Their gaze was global rather than local and their community took shape in the social spaces of the Internet.

What the two movements had in common was a sense of shared community and an ethical belief in the value of collaboration over proprietorship and access over ownership.

Now, 3D printing brings these two pivotal movements together, since it is both extremely high tech and appropriate tech. It is, for the most part, employed as an open-source technology. The software instructions for printing objects are globally shared rather than privately held, yet the material feedstocks are locally available, making the technology universally applicable. While 3D printing promotes self-sufficient local communities, the products can be marketed on websites at nearly zero marginal cost and made accessible to a global user base. Three-dimensional printing also bridges ideological borders, appealing to libertarians, do-it-yourselfers, social entrepreneurs, and communitarians, all of whom favor a distributed, transparent, collaborative approach to economic and social life rather than a centralized and proprietary one. 3D printing brings these various sensibilities together. The social bond is the deep abhorrence of hierarchical power and the fierce commitment to peer-to-peer lateral power.

It's not surprising that 3D printing is catching on in the most advanced industrial economies. While U.S. companies grabbed a quick lead in the new technology, Germany seems poised to catch up in the next several years because its 3D technology is viewed as an infofacturing model tailored for a distributed, collaborative, laterally scaled TIR infrastructure.

Germany is far ahead of the other major industrialized nations in advancing the IoT technology platform for 3D printing to plug into and play. As already mentioned, the country has surpassed the target of producing 20 percent of its electrical power with distributed renewable energy and is projected to generate 35 percent of its electricity from renewable energy by 2020.[32] Germany has also converted 1 million buildings to partial green micropower plants in the past ten years. E.ON and other power and utility companies are currently installing hydrogen and other storage technologies across the transmission grid. Deutsche Telekom is testing the Energy Internet in six regions of the country, and Daimler is establishing a network of hydrogen fueling stations across Germany in preparation for the company's launch of fuel-cell vehicles in 2017.[33]

Because they can connect into an IoT infrastructure across Germany, 3D printers can take advantage of the efficiencies and productivity potential afforded by the new Internet of Things. This allows German infofacturers to leap ahead of the United States, where 3D printing firms find themselves adrift in an inefficient and outdated Second Industrial Revolution infrastructure whose productivity capacity has long since peaked.

Germany's small- and medium-sized engineering companies have long been regarded as the best in the world in precision engineering, making them ideally positioned to lead in the advancement of 3D printing. Ten German companies are already out front in the development of 3D printing. EOS and Concept Laser, both based in Bavaria, are among the world-class players.[34] The German approach to shifting into a TIR infrastructure is both conventional, relying on a top-down implementation of the Internet of Things, and lateral, with local communities transforming their buildings to micropower plants, installing micropower grids, and introducing e-mobility transport.

It is in the developing world, however, that a Makers infrastructure is evolving in its purest form. In poor urban outskirts, isolated towns, and rural locales—where infrastructure is scant, access to capital spotty, at best, and technical expertise, tools, and machinery virtually nonexistent—3D printing provides a desperately needed opportunity for building a TIR Makers infrastructure.

Marcin Jakubowski, a graduate of Princeton University with a doctorate in fusion energy from the University of Wisconsin, is one of a growing number of socially motivated young inventors who are beginning to put together 3D blueprints for creating a TIR Makers infrastructure anywhere in the world. Jakubowski began by asking a rather simple question: What does any community need in the way of materials and machines to create a sustainable and decent quality of life? He and his team, who are impassioned advocates of open-source appropriate technology, have "identified 50 of the most important machines that allow modern life to exist—the tools we use every-day—everything from a tractor to a bread oven to a circuit maker," to farm, build habitats, and manufacture things.[35]

The group's primary focus is on the tools of production. The goal is to create open-source software that can use locally available feed-stock—mainly scrap metal—to print all 50 machines, giving every community a "global village construction kit" to make its own TIR society.

Thus far, Jakubowski's open-source ecology network of farmers and engineers have used 3D printing to make prototypes of 8 of the 50 machines: "bulldozer, rototiller, 'microtractor,' backhoe, universal rotor, drill press, a multi-purpose 'ironworker,' . . . and a CNC torch table for the precision cutting of sheet metal."[36] All the designs and instructions for 3D-printed machines are open sourced on the group's website for anyone to replicate. The team is currently working on the next eight prototype technologies.

Building a modern civilization from "scratch and scrap," from the ground up, would have been unthinkable a generation ago. While open-source ecology is taking an integrated, systemic approach de-signed to create an entire ecology of machines for making a modern economy, other 3D printing groups, including Appropedia, Howtope-dia, and Practical Action, are serving as repositories for open-source, 3D printing designs that will allow do-it-yourselfers to print a whole range of machines that are essential to build a TIR Makers economy.[37]

Three-dimensional printing of key tools and machines for farm-ing, building, and manufacturing, by themselves, can do very little. To be useful, they have to be plugged into an electricity infrastruc-ture. The real revolution comes when the 3D Makers Movement con-nects all the "things" in a 3D Makers economy to an Energy Internet. When that happens, the economic paradigm changes. Connecting 3D-printed things via an Energy Internet gives every community a mini-IoT infrastructure that can reach out nodally and connect contiguous communities across regions.

Microgrids—local Energy Internets—are already being installed in communities in the most remote regions of the world, transforming economic development overnight. In India, where 400 million people, mostly in rural areas, are still without electricity, the microgrid debuted in a big way in July 2012 when the country experienced the worst power blackout in history, leaving 700 million people without electricity. While much of the nation went into panic mode, one tiny village in rural Rajasthan enjoyed business as usual, without as much as a flickering of the lights. The villagers' newly acquired televisions stayed on, their DVD players worked, their buttermilk machines kept churning, and the fans kept them cool, all thanks to the green microgrid.

Just months earlier, a small start-up company called Gram Power, run by a 22-year-old social entrepreneur named Yashraj Khaitan, a graduate of the University of California, and Jacob Dickinson, a colleague, set up India's first smart microgrid in the tiny Indian village of Khareda Lakshmipura. The local electricity microgrid is powered by a bank of solar panels connected to a brick substation. Inside the substation are batteries that allow the village to store power during the night or when there is cloud cover. A small computer transmits data back to the company's offices in Jaipur. Wires on wooden poles transmit the electricity from the substation to scores of homes around the village, providing green electricity for more than 200 residents. Each home is equipped with a smart meter that informs the user how much electricity is being used and what it is costing at different times of the day.[38] Green electricity is far less expensive than electricity from India's national grid, and it eliminates the burning of highly polluting kerosene that is responsible for respiratory and heart diseases common throughout India.

A local mother interviewed by the *Guardian* described how electricity has transformed the life of the village. She explained that "now the children can study at night. Before, living here was like being in the jungle. Now we feel as though we are actually part of society."[39]

Gram Power, which was chosen by NASA as one of the top ten Clean Tech Innovators around the world in 2011, has since worked with ten other villages, installing microgrids, and expects to bring green electricity to an additional 40,000 villagers in 2014.[40] It is also looking to other sources of locally available renewable energy, including geothermal heat and biomass. The company is currently negotiating with the Indian government to extend microgrids to 120 additional villages, bringing power to more than 100,000 households.[41]

Gram Power is one of a slew of new start-up companies fanning out across rural India, helping local villages establish green microgrids to spread electricity. Husk Power Systems is a start-up company based in Bihar State, where 85 percent of the population is without electricity. The company is burning biomass from rice husks to power 90 local power plants. The power plants use microgrids to transfer electricity to 45,000 rural homes. The typical cost of installing a microgrid for a village of a hundred or so homes is as little as $2,500, allowing the community to pay off the investment in just a few years, after which the marginal cost of generating and delivering each additional kilowatt of electricity is nearly zero.[42]

As local microgrids come online, they also connect with one another, creating regional networks that eventually link up to the national grids, transforming the centralized power structure into a distributed, collaborative, laterally scaled power network. Microgrids are projected to account for more than 75 percent of the revenue for renewable energy generation globally by 2018.[43]

The proliferation of microgrids in the poorest regions of the developing world, powered by locally generated renewable energy, provides the essential electricity to run 3D printers, which can produce the tools and machinery needed to establish self-sufficient and sustainable twenty-first-century communities.

A NEO-GANDHIAN WORLD

Watching the transformation taking place in India and around the world, I can't help but reflect on Mahatma Gandhi's insight set forth more than 70 years ago. When asked about his economic vision, Gandhi replied, "Mass production, certainly, but not based on force. . . . It is mass production, but mass production in people's own homes."[44] E. F. Schumacher summarized Gandhi's concept as "not mass production but production by the masses."[45] Gandhi went on to outline an economic model that has even more relevance for India and the rest of the world today than when he first articulated it.

Gandhi's views ran counter to the wisdom of the day. In a world where politicians, business leaders, economists, academics, and the general public were extolling the virtues of industrialized production, Gandhi demurred, suggesting that "there is a tremendous fallacy behind Henry Ford's reasoning." Gandhi believed that mass production, with its vertically integrated enterprises and inherent tendencies to centralize economic power and monopolize markets, would have dire consequences for humanity.[46] He warned that such a situation

> would be found to be disastrous. . . . Because while it is true that
> you will be producing things in innumerable areas, the power will
> come from one selected centre. . . . It would place such a limitless
> power in one human agency that I dread to think of it. The con-
> sequence, for instance, of such a control of power would be that I
> would be dependent on that power for light, water, even air, and so
> on. That, I think, would be terrible.[47]

Gandhi understood that mass production was designed to use more sophisticated machines to produce more goods with less labor and at a cheaper cost. He saw, however, an inherent contradiction in the organizational logic of mass production that limited its promise. Gandhi reasoned that "if all countries adopted the system of mass production, there would not be a big enough market for their products. Mass production must then come to a stop."[48] Like Karl Marx, John Maynard Keynes, Wassily Leontief, Robert Heilbroner, and other distinguished economists, he argued that the capitalists' desire for efficiency and productivity would result in an unyielding drive to replace human labor with automation, leaving more and more people unemployed and without sufficient purchasing power to buy the products being produced.

Gandhi's alternative proposal was local production by the masses in their own homes and neighborhoods—what he called *Swadeshi*. The idea behind *Swadeshi* was to "bring work to the people and not people to the work."[49] He asked rhetorically, "If you multiply individual production to millions of times, would it not give you mass production on a tremendous scale?"[50] Gandhi fervently believed that "production and consumption must be reunited"—what we today call prosumers—and that it was only realizable if most production took place locally and much of it, but not all, was consumed locally.[51]

Gandhi was a keen observer of the power relations that governed the First and Second Industrial Revolutions. He watched the British industrial machine swarm over the Indian subcontinent, devouring its rich natural resources and impoverishing its citizenry to feed the consumer appetites of a wealthy elite and a growing middle class in Britain. He saw millions of his countrymen languish at the very bottom of a global industrial pyramid that wielded power from the top. It is no wonder he railed against a centralized capitalist system.

Gandhi was equally disenchanted with the Communist experiment in the Soviet Union, which gave lip service to the principle of communal solidarity while exercising an even more rigid centralized control over the industrialization process than its capitalist foes.

Gandhi never consciously articulated the concept that communication/energy/transportation matrices determine the way economic power is organized and distributed in every civilization. He intuited, however, that the industrial organization of society—be it under the aegis of a capitalist or socialist regime—brought with it a set of guiding assumptions, including centralized control over the production and distribution process; the championing of a utilitarian concept of human nature; and the pursuit of ever more material consumption as an end in itself. His philosophy, on the other hand, emphasized decentralized economic production in self-sufficient local communities; the pursuit of craft labor over industrial-machine labor; and the envisioning of economic life as a moral and spiritual quest rather than a materialist pursuit. For Gandhi, the antidote to rampant economic exploitation and greed is a selfless commitment to community.

Gandhi's ideal economy starts in the local village and extends outward to the world. He wrote:

My idea of village *Swaraj* is that it is a complete republic, independent of its neighbors for its own vital wants, and yet interdependent for many others which dependence is a necessity.[52]

He eschewed the notion of a pyramidically organized society in favor of what he called "oceanic circles," made up of communities of individuals embedded within broader communities that ripple out to envelop the whole of humanity. Gandhi argued that

> independence must begin at the bottom . . . every village has to be self-sustained and capable of managing its affairs even to the extent of defending itself against the whole world. . . . This does not exclude dependence on and willing help from neighbours or from the world. It will be a free and voluntary play of mutual forces. . . . In this structure composed of innumerable villages, there will be ever widening, never ascending circles. Life will not be a pyramid with the apex sustained by the bottom. But it will be an oceanic circle whose center will be the individual. . . . Therefore the outermost circumference will not wield power to crush the inner circle but will give strength to all within and derive its own strength from it."[53]

In championing this vision, Gandhi also distanced himself from classical economic theory. Adam Smith's assertion that it is in the nature of each individual to pursue his or her own self-interest in the marketplace and that "it is his own advantage, indeed, and not that of the society, which he has in view," was anathema to Gandhi.[54] He believed in a virtuous economy in which the community's interest superseded individual self-interest and argued that anything less depreciates the happiness of the human race.

For Gandhi, happiness is not to be found in the amassing of individual wealth but in living a compassionate and empathic life. He went so far as to suggest that "real happiness and contentment . . . consists not in the multiplication but, in the deliberate and voluntary reduction of wants," so that one might be free to live a more committed life in fellowship with others.[55] He also bound his theory of happiness to a responsibility to the planet. Nearly a half century before sustainability came into vogue, Gandhi declared that "Earth provides enough to satisfy every man's need but not enough for every man's greed."[56]

Gandhi's ideal economy bears a striking philosophical likeness to the Third Industrial Revolution and the accompanying Collaborative Age. His view of self-sufficient village communities joining together and rippling outward into wider oceanic circles that extend to all of humanity mirrors the community microgrids that connect in ever more distributed and collaborative lateral networks in the TIR economic paradigm. His concept of happiness as the optimization of one's relationships in shared communities rather than the autonomous pursuit of individual self-interest in the marketplace reflects the new dream of quality of life that is the hallmark of a Collaborative Age. Finally, Gandhi's belief that nature is a finite resource imbued with intrinsic value that requires stewardship rather than pillage fits the new realization that every human being's life is ultimately judged by the impact of his or her ecological footprint on the biosphere in which we all dwell.

While Gandhi espoused the idea of lateral economic power and understood that the Earth's environment is itself the overarching community that supports all life on the planet, he was forced to defend his philosophy of local economic power in an industrial era whose communication/energy/transportation matrix favored centralized, top-down management of commercial practices and the vertical integration of economic activity. That left him in the untenable position of championing traditional crafts in local subsistence communities that had kept the masses of Indian people mired in poverty and isolation over eons of history.

What Gandhi failed to perceive is that an even deeper contradiction lies at the heart of the capitalist system that would make possible the very distributed and collaborative laterally scaled economy he espoused—that is, the steadfast pursuit of new technologies whose increased efficiencies and productivity are driving marginal costs to nearly zero, making many goods and services potentially free and an economy of abundance a real possibility.

No doubt Gandhi would have been equally surprised to learn that capitalism's optimum point of ideal productivity at near zero marginal cost would be realized by introducing a new communication technology, a new energy regime, and an accompanying production-and-distribution model that is organized in a distributed and collaborative fashion and scaled peer to peer and laterally, allowing millions of people to become prosumers—not unlike the concept of production by the masses that he envisioned.

Today, the IoT infrastructure provides the means to advance the Gandhian economic vision, lifting hundreds of millions of Indians out of abject poverty and into a sustainable quality of life. Gandhi's quest for the good economy, brought forward and embedded in the Internet of Things, can serve as a powerful new narrative not only for India, but for emerging nations around the world in search of a just and sustainable future.

CHAPTER SEVEN
MOOCS AND A
ZERO MARGINAL
COST EDUCATION

A zero marginal cost society, in which scarcity has been replaced by abundance, is a far different world than the one we're accustomed to. Preparing students for an era in which capitalist markets play a secondary role to the Collaborative Commons is beginning to force a rethinking of the educational process itself. The pedagogy of learning is undergoing a radical overhaul. So too is the way education is financed and delivered. The near zero marginal cost phenomenon has penetrated deeply into the fabric of higher education in just the past two years with massive open online courses bringing the marginal cost of securing college credits to near zero for millions of students.

The capitalist era enshrined a model of teaching designed to prepare students to be skilled industrial workers. The classroom was transformed into a microcosm of the factory. Students were thought of as analogous to machines. They were conditioned to follow commands, learn by repetition, and perform efficiently. The teacher was akin to a factory foreman, handing out standardized assignments that required set answers in a given time frame. Learning was compartmentalized into isolated silos. Education was supposed to be useful and pragmatic.

The "why" of things was less discussed than the "how" of things. The goal was to turn out productive employees.

THE ONE-ROOM SCHOOLHOUSE WITH TWO BILLION STUDENTS

The transition from the capitalist era to the Collaborative Age is altering the pedagogy of the classroom. The authoritarian, top-down model of instruction is beginning to give way to a more collaborative learning experience. Teachers are shifting from lecturers to facilitators. Imparting knowledge is becoming less important than creating critical-learning skills. Students are encouraged to think more holistically. A premium is placed on inquiry over memorization.

In the traditional industrial classroom, questioning the authority of the teacher is strictly forbidden and sharing information and ideas among students is labeled cheating. Children quickly learn that knowledge is power, and a valuable resource one acquires to secure an advantage over others upon graduation in a fiercely competitive marketplace.

In the Collaborative Age, students will come to think of knowledge as a shared experience among a community of peers. Students learn together as a cohort in a shared-knowledge community. The teacher acts as a guide, setting up inquiries and allowing students to work in small-group environments. The goal is to stimulate collaborative creativity, the kind young people experience when engaged in many of the social spaces of the Internet. The shift from hierarchical power, lodged in the hands of the teacher, to lateral power, established across a learning community, is tantamount to a revolution in pedagogy.

While the conventional classroom treated knowledge as objective, isolated facts, in the collaborative classroom, knowledge is regarded as the collective meanings we attach to our experiences. Students are encouraged to tear down the walls that separate academic disciplines and to think in a more integrated fashion. Interdisciplinary and multicultural studies prepare students to become comfortable entertaining different perspectives and more adept at searching out synergies between phenomena.

The idea of learning as an autonomous private experience and the notion of knowledge as an acquisition to be treated as a form of exclusive property made sense in a capitalist environment that defined human behavior in similar terms. In the Collaborative Age, learning is regarded as a crowdsourcing process and knowledge is treated as a publically shared good, available to all, mirroring the emerging definition of human behavior as deeply social and interactive in nature. The shift from a more authoritarian style of learning to a more lateral learning environment better prepares today's students to work, live, and flourish in tomorrow's collaborative economy.

The new collaborative pedagogy is being applied and practiced in schools and communities around the world. The educational models are designed to free students from the private space of the traditional enclosed classroom and allow them to learn in multiple open Commons, in virtual space, the public square, and in the biosphere.

Classrooms around the world are connecting in real time, via Skype and other programs, and collaborating on joint assignments. Students separated by thousands of miles pair off in virtual-cohort teams, study together, make presentations, debate with one another, and even get graded together. The global collaborative classroom is quickly becoming a reality. Skype in the Classroom, a free online community, has already registered 60,447 teachers in its global classroom project and has set a goal of connecting 1 million classrooms across the world.[1]

Collaborative Classrooms, another Internet learning environment, allows thousands of teachers to cocreate curricula online and share the best lesson plans with one another—for free—in a global education Commons. More than 117,000 teachers are currently sharing open-source curricula, bringing learning communities together in a borderless global classroom.[2]

The learning experience is not only beaming up from the enclosed classroom into the virtual spaces of the Internet, but also seeping out into the surrounding neighborhoods that make up the public square. Today, millions of American students in elementary and secondary schools and in the nation's colleges and universities engage in "service learning" in the community. Service learning combines formal instruction with involvement in the civil society.

Service learning is predicated on the assumption that learning is never a solitary affair but ultimately a shared experience and a collaborative venture that is best practiced in real communities where people live and work. Students generally volunteer in nonprofit organizations where they learn by serving the larger interests of the community of which they are a part. This experiential-based learning provides students with a broader focus. They come to see that learning is more about the search for community than merely the amassing of proprietary knowledge to advance one's self-interest.

Students might learn a foreign language by serving in a neighborhood with a large immigrant population that speaks that particular tongue. If they are learning about the dynamics of poverty in their social studies class, they might volunteer at a food bank or homeless shelter. At the Einstein Middle School in Shoreline, Washington, four teachers representing the core subjects of social studies, English, math, and science brought together 120 eighth-grade students in a collaborative interdisciplinary service-learning project to study the issue of poverty and homelessness. The social studies teacher had the students enact an Oxfam hunger banquet and brought in speakers from several local agencies that assist community residents that live below the poverty line to acquaint them with the complex issues surrounding poverty. Students then volunteered once a week for five weeks at eight sites in downtown Seattle that serve underprivileged communities. The students helped prepare meals and collected and distributed food and other needed items to homeless people and engaged them in conversation, developing personal relationships. In their English classes, students read *Slake's Limbo*, a story about a young boy who runs away from home and lives in the tunnels of the New York City subway system, where he experiences what it's like to be homeless and hungry. In their math classes, students examined the economics of poverty. The eighth graders followed up with written reports about a specific local and global aspect of poverty, published zines, and organized an evening exhibit on issues relating to poverty for the students and the community.[3]

By extending the learning environment to the public Commons, students come to understand that the collaborative experience is the heart and soul of what it means to be a highly social creature endowed with an innate empathic capacity and a yearning to be part of a larger community.

The notion of a learning community is being extended not only to the edges of virtual space and to neighborhoods, but also to the farthest reaches of the biosphere. Students are learning that the biosphere is the indivisible Commons within which all our other communities are embedded. After nearly two centuries of industrial curricula that emphasized the idea of the Earth as a passive reservoir of useful resources to be harnessed, exploited, manufactured, and transformed into productive capital and private property for individual gain, a new collaborative curricula is beginning to re-envision the biosphere as a Commons made up of myriad relationships that act in symbiotic ways to allow the whole of life to flourish on Earth.

Students at the University of Wisconsin at Green Bay spend two weeks of the academic semester doing hands-on fieldwork in tropical conservation in the Carara National Park in Costa Rica. The students work with biologists and park staff to inventory local flora and fauna and monitor ecological conditions in the park. Along with their more technical pursuits, students also engage in unskilled work, repairing nature trails, building bridges, constructing biological field stations, and planting trees in the town abutting the park.

The service-learning experience is designed to both immerse the students in the complex biological dynamics of a tropical ecosystem and provide them an opportunity to assist in its management and preservation.[4]

Many of the nation's high schools are engaged in service-learning programs to protect the environment. At Exeter High School in New Hampshire, students monitoring air quality on school grounds and in adjoining neighborhoods found that car and bus idling had a significant impact on air quality and subsequently mobilized the community to enact a no-idling policy, which improved the air quality in and around the campus.[5]

In these examples, and countless other environmental-service programs, students are both learning about the myriad ways human activity impacts the environment and what remedial measures are needed to reverse the damage and restore local ecosystems back to health. Many students come away from such efforts with a very personal sense of responsibility for stewarding the biosphere community. A student in the Costa Rican service-learning program reflected on how the experience deeply affected his worldview and personal behavior:

> It is extremely important to protect the rainforest in Costa Rica and preserve the rich biodiversity of the area as well as keeping the

Earth's resources plentiful and pristine. Every day I rationalize in
my head what my actions are compromising in the world and I try to
limit my impact on the environment.[6]

The reductionist approach to learning that characterized an industrial era based on isolating and privatizing phenomena is giving way
to a more systemic learning experience designed to understand the
subtle relationships that bind phenomena together in larger wholes. In
learning environments all over the world, students are being prepared
to live in an open-biosphere Commons. More and more curricula are
emphasizing our species' deep biophilia connection to nature, exposing students to the diverse forms of life that inhabit the great oceans
and land masses, teaching them about ecosystem dynamics, and helping them reframe the human experience to live sustainably within the
requisites of the biosphere.

These and other educational initiatives are transforming the
learning experience from one that emphasized living in a closed
world of private property relations to one that prepares students to
live in the open Commons of virtual space, the public square, and
the biosphere.

Service learning has grown from a marginal activity at a handful of educational institutions 25 years ago to a centerpiece of the
American educational process. A recent survey of service learning in
U.S. colleges and universities by College Compact gives some idea
of both the level of commitment that institutions of higher learning are putting into service-learning curricula as well as the impact
that open-Commons learning is having on the communities where
students serve. The report, which covered 1,100 colleges and universities, found that 35 percent of the student body participated in
service-learning programs. Half of the colleges and universities surveyed require service learning as part of their core curriculum for
at least one major, and 93 percent of the schools reported offering
service-learning courses. In 2009 college students alone contributed
the equivalent of $7.96 billion worth of volunteer hours in service
to the community.[7] Equally impressive, studies of elementary schools
and high schools conducted in different regions of the country report
that service learning improved students' problem-solving skills and
understanding of cognitive complexity as well as their performance

in classroom work and on standardized tests, as compared to students who did not take part in service-learning programs.[8]

THE DECLINE OF THE BRICK-AND-MORTAR CLASSROOM

Education, like roads and mass transport, postal services, and health care, has remained, for the most part, in the public domain in industrialized countries and is treated as a public good administered by government.

The United States has been a partial exception in the delivery of education. Public primary and secondary schools have been the rule, but nonprofit private academies have long been part of the mix. Of late, profit-making schools, and especially charter schools, have entered the marketplace. In higher education, public and private nonprofit colleges and universities have dominated the landscape, with for-profit institutions playing only a small, insignificant role.

But now the escalating cost of higher education has created a crisis with millions of students increasingly unable to pay for a four-year college degree, which can cost up to $50,000 a year in the elite not-for-profit colleges and universities and as much as $10,000 per year in publicly funded institutions of higher learning.[9] Students who are able to secure college loans—even with government assistance—face the prospect of massive debt that will burden them well into midlife.

Colleges and universities strapped with ever-higher costs have increasingly turned to corporate sponsors for endowments and operating revenue. In return, the commercial sector has chipped away at the "independence" of these institutions of higher learning, requiring that more of their operations be privatized, from food services and resident and guest accommodations to general maintenance. Corporate advertising is rampant, with Fortune 500 logos adorning sports stadiums and lecture halls. University research facilities, especially in the natural sciences, are increasingly jointly managed, with companies leasing laboratories and contracting with academic departments to conduct proprietary research under various nondisclosure agreements.

Knowledge has been enclosed behind the walls of academic institutions whose price of admission excludes all but the wealthiest. That's about to change. The Internet revolution, whose distributed, collaborative, peer-to-peer power has begun to knock down the walls of once seemingly invincible enclosures across the societal spectrum, has unleashed its full fury on the academic community. The thrust of the assault is coming from inside the academy itself and has been ignited by the same combustible that is tearing asunder realm after realm—the implacable logic of a multifaceted technological revolution that's driving marginal cost to near zero everywhere there is vulnerability to exploit.

The revolution began when a Stanford University professor, Sebastian Thrun, offered a "free" course on artificial intelligence (AI) online in 2011, one similar to the course he taught at the university. Around 200 students normally enrolled in Thurn's course, so he anticipated that only a few thousand would register. But by the time it commenced, 160,000 students from every country in the world—with the exception of North Korea—were sitting at their computers in the biggest classroom ever convened for a single course in all of history. "It absolutely blew my mind," said Thrun. Twenty-three thousand of those students completed the course and graduated.[10]

Although thrilled that he was able to teach more students in one virtual course setting than he could reach in several lifetimes of teaching, Thrun was struck by the irony. While Stanford students were paying $50,000 or more per year to attend world-class courses like the ones he taught, the cost of making the course available to every other potential student in the world was nearly nothing. Thrun went on to launch an online university called Udacity, with the goal of providing a top-quality education for every young person in the world, especially the poor in developing countries who otherwise would never have the opportunity to be exposed to learning at this level. And so began the stampede to online learning.

Two of Thrun's computer-science colleagues, Andrew Ng and Daphne Koller, who participated with him in the online course experiment, set up a competing for-profit online university website called Coursera. While Udacity is developing its own courses, the Coursera founders have taken a different path—rounding up some of the leading academic institutions in a collaborative consortium to offer a full curriculum taught by some of the best college professors in the world.

Coursera's founders brought on the University of Pennsylvania, Stanford, Princeton, and the University of Michigan for starters, giving Coursera the academic heft to build out their vision. Coursera was followed by edX, a nonprofit consortium put together by Harvard and MIT. Coursera now has 97 participating universities as of this writing. EdX has also expanded to more than 30 universities. This new education phenomenon is called MOOCs, which, as mentioned in chapter 1, stands for Massive Open Online Courses.

The Coursera model, which is similar to the others, is grounded in three foundations. First, the course is made up of five- to ten-minute video segments presented by the professor and accompanied by various visual and graphic effects and even short interviews and news items to bring the experience alive and make it more appealing and vital. Students can pause and replay the lectures, allowing them to review material and absorb the work at their own pace. Students are also provided with preparatory materials in advance of each virtual-classroom session and optional material for those who are interested in diving deeper into the subject matter.

The second foundation is practice and mastery. After each video segment, students are required to answer questions. The system automatically grades students' answers on the quizzes, giving them immediate feedback on how they're doing. The research shows that these pop quizzes are powerful incentives to keep students involved—turning the course into more of an intellectual game than a drudgery to be endured. There are homework assignments after each class and grades are given out weekly. Courses that require human eyes to do the grading are evaluated by fellow students in a peer-to-peer process, making the students responsible for each other's performance.

The idea that students learn by judging the performance of their fellow classmates has gained traction within the online academic community. To assess the accuracy of peer-to-peer grading when compared with the grades the professor might give, Mitchell Duneier, a professor at Princeton University who teaches Introduction to Sociology at Coursera Online University, ran a test. He and his teaching assistants graded thousands of midterm and final examinations, compared their scores with the peer-to-peer grading, and found a correlation of 0.88. The average peer score came in at 16.94 of 24 possible points while the professors' score was 15.64—very close.[11]

The third and final foundation is the formation of virtual and real life study groups that are established across political boundaries and geographic terrains, transforming the learning process into a global classroom where students teach each other as much as they are being taught by a teacher. Universities that participate in edX augment their study groups by asking their own alumni to volunteer as online mentors and discussion group leaders. Harvard professor Gregory Nagy recruited ten of his former teaching fellows to help serve as online study group facilitators in the MOOC based on his popular course, Concepts of the Ancient Greek Hero.[12] Upon graduating the Coursera and edX courses, the students receive a certificate of completion.

The crowdsourcing approach to learning online is designed to foster a distributed, collaborative, peer-to-peer learning experience on the Commons—the kind that prepares students for the coming era. By February 2013, Coursera had approximately 2.7 million students from 196 countries enrolled in hundreds of courses.[13]

EdX's first course, in 2012, had an enrollment of 155,000 students. Anant Agarwal, edX's president and formerly the director of MIT's artificial-intelligence laboratory, noted that enrollment in the first virtual course nearly equaled the total number of MIT alumni in the university's 150 years of existence. Agarwal says he hopes to draw in a billion students in a decade.[14]

Like other academicians involved in the roll-out of MOOCs, Agarwal is convinced that this is merely the cusp of an education revolution that's going to sweep the globe. He argues that

> it's the biggest innovation to happen to education for 200 years. . . .
> It's going to reinvent education . . . transform universities [and] democratize education on a global scale.[15]

How does this virtual-learning experience compare to the intellectual fervor mustered in the traditional brick-and-mortar classroom? Carole Cadwalladr, a journalist for the *Guardian*, relates her own experience in preparing an article on MOOCs. Cadwalladr signed up for a Coursera course, Introduction to Genetics and Evolution, along with 36,000 other virtual classmates from every corner of the world. She says she wasn't all that excited about the video lectures. It's when she checked into the online class forum that she experienced her "being-blown-away moment." She writes:

The traffic is astonishing. There are thousands of people asking—and answering—questions about dominant mutations and recombination. And study groups had spontaneously grown up: a Colombian one, a Brazilian one, a Russian one. There's one on Skype, and some even in real life too. And they're so diligent!

Cadwalladr says, "If you are a vaguely disillusioned teacher, or know one, send them to Coursera: these are people who just want to learn."[16]

While student enthusiasm for MOOCs is running high, educators find that the number of participants that actually complete the courses and pass the tests is often substantially less than students in brick-and-mortar classrooms. One recent study found that 32 percent of the students failed or withdrew from online courses compared to only 19 percent that took the course in a traditional classroom. Educators have pinpointed a number of causes for the lower completion rates. At the top of the list is the feeling of isolation. Being engaged with other students in the classroom creates a sense of community and is a motivating factor in keeping individuals up to speed with the group. Students help each other along, not just in tackling the subject matter, but also in encouraging each other to stay involved. Studies also find that most MOOC students watch online lectures between midnight and 2 a.m., when they are often tired and less able to focus their attention on the course. MOOC students learning at home are also easily distracted and more likely to walk away from the screen to grab a snack in the kitchen or pick up on a more entertaining diversion around the house.

Participating MOOC universities are beginning to address the sense of isolation by offering what they call "blended classes" in which students enroll online and also take part in classroom projects with other students and faculty. New studies have found that by customizing MOOCs with the addition of limited teaching sessions on campus, student academic performance significantly improves over students that did not have an online component.

Another reason for low motivation was that early on, the MOOCs only offered "a statement of accomplishment" and a grade, but in 2013, they began to offer course credits as well. Coursera has formed partnerships with ten of the country's largest public university systems to deliver free online courses for credit, making online education available to more than 1.25 million students in public institutions. Some of the participating universities are requiring proctored exams on campus to secure the course credit. Faculty at the participating universities will also have the option of customizing the MOOCs with the addition of their own teaching sessions. The offer of credits for courses successfully completed has been a key factor in improving academic performance and completion of courses.

Stanford University courses cost approximately $10,000 to $15,000 to put online. Courses with video content can cost twice that amount. But the marginal cost of delivering the courses to students is simply the cost of bandwidth, which is nearly free. (The marginal cost is between three and seven dollars per person—about the same as a large cup of coffee and a cookie at Starbucks.)[17]

So how do the online universities pay for the fixed costs of MOOCs? The participating universities pay Coursera around $8 a student to use the Coursera platform and an additional $30 to $60 a student to take the course—all in all, nearly free.[18] By contrast, the University of Maryland, a typical public institution of higher learning, charges about $870 per course for in-state students and about $3,000 for out-of-state students.[19] Interestingly, educators find that if MOOC students are required to pay even a small token fee to verify both their participation in the course and that they passed the examination, they are far more likely to complete the course.[20] The MOOCs university consortiums also plan to provide "premium services" for fees. There is even discussion about "charging corporate recruiters for access to the best students."[21]

World-class universities are taking a gamble that the global reach and visibility that MOOCs give their "rock-star" faculties will draw the best and brightest students to their admissions offices. Like their counterparts in the commercial arena, they are hoping to grab hold of the long tail and profit by offering the courses free online to millions of students and corralling in a tiny percentage of those students to their campuses. Their rationale is that by giving their intellectual gifts away for free, they will be helping millions of online students who ordinarily couldn't afford such an education, while capturing a sufficient number of the best students to maintain their own brick-and-mortar operations.

The problem is, when the best education in the world can be delivered at near zero marginal cost and made nearly free online, what's to prevent any accredited university from accepting a MOOC's certification for credits for a very small fee so that students can be accredited with a college education? While employers might be skittish early on about credits from MOOCs, as more colleges and universities come on board, their doubts are likely to recede. Indeed, employers might look more favorably on credits obtained by graduating from MOOCs taught by some of the world's leading academics, rather than traditional credits earned by attending and passing courses taught by less renowned professors at undistinguished colleges.

Kevin Carey, policy director for the Education Sector, a think tank headquartered in Washington, D.C., got to the core of the dilemma facing colleges and universities in an essay in the *Chronicle of Higher Education*. He wrote:

> All of this points toward a world where economies of higher education are broken down and restructured around marginal cost. The cost of serving the 100,000th student who enrolls in a MOOC is essentially zero, which is why the price is zero, too. Open-source textbooks and other free online resources will drive the prices of supporting materials toward the zero line as well.[22]

What Carey is talking about is patently obvious. Whatever "marginal value" elite universities might exact on the long tail by providing free education to hundreds of millions of students is paltry compared to the loss of revenue to the brick-and-mortar system of higher education as a whole, when the marginal cost of teaching online is nearly zero and the courses are nearly free. Does any academic or social entrepreneur really believe that the traditional, centralized, brick-and-mortar education will survive as we know it in a world where the best education money can buy is made free online?

That is not to say that traditional colleges and universities will vanish—only that their mission will radically change and their role will diminish with the onslaught of MOOCs. Currently, university administrators and faculties still hold fast to the hope that world-class online university courses will draw students to a more conventional revenue-generating education. They have yet to fully realize the fact that the near zero marginal cost of education in a global virtual Commons they themselves are creating will increasingly become the new teaching paradigm for higher education, while brick-and-mortar learning eventually will play an ever more circumscribed and narrow supplementary role.

Why then, are so many universities so anxious to push forward? First, in their defense, there is a great deal of idealism involved here. It has long been the dream of educators to bring the knowledge of the world to every human being. Not to do so, once we have the means, would be considered unethical to many academics. But second, they recognize that if they hold out, others will rush in—which they already are. Like their counterparts in so many other sectors where new technologies are making possible a near zero marginal cost society and nearly free goods and services, they realize that the logic of optimizing the welfare of the human race in collaborative, networked Commons is so compelling that it is impossible to shut it out or turn away. The traditional colleges and universities will increasingly have to accommodate the MOOCs approach to learning and find their place in an ascending Collaborative Commons.

CHAPTER EIGHT
THE LAST WORKER STANDING

The same IT and Internet technology that is taking communications, energy, manufacturing, and higher education to near zero marginal cost is doing so with human labor as well. Big Data, advanced analytics, algorithms, Artificial Intelligence (AI), and robotics are replacing human labor across the manufacturing industries, service industries, and knowledge-and-entertainment sectors, leading to the very real prospect of liberating hundreds of millions of people from work in the market economy in the first half of the twenty-first century.

THE END OF WORK

In 1995, I published a book entitled *The End of Work* in which I made the argument that "more sophisticated software technologies are going to bring civilization ever closer to a near-workerless world."[1] *The Economist* ran a cover story on the end of work in which the editors suggested that we would have to see if my forecast will turn out to be prescient. In the interim years, the projections I had made back in 1995 of IT-generated automation leading to technology displacement in virtually every sector of the economy became a troubling reality, leaving millions of people unemployed and underemployed across every country in the world. If anything, my original forecast proved to be a bit too conservative.

In 2013, in the United States, 21.9 million adults are unemployed, underemployed, or discouraged and are no longer counted in the official statistics.[2] Worldwide, 25 percent of the adult workforce was either unemployed, underemployed, or discouraged and no longer looking for work in 2011.[3] The International Labor Organization reports that more than 202 million people will be without work in 2013.[4]

While there are many reasons for the unemployment, economists are just now waking up to the fact that technology displacement is a primary culprit. *The Economist*, among others, revisited the issue of the end of work 16 years after I published the book, asking, "What happens . . . when machines are smart enough to become workers? In other words, when capital becomes labour."[5] In an editorial *The Economist* noted that

> this is what Jeremy Rifkin, a social critic, was driving at in his book *The End of Work*, published in 1995. . . . Mr. Rifkin argued prophetically that society was entering a new phase—one in which fewer and fewer workers would be needed to produce all the goods and services consumed. . . . The process has clearly begun.[6]

It wasn't that I was clairvoyant. The signs were everywhere, but in the growth years, most economists were so attached to conventional economic theory—that supply creates demand and that new technologies, while disruptive, reduce costs, stimulate consumption, spur more production, increase innovation, and open up opportunities for new kinds of jobs—that my message fell largely on deaf ears. Now, economists are taking notice.

In the period of the Great Recession, economists discovered that while millions of jobs were irreversibly lost, productivity was reaching new peaks and output was accelerating around the world, but with fewer workers at their stations. The U.S. manufacturing sector is a prime example. Even before the Great Recession, the mounting statistics were confounding economists. Between 1997 and 2005, manufacturing output increased by 60 percent in the United States while 3.9 million manufacturing jobs were eliminated during roughly the same period, between 2000 and 2008. The economists attribute the dichotomy to a dramatic 30 percent increase in productivity from 1993 to 2005 that allowed manufacturers to produce more output with fewer workers. Those productivity advances came about by "the application of new technologies such as robotics and the use of computing and software on the factory floor . . . [which] increased quality and cut prices, but also led to ongoing layoffs."[7] By 2007 manufacturers were using more than six times as much equipment—computers and software—as they did 20 years earlier while doubling the amount of capital used per hour of employee work.[8]

Between 2008 and 2012, while the Great Recession was bleeding workers, industry was piling on new software and innovations to boost productivity and keep profitable with smaller payrolls. The effect of these efforts is striking. Mark J. Perry, a University of Michigan economics professor and visiting scholar at the American Enterprise Institute, a conservative think tank based in Washington, D.C., ran the numbers. By the end of 2012, according to Perry, the U.S. economy had made a complete recovery from the 2007–2009 recession, with a gross domestic output of $13.6 trillion (in 2005 dollars). That was 2.2 percent higher, or $290 billion more real output, than in 2007, just before the recession, when the GDP was at $13.32 trillion. Perry observes that, while real output was 2.2 percent above the recession level in 2007, industry churned out the increase in goods and services with only 142.4 million workers in 2012—or 3.84 million fewer workers than in 2007. Perry's conclusion: "The Great Recession stimulated huge productivity and efficiency gains as companies shed marginal workers and learned how to do 'more with less (fewer workers).'"[9]

Although Perry and others are just now discovering the disquieting relationship between increased productivity and fewer workers—again, economists always believed in the past that increased productivity drives growth in jobs—evidence of the disconnect was building for more than 50 years.

The first indications of the paradox surfaced at the very beginning of the IT revolution in the early 1960s, with the introduction of the computer on the factory floor. It was called computer numerical control technology. With numerical control, a computer program stores instructions on how a piece of metal should be rolled, lathed, welded, bolted, or painted. The computer program instructs a machine on how to produce a part and directs robots on the factory floor in shaping or assembling parts into products. Numerical control was quickly perceived as "probably the most significant new development in manufacturing technology since Henry Ford introduced the concept of the moving assembly line."[10]

Computer numerical control led to a dramatic boost in productivity and was the first leg in the long process of steadily replacing human labor with computerized technology, programmed and managed by small professional and technical work forces. The Chicago management consulting firm Cox and Cox sized up the significance of substituting the computer and IT for workers, announcing that with numerically controlled machine tools, a "management revolution is here. . . . The management of machines instead of the management of men."[11] Alan Smith of Arthur D. Little was a bit more blunt and candid, declaring that computer-driven numerical control tools signaled management's "emancipation from human workers."[12]

Fast forward 50 years. Today, near workerless factories run by computer programs are increasingly the norm, both in highly industrialized countries and developing nations. The steel industry is a typical example. Like the auto industry and other key Second Industrial Revolution manufacturing enterprises that were the staples of blue-collar employment, the steel industry is undergoing a revolution that is quickly eliminating workers on the factory floor. Computerized programs and robotics have allowed the steel industry to slash its workforces in recent decades. In the United States, between 1982 and 2002, steel production rose from 75 million tons to 120 million tons, while the number of steel workers declined from 289,000 to 74,000.[13]

American and European politicians, and the general public, blame blue collar job losses on the relocation of manufacturing to cheap labor markets like China. The fact is that something more consequential has taken place. Between 1995 and 2002, 22 million manufacturing jobs were eliminated in the global economy while global production increased by more than 30 percent worldwide. The United States lost 11 percent of its manufacturing jobs to automation. Even China shed 16 million factory workers while increasing its productivity with IT and robotics, allowing it to produce more output, more cheaply, with fewer workers.[14]

Manufacturers that have long relied on cheap labor in their Chinese production facilities are bringing production back home with advanced robotics that are cheaper and more efficient than their Chinese workforces. At Philips's new electronic factory in the Netherlands, the 128 robot arms work at such a quick pace that they have to be put behind glass cases so that the handful of supervisors aren't injured. Philips's robotized Dutch factory produces the equivalent output of electronics products as its Chinese production facility with one-tenth of the number of workers.[15]

Anxious not to be left behind, many of China's largest manufacturers are quickly replacing their cheap workers with even cheaper robots. Foxconn, the giant Chinese manufacturer that produces iPhones, plans to install one million robots in the next few years, eliminating a large portion of its workforce. Terry Gou, CEO of Foxconn, whose global workforce totals more than one million, joked that he would prefer one million robots. "As human beings are also animals, to manage one million animals gives me a headache."[16]

The robot workforce is climbing around the world. Robot sales grew by 43 percent in both the United States and the European Union in 2011, moving the manufacturing sector ever closer to near workerless production, or what the industry calls "lights-out" production.[17] China, India, Mexico, and other emerging nations are learning quickly that the cheapest workers in the world are not as cheap, efficient, and productive as the information technology, robotics, and artificial intelligence that replaces them.

Even manufacturing industries once deemed too complex to be automated are falling victim to computerization. The textile industry was the first industrialized sector. While steam-powered technology and, later, electrification and electric power tools increased productivity, much of the work in making the garments was done by hand. New information technologies, computerization, and robotics have begun to take over an increasing number of the processes that formerly required human labor. Computer-aided design (CAD) has reduced the time to design garments from weeks to minutes. Computerized drying and finishing systems have also replaced traditional hand labor. The computerization of storage, handling, packing, and shipping of garments has also greatly increased efficiency and productivity.

The making of the garment itself is being handled by fewer workers aided by computerized programs. Fifty years ago, a single textile worker operated five machines, each able to run a thread through the loom at 100 times per minute. Today, machines run at six times that speed and one operator supervises 100 looms—a 120-fold increase in output per worker.[18]

And now, the Defense Advanced Research Projects Agency (DARPA), the same U.S. Department of Defense agency that invented the Internet, is turning its attention to automating the sewing process itself—long considered the holy grail of textile innovation. With an annual budget of $4 billion for military clothing, the Department of Defense is anxious to cut labor costs in producing uniforms to near zero direct labor and has awarded SoftWear Automation, Inc. a grant to fully automate the last remaining hand-manufactured part of making a garment by substituting computer-driven robots to undertake the delicate task. If successful, the new automated system will eliminate the nearly 50,000 workers employed by contractors to produce military garb and be able to do so at near zero marginal labor costs.[19]

For many years automation was an expensive up-front cost and out of reach for all but the biggest manufacturing enterprises. In recent years, however, costs have declined dramatically, allowing small- and medium-sized manufacturers to reap handsome productivity gains while reducing payrolls. Webb Wheel Products is a U.S. company that makes parts for truck brakes. The company's newest employee, a Doosan V550M robot, has churned out 300,000 more drums annually in just three years—a 25 percent increase in production—without having to add a single worker on the factory floor.[20]

If the current rate of technology displacement in the manufacturing sector continues—and industry analysts expect it to only accelerate—factory employment, which accounted for 163 million jobs in 2003, is likely to be just a few million by 2040, marking the end of mass factory labor in the world.[21] While some human labor is required to manufacture robots, create new software applications to manage production flows, and maintain and upgrade programs and systems, even that professional and technical labor is diminishing as intelligent technology is increasingly able to reprogram itself. Up-front costs aside, the marginal labor cost of automated production of additional units of a good is edging closer to zero with each passing day.

Logistics is another of the sectors that, like textiles, was able to automate much of its processes, but still relied heavily on human labor to pick up and deliver items. Delivering e-mail in seconds around the world, at near zero marginal labor costs, has eviscerated the postal services in every country. The U.S. Postal Service, which just ten years ago was the largest U.S. enterprise, with over 700,000 employees, has tumbled to less than 500,000 employees in 2013. And even though the USPS took pride in the automation of its sorting and handling systems, once praised as the most advanced in the world, it is now facing near-extinction as more of its letter-carrying business is shifting over to e-mail.[22]

Automation is replacing workers across the entire logistics industry. Amazon, which is as much a logistics company as a virtual retailer, is adding intelligent automated guided vehicles, automated robots, and automated storage systems in its warehouses, eliminating less efficient manual labor at every step of the logistical value chain with the goal of getting as close as possible to near zero marginal labor costs.

That goal is now within sight with the introduction of driverless vehicles. The prospect of eliminating human driving with the substitution of driverless vehicles operating on smart roads, once relegated to the realm of science fiction, will soon be operational. There are currently over 2.7 million truck drivers in the United States alone.[23] By 2040, driverless vehicles, operating at near zero marginal labor costs, could eliminate much of the nation's truckers. (Driverless vehicles will be discussed in greater detail in chapter 13.)

Automation, robotics, and artificial intelligence are eliminating human labor as quickly in the white-collar and service industries as in the manufacturing and logistics sectors. Secretaries, file clerks, telephone operators, travel agents, bank tellers, cashiers, and countless other white-collar service jobs have all but disappeared in the past 25 years as automation has driven the marginal cost of labor to near zero.

The Hackett Group, a consultant on back-office employment, estimates that 2 million of the jobs lost in the United States and the European Union since the onset of the Great Recession have been in human resources, finance, information technology and procurement, and that more than half of those job losses were the result of technology displacement due to automation.[24]

Automation is also making deep inroads into the retail sector, which employs one out of every ten Americans. While back-office work, warehousing, and shipping were surefire candidates for automation, observers of the retail industry long assumed that salespeople, at least, would be spared the ax because of the very social nature of their relationships with customers. Wishful thinking.

Vending machines and kiosks now sell everything from bathing suits to iPods and even gold coins. In 2010, $740 billion in retail sales were transacted by self-service machines. Industry watchers expect that figure to jump to $1.1 trillion by 2014.[25]

Walmart already has self-checkout terminals and plans to install 10,000 additional terminals in more than 1,200 of its stores by the end of 2013. The giant retailer is also expanding its Scan and Go self-checkout system in 40 of its stores in the Denver, Colorado, area. Shoppers scan the bar code of the products they take off the shelves on their iPhone app before putting them in their shopping carts. When they are finished shopping, they press the "done" button and the app provides them with a custom QR (quick response) code. The self-checkout terminal scans the QR code on the smart phone, adds up the price of the items, and asks the customer to pick a payment option.[26]

Despite efforts by brick-and-mortar retailers to automate more and more of their operations to reduce their labor costs, they continue to lose ground to online retailers whose marginal labor costs are heading to near zero. On the surface, brick-and-mortar sales appear healthy, if not robust. They made up 92 percent of retail sales in 2011, versus only 8 percent online.[27] It's only when we probe a little deeper and look at growth rates that we begin to see the handwriting on the wall. According to the National Retail Federation, brick-and-mortar sales are only growing at 2.8 percent per year while online retailers are growing at 15 percent per year, raising the question of how long physical retailing, with its significant fixed costs and sizable payrolls, can compete with much lower marginal labor costs online.[28] The casualty list is already mounting. Borders books and Circuit City, once giant brick-and-mortar retailers, have already fallen victim to the low marginal labor costs of online retailing. With online retail stores expected to double by 2020, many more brick-and-mortar retailers, already stretched by falling profit margins, are likely to succumb to virtual retailing.[29]

Brick-and-mortar retailers are caught in a bind, unwittingly becoming free showroom spaces for customers to browse and handle products and clothes that they then purchase online. Price-check iPhone apps allow customers to scan a product in the store and then compare it on the spot to prices online, where they are sure to get the item at a cheaper price at Amazon or other virtual retailers—often with free shipping thrown in.

Some brick-and-mortar retailers are fighting back against "fit-lifters" who try on clothes and shoes in their stores to get the right size and then order them online. Gary Weiner, the owner of Saxon Shoes in Virginia and a board member of the National Shoe Retailers Association, shares the concern of a growing number of retailers who resent what they call showrooming—the practice of online customers using stores to try on things they then buy online. Weiner says that it's common for young people to come in the store and say, "My mother sent me in to get my size fitted so she can buy them online."[30] A few stores are beginning to charge a browser fee to discourage fit-lifting. Other retailers worry, probably rightly so, that if they charge for browsing and fitting it will only result in consumers abandoning their stores altogether.[31]

A number of retailers are attempting an accommodation with online shopping by encouraging their customers to buy from their online shop and pick up their merchandise in the brick-and-mortar store—so the stores become, in effect, mini-distribution centers. Still, such efforts are likely to be only a stopgap measure because of the steep overhead costs in maintaining brick-and-mortar operations.

Many of the big-box retailers, including Best Buy, Target, and Walmart, will likely attempt to get ahead of the curve by pushing more of their business online. Others—especially traditional department stores like Macy's, Nordstrom, and Neiman Marcus—are going to pare down or simply die off as more and more retail goes virtual. Online clothiers already offer virtual fitting. Online customers can create a virtual model of themselves, providing information on their size, gender, age, chest, waist, and hip size. Using a mouse, the customer can even check the fitting from different angles.

A growing number of retail industry analysts are forecasting the imminent death of large segments of the brick-and-mortar retail trade. Jason Perlow, technology editor at ZDNet, says that convenience stores like 7-Eleven, drug stores like Walgreens, and supermarket chains like Kroger will continue to keep their doors open, along with high-end specialty and luxury stores like Crabtree & Evelyn, and a few big box stores like Walmart. Much of the brick-and-mortar retail business, however, is going to shrink, especially as a younger generation weaned on purchasing online comes of age.

Perlow says that while brick-and-mortar retail will not disappear, in "ten years hence [the] retail footprint will be a shadow of its former self and heavy competition from online will allow only the strongest brick-and-mortar businesses to survive."[32]

As in other industries where automation is quickly reducing human labor, virtual retailing is following suit. At best we can say that the future does not look good for the 4.3 million workers in brick-and-mortar retail as we move closer to near zero marginal labor costs and a near workerless world.[33]

EVEN KNOWLEDGE WORKERS ARE EXPENDABLE

By 2005, the anecdotal evidence of automation replacing workers in the manufacturing and service industries was no longer an object of curiosity. Automation had become pervasive. Everywhere we turned, it seemed, workers had disappeared and we found ourselves surrounded by intelligent-machine surrogates talking to us, listening to us, directing us, advising us, doing business with us, entertaining us, and watching over us. Early on, the experience of a workerless presence was often amusing, sometimes irksome, and even eerie. Now it's commonplace. Still, it was not until around 2010 that an avalanche of new books came out with alarming titles like *The Race Against the Machine*, *Light at the End of the Tunnel*, and *Automate This*, warning of automation's impact on jobs. Their authors took to the talk shows, and their message of a coming workerless world began to gain attention in social media outlets, even attracting some comments from policy makers, think tank researchers, economists, and President Barack Obama.

We are just beginning to hear the rumble of what's likely to become a global policy debate on automation and the future of jobs. In part, that discussion is starting to happen because of the jobless recovery that followed the Great Recession. The disconnect between a rising GDP and diminishing jobs is becoming so pronounced that it's difficult to continue to ignore it, although I'm still somewhat amazed at how few economists, even at this stage, are willing to step forward and finally acknowledge that the underlying assumption of classical economic theory—that productivity creates more jobs than it replaces—is no longer credible.

The other reason I suspect that the great automation debate may be about to take flight is that the new innovations in the use of Big Data, the increasing sophistication of algorithms, and advances in AI are, for the first time, crawling up the skill ladder and affecting professional work itself, long considered immune from the forces of automation and the advances of technology displacement. Computers are being programmed to recognize patterns, advance hypotheses, self-program responses, implement solutions, and even decipher communication and translate complex metaphors from one language to another in real time with accuracy approaching that of the best translators in the world.

Advances in AI are now being employed across a range of professional disciplines to increase efficiency and productivity and reduce human labor. EDiscovery is a software program that can sift through millions of legal documents, looking for patterns of behavior, lines of thought, concepts, and the like, at speeds that would trump the best Harvard-educated lawyers and with crisp analysis that even the most well-trained legal scholars might miss. The savings in labor cost is equally impressive.

The *New York Times* journalist John Markoff cites the example of a blockbuster lawsuit in 1978 involving five television studios, the U.S. Justice Department, and CBS. The studios' lawyers and paralegals had the unenviable task of reading through more than 6 million documents over months at a cost of $2.2 million in labor time. In January 2011 BlackStone Discovery, a Palo Alto, California, enterprise, analyzed 1.5 million legal documents using eDiscovery software for less than $100,000. Bill Herr, an attorney at a U.S. chemical company who used to pack an entire army of lawyers in an auditorium to read documents for weeks at a time, says that "from a legal staffing viewpoint, it means that a lot of people who used to be allocated to conduct document review are no longer able to be billed out."[34] Mike Lynch, founder of Autonomy, another eDiscovery firm, calculated that with the new search software, one lawyer can do the work of 500 lawyers, and with greater accuracy. Using eDiscovery software, Herr found only 60 percent accuracy when attorneys were doing the research, leading him to gripe: "Think about how much money had been spent to be slightly better than a coin toss."[35]

Very few professional skills are being spared the long arm of IT and Big Data–crunching by algorithms. Knowledge workers of every stripe and variety—radiologists, accountants, middle managers, graphic designers, and even marketers—are already feeling the heat as pattern-recognition software begins to penetrate every professional field. Mike McCready is the head of a startup company called Music Xray, a firm that uses Big Data and algorithms to identify potential musical hits. The company, which has secured recording contracts for more than 5,000 artists in less than three years, uses sophisticated software to compare the structure of a song to songs previously recorded to assess its potential to break out and hit the charts. His company already has an impressive track record of spotting songs by unknown artists and accurately predicting their success. A similar software program developed by Epagogix analyzes movie scripts to project box office hits for the film industry.[36] Its success in identifying winners has made algorithm assessment standard fare in the industry. In the future, these kinds of forecasting tools will eliminate the need to hire pricey marketing agents to conduct expensive focus-group encounters and other marketing-research initiatives, the accuracy of which might pale against the crowdsourcing accuracy of Big Data filtered by algorithms.

Big Data and algorithms are even being used to create copy for sports stories that are chatty, chock full of information, and engaging. The Big Ten Network uses algorithms to create original pieces posted just seconds after games, eliminating human copywriters.[37]

Artificial intelligence took a big leap into the future in 2011 when an IBM computer, Watson—named after IBM's past chairman—took on Ken Jennings, who held the record of 74 wins on the popular TV show *Jeopardy*, and defeated him. The showdown, which netted a $1 million prize for IBM, blew away TV viewers as they watched their *Jeopardy* hero crumble in the presence of the "all-knowing" Watson. Watson is a cognitive system that is able to integrate "natural language processing, machine learning, and hypothesis generation and evaluation," says its proud IBM parent, allowing it to think and respond to questions and problems.[38]

Watson is already being put to work. IBM Healthcare Analytics will use Watson to assist physicians in making quick and accurate diagnoses by analyzing Big Data stored in the electronic health records of millions of patients, as well as in medical journals.[39]

IBM's plans for Watson go far beyond serving the specialized needs of the research industry and the back-office tasks of managing Big Data. Watson is being offered up in the marketplace as a personal assistant that companies and even consumers can converse with by typed text or in real-time spoken words. IBM says that this is the first time artificial intelligence is graduating from a simple question-and-answer mode to a conversational mode, allowing for more personal interaction and customized answers to individual queries.[40]

AI scientists will tell you that the most challenging hurdle for their industry is breaking through the language barrier. Comprehending the rich meaning of complex metaphors and phrases in one language and simultaneously retelling the story in another language is perhaps the most difficult of all cognitive tasks and the most unique of all human abilities. I have spent quite a bit of time over the years with translators at lecture presentations, in meetings, and even, when required, at social functions. I marvel at their ability to take what I'm saying—not just the text, but the subtle inferences in my tone of voice, my accentuations, and even my facial expressions and body language—and without hesitation convey its layers of meaning to others in words that resonate with the same intent that I expressed. Mediocre translators are literalists, attempting merely to match words and phrases in two different languages. Their translations seem machinelike and the meanings are garbled and confused. The best translators are artists who are able to live in two different cognitive personas simultaneously.

I have long been a skeptic when it comes to the prospect of AI besting world-class translators. Still, recent advances in AI are bringing that day ever closer. Lionbridge is a company that provides real-time translation for online customer support, allowing consumers to speak across languages via instant translation of user-generated content. Its GeoFluent plug-in software-as-a-service solution, which uses Microsoft translation technology, provides translations between 39 languages. While not yet as proficient as the best translators, GeoFluent is good enough to break the language barrier and bring one-third of the human race already online together in the first truly shared global conversation in all of history, speeding the transition into a universal Commons and Collaborative Age.[41]

Within a decade or so, businesspeople, workers, and travelers will be equipped with mobile apps allowing them to effortlessly have conversations online or face to face with someone who speaks a different language. Most of the 150,000 to 300,000 highly educated and costly translators will go the way of cashiers, file clerks, and secretaries, as AI provides translation services at near zero marginal labor costs, dead-ending still another professional labor category.[42]

WE ARE IN THE MIDST OF AN EPIC CHANGE in the nature of work. The First Industrial Revolution ended slave and serf labor. The Second Industrial Revolution dramatically shrank agricultural and craft labor. The Third Industrial Revolution is sunsetting mass wage labor in the manufacturing and service industries and salaried professional labor in large parts of the knowledge sector.

IT, computerization, automation, Big Data, algorithms, and AI embedded in the Internet of Things are quickly reducing the marginal labor costs of producing and delivering a wide range of goods and services to near zero. Barring an unforeseen blowback, much of the productive economic activity of society is going to be increasingly placed in the "hands" of intelligent technology, supervised by small groups of highly skilled professional and technical workers as we journey further into the twenty-first century.

The wholesale substitution of intelligent technology for mass wage labor and salaried professional labor is beginning to disrupt the workings of the capitalist system. The question economists are so fearful to entertain is, what happens to market capitalism when productivity gains, brought on by intelligent technology, continue to reduce the need for human labor? What we are seeing is the unbundling of productivity from employment. Instead of the former facilitating the latter, it is now eliminating it. But since in capitalist markets capital and labor feed off of each other, what happens when so few people are gainfully employed that there are not enough buyers to purchase goods and services from sellers?

For starters, the emerging zero marginal cost economy radically changes our notion of the economic process. The old paradigm of owners and workers, and of sellers and consumers, is beginning to break down. Consumers are becoming their own producers, eliminating the distinction. prosumers will increasingly be able to produce, consume, and share their own goods and services with one another on the Collaborative Commons at diminishing marginal costs approaching zero, bringing to the fore new ways of organizing economic life beyond the traditional capitalist market model.

Secondly, the automation of work across every sector of the market economy is already beginning to free up human labor to migrate to the evolving social economy. In the coming era, deep play in the Collaborative Commons becomes as important as hard work was in the market economy, and the amassing of social capital becomes as valued as the accumulation of market capital. Attachment to community and the search for transcendence and meaning comes to define the measure of one's life rather than one's material wealth.

Lest this sounds fanciful and out of reach, know that millions of young people are just beginning to make their way from the old order to the new. Members of the Internet generation see themselves more as players than workers, regard their personal attributes more as talents than skills, and prefer to express their creativity in social networks rather than laboring away in cubicled assignments, performing autonomous tasks in markets. For an increasing number for young people, the emerging social economy on the Commons offers greater potential opportunity for self-development and promises more intense psychic rewards than traditional employment in the capitalist marketplace. (The migration of employment from the capitalist market economy to the social economy on the Collaborative Commons will be addressed more fully in chapter 14.)

If the steam engine freed human beings from feudal bondage to pursue material self-interest in the capitalist marketplace, the Internet of Things frees human beings from the market economy to pursue nonmaterial shared interests on the Collaborative Commons. Many—but not all—of our basic material needs will be met for nearly free in a near zero marginal cost society. Intelligent technology will do most of the heavy lifting in an economy centered on abundance rather than scarcity. A half century from now, our grandchildren are likely to look back at the era of mass employment in the market with the same sense of utter disbelief as we look upon slavery and serfdom in former times. The very idea that a human being's worth was measured almost exclusively by his or her productive output of goods and services and material wealth will seem primitive, even barbaric, and be regarded as a terrible loss of human value to our progeny living in a highly automated world where much of life is lived on the Collaborative Commons.

CHAPTER NINE

THE ASCENT OF THE PROSUMER AND THE BUILD-OUT OF THE SMART ECONOMY

I n a Collaborative Commons, sellers and buyers give way to prosumers, property rights make room for open-source sharing, ownership is less important than access, markets are superseded by networks, and the marginal cost of producing information, generating energy, manufacturing products, and teaching students is nearly zero. A central question arises: How is the new Internet of Things infrastructure that makes all of this possible going to be financed? (The issue of how a near zero marginal cost society is going to be governed and managed will be addressed separately in chapter 12.)

THE MARGINAL COST CONTROVERSY

This question of financing infrastructure has come up before, back in the 1930s and 1940s. It was referred to at the time as the "marginal-cost controversy" and unleashed a contentious debate among economists, business leaders, and government policy makers. At the time, it was more of an abstract issue. Today, it's one of the most important political issues facing society. How we choose to finance a near zero marginal cost society will likely determine the way we organize economic, social, and political life for the remainder of the twenty-first century.

In December 1937, the economist Harold Hotelling, the retiring president of the Econometric Society, presented an esoteric paper called "The General Welfare in Relation to Problems of Taxation and of Railway and Utility Rates" at the association's annual meeting.

Hotelling began with the observation that "the optimum of the general welfare corresponds to the sale of everything at marginal cost."[1] Of course, if firms were to sell their products at the marginal cost, they would soon be out of business because they would be unable to recoup their capital investment, so every entrepreneur builds in the up-front costs in the sale of each unit.

Hotelling observed, however, that there are certain kinds of goods—public goods—that are nonrivalrous because everyone needs to have access to them—for example, roads and bridges, water and sewage systems, railroad lines, electricity grids, etc. These public goods are generally of the kind that establish infrastructure for conducting all other economic activity and require significant capital expenditures. And because they are nonrivalrous goods, they favor natural monopoly. Competing grids for roads, bridges, water and sewage systems, and electricity transmission would be a colossal waste of resources.

All of which raises the question: How should infrastructure and public goods be paid for? Hotelling argued that since the general public would greatly benefit from only having to pay for the marginal cost of what they are using, the best way to finance the fixed costs of creating the public goods is through general taxation. Hotelling favored income taxes, inheritance taxes, and taxes on the value of land to pay for public goods. He reasoned that if government were to finance the overhead cost of nonrivalrous infrastructure development up front with taxes, "everyone would be better off."[2]

Hotelling used the illustration of a bridge to make his case.

A free bridge costs no more to construct than a toll bridge, and costs less to operate; but society, which must pay the cost in some way or other, gets far more benefit from the bridge if it is free, since in this case it will be more used. Charging a toll, however small, causes some people to waste time and money in going around by longer but cheaper ways, and prevents others from crossing.[3]

Hotelling acknowledged that while using taxes to finance the overhead of public goods might adversely affect some taxpayers—depending on the type of tax—and especially the well-to-do, in the case of inheritance and land taxes, it would be a small burden for the nation's wealthiest members to bear when measured against the gains to the general welfare.

Hotelling concluded that general government revenue should "be applied to cover the fixed costs of electric power plants, waterworks, railroads, and other industries in which the fixed costs are large, so as to reduce to the level of marginal cost the prices charged for the services and products of these industries."[4] Many of the leading economists of the day agreed with Hotelling's argument, convinced that it was the most rational approach to achieving the public good.

Not all economists, however, were won over to Hotelling's pleadings. More traditional advocates of free enterprise recognized that public goods—especially those that constitute infrastructure—were non-rivalrous, and in those instances the average cost of bringing additional units to market continued to decline with prolonged demand. Charging for "declining average cost," they argued, was more sensible, allowing firms to recoup their investment while keeping the government's hands off the economic life of the nation.

In 1946, economist Ronald Coase stepped into the fray, taking exception to Hotelling's thesis by arguing that the social subsidies Hotelling advocated "would bring about a maldistribution of the factors of production, a maldistribution of income, and probably a loss similar to that which the scheme was designed to avoid."[5]

Coase did not disagree with Hotelling that price should equal marginal cost, but he also believed that the total cost needed to be covered. He suggested a multipart pricing scheme in which those using the public good paid an additional fee on top of the marginal cost price for carriage charges. That way, those using the service would pay a little extra for carriage rather than taxpayers, some of whom wouldn't even use the service. Multipart pricing, Coase believed, would allow both the marginal cost and total cost to be covered.[6]

Without going into laborious detail on the nuances of the marginal cost controversy, suffice it to say that Coase turned the tide in favor of the free market. By 1946, conventional wisdom had seesawed back to the champions of the unencumbered market, who argued that natural monopolies should remain in the hands of the private sector and, in lieu of public subsidies, firms should be able to set prices above marginal costs to recoup their investments. That line of reasoning still holds sway today. John Duffy, a professor of law at the George Washington University Law School, says that "in short, modern public utility theorists generally do not recommend using pervasive public subsidies to chase the Holy Grail of global marginal cost pricing."[7]

In reality, the argument that governments ought not to finance infrastructure that creates public goods and services and that natural monopolies ought to be able to set their prices above marginal costs to recoup fixed costs is more than a bit disingenuous. Many of the same market economists who oppose government subsidies turn a blind eye to the fact that the private firms characterized as public utilities and that enjoy near monopoly status are the most heavily subsidized by government taxes.

In the United States, over half of all federal tax subsidies go to just four industries—finance, utilities, telecommunications, and oil, gas, and pipelines. With the exception of finance, they bear all the earmarks of public utilities. Between 2008 and 2010, gas and electric utilities received more than $31 billion in government subsidies, telecommunications got more than $30 billion, and oil, gas, and pipelines weighed in with $24 billion.[8]

Before the move to deregulation and privatization in the 1980s, these three industries were, in fact, government owned and financed in most industrialized nations—allowing the consumer to enjoy relatively cheap prices. In the United States, however, they remained, for the most part, in the private sector. Electricity and gas utilities were regulated by government but allowed to set prices above the marginal costs, allowing them to make profit while enjoying rich government subsidies.

Those subsidies don't even include intellectual-property protection afforded by the government in the form of patents. Although originally conceived to encourage invention and allow entrepreneurs to recoup their investments, intellectual property has long since served a different function, allowing natural monopolies to enjoy a second monopoly over goods and services they deliver, enabling them to charge prices far in excess of their marginal costs.

All of this might have gone unseen were it not for the meteoric rise of the Internet, which brought the marginal cost of securing information to near zero. This was followed in quick succession by the plunging marginal cost of harvesting the sun and wind and other abundant renewable energies, the 3D printing of "things," and online courses in higher education.

The Internet of Things is the first general purpose technology platform in history that can potentially take large parts of the economy to near zero marginal costs. And that's what makes the marginal cost controversy so pivotal to humanity's future. Whether the new potential inherent in the IoT infrastructure can be realized will be determined by who finances the platform. The struggle for control is already well underway, mostly behind the scenes, in regulatory commissions, courtrooms, legislatures, corporate boardrooms, civil society organizations, and academic circles all over the world. As of yet, only snippets of the discussion have bubbled up to public consciousness. That is likely to change in the next few years as a younger generation squares off with itself on what kind of economic future it favors.

POWER TO THE PEOPLE

The question is whether, on the one hand, prosumers weaned on open-source access and peer-to-peer collaboration will find a financing model that can optimize the new infrastructure's potential of achieving a near zero marginal cost society. Or, on the other hand, whether corporate interests wedded to an older capitalist model will use intellectual-property protection, regulatory policy, and other legislation to bend the infrastructure their way, keeping prices well above near zero marginal costs and profits flowing.

To get a handle on which of these two forces is likely to triumph, follow the money. In the First and Second Industrial Revolutions, the amassing of private capital allowed a growing entrepreneurial class to underwrite and seize control of the vital infrastructure and, along with it, the legislative, judicial, and executive powers that would regulate it. Although the government subsidized much of the infrastructure development as well as the critical industries that grew up around it, private capital ran the game, at least in the United States. As mentioned, in Europe and elsewhere, governments owned many of the critical infrastructure industries, particularly those involved in the delivery of nonrivalrous public goods—that is, until the Reagan/Thatcher push to sell off public enterprises to the private sector in the great deregulation shuffle. The selloff continued for nearly 30 years under the guise of encouraging free markets.

The financing of the IoT infrastructure, however, is coming not so much from wealthy capitalists or corporate shareholders, but from hundreds of millions of consumers and taxpayers. First, let's begin with the Internet, the communication medium of the IoT infrastructure. Who owns it? Actually, everyone and no one. The Internet is a system organized by an agreed-upon set of protocols that allows computer networks to communicate with one another. While there is a physical network—an Internet backbone—made up of big companies that lay the cable, provide wired and wireless connections, route the traffic, and store the data, the companies are merely providers and facilitators. There are also Web companies and nonprofit Web organizations that inhabit the Internet and coordinate the content. The Internet itself, however, is a virtual public square where anyone who pays for an Internet connection can gain admission and join the conversation. The Internet has already brought 2.7 billion people into the coveted zone where the marginal cost of accessing and sending various forms of communication is nearly zero.[9]

Now that the Internet is converging with distributed renewable energies to create a nervous system for a new economic paradigm, the question shifts to who is financing the Internet of Things? By and large, the evolving smart infrastructure—and especially the Energy Internet—is being financed by consumers, with lesser amounts being ponied up by governments, primarily to stimulate research and development of new enabling technologies.

The green feed-in tariff has become the primary tool for advancing distributed renewable energies. Local, regional, and national governments guarantee a premium price above the market value of other energies for a set period of usually 15 to 20 years to encourage early adopters to invest in the installation of wind, solar, geothermal, biomass, and small hydro renewable energy generation and feed the new green electricity back to the transmission grid. As more individuals bring renewable energy online, the industry scales, encouraging new investments by manufacturers to innovate their harvesting technologies, increase their efficiency and productivity, and drop their costs, all of which stimulates a growing market.

Increased efficiency and productivity reduces the cost of generating renewable electricity, allowing the new green-sourced electricity to move closer and closer to parity with the market price of conventional fossil fuels and nuclear electricity. As the new renewable electricity approaches parity, governments can begin to reduce the feed-in tariff premium and, eventually, when parity is reached, phase out the tariff altogether.

Sixty-five countries have instituted feed-in tariffs, and over half of them are in the developing world.[10] Feed-in tariffs have proven to be a powerful policy instrument in moving renewable energy online. Nearly two-thirds of the global wind and 87 percent of global photovoltaic capacity has been spurred by feed-in tariffs.[11]

The funding for feed-in tariffs generally comes from a slight increase in the price of electricity on everyone's monthly electricity bill or from taxes. In other words, either the power companies pass the additional cost along to the consumers, who finance the shift to renewable energies, or the taxpayers pay via government subsidies of the feed-in tariffs. In the early years of the feed-in tariffs, big solar and wind companies were the most likely to take advantage of the premium by establishing large, concentrated solar and wind energy parks and reaping profits, all financed by rate hikes charged to millions of small electricity consumers. On occasion, power and utility companies even set up their own subsidiaries to generate wind and solar energy, which they fed back to the parent company at a premium, all paid for by the company's electricity consumers—allowing the company to profit at the expense of the millions of ratepayers.

The increasing public awareness of both the corporate "rip-off" and the opportunity of becoming a prosumer—a producer and consumer of one's own green electricity—has turned the tide toward millions of small-business owners and homeowners who are becoming the primary drivers of a shift to distributed renewable energies. A growing number of the millions of consumers of electricity who are footing the bill for the feed-in tariffs are also beginning to reap the benefits. They are investing their own capital to install renewable energy harvesting technologies on site. While the up-front capital investment is significant, they are beginning to receive low-interest-rate green loans from banks and credit unions. The lenders are more than willing to lend money at reduced interest rates because the premium in selling green electricity back to the grid virtually ensures the loan will be honored.

The shift from being a consumer to being a prosumer of energy marks a tipping point in the way power is generated and used. The giant oil, coal, and gas companies of the twentieth century, often in collusion with banks and other financial institutions and abetted by favorable government subsidies, were able to amass and employ huge sums of financial capital to gain control of the nation's power supply. Today, millions of little players are underwriting their own renewable energy revolution by taking advantage of feed-in tariffs financed by the slight monthly rate hike attached to their electricity bill.

In Germany, which is setting the pace for transitioning into green electricity in Europe, the big traditional power and utility companies—E.ON, RWE, EnBW, Vattenfall Europe—owned only 7 percent of the renewable-energy capacity installed by the end of 2011. Individuals, however, "owned 40 percent of the renewable energy capacity, energy niche players 14 percent, farmers 11 percent, various energy-intensive industrial companies 9 percent, and financial companies 11 percent. Small regional utilities and international utilities owned another 7 percent."[12] Nearly half of the German wind turbines are owned by residents of the regions.[13] In other EU countries, the pattern is the same. Consumers are becoming prosumers and generating their own green electricity.

Gérard Mestrallet, CEO of GDF Suez—the French gas utility—says that just ten years ago the European energy market was dominated almost exclusively by a handful of regional monopolies. "Those days are gone forever," says Mestrallet, now that "some consumers have become producers."[14] Peter Terium, CEO of RWE, the German-based energy company, acknowledges the massive shift taking place in Europe from centralized to distributed power, and says that the bigger power and utility companies "have to adjust to the fact that, in the longer term, earning capacity in conventional electricity generation will be markedly below what we've seen in recent years."[15]

Had anyone suggested ten years ago that the big power and utility companies of Europe would begin to crumble as millions of small, distributed, renewable-energy micropower players began to generate their own green electricity for the grid, it would have been dismissed as fantasy by the powers that be. Not now. "It is a real revolution," says Mestrallet.[16]

Consumers and small business owners are not only paying most of the costs for bringing green electricity online through rate hikes in their electricity bills and taxes. They are also paying the lion's share of costs in the build-out of the Energy Internet. Just recently, the U.S. government shelled out $3.4 billion in Federal Recovery Act funds, which will be leveraged with an equal or greater amount of private sector resources, for a total $7.8 billion investment to support grid modernization.[17] If this sounds like a lot of money, consider for a moment the cost to businesses and consumers in power interruptions, brownouts, and blackouts each year resulting from an underperforming and inefficient power grid. "Power outages and interruptions . . . cost Americans at least $150 billion each year—about $500 for every man, woman and child."[18]

Most power interruptions in the United States stem from the fact that the old electricity transmission lines are still above ground, with wire strung across decaying wood poles. The problem is that more extreme weather events brought on by climate change—winter snow storms, torrential spring storms and floods, hurricanes, etc.—are downing transmission lines on a much more frequent basis, forcing brownouts and blackouts across wide areas. Power losses, which used to be occasional events, are now the new normal across large parts of the United States, as extreme weather events take a ruthless toll on old sagging transmission lines that should have been tucked underground a long time ago. If this weren't enough, "more than 10% of all the electricity used is ultimately lost due to conversion inefficiencies."[19] Installing a secure, twenty-first-century, digitalized, distributed smart grid underground would dramatically reduce electricity losses and power blackouts while increasing the efficiency of electricity transmission along the lines.

A study carried out by the Electric Power Research Institute (EPRI), the nonprofit think tank of the U.S. electricity industry, estimates that it will cost between $17 and $24 billion a year over the next 20 years, or about $476 billion, to phase in a national Energy Internet.[20] Not cheap, but then again, not overly expensive either, especially when you consider the return. That's approximately the same amount of money per year as the Department of Defense spends to build two new aircraft carriers—or, to put it in energy terms, Royal Dutch Shell's annual revenue of $470 billion in 2011 nearly equals the cost of building a national Energy Internet over 20 years.[21]

The EPRI price tag is probably too low. It assumes a bargain-basement, no-frills approach to smartening up the energy grid by installing smart meters and laying out additional power lines. Other studies suggest the price could be as high as $2.5 trillion when we take into account energy storage, the wiring of every machine, appliance, and thermostat to the grid, and the cost of IT management of Big Data feedback from billions of nodes across the Energy Internet. Vaclav Smil, a leading energy analyst, reminds us that even this figure doesn't include the write-off of the existing fossil fuel and nuclear power plants, whose replacement value is at least $1.5 trillion.[22]

In reality, the costs are probably going to be somewhere in the neighborhood of $1.2 trillion, stretched out over three decades. Power companies will pass on some of the costs of constructing an Energy Internet to their customers in the form of increased charges. Still, the hikes will be tiny and easily manageable. The rest of the costs will be absorbed by the local, state, and federal governments in the form of direct outlays, subsidies, incentives, and allowances. This is how the communication/energy/transportation infrastructure of both the First and Second Industrial Revolutions were financed, through a combination of private and public investment.

The EPRI study shows that the increase in "energy savings" to customers in the installation of a continental Energy Internet would be in the neighborhood of $2 trillion, well worth the up-front infrastructure costs.[23] However, that $2 trillion doesn't even begin to take into account the dramatic increase in potential productivity that will result from embedding all economic activity in an intelligent, networked IoT infrastructure that is continually using Big Data feedback and state-of-the-art analytics and algorithms to increase thermodynamic efficiency and productivity in every corner of society. As mentioned earlier, it's the steep rise in overall aggregate energy efficiency from the peak level of 14 percent in the Second Industrial Revolution to

40 percent in the Third Industrial Revolution and the accompanying productivity gains that are going to move us ever closer to a near zero marginal cost society.

Fourteen countries are currently implementing smart grids, and, in the majority of the cases, the Energy Internet is being financed by raising the electricity bill to consumers and by taxes paid by its citizens and businesses.[24] A significant part of the financing of the Energy Internet will go to reconfiguring electricity lines and establishing the substations and other hardware components that make up the physical operating systems. Much of the rest of the financing will be dedicated to the intelligent communication technologies that will coordinate the complex flow of green electricity being generated, stored, and shared by millions of individual prosumers.

As mentioned in chapter 5, every device in every building will be equipped with sensors and software that connect to the Internet of Things, feeding real-time information on electricity use to both the on-site prosumer and the rest of the network. The entire network will know how much electricity is being used by every appliance at any moment—thermostats, washing machines, dishwashers, televisions, hair dryers, toasters, ovens, refrigerators, and so on. The continuous feedback of information allows on-site prosumers to optimally program their own electricity use while the distributed and collaborative nature of the system allows millions of energy players to share electricity in ways that optimize the efficiency of the entire network. For example, millions of energy prosumers can preprogram their nodes— it's a voluntary system—so that if the demand for air conditioning spikes because of a heat wave across the region, their thermostat will automatically take itself up by one or two degrees or their washing machine will automatically shift down to a shorter rinse cycle to save on electricity use, allowing the system to level off the increase in electricity demand. Prosumers who assist the grid receive a credit on their next electricity bill.

Utility companies, anxious to profit from the smart grid, would prefer to control the communications across the network. The smart meters installed in millions of buildings are owned by the utility, even though the customers end up paying for them because the cost is passed on in their monthly bill. By locking up the communications that are essential to the management of the Energy Internet, the utility companies can prevent millions of businesses and home owners from fully benefiting from the smart electricity system they are funding.

Their efforts are likely to fail. Dozens of companies are coming to the market with new Web-connected smart energy devices that allow prosumers to connect every appliance in their building and communicate via wireless networks with the power grid.[25] Dave Martin is the president of Intwine Energy, a U.S. start-up company that facilitates wireless smart grid connection. Like others who have put their faith in wireless interfaces with the Energy Internet, Martin sees the opportunity of bypassing the old centralized and proprietary approach to communications in favor of a distributed, open, collaborative, and lateral model:

> We believe being able to tap into the existing Internet connectivity in broadband-equipped homes and use the World Wide Web, rather than having to rely so much on proprietary, "closed" systems, offers significant benefits to homeowners and utilities.[26]

Martin points to the agility, mobility, and simplicity, and the reduction in costs that come with using wireless networks and remote devices to program, manage, and distribute energy across an Energy Internet. He explains the rationale behind wireless smart grid connection:

> Our systems enhance collaboration between the homeowner and the utility. As a result, energy users can customize their energy management practices based on their lifestyle, and energy producers can meet their demand management commitments without having to engineer and deploy their own proprietary systems.[27]

Wireless network devices will empower millions of people to take direct control over their energy generation and use and enable them to reduce the marginal costs of managing energy to near zero on a continental Energy Internet.

Transforming the entire infrastructure of society into a Third Industrial Revolution seems daunting—but no less so than the First and Second Industrial Revolutions. Both came to fruition in less than 40 years. This time around, the process is likely going to evolve more quickly, in large part because the global connectivity of the Internet makes possible the active engagement of billions of people in the build-out of the new communication/energy/transportation matrix. That level of involvement allows for the lateral scale-up of the Energy Internet and Transportation Internet at speeds that resemble the exponential growth of the Communication Internet over the past two decades.

THE CLEAN WEB

A young generation of social entrepreneurs are just now beginning to use social media to mobilize their peers to become as engaged with the Energy Internet as they are with the Communications Internet itself. In the process, they are creating new technologies that will unleash the thermodynamic efficiencies and productivity potential inherent in the IoT infrastructure.

It's called the Cleanweb, a grassroots movement that took off in 2011 in the United States and countries around the world. Writing on the *MIT Technology Review* website, Sunil Paul and Nick Allen, two young venture capitalists, describe the Cleanweb vision:

> We believe the next opportunity is what we call the "cleanweb"—a form of clean tech that takes advantage of the Internet, social media, and mobile communications to alter how we consume resources, relate to the world, interact with each other, and pursue economic growth.[28]

The Cleanweb Movement, also called energy IT or clean IT, is likely going to drive the paradigm change with lightning speed, leaving conventional business practices at the side of the road, with business leaders wondering how they failed to pick up on the cues—just as was the case when the Internet generation began to create applications and employ social media to share music, videos, news, and information, leaving much of the media and entertainment industries in the dust.

To understand the speed at which this change is going to take place, we need to step back for a moment and look at Zuckerberg's law, named after Mark Zuckerberg, founder of Facebook. Zuckerberg has discovered an exponential curve in social media, not unlike Moore's discovery in computing power and Swanson's discovery in solar technology. Using data assembled internally on Facebook, Zuckerburg shows that the amount of information shared on the Web has been doubling every year and he predicts that the doubling process will continue for the foreseeable future. The proliferation of cheap computers and mobile devices makes it easier to share every moment of our daily lives with one another through social media. For example, Spotify, a music-streaming service, can automatically post every song you listen to on Facebook. In the first few months of its introduction, 1.5 billion "listens" were shared through Spotify and other apps. Apple now has an iPhone feature called Find My Friends, which allows Apple to track an individual's location and share it with others in their network.[29] Similar apps are now being created to allow people to co-generate and share green electricity across an Energy Internet.

The Cleanweb Movement is hosting weekend hackathons all over the world. These events bring together software developers, social entrepreneurs, and environmental activists in deep collaboration to create apps that will allow hundreds of millions of people to become players on the Energy Internet. Prizes are awarded to the developers of the best apps.

At the New York Clean Web Hackathon, several hundred developers broke up into 15 teams and, after 28 intensive hours, came up with inventive new apps for using Internet technology to manage green energy. The winner of the New York Hackathon was a group called Econofly. Their website allows consumers to compare appliances by their energy efficiency ratings. Another winner, Parkifi, is an app that helps users locate a New York park with a Wi-Fi hotspot. A third winner, nycbldgs.com, uses energy data created by the city of New York to put together a map of all the municipal buildings, ranking them on energy usage and carbon dioxide (CO_2) emissions. The goal is to identify buildings that can be retrofitted and converted to micropower plants and feature "best in show" buildings that can highlight state-of-the-art green design and energy efficiencies.[30]

The idea behind the Cleanweb Movement is to use IT, the Internet, and social media to cluster like-minded people together to create lateral economies of scale in the implementation of energy efficiencies and the introduction of renewable-energy harvesting technology. This means simplifying the process of gathering information on energy efficiencies and making it easier and cheaper to invest in renewable-energy technologies.

Mosaic is a Cleanweb company that uses Web-based crowdfunding to install solar panels on roofs. Much of the cost in financing renewable energy, interestingly enough, is not in the solar panels themselves—they're getting cheaper and cheaper—but in the "soft costs," which include customer prospecting, site evaluations, and financing. In the United States, solar companies spend approximately $2,500 to acquire each new customer. It is estimated that IT solutions—using social media—could drive the cost of solar down by 75 percent, making it cheaper than coal.[31]

The Cleanweb Movement in the United States is getting Big Data help from a new federal government initiative called Green Button. The program, which was launched in 2011, encourages power and utility companies to voluntarily provide easy access to real-time energy usage data now available for the first time because of the installation of millions of smart meters in homes and businesses. Smart meters are vital data collection points in the Energy Internet infrastructure. That data can be downloaded by the companies' customers so they can have the information they need to more efficiently manage their energy use. In less than a year, the number of customers with instant access to their own energy use data ballooned to 31 million.[32]

Companies like Opower, Itron, First Fuel, Efficiency 2.0, EcoDog, Belkin, and Honest Buildings are scurrying to develop new applications and Web services that can use Green Button data to empower users to take control of their own energy future.[33]

This wealth of data on individual energy usage is now being leveraged through social media. Studies show that money is often not the critical factor in moving people to change their energy lifestyle. Instead, researchers have found that altering one's energy profile is more often stimulated by the desire to cooperate in a shared commitment to sustainable living and by a sense of collective empowerment.

Being able to share one's energy data on social media is a powerful way to begin a peer-to-peer conversation about new ways to manage energy. Sharing energy tips, alerting each other to new apps to increase energy efficiency, clustering together in energy cooperatives to install renewable energy more cheaply, or just taking pleasure in a little friendly competition greatly strengthens the global community of sustainability activists.

Facebook launched the "Social Energy App" in 2012 in cooperation with the Natural Resources Defense Council (NRDC), Opower, and 16 utility companies. Participants can sign up on the Green On Facebook energy app or on Opower's website. The app uses data from your energy bill to show how your home ranks against similar homes across America as well as the homes of your Facebook friends. Participants can compete with others to increase their energy efficiency and reduce their energy use and set up groups interested in exploring various green energy initiatives. The social energy app also provides tips and a platform for all the participants to share energy advice. Facebook's Mary Scott Lynn, who leads the company's sustainability programs, remarked that "the app is intended to make saving energy social and creates a conversation about the merits of energy efficiency that doesn't currently happen." Lynn believes that "adding the social aspect of environmental action could be the missing piece to previous attempts to create an online community on energy."[34]

By bringing together IT, the Internet, mobile communications, and social media with renewable energy, the Cleanweb Movement has created a powerful mix. One pioneer of the new movement touched on the implications of the convergence of Internet communication with renewable energy. "Think of the Cleanweb as what happens when green energy meets Moore's Law," says Dominic Basulto. Writing on the blog *Big Think*, he observed that social entrepreneurs who

> once viewed "clean tech" and "the Web" as an either/or investment
> proposition now have the best of both worlds: they can invest in so-
> lar companies at the same time as they are investing in the future of
> Web or mobile. If Silicon Valley can get the Cleanweb to scale in the
> same way that raw computing power has scaled over the past two
> decades, just think of the possibilities.[35]

FREE WI-FI FOR EVERYONE

The prospect of prosumers financing the generation of their own green energy and overseeing its use and distribution with their own wireless devices at near zero marginal cost has come a step closer to reality with the recent recommendation of free Wi-Fi for everyone. In February 2013, the Federal Communications Commission (FCC), the oversight body that regulates the U.S. telecommunications industry, dropped a bombshell. The commission published a proposal that would create "super Wi-Fi networks" across America, making wireless connection free for everyone. The FCC plan is to require television stations and other broadcasters to sell back to the government unused airwaves so they can be reemployed for public Wi-Fi networks. The reused broadcast frequencies would have a reach of a mile or more, be able to penetrate walls and enclosures, and allow users to make free calls from their mobile phones on the Internet, as well as use the Wi-Fi connection in their homes and businesses for free, slashing the cost of Internet bills.[36]

The harnessing of near zero marginal cost communications to manage near zero marginal cost renewable energy gives society the critical operating platform to build out the Internet of Things infrastructure and change the economic paradigm. The controversial FCC proposal has pitted the wireless carriers of the nation's great telecommunications companies, including AT&T, T-Mobile, Intel, and Verizon, against the equally formidable Internet and IT companies like Google and Microsoft. The former, which have paid out billions of dollars to secure FCC spectrum licenses, risk heavy losses to their $178 billion wireless industry.[37] The latter argue that free Wi-Fi connection will spur the introduction of "millions of devices that will compose the coming Internet of Things."[38] Google is already providing free Wi-Fi in the Chelsea section of Manhattan and in some neighborhoods in Silicon Valley.[39]

Industry analysts are predicting that free Wi-Fi "could replace carrier service."[40] The FCC is of a like mind. One FCC official says, "We want our policy to be more end-user-centric and not carrier-centric."[41]

The FCC proposal comes as a result of dramatic technological advances over the past decade that have transformed the electromagnetic spectrum from a scarce resource to a potentially infinitely available one, just like solar, wind, and geothermal heat. When broadcast radio emerged in the 1920s, if two or more broadcasters in close proximity to each other were using the same spectrum frequency or a very close one, they would continually interrupt and interfere with one another's broadcast signals, making the communication unintelligible. By 1927, the proliferation of radio broadcasters was creating chaos in radio reception, forcing Congress to pass the Radio Act to establish the Federal Radio Commission (FRC), whose mission was to determine which frequencies could be used and who could use them.[42] The subsequent Communications Act of 1934 vested the spectrum allocation to the newly established Federal Communications Commission.[43] The FCC took on the responsibility of managing the spectrum, which meant licensing a specific frequency in a given location to a broadcaster or other parties for their exclusive use. The spectrum itself was viewed as a scarce resource and therefore regarded as a valuable commercial asset.

Today, new technologies for managing communications over the radio frequencies have made the concept of the spectrum as a scarce resource null and void. That new reality is changing the very nature of broadcast communications. Smart antennas, dynamic spectrum access, cognitive radio technologies, and mesh networks are among the new technologies that are expanding the spectrum to an abundant resource by using it more efficiently and with greater agility. The new technologies can concentrate a transmitted signal so that it goes only to the user's antenna, avoiding interference with other antennas. They can also sense other transmissions and share unused spectrum. They can scan the spectrum, searching for temporarily unused holes to use. In a wireless network, the radios can even coordinate information with each other, allowing for parallel transmissions and an optimization of a particular time-frequency slot.

A report by the National Telecommunications and Information Administration (NTIA) in 2010 on the future use of unlicensed spectrum observed that "when such technology is available, the capacity of the radio-frequency spectrum will be multiplied exponentially" and by "many orders of magnitude."[44] The NTIA report concluded that "if even a small part of this potential is realized, today's concept of spectrum shortage may dissipate and the need for traditional frequency regulation based on licensing may be dramatically altered."[45]

Many industry observers say that the new technologies are going to make the airwaves "so abundant that there would be no justification for the government to ration access to spectrum or to give some services priority over others."[46] In the near future, everyone will be able to share Earth's abundant free air waves, communicating with each other for nearly free, just as we will share the abundant free energy of the sun, wind, and geothermal heat.

Open wireless communication, carried over Wi-Fi networks, is quickly surpassing traditional licensed wired communications. A study by comScore found that "in December 2011, Wi-Fi connections drove 40.3 percent of mobile Internet connections and 92.3 percent of tablet Internet connections in the US."[47] Even more interesting, a Cisco report uncovered the fact that only 35 percent of mobile data use was "on the move," while 40 percent was from home, and 25 percent from work.[48] And in 2012, 33 percent of all the mobile data was offloaded to Wi-Fi networks. The Cisco study forecasts that the percentage will exceed 46 percent by 2017.[49]

The impact of open wireless communication via Wi-Fi networks is going to be most pronounced in the management of the smart grid. Open wireless strategies already account for over 70 percent of smart grid communication.[50]

The use of open wireless connections over a free Wi-Fi network is likely going to become the norm in the years to come, not only in America, but virtually everywhere. It's just too beneficial for the human race to turn down, regardless of the push back by conventional wired carriers. The notion of communicating over proprietary, centralized, wired communications networks is going to be little more than a historical curiosity to young people living in the mid-twenty-first century.

BEYOND GOVERNMENTS AND MARKETS

We are waking up to a new reality that is difficult to fathom. We have been so convinced of the economics of scarcity that we can hardly believe that an economy of abundance is possible. But it is. New communications technologies are turning the broadcast spectrum from a scarce resource to an abundant one, just as with information, renewable energy, 3D printing, and online college courses. The journey to an economy of abundance, however, is cluttered with roadblocks that could delay and even derail the collaborative era. The challenge is finding a governance model that can take society into the new paradigm. That search takes us right back to the marginal cost controversy that put two great economists at loggerheads nearly seven decades ago.

Hotelling and Coase squared off over two distinct governing models for society. Hotelling argued passionately for government management of public infrastructure goods while Coase championed governance by markets.

As fate would have it, Coase's singular achievement, which helped secure him the Nobel Prize in economics, came after the controversy over marginal costs, when he penned his treatise on privatizing the spectrum. He argued for a one-time sell-off of the entire spectrum, putting it in the hands of commercial enterprises for proprietary use and exchange in the marketplace.

Coase believed that the market was a far more efficient mechanism for determining how resources should be allocated than government regulators and bureaucracies. Or, in today's parlance, "the government should not be in the business of picking winners and losers," not only because it lacks the vital up-to-the-moment information on value propositions that sellers and buyers bring to the market, but also because government policy makers are subject to influence peddling by special interests.

Most economists bought into Coase's thesis, and eventually the FCC itself began to fall in line with Coase's argument by allocating spectrum leases through public auctions to the highest bidder.[51] The FCC's decision to auction leases wasn't entirely devoid of self-interest. The government reasoned that from a purely financial perspective, it made far more sense to sell valuable spectrum leases, which could put billions of dollars into the federal coffers, than to just give it away for free. The idea was that by selling spectrum leases, both the government and private enterprise came out on top.

The win-win collaboration was predicated on the assumption, however, that the spectrum is a highly valuable commercial asset because it is a scarce resource. That assumption began to crumble in the late 1990s with the introduction of the new technologies that transformed the spectrum from a scarce resource to an abundant one. Engineers argued that the spectrum, if not an infinite resource, was certainly a renewable one with untapped capacity that could drive the cost of using it to nearly zero.

Social critics and a small but influential group of economists seized on the opportunity of an abundant spectrum and began to frame the issue in social terms, arguing that denying millions of people the ability to communicate with each other at near zero marginal cost constituted a denial of their right to free speech. After all, much of the communication that goes on today in the United States and around the world is via e-mail, smartphones, and tablets. In the Collaborative Age, social media like Facebook and Twitter are the indispensable means by which people increasingly communicate with each other.

A new generation of scholars like Eli Noam of Columbia University, Yochai Benkler of Harvard University, and Kevin Werbach of the Wharton School at the University of Pennsylvania found common cause with the traditional market economists. All of them argued that the FCC command and control of the radio bands was, at best, inefficient and wasteful. The new activists disagreed, however, with Coase's disciples, who argued that market management was the only viable alternative to government control. They argued that if the remaining airwaves were leased or sold to the private sector, the telecom giants would stow away large chunks of the spectrum, monopolize the rest, and assert an iron grip over the communication channels of the country—denying millions of prosumers and hundreds of thousands of businesses nearly free communications and the economic, social, and political benefits that accompany it. They support a third alternative that would take the nation's communications beyond both government and market control. They call the new governing model the Networked Commons. Web activists are not talking about the quaint old ancestral commons of feudal yore, but a high-tech, twenty-first-century Commons that can manage the distributed, peer-to-peer, laterally scaled economic activities made possible by the Internet of Things. The Networked Commons becomes the governing body for a new collaborative economic paradigm.

What they're advocating extends far beyond governance of the airwaves. Because IT computing, wireless telecommunications, and Internet technology are increasingly being deployed to organize and manage information, green energy and electricity, 3D printing of infofactured products, online higher education, social media marketing, and plug-in clean transport and logistics, the networked Commons becomes the governing model that envelopes the entirety of the Internet of Things. While none of the new digital commoners expect

government or markets to suddenly shrivel, they see them making
room for a third alternative that will come to play an increasingly
mainstream role in managing much of the economic, social, and political affairs of every locale and region in a near zero marginal cost
world. The Collaborative Commons has entered onto the world stage.

PART III
THE RISE OF THE COLLABORATIVE COMMONS

CHAPTER TEN

THE COMEDY OF
THE COMMONS

Although most people know little about Commons governance (as described in chapters 1 and 2), it predates the capitalistic system and proved to be an effective governing model for organizing economic life during the feudal and medieval eras. Unfortunately, in modern times, its reputation has been tarnished, first by Enlightenment philosophers and, more recently, by conventional economists committed to replacing it with a ubiquitous private property regime and market exchange model.

Likely the most well-known contemporary depiction of the Commons—albeit a thoroughly negative one—is Garrett Hardin's essay entitled "The Tragedy of the Commons," which appeared in the journal *Science* in 1968. A professor of ecology at the University of California, Santa Barbara, Hardin posed the hypothetical situation of a pasture "open to all." Each herder benefits from grazing as many cows on the pasture as he can. Yet he suffers the negative consequences of a deterioration of the pasture if every other herder attempts to optimize his benefits by similarly grazing as many cows as they can on the same open pasture. As the land continues to erode, the struggle between the herders only escalates, as each attempts to maximize his own grazing before the pasture becomes barren. The short-term race for gain dictates the inevitable diminishment of the resource. Hardin writes:

Therein is the tragedy. Each man is locked into a system that compels him to increase his herd without limit—in a world that is limited. Ruin is the destination toward which all men rush, each pursuing his own best interest in a society that believes in the freedom of the commons. Freedom in a commons brings ruin to all.[1]

Even if the open pasture was being taken care of by some of the herders, the tragedy of the Commons could not be prevented because of the "free riders dilemma." That is, if the pasture were open to everyone, then free riders would take advantage of the good will of others, who were attempting to steward the resources, by grazing more of their herd without contributing to the general effort of taking care of the pasture. If the free riders prevail over the stewards, the result is the ruin of the Commons.

Hardin concluded with an ominous declaration that "the alternative of the Commons is too horrifying to contemplate."[2] An ardent ecologist, Hardin was convinced that the only effective way to restore the Earth's deteriorating ecosystems was to impose the heavy hand of centralized government command and control:

> If ruin is to be avoided in a crowded world, people must be responsive to a coercive force outside their individual psyches, a "Leviathan," to use Hobbes's term.[3]

Hardin's description of the Commons contained more than a modicum of truth. However, it omitted the most salient factors of the Commons model that allowed it to persevere over eons of history—that is, the self-regulating, self-enforcing protocols and accompanying punishments agreed to by its members as a condition of participation. Without those protocols and punishments, the tragedy of the Commons is likely, if not inevitable. In other words, Hardin left out governance.

What I find so strange is that Hardin chose to cast the Commons as the villain responsible for the unleashing of wanton greed and destruction in the modern era. In fact, it was the excesses of a market-driven capitalist system motivated by the dogged pursuit of profit and abetted by the heavy hand of government-directed colonial and neocolonial policies that led to the pillage of resources and the wholesale exploitation of humanity in the developing world over the course of the eighteenth, nineteenth, and twentieth centuries.

REDISCOVERING THE COMMONS

Until very recently, economists and historians regarded the Commons as a unique economic model whose relevance was inextricably tied to a feudal society. Over the past 25 years, however, a younger generation of scholars and practitioners has begun to reexamine the Commons as a governing model. They sense that its guiding principles and assumptions, if updated and reworked, might offer a more practical organizational model for a transitioning economy where centralized command and control of commerce is capitulating to distributed, laterally scaled, peer-to-peer production, where property exchange in markets is becoming less relevant than access to sharable goods and services in networks, and where social capital is becoming more valued than market capital in orchestrating economic life.

In 1986—18 years after Hardin's essay seemed to put the last proverbial nail in the coffin of Commons theory—Carol Rose pried open the casket, breathing new life into what many had already concluded was a dead idea. The Northwestern University law professor entitled her salvo "The Comedy of the Commons," a scathing rejoinder to Hardin's earlier thesis. Her spirited and rigorous defense of Commons governance rousted the academic community, spurring a revival of Commons scholarship and practice.

Rose began by reminding her readers that not everything is amenable to private ownership. The oceans and submerged lands at high tides, lakes and rivers, forests, glens, mountain passes, open lands, country lanes, roads and bridges, and the air we breathe are all in the nature of public goods. While they can be privatized in the form of property exchanged in markets, they have more often been overseen by government, but not always. Rose points out that

> there lies outside purely private property and government-controlled "public property" a distinct class of "inherently public property" which is fully controlled by neither government nor private agents.

[This is] property collectively "owned" and "managed" by society at
large, with claims independent of and indeed superior to the claims
of any purported governmental manager.[4]

In the legal field, these claims are known as customs claims and
can be found in British and American law, as well as in legal doctrines
in countries around the world. They are generally rights that have existed beyond memory—for example, a community's right to use land
in common to graze animals, or gather wood from local forests, or cut
peat or turf from bogs and fields, or use roads, or fish in local streams,
or assemble for festivals on the "public commons." The interesting
aspect of customary rights is that they are most often accompanied by
informal or formal management protocols to ensure a proper stewardship of the commons.

The late University of Toronto professor Crawford Macpherson,
one of the twentieth century's distinguished authorities on the history of property, notes that we are so used to thinking of property as
the right to exclude others from the use or benefit of something that
we have lost sight of an older conception of property, the customary
right of access to property held in common—to wit, the right to freely
navigate waterways, or walk along country roads, or enjoy access to
the public square.[5]

Rose cites the customary right to participate in the public square,
noting that it has long been regarded as indispensable to social life.
The public square—at least before the Internet—is where we communicate, socialize, revel in each other's company, establish communal
bonds, and create social capital and trust, the indispensable elements
for nurturing community. For that reason, the right to attend festivals
and sporting events or assemble on the promenade has traditionally
been the most basic of all rights. The right to be included, to have
access to one another, which is the right to participate "in common,"
is the fundamental property right, while private property, the right
to enclose, own, and exclude is merely a qualified deviation from the
norm—although in modern times the qualification has all but sub-
sumed the norm.

Rose makes a poignant observation about the customary right to
hold public festivities on the commons that has deep relevance to the
current debate on the right to universal access to networked social

spaces on the Internet. In regard to festivals, dances, sporting events, and other social activities in the public square, the more individuals that participate, says Rose, "the higher its value to each participant."[6] Rose says that "this is the reverse of the 'tragedy of the commons': it is a 'comedy of the commons,' as is so felicitously expressed in the phrase 'the more the merrier.'"[7]

What makes Rose's insight so uncanny is she wrote it in 1986, before the emergence of the World Wide Web. Rose, in simple prose, addressed the most important question of all: When should property claims rest in private hands and when in public trust on the Commons? The properties in question, said Rose, have to be physically capable of being monopolized by private persons. But "the public's claim had to be superior to that of the private owner, because the properties themselves were most valuable when used by indefinite and unlimited numbers of persons—by the public at large."[8] Rose saw that the "publicness" of goods and services "created the 'rent' of the property, and public-property doctrines—like police-power doctrines—protected that publicly created rent from capture through private holdout."[9]

Rose's blistering attack on Hardin's tragedy of the commons thesis and her equally spirited defense of the comedy of the commons was followed, just four years later, by the publication of Elinor Ostrom's *The Governing of the Commons*. Ostrom, an economist who served on the faculties of both Indiana University and Arizona State University, wrote the first comprehensive economic and anthropological analysis on the history of the commons, covering a thousand-year span. Her work dazzled the intellectual community and even the economic academy. Ostrom's insightful analysis of why commons governance had succeeded and failed in the past, and her pragmatic prescriptions for ensuring the success of future Commons management, won her the coveted Nobel Prize in economics in 2009—making her the first woman ever to receive the honor.

Ostrom, although every bit the economist, was not shy about taking on the role of an anthropologist. She studied commons management schemes from the Swiss Alps to Japanese villages to discover the underlying principles that made them effective governing models. At the very onset of her work, she took care to explain that many of the commons institutions she cataloged had, in her words, "survived droughts, floods, wars, pestilence, and major economic and political changes" over long sweeps of history, making it crystal clear that the commons has proven itself to be a formidable governing institution and worthy of reconsideration in light of the environmental, economic, and social challenges and opportunities facing humanity in an increasingly connected global world.[10]

Her research contradicted Hardin's assertion that "all" commons were destined to ruin because of free riding and cast doubt on the long-held shibboleth among economists—dating back to Adam Smith—that each individual seeks only his or her own immediate self-interest in the market.[11]

What Ostrom found instead is that in managing common-pool resources—pastures for grazing animals, fisheries, irrigation systems, forests, and the like—individuals, more often than not, put the community's interest before self-interest and the long-term preservation of the common resource above each person's immediate circumstances, even when their plight was dire. In each instance, the glue that kept the commons viable was the agreed-upon self-management protocols entered into voluntarily by the democratic participation of all the members. It was the continuous collaboration and feedback that created bonds of social trust, generation after generation. The social bonds kept the commons from ossifying and falling apart. In the worst of times, the "social capital" proved to be the central asset that allowed the commons to soldier on. Ostrom observed in her historical research of commons management that

> thousands of opportunities have arisen in which large benefits could have been reaped by breaking the rules, while the expected sanctions were comparatively low. Stealing water during a dry season in the Spanish *huertas* might on occasion save an entire season's crop from certain destruction. Avoiding spending day after day maintaining the Philippine irrigation systems might enable a farmer to earn needed income in other pursuits. Harvesting illegal timber in the Swiss or Japanese mountain Commons would yield a valuable product. Given the temptations involved, the high levels of conformance to the rules in all these cases have been remarkable.[12]

All the commons build in sanctions and punishments to enforce the agreed-upon management protocols. Yet it's striking, says Ostrom, that in almost every case study, the fines imposed for violations of the norms are "surprisingly low" and "rarely are they more than a small fraction of the monetary value that could be obtained by breaking the rules."[13]

The monitoring of each other's activities is almost always by the members themselves. The intimacy of the monitoring makes any potential violation less likely, not only because "there is no place to hide" but also because of the sense of shame and guilt a would-be violator might feel in betraying the trust of his or her neighbors and friends.

The village of Törbel, Switzerland, with a population of 600, is one of the many examples cited by Ostrom of a successful commons that has endured for more than 800 years. Törbel farm families plant their own privately owned plots, producing vegetables, grains, fruits, and hay for feeding their cows during the winter. Local herdsmen pasture their cows in communally owned Alpine meadows in the summer months. The cows produce cheese, which is a vital part of the local economy.[14]

The Törbel Commons covenant agreement of 1483, which has been repeatedly updated and revised over the centuries, describes the governing protocols for maintaining the Alpine grazing meadows, the forests, wastelands, irrigation systems, and lanes and roads that connect private and communally owned properties.[15]

This Swiss commons has well-established boundaries, allowing only local citizens the right to use common's resources. Specific rules ensure that there won't be overgrazing. A covenant restriction first laid down in 1517 states that "no citizen could send more cows to the alp than he could feed during the winter."[16] Cows sent to the mountain for summer grazing are counted at the beginning of the seasonal retreat in order to ascertain how much cheese each family will be given at the annual distribution.[17]

The commons association holds annual meetings to discuss management, review rules, and elect governing officials. The association is responsible for imposing fines, organizing the maintenance of paths and roads, repairing infrastructure, and collecting members' fees for the work performed. Fees are generally proportional to the number of cows owned by each household. The association also marks the trees that will be cut for timber for construction and heating and assigns them by lot to households that then harvest the trees. While each household owns its own farm plots—gardens, vineyards, and grain fields—commons-type arrangements allow for the sharing of commons infrastructure, including barns, granaries, and multistory housing units.[18]

Törbel has maintained a consistently high level of productivity over the centuries by a careful management of its commons. Although each family enjoys private ownership of its land, it has continued to prefer communal tenure of other resources for the very practical reason, wrote Robert McC. Netting in a study published in *Human Ecology,* that it "promotes both general access to and optimum production from certain types of resources while enjoining on the entire community the conservation measures necessary to protect these resources from destruction."[19] Törbel is not an anomaly. More than 80 percent of the Alpine region of Switzerland is managed by a mixed system combining private property for agriculture and commons property for the use of meadows, forests, and wasteland.[20]

My wife, Carol, and I have had the pleasure of visiting these Alpine communities countless times over the years. What always impresses us is the high quality of life in these villages. The citizenry seems to have struck just the right balance between the traditional and the contemporary, mixing state-of-the-art commons management, market savvy, and enlightened local governance. The Swiss Alpine villages are an advertisement for sustainable practices and a clear demonstration of what can be achieved when the commons is a vital centerpiece of local life.

Nor are the Swiss Alps commons just a precious oddity. There are literally thousands of similar examples of such commons arrangements, stretching from traditional farming communities in developing countries to the most sophisticated condominium arrangements that govern common-interest developments in suburban communities across America.

In studying the strengths and weaknesses of the three dominant management models of government, the private sector, and the commons, it is far from clear that one is necessarily always better or worse than the other. Which management model is best depends largely on the particular context.

Private-property arrangements are quite efficient for some purposes. But to believe that placing virtually everything on earth in private hands—which most free-market economists advocate—is the best way to go doesn't pass the smell test, especially when dealing with public goods that everyone needs to have access to in order to flourish. Would we want to fence off every beachfront, lake and river, every forest, every suburban community, every road and bridge, and put the whole of the Earth's diverse ecosystems into private hands, allowing property owners the exclusive right to charge an access fee for admission and use of the resources, or worse, deny admission altogether? Anyone who has ever experienced the rapacious destruction of ecosystems and resources at the hands of commercial and residential developers would be hard pressed to argue that the private market is always the most efficient means of optimizing the general welfare.

Likewise, while governments have performed laudably in overseeing the management of many public goods, from roads and water systems to postal delivery and public schools, they have often fallen short when it comes to understanding the very complex dynamics that make every local situation a unique experience. A "one size fits all" box of prescriptions and protocols can often lead to horrendous mismanagement—especially when those responsible for oversight are anonymous bureaucrats, without ties to the communities they are administering.

If there is an essential theme to the commons, it is that the people who know best how to govern their lives are the members of the community themselves. If there are resources, goods, and services that are public in nature and are best optimized by public access and use, then they are often best managed by the community as a whole.

After years of field investigations and research on what makes commons work, Ostrom and her colleagues came up with seven "design principles" that seem to be integral to every effective commons surveyed.

First, effective management of a commons requires "clearly defined boundaries" on who is allowed to appropriate from the commons and who is not.

Second, it's necessary to establish appropriation rules restricting the time, place, technologies, and quantity of the resources that can be used as well as setting up the rules on the amount of labor, materials, and money that can be allotted to the appropriation.

Third, a commons association needs to guarantee that those affected by the appropriation rules jointly and democratically determine those rules and their modifications over time.

Fourth, the commons association should ensure that those monitoring the activity on the commons are the appropriators or are accountable to them.

Fifth, appropriators who violate the rules should, in principle, be subject to graduated sanctions by the other appropriators or officials accountable to the appropriators, to guard against overly punitive punishment that sours their future participation and creates ill will in the community.

Sixth, the commons association ought to build in procedures for rapid access to low-cost private mediation to quickly resolve conflict among appropriators or between appropriators and public officials.

Seventh, it is vital that government jurisdictions recognize and condone the legitimacy of the rules established by the commons association. If government authorities do not provide a minimum recognition of the authority of the commons association to self-manage and, in effect, treat it as illegitimate, the self-rule of the commons is not likely to be able to sustain itself over time.[21]

These seven design principles appear over and over again in Commons arrangements all over the world. Long before the age of global communications, isolated communities, with little outside contact, came up with similar management models, which raises the interesting question of whether there is a universal constant in play.

Ostrom and her colleagues put this notion to the test in laboratory experiments. They found that when subjects are faced with a common-pool resource problem and are kept from communicating with one another and forced to make decisions independently and anonymously, they invariably overuse resources. However, when they are allowed to openly communicate with one another, overharvesting is dramatically cut. The laboratory studies also reveal that the subjects are willing to pay fees to fine other violators, demonstrating a commitment to "sanction others at a cost to themselves."[22] Ostrom also found that when subjects are able to make their own rules about withdrawals and whether or not they will punish others and how much, they move toward a withdrawal system in the lab that is very close to optimal. They also rarely have to punish another member, but are willing to do so if necessary. What the lab experiments suggest is that when people are able to design their own rules for managing common-pool resources, they intuitively reach for some variation of the design principles that have given form and direction to commons management around the world.[23]

Most economists would be nonplussed because their discipline is so wedded to the idea that human nature is purely self-interested and that each individual seeks to optimize his or her autonomy. The very idea of freely choosing to pursue the collective interest is anathema to many market-oriented economists. They might be well served by boning up on the findings of evolutionary biologists and neurocognitive scientists. A spate of studies and discoveries over the past 20 years is shattering the long-held belief that human beings are, at their core, utilitarian-seeking loners prowling the marketplace for opportunities to exploit their fellow human beings and enrich themselves.

We are learning that our species is the most social of beings, boasting a very large and extremely complex neocortex. The worst punishment that can be imposed on a human being is ostracism. Cognitive scientists tell us that our neural circuitry is soft wired for experiencing empathic distress and that evolutionary survival has depended far more on our collective sociability than our self-directed proclivities. Far from being an anomaly, the Commons approach to marshaling economic activity appears to be much better suited to our biological instincts than the stark picture of an anonymous marketplace where an invisible hand mechanically rewards selfish behavior in a zero-sum game.

Why, however, this sudden interest in retrieving the commons as a governance model for society? There is no easy answer, but let me suggest at least some of the relevant parameters.

The Reagan/Thatcher-led economic movement to privatize public goods and services by selling off telecommunications networks, radio frequencies, electricity generation and transmission grids, public transport, government-sponsored scientific research, postal services, rail lines, public lands, prospecting rights, water and sewage services, and dozens of other activities that had long been considered public trusts, administered by government bodies, marked the final surrender of public responsibility for overseeing the general welfare of society.

Deregulation and privatization spread quickly to other countries. The magnitude of the capitulation was breathtaking in scope and scale. Governments were hollowed out overnight, becoming empty shells, while vast power over the affairs of society shifted to the private sector. The public, at large, was stripped of its "collective" power as citizens and reduced to millions of autonomous agents forced to fend for themselves in a marketplace increasingly controlled by several hundred global corporations. The disempowerment came with lightning speed, leaving little time for public reaction and even less time for public engagement in the process. There was virtually no widespread debate at the time, despite the breadth of the shift in power from the government to the private sector, leaving the public largely unaware and uninvolved, although deeply affected by the consequences.

For the most part, free-market economists, business leaders, neoliberal intellectuals, and progressive politicians—like President Bill Clinton of the United States and Prime Minister Tony Blair of the United Kingdom—were able to prevail by portraying the market as the sole key to economic progress and castigating critics as old fashioned and out of touch or, worse, as Soviet-style apologists for big government. The collapse of the Soviet empire, with its widespread corruption, inefficiencies, and stagnant economic performance was trotted out at every occasion as a whipping boy and proof positive that the well-being of society would be better assured by placing all the economic marbles in the hands of the market and letting government shrivel to the most rudimentary of public functions.

Large segments of the public acquiesced, in part because they shared a sense of frustration and disappointment with government management of goods and services—although much of the ill feeling was contrived by a business community anxious to penetrate and mine a lucrative economic largesse that had long remained under government auspices and beyond the reach of the market. After all, in most industrialized countries, publicly administered goods and services enjoyed an enviable track record. The trains ran on time, the postal service was dependable, government broadcasting was of a high quality, the electricity networks kept the lights on, the telephone networks were reliable, the public schools were adequate, and so forth.

In the end, free-market ideology prevailed. But it wasn't long before various segments of the public—trade unions, small businesses, nonprofit organizations, and grassroots activists in the industrialized and developing world—began to catch their breath, take stock, and realize that the private sector had seized and gulped down, in one big bite, much of the wealth-producing endowment of the planet in the blink of an eye, transforming it into corporate fat and muscle, with sufficient clout to flick off any challenge to its supremacy.

With governments eviscerated and no longer able to offer a viable counterweight to the private market, affected constituencies began to search for another governing model that better reflected their interests and sensibilities. Disenchanted by centralized and sometimes impersonal bureaucratic government management on one extreme and a manipulative and tight-fisted commercial juggernaut determined to capture every aspect of life in the folds of its income stream and profit margins on the other, those constituencies began looking for a governing model that would allow for a more democratic and collaborative way of organizing economic life. They rediscovered the commons.

Communities were also beginning to experience the growing degradation of local ecosystems, first at the hands of governments wielding geopolitical power and then, with deregulation, global companies bullying every region of the world into compliance with their thirst for cheap labor and lax environmental regulatory oversight.

Community after community began to fall victim to the terrifying toll exacted by the decline in environmental resources and the devastating impact that real-time climate change was beginning to have on local agricultural productivity and infrastructure, threatening the very survival of their communities. Lacking effective government responses and at the mercy of a global corporate machine that was unaccountable to local communities, civil society organizations and local businesses saw in the commons a third model of governance they could begin to depend on to recapture their economic balance.

Finally, a new genre of technologies emerged in the last quarter of the twentieth century that opened up vast new economic veins and claims, igniting a global debate on how much of Earth's remaining endowment could and should be allowed to be enclosed and privatized or put into public trusts. This time, the push for enclosure penetrated to the very core building blocks that comprise Earth.

The biotechnology industry sought to patent the genes that make up the blueprints for all of life. The telecommunications industry pushed for a selloff of the electromagnetic spectrum to the private sector, giving it exclusive control of the radio frequencies over which much of the communication and information of society is channeled.

And now, the nanotechnology industry is seeking patents on processes for manipulating the physical world at the atomic level.

HOW I DISCOVERED THE COMMONS

My first introduction to the new high-tech enclosures came in 1979. Ananda Chakrabarty, a microbiologist employed by General Electric, applied to the U.S. Patents and Trademark Office (PTO) for a patent on a genetically engineered microorganism designed to consume oil spills on the oceans.[24] The PTO turned down Chakrabarty's claim, arguing that living things are not patentable under U.S. law—with the exception of asexually reproduced plants, which had been granted a special patent protection by an act of Congress.

Chakrabarty's case made its way to the U.S. Supreme Court. This is where I jumped in, through a nonprofit organization, the People's Business Commission (shortly thereafter renamed the Foundation on Economic Trends). Our organization filed the main *amicus curiae* brief on behalf of the PTO. We argued—along with the PTO—that genes are not inventions but merely discoveries of nature, even if sequestered, purified, isolated, and identified by use and function. After all, the chemists were never allowed to patent the chemical elements in the periodic table, even though they too argued that by the sheer act of isolating, purifying, and identifying the functional qualities, the elements were more inventions than discoveries. The PTO, nonetheless, refused to grant any patents on the basic chemical elements.[25]

In our brief, prepared by my colleague Ted Howard, we warned that if patents were granted, the floodgates would be opened to the patenting of all the genetic building blocks that make up the evolutionary schema of biological species. Giving private enterprises ownership of the genetic code would enclose the most precious resource of all—life itself—reducing it to a mere commodity for exploitation, sale, and profit in the marketplace.[26] I sat in the Supreme Court chamber along with a smattering of corporate lobbyists, listening to the oral arguments and thinking to myself that the potential enclosure of the Earth's gene pool was a momentous turning point for the human race, destined to affect our species and our fellow creatures far into the future.

The court, by a slim 5-to-4 margin, awarded the patent on the first genetically engineered organism. Chief Justice Warren Burger specifically referred to the arguments in our amicus brief as "the grue-some parade of horribles" and argued that we were wrong in believing that this decision would transfer the genetic inheritance of Earth to private enterprise, with innumerable consequences for society.[27]

Within months of the Supreme Court decision, Genentech, the first biotech company, went public in 1980 offering a million shares of stock at $35 per share. The share price quickly jumped to $88 within the first hour on the market. By the end of the day, Genentech had raised $35 million in "one of the largest stock run ups ever" and had not yet produced a single product for sale.[28] Agribusiness, the pharmaceutical industry, chemical companies, and biotech start-up companies joined the race, determined to lay claim to the genetic code.

Seven years later, "the parade of horribles" we had warned of materialized. In 1987, the PTO reversed its long-standing position that life was not patentable, ruling that all genetically engineered, multicellular living organisms, including animals, are potentially patentable. The commissioner of patents and trademarks, Donald J. Quigg, in an effort to quell a public outcry, made it clear that human beings were excluded, only because the Thirteenth Amendment to the Constitution forbids human slavery.[29] Nonetheless, genetically altered human embryos, as well as human genes, cell lines, tissues, and organs, are potentially patentable, leaving open the option of patenting all the parts of the whole human being.

In the years since, Life Science companies have fanned out across the world, "bioprospecting" in every corner of the planet for rare and valuable genes and cell lines—including genes from indigenous human populations—that could be of potential commercial value in fields ranging from agriculture to pharmaceuticals and medicine, quickly securing patent protection on every "discovery." The Foundation on Economic Trends (FOET) has spent the better part of the past 32 years fighting the enclosures, in patent offices, courtrooms, and legislative chambers.

In 1995, FOET assembled a coalition of more than 200 U.S. religious leaders, including the titular heads of virtually all the major Protestant denominations, Catholic bishops, and Jewish, Muslim, Buddhist, and Hindu leaders, to voice their opposition to the granting of patents on animal and human genes, organs, tissues, and organisms. It was the largest coalition of American religious leaders to come together on any issue in the twentieth century—but to little avail.[30]

Years earlier—around the mid-1980s—I began to realize that opposing patents on life in a capitalist system whose laws and government regulatory oversight were all conditioned to encourage the commercial enclosure of Earth's commons was a futile exercise. If both government and the private sector were in lock step, what other institutional avenue might be available for stewarding Earth's biology and, for that matter, the rest of the planet's resources? The search led me to a rediscover the commons.

I found small bits of information on commons, mostly in esoteric anthropological studies and even less in formal histories. For the most part, the history of the commons was relegated to a few paragraphs in textbooks on the feudal economy of England. As I continued to explore, however, I began to find more stories about commons in various parts of the world, almost all of them devoted to feudal economic arrangements. It dawned on me that "the Commons" was potentially a much broader metaphor that applied to far more diverse phenomena, so I set out to write a book on the history of the commons and enclosures starting with the feudal enclosures of agricultural lands in Europe. I then proceeded to the enclosure of the ocean Commons, in the age of exploration and discovery in the sixteenth century; the enclosure of the knowledge Commons with the introduction of intellectual property in the form of patents, copyrights, and trademarks in the late eighteenth century; the enclosure of the electromagnetic-spectrum Commons in the early twentieth century with the licensing of radio bands to private enterprises; and finally the enclosure of the genetic Commons in the later part of the century with the conferring of patents on genes.

By framing the historical narrative in terms of commons and enclosures, I discovered a more compelling account of the human journey over the past half millennium of history. I published my findings in a book titled *Biosphere Politics* in 1991. In the book, I urged a reopening of the global Commons and suggested that a rethinking of the Commons model for the twenty-first century might be a rallying point for bringing together diverse interests from disparate fields into a common cause.

In 2002, FOET put theory into practice, bringing together 250 organizations from 50 countries at the World Social Forum in Porto Alegre, Brazil, in support of a Treaty to Share the Genetic Commons.

The organizations included farm associations, women's groups, fair-trade advocates, biotech activists, organic food associations, religious groups, environmental organizations, and hunger and emergency-aid organizations. The preamble to the proposed treaty declared the genetic heritage of Earth to be a shared Commons, held in trust by the human race on behalf of our species and our fellow creatures. It reads:

We proclaim these truths to be universal and indivisible;

That the intrinsic value of the Earth's gene pool, in all of its biological forms and manifestations, precedes its utility and commercial value, and therefore must be respected and safeguarded by all political, commercial and social institutions,

That the Earth's gene pool, in all of its biological forms and manifestations, exists in nature and, therefore, must not be claimed as intellectual property even if purified and synthesized in the laboratory,

That the global gene pool, in all of its biological forms and manifestations, is a shared legacy and, therefore, a collective responsibility,

And,

Whereas, our increasing knowledge of biology confers a special obligation to serve as a steward on behalf of the preservation and well being of our species as well as all of our other fellow creatures,

Therefore, the nations of the world declare the Earth's gene pool, in all of its biological forms and manifestations, to be a global commons, to be protected and nurtured by all peoples and further declare that genes and the products they code for, in their natural, purified or synthesized form as well as chromosomes, cells, tissue, organs and organisms, including cloned, transgenic and chimeric organisms, will not be allowed to be claimed as commercially negotiable genetic information or intellectual property by governments, commercial enterprises, other institutions or individuals.[31]

In the years since, a number of associations and organizations have been established to both manage a global genetic Commons and prevent its further enclosure.

The Global Crop Diversity Trust, an independent nonprofit association founded by Cary Fowler, works with research institutions, germplasm preservation groups, farm associations, independent plant breeders, and other agricultural interests to preserve the world's dwindling plant genetic resources. As part of its mission, the trust has erected an underground vault deep beneath the ice in the small island of Svalbard, Norway, high up in the Arctic, in one of the most remote regions of the world. The maze of tunnels inside the air-conditioned, sealed vault houses thousands of rare seeds from around the world for potential use by future generations. The vault is designed as a fail-safe depository that can store up to 3 million seed varieties used in agriculture to ensure their safekeeping in a world of wars and increasing human-induced catastrophes. The trust operates as a self-managed Commons on a global scale. Its network of thousands of scientists and plant breeders is continually searching for heirloom and wild seeds, growing them out to increase seed stock, and ferrying samples to the vault for long-term storage.[32] In 2010, the trust launched a global program to locate, catalog, and preserve the wild relatives of the 22 major food crops humanity relies on for survival.

The intensification of genetic-Commons advocacy comes at a time when new IT and computing technology is speeding up genetic research. The new field of bioinformatics has fundamentally altered the nature of biological research just as IT, computing, and Internet technology did in the fields of renewable-energy generation and 3D printing. According to research compiled by the National Human Genome Research Institute, gene-sequencing costs are plummeting at a rate that exceeds the exponential curves of Moore's Law in computing power.[33] Dr. David Altshuler, deputy director of the Broad Institute of Harvard University and the Massachusetts Institute of Technology, observes that in just the past several years, the price of genetic sequencing has dropped a million fold.[34] Consider that the cost of reading one million base pairs of DNA—the human genome contains around three billion pairs—has plunged from $100,000 to just six cents.[35] This suggests that the marginal cost of some genetic research will approach zero in the not-too-distant future, making valuable biological data available for free, just like information on the Internet.

Gene sequencing and other new biotechnologies are putting us on the road to the democratization of research. *Washington Post* science reporter Ariana Eunjung Cha observes that

[a] generation ago, the process of manipulating an organism's genes required millions of dollars in sophisticated equipment and years of trial and error.

Now, it can be done in a garage with second-hand parts ordered off the Internet in a few days.[36]

Biological research and the accompanying expertise, which just two decades ago were available to only an elite group of scientists working for governments or in industry, are now within reach of thousands of university students and hobbyists. Worried that global Life Science companies are quickly maneuvering to convert the biological information of the planet into intellectual property, environmentalists are pushing hard to prevent what they regard as the ultimate Enclosure Movement. Their efforts are gaining traction among a younger generation of researchers who grew up with the Internet and regard the open sharing of genetic information as a right, no less important than the right to freely access other information.

The specter of nearly free genome research and just-as-cheap applications in the future makes the prospect of Commons management of scientific endeavors a very real option. Scientific papers and proposals on Commons management of genetic research and applications are flooding social media spaces, and new Commons associations to manage genetic innovations are proliferating.

The push to open up the genetic Commons by a younger generation of scientists has forced the issue onto the public agenda. The growing popular support for sharing genetic information pressured the U.S. Supreme Court to partially reverse its earlier ruling granting patents on life. In June 2013 the court unanimously ruled that genes linked to breast cancer are discoveries of nature and not human inventions, thereby invalidating a patent on the genes issued to Myriad Genetics. The decision, although an important first step in reopening the genetic Commons, is not as significant as it might seem, because new cloning technologies that slightly modify naturally occurring genes are still held to be human inventions and therefore patentable, allowing biotech, pharmaceutical, and Life Science companies to continue to partially enclose the planet's gene pool.

The rush to freely share the accumulating knowledge of the biology of the planet echoes a similar surge between 1992 and 2008 to

freely share software, music, entertainment, and news when the plummeting marginal costs of generating information gave rise to open
Commons like Linux, Wikipedia, Napster, and YouTube.

THE ENVIRONMENTALISTS AND SOFTWARE
HACKERS BECOME KINDRED SPIRITS

The "free genetics" movement has run parallel to the "free software"
movement for the past 30 years. They both champion the open sharing
of information over conventional intellectual-property protection—
and each faces formidable foes. The early leaders of the Free Software
Movement realized that big media, the telecommunications industry,
and the entertainment community would circle the wagons and do
what it took to tighten up any holes in intellectual-property law that
might provide an opening for the insurgency. Environmentalists faced
a similar situation with the Life Science industry, pharmaceutical companies, and agribusiness.

While the dual movements shared common philosophical ground,
they also began to share technological ground with the birth of the
new field of bioinformatics. Researchers began using computing technology to decipher, download, catalog, store, and reconfigure genetic
information, creating a new kind of genetic capital for the Bioindus-
trial Age. Computing and sophisticated software programs provided a
new language for conceptualizing biology as well as an organizing medium to manage the flow of genetic information in a biotech economy.
As I noted in my 1998 book, *The Biotech Century*, "Computational
technologies and genetic technologies are fusing together into a powerful new technological reality."[37]

Today, molecular biologists around the world are busily engaged
in the most extensive data-collection project in history. In government,
university, and corporate laboratories, researchers are mapping and
sequencing the entire genomes of creatures from the lowliest bacteria
to human beings, with the goal of finding new ways of harnessing and
exploiting genetic information for economic purposes.

By midcentury, molecular biologists hope to have downloaded and
cataloged the genomes of tens of thousands of living organisms—a vast
library containing the evolutionary blueprints of many of the microor-
ganisms, plants, and animals that populate the Earth. The biological

information being generated is so massive that it can only be managed by computers and stored electronically in thousands of databases around the world. For example, were the complete human sequence to be typed out in the form used in a telephone directory, it would take up the equivalent of 200 volumes of Manhattan's thousand-page directory.[38] That's a database containing more than 3 billion entries. Taking the analogy one step further, if we were to print out the data on all human diversity, the database would be at least four orders of magnitude bigger—or 10,000 times the size of the first database.

Mapping and sequencing the genomes is just the beginning. Understanding and chronicling all the relationships between genes, tissues, organs, organisms, and external environments, and the perturbations that trigger genetic mutations and phenotypical responses, is so far beyond any kind of complex system ever modeled that only an interdisciplinary approach, leaning heavily on the computational skills of the information scientists, can hope to accomplish the task.

Titans in the computer field like Bill Gates and Wall Street insiders like Michael Milken poured funds into the new field of bioinformatics in hopes of advancing the collaborative partnership of the information and Life Sciences.

Computers are not only being used to decipher and store genetic information. They are also being used to create virtual biological environments from which to model complex biological organisms, networks, and ecosystems. The virtual environments help researchers create new hypotheses and scenarios that will later be used in the laboratory to test new agricultural and pharmaceutical products. Working in virtual laboratories, biologists can create synthetic molecules with a few keystrokes, bypassing the often laborious process—which can take years—of attempting to synthesize a real molecule on the lab bench. With 3D computer models, researchers can play with various combinations on the screen, connecting different molecules to see how they interact.

Scientists plan to create all sorts of new molecules in the future using the new Information Age computing technologies. Chemists are already talking about the potential for developing compounds that could reproduce themselves, conduct electricity, detect pollution, stop tumors, counter the effects of cocaine, and even block the progress of AIDS.

Gates is enthusiastic about the coming together of information technology and the Life sciences, saying that: "This is the information age, and biological information is probably the most interesting information we are deciphering and trying to decide to change. It's all a question of how, not if."[39]

At present, computational technology is spreading to every other field, becoming the communication medium for organizing renewable energy, 3D printing, work, marketing, logistics, transport, health care, and online higher education. The new computing language for reorganizing society has brought together varied interests, including info-hackers, bio-hackers, 3D-hackers, and Cleanweb-hackers. The bond that unites all these groups is a deep commitment to a collaborative open-source economy and a Commons-governing model. While markets aren't altogether dismissed, or governments left entirely out of the equation, the new movements share a passionate belief in the superiority of peer-to-peer Commons management as the best governing model to ensure that the benefits of a near zero marginal cost society are realized rather than stymied.

CHAPTER ELEVEN
THE COLLABORATISTS
PREPARE FOR BATTLE

The new commoners make up far more than a political movement. They represent a deep social transformation whose impacts are likely to be as significant and long lasting as those that catapulted society from a theological to an ideological worldview at the onset of the capitalist era.

The struggle between prosumer collaboratists and investor capitalists, while still nascent, is shaping up to be the critical economic battle of the first half of the twenty-first century. Recall that in Part I we examined how the shift to the communication/energy/transportation matrix of the First Industrial Revolution was accompanied by the severing of workers from their own tools and shareholder investors from the management of the companies they owned. Today, the new Third Industrial Revolution communication/energy/transportation matrix is enabling consumers to become their own producers. The new prosumers, in turn, are increasingly collaborating and sharing goods and services in globally distributed networked Commons at near zero marginal costs, disrupting the workings of capitalist markets. The unfolding economic clash between the collaboratists and capitalists is a manifestation of a cultural conflict that will likely redefine the nature of the human journey in the years ahead. If there is an underlying theme to the emerging cultural narrative, it is the "democratization of everything."

The Free Culture Movement, the Environmental Movement, and the movement to reclaim the public Commons are the coproducers, if you will, of this unfolding cultural drama. Each brings its own distinct set of metaphors to the script. And at the same time, they are increasingly borrowing each other's metaphors, strategies, and policy initiatives, bringing them ever closer into a single frame.

If there was a trigger point for the Free Culture Movement, a moment in time that galvanized the hopes and imaginations of hackers, it was probably when one of their own turned on them, exposing the rank commercial side of the computing and software revolution. In 1976, an angry young Bill Gates denounced his fellow hackers, unleashing a nasty diatribe along with a veiled warning:

> As the majority of hobbyists must be aware, most of you steal your software. Hardware must be paid for, but software is something to share. Who cares if the people who worked on it get paid? Is this fair? . . . Who can afford to do professional work for nothing? . . . The fact is, no one besides us has invested a lot of money in hobby software . . . but there is very little incentive to make this software available to hobbyists. Most directly, the thing you do is theft.[1]

Gates's venting didn't just come out of the blue. The computing and software industry was maturing. The hobby-hacker cultures at university tech hubs like MIT, Carnegie Mellon, and Stanford, which had enjoyed a collegial and collaborative sharing of computing and software in a more relaxed, playful, and creative academic milieu, were faced with new actors in their midst, who were determined to take this new communications revolution into the marketplace. Gates was the first to draw the line in the sand. Another young hacker, Richard M. Stallman, who worked at MIT's Artificial Intelligence Laboratory, took the challenge and crossed the line.

RALLYING AROUND FREE SOFTWARE

Stallman argued that software code was quickly becoming the language of communication between people, and between people and things, and that it was immoral and unethical to enclose and privatize the new communications media, allowing a few corporate players to determine the conditions of access while imposing rent. Stallman proclaimed that all software should be free, by which he meant as in "free speech, not free beer." Stallman and Gates couldn't be further apart in their positions—Gates viewed free software as theft and Stallman saw it as free speech.

Determined to create the technological means of keeping software distributed, collaborative, and free, Stallman assembled a consortium of the best software programmers around. They erected an operating system called GNU made up of free software that could be accessed, used, and modified by anyone. Stallman and others then founded the Free Software Foundation in 1985 and established the four freedoms that underlay the organization's credo:

> The freedom to run the program, for any purpose. The freedom to study how the program works, and change it so it does your computing as you wish. . . . The freedom to redistribute copies so you can help your neighbor. [And] the freedom to distribute copies of your modified versions to others. By doing this you can give the whole community a chance to benefit from your changes.[2]

Stallman put flesh on his manifesto by creating a free software licensing scheme that he called a GNU General Public License (GPL) that would ensure the four freedoms stated above. These licenses, which Stallman dubbed "copyleft," were conceived as an alternative way to use copyright law.[3] Unlike conventional copyrights that give the holder the right to prohibit others from reproducing, adopting, or distributing copies of an author's work, copyleft licenses allow an author to "give every person who receives a copy of a work permission to reproduce, adapt or distribute it and require that any resulting copies or adaptations are also bound by the same licensing agreement."[4]

The GPL became the vehicle for the establishment of a Commons for the free sharing of software. The license incorporated many of the paramount features Elinor Ostrom proposed for effective management of any Commons, most importantly the conditions of inclusion and the restrictions for exclusion; the rights governing access and withdrawal; monitoring sanctions and protocols for self-management; enhancement and stewardship of the resources, which, in this instance, is the code itself. The GPL and other free software licenses that followed gave

millions of people in a software Commons the legal means to collaborate freely, with a formally agreed-upon set of operating principles.
The GPL also laid the foundation for what would later metamorphose
into the Free Culture Movement. Lawrence Lessig, a professor of law
at Harvard University who came to personify the Free Culture Movement, coined the apt phrase "Code is Law."[5]

Just six years after Stallman went public with his GNU operating
system and the GPL, a young college student at the University of Hel-
sinki, Linus Torvalds, designed a free software kernel for a Unix-like
operating system for personal computers (PCs) that was compatible
with Stallman's GNU project and distributed it under the Free Software Foundation's GPL. The Linux kernel made it possible for thousands of prosumers around the world to collaborate via the Internet on
improving free software code.[6]

Today, GNU/Linux is used in more than 90 percent of the fastest
500 supercomputers, as well as by Fortune 500 companies, and even
runs on embedded systems like tablet computers and mobile phones.[7]

Eben Moglen, professor of law and legal history at Columbia
University, wrote in 1999 of the seminal importance of the Linux
achievement:

> Because Torvalds chose to release the Linux kernel under the Free
> Software Foundation's General Public License . . . the hundreds and
> eventually thousands of programmers around the world who chose
> to contribute their effort towards the further development of the
> kernel could be sure that their effort would result in permanently
> free software that no one could turn into a proprietary product. Ev-
> eryone knew that everyone else would be able to test, improve, and
> redistribute the improvements.[8]

GNU/Linux demonstrated something else of even greater significance—that free-software collaboration in a global Commons could
best proprietary software development in the capitalist marketplace.
Moglen continued:

> The development of the Linux kernel proved that the Internet
> made it possible to aggregate collections of programmers far larger
> than any commercial manufacturer could afford, joined almost

non-hierarchically in a development project ultimately involving more than one million lines of computer code—a scale of collaboration among geographically dispersed unpaid volunteers previously unimaginable in human history.[9]

The Free Software Movement was not without critics even inside the IT community. In 1998, some of the principal players in the movement split off to create what they called the Open Source Initiative (OSI). The founders, Eric S. Raymond and Bruce Perens, warned that the philosophical baggage that came with free software was frightening away commercial interests. They were particularly concerned that free software might become linked to the idea of zero cost. Zero cost, in the minds of private firms, conjured up the notion of zero margins, the elimination of profit, and free goods—too big a philosophical leap, they reasoned, for the business community to make.[10]

Their alternative was open-source software. The difference between free and open-source software is more perception than substance. Both rely on substantially the same types of licensing agreements. Raymond and Perens, however, were anxious to draw in the business community and believed that it would be easier to convince them of the merits of open-source code as a practical business proposition if the licensing was not attached to a philosophy that regarded the holding of proprietary information as immoral and unethical.[11]

Both Stallman and Raymond acknowledged that there was little difference in practice between free and open-source software. Stallman, however, believed that the shift in terminology weakened the concept, undermined the movement, and opened the door for the business community to whittle away at the gains of the Free Software Movement over the long run by encouraging subtle changes in the licensing agreements. Stallman summed up the differences in approach by asserting that "open source is a development methodology; free software is a social movement."[12]

Stallman granted that open source would bring many more businesses to use free software, not because they agreed with its premises but only because they could fundamentally benefit from its deployment by bringing in more users. "Sooner or later," he warned, "these users will be invited to switch back to proprietary software for some practical advantage."[13] Nonetheless, open-source software has been a runaway success and has drawn in large segments of the business community while continuing to pick up support in academic circles and civil society.

Still, the free and open-source software initiatives focused more on ensuring universal access to code—the language of the new media. What started as a geek exercise transformed into a social movement with the maturing of the Internet. Overnight, millions of people were connecting and creating new virtual salons for socializing. The emergence of social media shifted the discussion from code to conversation. The Internet became the global virtual public square, the meeting place to share music files, videos, photographs, news, and gossip. Suddenly, the Free Software Movement became part of a much larger Free Culture Movement. Eric Raymond used the metaphor of "the bazaar" to capture the buzzing virtual space where ideas, aspirations, and dreams melded with the myriad forms and expressions human beings employ to engage one another in deep play.[14] There was a growing awareness of the Internet as a place where human beings create social capital rather than market capital. Every young person in the world wanted to get in on the act, creating videos and photos for each other to look at, sharing music tips, blogging ideas and observations, and contributing academic snippets on Wikipedia, with the hope that their input might be of value to other users.

This metamorphosis of human sociability is taking us beyond blood ties, religious affiliations, and national identities to global consciousness. This is a cultural phenomenon on an unprecedented scale, and is being led by 2.7 billion amateurs. The global democratization of culture is made possible by an Internet communication medium whose operating logic is distributed, collaborative, and laterally scaled. That operating logic favors an open Commons form of democratic self-management.

Lawrence Lessig was one of the first to see the deep social significance of a medium that was democratizing culture. The very word *culture*, at least in the past century, was segmented into high and low, with the implicit understanding that the former creates social capital of lasting value while the latter is relegated to cheap entertainment for the masses.

The Internet has tipped the cultural scales. The amateurs—2 billion strong—now find themselves on top, redirecting the social narrative from the professional elites to the masses. But the democratization of culture is not assured. Lessig and others warn of backlash as commercial and professional interests band together to tighten protection of intellectual property and close off the unique collaborative potential of the Internet as a forum for peer-to-peer creativity.

THE MEDIUM IS THE DOMAIN

Whether culture is created by elites or masses depends largely on the nature of the medium. The coal-powered steam printing revolution, and its offshoots of books and periodicals, and later, the electricity revolution, and its progeny of film, radio, and television, favored copyright protection. The centralized nature of the media and the boundaried contours of the contributions "individualized" cultural content.[15]

Print introduced the idea of individual authorship. While individual authors existed previously—such as Aristotle or St. Thomas Aquinas—they were rare. In script culture, manuscripts were often written by hundreds of anonymous scribes over long periods of time. A scribe might slightly change the meaning of a small portion of the text by amplifying a sentence or two—hardly qualifying as a significant authorial contribution. Scribes saw their role as copiers. Even the few writers whose names are associated with an entire work did not so much think of themselves as creators of their own thoughts. Rather, they felt that ideas came from without in the form of a vision or inspiration—that they were struck by an idea. The very notion that an idea might come solely from within, as a unique creative insight, would have seemed strange, if not completely incomprehensible.

Print democratized writing by allowing anyone to write down their thoughts, then print and circulate them widely for others to read. The introduction of copyright laws, in turn, introduced the novel idea of owning one's thoughts and words. Owning one's words led inevitably to the idea that one's thoughts were the product of one's labor and therefore personal achievements that could be sold in the marketplace. Print and the accompanying copyright laws partially enclosed the Communications Commons for the first time in history. (In a script or oral culture, the concept that one could own his or her own words and charge other people to listen to them would have been simply unbelievable.)

The printed book also enclosed communications on still another level. In oral cultures, communication between people took place in real time. Thoughts flowed back and forth between people in an open-ended way, often drifting from one theme to another. A book, by contrast, is a one-way conversation, generally highly structured around a central theme or set of ideas, fixed forever on the printed page, and enclosed and bound by the front and back jackets.

While language is meant to be a shared experience between people, what's so unusual about print is that it is experienced alone. Print privatizes communication. One reads a book or newspaper in isolation from others. A reader can't carry on a conversation with the author. Both the author and the reader are entrenched in their own separate worlds, unable to participate in a "real-time" dialogue. The solitary nature of reading reinforces the idea of communication as an autonomous act that takes place purely in one's mind. The social quality of communication is severed. When reading, one recedes into an enclosed space, shunted away from the Commons. The enclosure of communication, in effect, creates millions of autonomous worlds. The historian Elizabeth Eisenstein notes that a reading culture is more individualistic and autonomous than an oral culture. She writes:

> The notion that society may be regarded as a bundle of discrete units
> or that the individual is prior to the social group seems to be more
> compatible with a reading public than with a hearing one.[16]

The Internet, by contrast, dissolves boundaries, making authorship a collaborative, open-ended process over time rather than an autonomous, closed process secured by copyright through time. Lessig draws attention to the pastiche nature of cultural creation on the Internet. For starters, the Internet generation does not write with words as much as it communicates with images, sounds, and video. The distributed nature of the medium makes it easy to mix and match and cut and paste within and across genres. Because the marginal cost of copying anything on the Internet is nearly free, kids grow up with the idea that sharing information is little different than sharing conversation. The interconnectivity and interactivity of the medium cries out for collaboration and gives rise to what Lessig calls the "remix" culture, in which everyone is playing off everyone else, using a mix of media and adding their own variations to a theme, and passing it down the line in a never-ending game. "These remixes are conversations," says Lessig, and just as previous generations didn't charge one another when they conversed, the Internet generation feels the same way, except their conversation is of a different nature.[17]

The new remix form of communication has become almost as cheap as oral communications, although now the conversation is among 2.7 billion human beings.[18] Ensuring that the global conversation and the collaborative culture it creates are not cut off requires finding the legal means to keep the new Commons open. Lessig and a number of colleagues founded Creative Commons, a nonprofit organization, in 2001. The organization followed the lead of Stallman and others in the Free Software Movement by issuing copyleft licenses, known as Creative Commons licenses, free of charge to anyone involved in creating cultural content. The licenses provide a number of options by which authors can mark their content and determine the freedoms they would like to extend to others. In place of "all rights reserved," the critical feature of copyrights, the Creative Commons licenses substitute "some rights reserved." Lessig explains:

> The freedoms could be to share the work, or to remix the work, or both. The restrictions could be to use the work only for noncommercial purposes, or only if the user shares alike (giving others the freedom inherited), or both. The creator can mix these freedoms and restrictions, resulting in six licenses, which come in three layers.[19]

Lessig gives his favorite example of how the Creative Commons license rolls out in practice.

> [It's] a song, "My Life," written by the artist Colin Mutchler. He uploaded the guitar track to a free site that allowed other people to download it under a Creative Commons license. A 17-year-old violinist named Cora Beth downloaded it, added a violin track on top, renamed the song "My Life Changed," and then re-uploaded the song to the site for other people to do with as they wanted. I've seen a whole bunch of remixes of the song. The critical point is that these creators were able to create, consistent with copyright law and without any lawyer standing between them.[20]

The Creative Commons license has gone viral. By 2008, there were 130 million works licensed under Creative Commons, including some big names in the recording business.[21] Flickr alone showcased 200 million Creative Commons licensed photos.[22] In 2012, just one year after YouTube launched its Creative Commons video library, 4 million licensed videos were listed on the site.[23] In 2009, Wikipedia relicensed all of its content under a Creative Commons license.[24]

Creative Commons has also established a science Commons. Researchers argue that copyright law and especially patents prohibit the timely sharing of information, slow down research, discourage collaboration among scientists, and hold back new innovations. At worst, intellectual property protection gives big players—Life Science companies, agribusiness, pharmaceutical companies, etc.—a means to thwart creativity and dampen competition. More and more scientists in universities and foundation-sponsored laboratories around the world are abandoning the idea of patenting genetic information in favor of uploading their research in open-source networks to be shared freely with colleagues in managed Commons.

The Creative Commons license has been implemented by the Harvard University Medical School in its Personal Genome Project.[25] This is a long-term cohort study that aims to sequence and publicize the genome and records of 100,000 volunteers in order to advance research in the field of customized personal medicine.[26] All the genome data covered by a Creative Commons license will be put in the public domain and be made available on the Internet to allow scientists open and free access for their laboratory research.[27]

Despite the success of the Creative Commons licensing, Lessig takes every opportunity to distance himself from what he calls "a growing copyright abolitionist movement."[28] He believes that copyright will remain a viable part of the coming era but will need to make room for open-source licensing in a world that will be lived partially in the market and partially on the Commons. I suspect he's right in the short run, but not in the long run.

Patents and copyrights thrive in an economy organized around scarcity but are useless in an economy organized around abundance. Of what relevance is intellectual-property protection in a world of near zero marginal cost, where more and more goods and services are nearly free?

The spectacular rise of open-source licensing is already posing a serious challenge to traditional copyright and patent protection as creative works are migrating from single authorship to multiple collaborative inputs over time. Concurrently, an increasing amount of Big Data is being shared by millions of individuals whose personal information is contributed to the mix. Just as information wants to be free, "Big Data wants to be distributed." What makes Big Data valuable is the information inputted from millions of individual contributors and sources that can be analyzed and used to find patterns, draw inferences, and solve problems. In a distributive, collaborative society, the millions of individuals whose data contributes to the collective wisdom are increasingly demanding that their knowledge be shared in open Commons for the benefit of all, rather than being siphoned off and enclosed in the form of intellectual property owned and controlled by a few.

A NEW COMMONS NARRATIVE

Open-source licenses, designed to encourage a democratization of culture, are all well and good. Attaching such legal instruments to a Commons approach to management is even better. The idea that much of the social life of our species is best optimized in the public domain makes "common" sense—after all, it is the arena in which we create social capital and trust. But can we lean on open-source licenses, Commons management, and a vague notion of the public domain to build out a new society? These are legal tools and management prescriptions but hardly qualify, in and of themselves, as a worldview. Missing from the script is an overarching narrative, a new story about the future of the human journey that can make sense of the reality unfolding.

The leaders of the IT, Internet, and Free Culture Movement became aware of the missing narrative element in the midst of their mounting successes with free software licenses and Creative Commons agreements. While they had momentum, their activism was more reactive than visionary. They found themselves putting out fires rather than claiming new ground. Being restrained by having to maneuver inside an older paradigm of centralized, proprietary relationships in capitalist markets made it difficult to break out and create something new from whole cloth.

Free-culture theoreticians began to wrestle with the larger question of finding a narrative to frame their intuitive but still inchoate vision. In 2003, James Boyle, a professor of law at Duke University and a founder of Creative Commons, published an essay entitled "The Second Enclosure Movement and the Construction of the Public Domain." The essay touched off a debate around finding that narrative.

Although I don't know Boyle personally, his essay refers to the work done by the Foundation on Economic Trends and other environmental and genetic activists to keep the genetic Commons open—referring to our claim that the human genome, and all other genomes, are the "common heritage" of evolution and therefore cannot be enclosed as private property.[29]

Boyle sensed that while the new field of "bioinformatics blurs the line between computer modeling and biological research," it might be possible that open-source genomics could liberate biological research from narrow corporate interests, making the stewardship of Earth's genetic resources the "common" responsibility of the human race.[30]

With this example in mind, Boyle stepped outside the day-to-day struggle between free-culture activists and traditional market defenders to muse on the prospect of an alternative future for the human race—one utterly different from the current course we find ourselves on. His thoughts were more contemplative than declarative—and put forth in the form of an observation. He wrote:

> At the very least, there is some possibility, even hope, that we could have a world in which much more of intellectual and inventive production is free. "'Free' as in 'free speech,'" Richard Stallman says, not "'free' as in 'free beer.'" But we could hope that much of it would be *both* free of centralized control *and* low cost or no cost. When the marginal cost of production is zero, the marginal cost of transmission and storage approaches zero, the process of creation is additive, and much of the labor doesn't charge—well, the world looks a little different. This is at least a *possible* future, or part of a possible future, and one that we should not foreclose without thinking twice.[31]

How do we get to that future? Certainly not by moving back to the vague legal concept of the public domain as justification for a new way to live in society. Boyle and others realized that they needed a general theory that could tie up the loose ideas and give them a framework for talking about the world they wanted to build.

It dawned on Boyle that the Environmental Movement, which had been paralleling the Free Culture Movement for two decades, had successfully developed a rigorous general theory that could be instructive for their own movement—maybe even bring the two movements together in a larger narrative.

The modern Environmental Movement has always been a dual phenomenon. Ecological science continues to hone in on the patterns and relationships that make up the complex dynamics of Earth's living systems, while activists use the knowledge gained to push for new ways of reorganizing human beings' relationship with nature. For example, early activists focused much of their effort on protecting individual species threatened with extinction. As ecologists learned more about the intricate relationships between organisms and their environments, they began to realize that if they were to save individual species they would have to focus on saving their habitats. This led to the further realization that threatened species were often in jeopardy because of the imposition of arbitrary political, commercial, and residential boundaries that severed ecosystems and undermined complex ecological dynamics, resulting in a diminishing of the natural flora and fauna. In the 1990s, activists seized on the data and began pushing for transborder peace parks, a new development concept that is being implemented around the world. The mission is to reconnect natural ecosystems that were formerly severed by national boundaries in order to restore not only migratory patterns but also the many other complex biological relationships that exist in various ecosystems.

The transborder parks are a departure from the existing narrative that emphasizes enclosure, privatization, and commercial development of the environment in favor of restoring and managing biodiversity in regional ecosystem Commons, making them whole again. The very idea that nature's boundaries supersede political and commercial boundaries in importance has the effect of redirecting the social narrative away from individual self-interests, commercial pursuits, and geopolitical considerations to the general well-being of nature.

Transborder parks represent the very tentative beginnings of a great reversal. After a half millennium characterized by the increasing enclosure of Earth's environmental Commons, transborder parks re-open the Commons, even if only in a very limited way.

What makes ecology so radical as a discipline is its emphasis on Earth as a complex system of interrelationships that function symbiotically and synergistically to maintain the functioning of the whole. Where Darwin concentrated more on the individual organism and species, and relegated the environment to a backdrop of resources, ecology views the environment as all the relationships that make it up.

Ecology grew out of the study of local habitats and ecosystems. In the early twentieth century, Russian scientist Vladimir Vernadsky expanded the concept of ecology to include the ecological workings of the planet as a whole. Vernadsky parted ways with the conventional scientific thinking of the day, which held that Earth's geological processes evolved independently of biological processes, providing the environment in which life evolved. He published a seminal book in 1926, positing the radical theory that geological and biological processes evolved in a symbiotic relationship. Vernadsky proposed that the cycling of inert chemicals on Earth is affected by the quality and quantity of living matter. That living matter, in turn, is affected by the quality and quantity of inert chemicals cycling Earth. He called his new theory the Biosphere.[32] His ideas about the way Earth evolves changed the very framework by which scientists understand and study the workings of the planet.

The biosphere is described as an

integrated living and life-supporting system comprising the peripheral envelope of the planet Earth together with its surrounding atmosphere so far down and up as any form of life exists naturally.[33]

The biosphere sheath extends only about 40 miles up from the ocean floor, inhabited by the most primitive life forms, to the stratosphere. Within this narrow realm, Earth's biological and geochemical processes are continually interacting in a complex choreography that determines the evolutionary path of life on the planet.

Biosphere science gained greater prominence in the 1970s with the growing public awareness of global pollution and the destabilization of Earth's ecosystems. The publication of the Gaia hypothesis by the British scientist James Lovelock and the American biologist Lynn

Margulis sparked a new wave of interest within a scientific community that was increasingly concerned with the impact industrial pollution was having on the biosphere.

Lovelock and Margulis argued that Earth operates much like a self-regulating living organism in which geochemical and biological processes interact and check each other to ensure a relatively steady balance in Earth's temperature, making possible a planet hospitable to the continuation of life. The two scientists cite the example of the regulation of oxygen and methane. Oxygen levels on Earth have to stay within a narrow range. Too much oxygen risks global conflagration, too little risks choking off the life force. Lovelock and Margulis theorized that when oxygen climbs above an acceptable level, some kind of warning signal triggers microscopic bacteria to release more methane into the atmosphere to reduce the oxygen content until a steady state is reached.[34]

The Gaia hypothesis has been taken up by scientists across a wide range of disciplines, including geochemistry, atmospheric science, and biology. The study of the complex relationships and symbiotic feedback loops between geochemical and living processes that maintain Earth's climate in a steady state, allowing life to flourish, has led to a consensus of sorts. The new, more holistic approach to ecology views the adaptation and evolution of individual species as part of a larger, more integrative process—the adaptation and evolution of the planet as a whole.

If Earth functions more like a self-regulating organism, then human activity that undermines the biochemical balance of the planet can lead to the catastrophic destabilization of the entire system. The spewing of massive amounts of carbon dioxide, methane, and nitrous oxide into the atmosphere over the course of the First and Second Industrial Revolutions has done just that. The rising temperature from industrial emissions of global warming gases has now dramatically altered Earth's hydrological cycle, throwing ecosystems into rapid decline and ushering in the sixth extinction event in the past 450 million years, with dire consequences for both human civilization and the future health of the planet.

Humanity is quickly becoming aware that the biosphere is the indivisible overarching community to which we all belong and whose well-being is indispensable to assuring our own well-being as well as our survival. This dawning awareness comes with a new sense of responsibility—living our individual and collective lives in our homes, businesses, and communities in ways that advance the health of the larger biosphere.

James Boyle and his colleagues pinned their intellectual hopes on using the environmental perspective as an analogy from which to draw lessons for creating what they call cultural environmentalism— a systems theory of the indivisibility of the public domain that might unite all the disparate interests and initiatives in an overarching general theory. They're still looking because what they regarded as an analogy is, in fact, a common frame that unites our species. The same general theory that governs the biosphere dictates the general welfare of society.

While the enclosure, privatization, and commercial exploitation of Earth's ecosystems in the capitalist era has resulted in a dramatic rise in the standard of life of a significant minority of the human race, it has been at the expense of the biosphere itself. When Boyle, Lessig, Stallman, Benkler, and others lament the consequences of enclosing the various Commons in the form of private property that is exchanged in the market, the damage inflicted penetrates more deeply than just the question of freedom to communicate and create. The enclosures of the land and ocean Commons, the fresh water Commons, the atmosphere Commons, the electromagnetic spectrum Commons, the knowledge Commons, and the genetic Commons has severed the complex internal dynamics of Earth's biosphere, jeopardizing every human being's welfare and the well-being of all the other organisms that inhabit the planet. If we are looking for a general theory that brings everyone's interests together, restoring the health of the biosphere community seems the obvious choice.

The real historical significance of the Free Culture Movement and Environmental Movement is that they are both standing up to the forces of enclosure. By reopening the various Commons, humanity begins to think and act as part of a whole. We come to realize that the ultimate creative power is reconnecting with one another and embedding ourselves in ever-larger systems of relationships that ripple out to encompass the entire set of relationships that make up the biosphere Commons.

If by advancing culture we mean the search for meaning, it is likely to be found in exploring our relationship to the larger scheme of things, of which we are irrevocably intertwined—our common biosphere and what lies beyond. "Free speech" is not "free beer," but what is its purpose if not to join together and collaboratively reimagine the nature of the human journey in a way that celebrates life on Earth? The opposite of enclosure is not merely openness, but transcendence.

The distributed, collaborative, laterally scaled nature of Internet communications is indeed both the medium and the domain. The domain, in turn, is the social Commons. It is the meeting place where our species comes together and creates the necessary social capital to cohere as a whole and hopefully to expand our empathic horizon to include the many other communities we live with, but often fail to recognize, that make up the biosphere Commons.

The social Commons is merely our species' habitat and a subregion of the biosphere, and, it turns out, the same laws of energy that determine the optimum well-being of nature's mature ecosystems operate in the public domain. In a climax ecosystem like the Amazon, the thermodynamic efficiency is optimized. The consumption of matter does not significantly exceed the ecosystem's ability to absorb and recycle the waste and replenish the stock. In a climax ecosystem, the symbiotic and synergistic relationships minimize energy loss and optimize resource use, providing abundance for each species' needs. Similarly, in the economy, the optimal efficient state is reached when marginal costs approach zero. That is the point at which the production and distribution of each additional unit and the recycling of waste requires the least expenditure of energy in the form of time, labor, capital, and power generation, optimizing the availability of resources.

Even the legal tools used to open up both the cultural Commons and the environmental Commons are uncannily similar. Conservation easements, for example, operate by a set of legal conventions that mimic Creative Commons licenses in the cultural sphere. My wife and I own land near the Blue Ridge Mountains of Virginia. The land is being converted into a wildlife refuge for the black bear, white-tailed deer, red foxes, wild turkeys, raccoons, and other species native to the region. The land is in a conservation easement. That means that our title of ownership comes with restrictions governing how it can be used. While my wife and I own the land, we cannot subdivide it for sale, or build certain kinds of structures on it.

Conservation easements might require that the land be maintained in a pristine state as a wildlife habitat or that it be preserved as open space for scenic and aesthetic reasons. Like Creative Commons licenses, the purpose of the easement is to promote the Commons by separating the right to own the land from the right to enjoy exclusive use of it.

Conservation easements modify enclosures by transforming some of the uses to the public domain. The legal instrument is not unlike open-source creative licenses that perform much the same function. In both instances, the thrust is reversing enclosures of Earth's various Commons—the central feature of the capitalist era—and reopening and restoring the Commons to allow the biosphere to reheal and flourish.

The point is, the Commons doesn't stop at the public square, but extends ever outward to the very edge of Earth's biosphere. We human beings are members of an extended evolutionary family of species that fills the planet. The ecological sciences are teaching us that the well-being of the entire biological family depends on the well-being of each of its members. The symbiotic relationships, synergies, and feedbacks create a form of mass collaboration that keeps the extended family vibrant and the biosphere household viable.

Let me share a personal anecdote relating to the notion of the Commons. When I first began writing about the evolution, devolution, and reconstruction of the Commons nearly 25 years ago, my near obsession, I suspect, got the better of me. I was seeing enclosures everywhere I turned, and being a social activist, I couldn't help thinking about new Commons possibilities every time an opportunity lent itself to push forward what we used to call "participatory democracy"— this was before peer-to-peer engagement nudged the term to the side. My intellectual musings became the butt of jokes among my friends and colleagues, not to mention my wife. If I mentioned a new book I was writing or initiative my office was undertaking, I would be mercilessly ribbed with the refrain "not the Commons again . . . please say it ain't so."

Around the mid-1990s, I was beginning to hear of others who suffered from this rare "Commons affliction." The affliction began to spread. I was hearing the words *enclosure* and *commons* everywhere I turned. The terms were floating across the social ether and spreading like an epidemic across the public square and even more quickly in virtual space. The breeding ground was globalization, a grossly misnamed metaphor that disingenuously cloaked government deregulation and the privatization of public goods and services in the wrap of a new global "interconnectivity."

The contradiction of privatizing the human and natural resources of the planet in the hands of several hundred commercial enterprises and labeling it *globalization* was not lost on a generation of scholars and activists whose ideas of globalization went in the opposite direction—toward greater participation by the marginalized and disenfranchised throngs of humanity in the sharing of Earth's largesse.

GLOBALIZATION VERSUS REOPENING THE GLOBAL COMMONS

In 1999, tens of thousands of activists representing a panoply of nongovernmental organizations (NGOs) and interests, including labor unions, feminists, environmentalists, animal rights activists, farm organizations, fair-trade activists, academics, and religious groups, took to the streets of Seattle in a mass protest at the World Trade Organization (WTO) conference being held there. Their objective was to reclaim the public Commons. Protestors filled the downtown streets around the Washington State Convention and Trade Center, blocking intersections and preventing WTO delegates from attending the scheduled meetings. The protestors were joined by the Seattle City Council, which passed by unanimous vote a resolution declaring the city a Multilateral Agreement on Investment (MAI) free zone. The international press joined in, not a few siding with the protestors. In the days leading up to the global convention, the London *Independent* wrote a scathing editorial attacking the WTO itself:

> The way [the WTO] has used [its] powers is leading to a growing
> suspicion that its initials should really stand for World Take Over.
> In a series of rulings it has struck down measures to help the world's
> poor, protect the environment, and safeguard health in the interest
> of private—usually American—companies.[35]

The protests led to over 600 arrests and marked a turning point in the headlong rush to globalization. Now, there was an identifiable public opposition.[36]

The street demonstrations were notable in another respect. Many of the activists were computer hackers who helped organize the logistics of the demonstrations. This was one of the first protests to use e-mail, chat rooms, live Internet broadcasts, virtual sit-ins, and cell phones to coordinate the mobilization leading up to the event. The synchronization of logistics using IT and Internet media during the street demonstrations was a preview of what would unfold on the streets of Cairo and other Middle Eastern hot spots 12 years later in the Arab Spring.

The hackers had good reason to join with the environmentalists, trade unionists, and fair-trade activists. A year earlier, the U.S. Congress passed the Sonny Bono Copyright Term Extension Act, signed into law by President Bill Clinton.[37] The act extended copyright protection to an author's work for 70 years after his or her death. That same year, the U.S. Senate ratified and Clinton signed the Digital Millennium Copyright Act (DMCA), implementing two treaties of the World Intellectual Property Organization (WIPO).[38] The treaties and national law made it illegal to use technologies and other means to circumvent practices that secure copyright protection. These practices are referred to as digital rights management (DRM).

The Free Culture Movement arose out of these two landmark pieces of legislation, whose sole purpose was to prevent the free distribution of copyrighted material over the Internet. In 1999 Lessig challenged the Sonny Bono Act, taking the case all the way to the Supreme Court.

The protestors who came together in Seattle were clear about what they opposed—the privatization of human knowledge and Earth's resources. The anti globalization banner cry was a repudiation of an existing paradigm. But the question it raised internally and to the general public was, what are they for? If not for globalization via privatization, what? It was around this time that the idea of reversing enclosures and reinstating the Commons across every facet of human life ascended from an academic whisper to a public roar. There were calls for opening up the public square Commons, the land Commons, the knowledge Commons, the virtual Commons, the energy Commons, the electromagnetic spectrum Commons, the Communications Commons, the ocean Commons, the fresh water Commons, the atmosphere Commons, the nonprofit Commons, and the biosphere Commons. Virtually every Commons that had been enclosed, privatized, and commodified in the market during the 200-year reign of capitalism suddenly came under scrutiny and review. NGOs were formed and initiatives were launched to champion the reopening of the many Commons that embed the human race in the biosphere. Globalization had met its nemesis in the form of a diverse movement committed to reversing the great enclosures and reestablishing the global Commons.

Lord Harold Samuel, a British real estate magnate, once remarked that "there are three things that matter in property: location, location, location." This now well-worn cliché is particularly apt when it comes to understanding the wave of spontaneous public demonstrations over the past 14 years that have snaked their way around the world since activists first took to the streets in Seattle. Mass demonstrations have erupted—seemingly out of nowhere—toppling governments and triggering social upheavals on every continent. Although the protests speak to a range of social issues, they share a common profile. The demonstrations are more like swarms than orchestrated protests, are largely leaderless, and are informal and networked in nature. In every case, the participants flood into the central squares of the world's great cities, where they set up camp, confront the powers that be, and create an alternative community designed to celebrate the social Commons.

Jay Walljasper, an author and early leader in the global movement to reclaim the public Commons, observed that while the media was devoting a great deal of attention to young people's use of Facebook, Twitter, and other social media on the virtual Commons to organize the protests across the Middle East in 2011, "the importance of a much older form of commons in these revolts has earned scant attention—the public spaces where citizens rally to voice their discontent, show their power and ultimately articulate a new vision for their homelands."[39] Walljasper makes the important point "that the exercise of democracy depends on having a literal commons where people can gather as citizens—a square, main street, park, or other public space that is open to all."[40]

The activists support many agendas but are united around a shared symbolism—their determination to reclaim the public square and, by so doing, reopen the many other Commons that have been expropriated, commodified, politicized, and enclosed by special interests and a privileged minority. The alienated youth at Tahrir Square in the Arab Spring, the Occupiers on Wall Street, the demonstrators at Gezi Park in Istanbul, and the angry underclass on the streets of São Paulo are on the front line of an unfolding cultural phenomenon whose underlying theme centers around countering enclosures in all their various forms and establishing a transparent, nonhierarchical, and collaborative culture. These are the new commoners.

The late Jonathan Rowe, one of the visionaries of the new networked Commons, best explained the idea of what a Commons is all about. He wrote:

> To say "the commons" is to evoke a puzzled pause. . . . Yet the commons is more basic than both government and market. It is the vast realm that is the shared heritage of all of us that we typically use without toll or price. The atmosphere and oceans, languages and cultures, the stores of human knowledge and wisdom, the informal support systems of community, the peace and quiet that we crave, the genetic building blocks of life—these are all aspects of the commons.[41]

I am particularly fond of a quip by a naturalist, Mike Bergan, about the nature of a Commons that goes to the heart of the current struggle between the capitalists and the collaboratists. He warned,

> Don't trust anyone who wants to take something that we all share and profit from equally and give it to someone else to profit from exclusively.[42]

Charlotte Hess, a protégé of the late Elinor Ostrom and associate dean at the Bird Library at Syracuse University, has cataloged the many branches of the Commons tree. She is quick to differentiate the "new Commons" from the old, noting the similarities, while highlighting the differences.

The Commons, old and new, define the way human beings manage Earth's bounty. To say something is a Commons is to mean that
it is held in common and collectively managed. The term *Commons*
describes a form of governance. Hess reminds us that something can't
become a Commons until the technological means are available to
manage it. Forager/hunters enjoyed the bounty of nature, but did not
manage it. The Commons begins with agriculture and pastoralism.
The oceans didn't become a Commons until the invention of vessels
to travel on them.

The modern era brought with it a spate of new technologies that
allowed for the management of new parts of Earth's biosphere that
were previously not subject to supervision. The printed word, the discovery of electricity (and later the electromagnetic spectrum), flight
in the atmosphere, and the discovery of the gene and nanotechnology
all opened up previously unknown or unexplored realms for management. These new realms can be managed by government, by the private marketplace, or by way of a Commons.

As described in chapter 3, the communication/energy/transporta-
tion matrices of the First and Second Industrial Revolutions required
huge influxes of financial capital and relied on vertically integrated
enterprises and centralized command and control mechanisms to
achieve economies of scale, all of which put the economy in the lap of
capitalism, aided by government. The communication/energy matrix
of the Third Industrial Revolution—the Internet of Things—is facili-
tated more by social capital than by market capital, scales laterally,
and is organized in a distributed and collaborative fashion, making
Commons management with government engagement the better governing model.

Yochai Benkler says that while an inordinate amount of attention
is being placed on free software,

> it is in fact only one example of a much broader social-economic phe-
> nomenon. I suggest that we are seeing the broad and deep emergence
> of a new, third mode of production in the digitally networked en-
> vironment. I call this mode "Commons-based peer-production," to
> distinguish it from the property- and contract-based modes of firms
> and markets. Its central characteristic is that groups of individuals

successfully collaborate on large-scale projects following a diverse
cluster of motivational drives and social signals, rather than either
market prices or managerial commands.[43]

Expectations notwithstanding, it would be a mistake to believe
that a Commons model will invariably govern the next chapter in the
human journey. While the collaboratists are ascendant, the capitalists are split. The global energy companies, the telecommunications
giants, and the entertainment industry—with a few notable exceptions—are entrenched in the Second Industrial Revolution and have
the gravitas of the existing paradigm and political narrative to back
them up. However, the electricity transmission companies, the construction industry, the IT, electronics, Internet, and transport sectors
are all quickly creating new products and services and changing their
business models to gain market share in the emerging Third Industrial
Revolution hybrid of market and Commons arrangements, aided in
various ways by government.

In my social enterprise, the TIR Consulting Group, we experience this new hybrid governing reality every day in our development of
Third Industrial Revolution Master Plans for cities, regions, and countries. The new initiatives we are engaged in to help communities build
out IoT infrastructure are collaborative arrangements in which markets
and Commons operate on parallel tracks, provision each other, or collaborate in joint management structures, generally with government
involved in establishing regulatory standards, codes, and financial incentives. Peter Barnes, in his book *Capitalism 3.0: A Guide to Reclaiming the Commons*, envisions a future that mirrors our day-to-day
work on the ground in countries around the world. He explains that

> the key difference between versions 2.0 and 3.0 is the inclusion in
> the latter of a set of institutions I call the *Commons sector*. Instead
> of having only one engine—that is, the corporate-dominated pri-
> vate sector—our improved economic system would run on two: one
> geared to managing private profit, the other to preserving and en-
> hancing common wealth.[44]

I can also tell you with near certainty that in the real world,
the struggle to define the economic future pivots on the kind of

infrastructure that will be put in place to serve the coming era. While both the capitalist market and the Collaborative Commons will co-exist—sometimes synergistically, and at other times competitively or even adversarily—which of the two management models ultimately prevails as the dominant form and which as the niche player will depend largely on the infrastructure society erects.

CHAPTER TWELVE

THE STRUGGLE TO DEFINE AND CONTROL THE INTELLIGENT INFRASTRUCTURE

Yochai Benkler is one of the most ardent and articulate advocates of the Commons approach. He also realizes that a Communications Commons will remain elusive if tied to a proprietary infrastructure. In the last few pages of his eloquent book *The Wealth of Networks*, Benkler argues that if future generations are to enjoy the immense benefits that come with a networked information economy, it will be necessary to create a common infrastructure. He writes:

> To flourish, a networked information economy rich in social production practices requires a core common infrastructure, a set of resources necessary for information production and exchange that are open for all to use. This requires physical, logical, and content resources from which to make new statements, encode them for communication, and then render and receive them.[1]

No disagreement here. But a key element is missing from Benkler's analysis. Brett M. Frischmann, whose own book *Infrastructure: The Social Value of Shared Resources* is equally meaty and dovetails with

Benkler's analysis and prescriptions, hits on the lapse. He says that "Benkler does not fully examine what constitutes core common infrastructure or the challenges to ensuring sustainable public access to common infrastructure."[2] Frischmann goes on to explain that

> core common infrastructure refers to those foundational infrastructural resources that should be available to all on a nondiscriminatory basis. . . . The first difficulty is in identifying which resources are truly foundational and explaining why this critical subset of infrastructure resources should be managed on a nondiscriminatory basis . . . once that obstacle is surmounted . . . by what institutional means should commons management be achieved?[3]

Frischmann notes that Benkler has championed open wireless networks and some forms of public provisioning of a communications infrastructure, but wonders whether that's enough. To Benkler's credit—and that of Eli Noam, David Bollier, Kevin Werbach, and others who have pushed for open wireless networks—the recent FCC proposal to create an unlicensed spectrum for a free nationwide Wi-Fi communications network is to no small extent a testimonial to their tireless determination and persuasive arguments in favor of an open Communications Commons.

If there is a failure of imagination here, it lies in a misunderstanding of the critical role energy plays in foundational infrastructure. As I mentioned at the very beginning of this book, the great economic revolutions in history are infrastructure revolutions, and what makes the great infrastructure revolutions transformational is the convergence of new communications media with new energy regimes. Every energy revolution in history has been accompanied by its own unique communications revolution. Energy revolutions change the temporal and spatial reach of society and make possible more complex living arrangements, all of which require new communication media to manage and coordinate the new opportunities. Try to imagine organizing the production and distribution complexities of a steam-powered urban industrial revolution without cheap and quick steam-powered printing and the telegraph, or organizing the managerial complexities of an oil, auto, and suburban mass-consumer culture without centralized electricity and especially telephone communication, radio, and television.

Or, to bring it up to the moment, consider this. Benkler and others argue that the new Internet communications favors a networked Commons form of management because the nature of the media is distributed and collaborative and makes possible peer-to-peer production and the lateral scaling of economic activity. Let's assume for the sake of argument that the United States remains yoked to a vertically integrated and highly centralized fossil fuel energy regime that requires ever greater infusions of finance capital to operate. As long as fossil fuel energies underlie every aspect of the global economy, every other commercial enterprise that relies on these fuels for its materials, power generation, and transportation and logistics will be forced by necessity to continue using a vertically integrated business model and centralized management to achieve its own economies of scale and stay alive.

Can the advocates of a networked infrastructure Commons imagine how a distributed, collaborative, peer-to-peer, laterally scaled communications revolution might prosper in a highly capitalized and centralized fossil fuel-based energy regime? To put it another way, is it likely that a highly capitalized and centralized fossil fuel energy regime would welcome a communications revolution that offers the potential of open-source, peer-to-peer management of renewable energies, 3D printing, and the like with the aim of pushing ever closer to a near zero marginal cost society and the diminution of the capitalist system?

On the other hand, a distributed, collaborative, peer-to-peer, laterally scaled communications medium is ideally suited to manage renewable energies that are distributed in nature, are best organized collaboratively, favor peer-to-peer production, and scale laterally across society. Together, Internet communication and renewable energies form the inseparable building blocks for a foundational infrastructure whose operating logic is best served by Commons management. As outlined in chapter 1, that intelligent infrastructure is comprised of three interlocking Internets: a Communications Internet, an Energy Internet, and a Transportation Internet. When linked together in a single interactive system—the Internet of Things—these three Internets provide a stream of Big Data on the comings and goings of society that can be accessed and shared collaboratively on an open global Commons by the whole of humanity in the pursuit of "extreme productivity" and a zero marginal cost society.

The struggle over governance of the three interlocking Internets that make up the Internet of Things is being aggressively waged among governments, capitalist enterprises, and champions of the nascent social economy on the Commons, each with ambitions to define the coming era.

THE COMMUNICATIONS COMMONS

Let's start with the Communications Internet of the new Commons infrastructure. The Internet is a hybrid infrastructure made up of three primary stakeholders—the government, the private sector, and civil society. Up until now, the Internet has been managed as a global Commons with all three of the primary stakeholders playing a collaborative role in its governance.

Technological governance of the Internet, which includes establishing standards and management protocols, has been handed off to nonprofit organizations, including the Internet Engineering Task Force, the World Wide Web Consortium, and the Internet Corporation for Assigned Names and Numbers (ICANN). Although ICANN was initially a creature of the U.S. government and nominally under its jurisdiction, in 2009 the United States gave up its oversight function. ICANN is currently governed by an international board made up of academics, businesses, and civil society interests.[4] All the above organizations are, at least in theory, open for anyone to take part in, yet because of their highly technical nature, it is generally people with technical expertise who make decisions about management operations by consensus.

Still, governance of the Internet is a bit more thorny and less clear-cut than one might suspect. In 2003, representatives of the three primary stakeholder groups convened a World Summit on the Information Society in Geneva to discuss Internet governance, followed by a second meeting in June 2005 in Tunis. A working group on Internet governance was established by the U.N. secretary general to "investigate and make proposals for action, as appropriate, on the governance of the Internet."[5]

The working group came up with an agreed-upon governing framework that was subsequently adopted by 174 member countries. It states,

> Internet governance is the development and application by govern-
> ments, the private sector and civil society, in their respective roles,
> of shared principles, norms, rules, decision-making procedures, and
> programs that shape the evolution of the Internet.[6]

This three-stakeholder model is deeply significant. In the past, the
parties at the table in global-governance issues were limited to government and the private sector—with civil society given, at best, observer
status and unofficial representation. With the Internet, however, there
was an understanding that excluding civil society would have been
indefensible since many of the players and participants who engage in
peer-to-peer production on the new medium are drawn from the third
sector.

Having agreed on tripartite governance, a multi stakeholder body
was set up under a United Nations umbrella group, called the Internet Governance Forum (IGF), to deliberate on governance policies.
The IGF meets regularly to ensure that policy deliberations reflect the
distributed, collaborative, laterally scaled nature of the Internet. Regional and national IGF bodies have been created in countries all over
the world, providing a networked approach, rather than a top-down
governing model, for collective self-management of this sprawling new
communications medium.[7]

The United Nations, however—which is, after all, a body representing the governments of the world—slipped an article into the formal document that was agreed to at the Tunis meeting of the World
Summit on the Information Society that gave the Secretary General
the authority to begin a process of "enhanced cooperation" that would

> enable governments, on an equal footing, to carry out their roles
> and responsibilities, in international public policy issues pertaining
> to the Internet, but not in the day-to-day technical and operational
> matters, that do not impact on international public policy issues.[8]

National governments, concerned over a spate of Internet-related
policy issues that affect their general welfare and sovereign interests,
including taxing commercial activity in virtual space, protecting intellectual property, maintaining security against cyberattacks, and sti-
fling political dissent, are enacting national legislation, some of which

is threatening an essential feature of the medium—its open, universal, and transparent nature. Not surprisingly, the nations pushing for new forms of government control over the Internet include Russia, Iran, China, South Africa, and Saudi Arabia, as well as India and Brazil.

In 2011, Russia, China, Uzbekistan, and Tajikistan submitted a proposal to the U.N. General Assembly calling for an international code of conduct for the information society. The proposal, which has no provisions for a multistakeholders approach, would have the effect of increasing government control of the Internet.[9] The preamble to the proposal states unequivocally that the "policy authority for Internet-related public issues is the sovereign right of States."[10]

The private sector is also beginning to stray from the three-party stakeholder alliance, seeking increased income and profits by way of price discrimination—a move that threatens to undermine one of the guiding principles of the Internet: network neutrality, a principle that assures a nondiscriminatory, open, universal Communications Commons in which every participant enjoys equal access and inclusion.

The concept of network neutrality grew out of the end-to-end design structure of the Internet, which favors the users rather than the network providers. While users pay for Internet connection, and the price they pay can depend on the speed or quality provided by their Internet service provider, once they're connected, their transmitted packets are treated the same way as everyone else's by the network providers.

Network providers—the major telecom and cable companies—would now like to change the rules of the game and secure control of information exchanged over the Internet for commercial gain. That control would allow them to charge different prices for access to specific information or to prioritize transmissions, putting time-sensitive packets at the front of the line for a higher price, or charge application fees, or block specific applications from their networks in favor of others, again based on exacting discriminatory payments.

Proponents of network neutrality argue that the network should remain "stupid," thereby allowing millions of end users to collaborate and innovate by developing their own applications. It's this kind of "distributed intelligence" that makes the Internet such a unique communications medium. If network providers were to gain centralized control over access to content and how it is delivered, it would disempower end users and undermine the creativity that comes with distributed collaboration and laterally scaled intelligence.

Network providers feel differently, of course. In the United States, AT&T, Verizon, and cable TV companies argue that they are being unfairly limited in their pursuit of new profit-generating schemes. Ed Whitacre, former CEO of AT&T, vented his frustration in an interview with *BusinessWeek*:

> Now what they would like to do is use my pipes [for] free, but I ain't going to let them do that because we have spent this capital and we have to have a return on it.[11]

In fact, AT&T is paid for the transmission of information packets by either Internet service providers who are using their lines or by their own customers. Still, AT&T and other network providers would like to use various discriminatory mechanisms to squeeze additional money out of the process.

Deutsche Telekom, the giant German communications company that controls 60 percent of the country's Internet connections, created an uproar in May 2013 when it announced that it would impose download limits on all the customers that use its home Internet service. The company said it was imposing the restriction because of escalating data traffic, which is expected to quadruple by 2016. More controversial still, the company said it would sell upgrades to those customers that wanted to increase their limits. Even more troubling, it announced it would be accepting the traffic from its own Internet-television service but not from its competitors, which include Google, YouTube, and Apple.[12]

Deutsche Telekom's flagrant attempt to undermine network neutrality drew an immediate response from German regulatory bodies. The Bundesnetzagentur—the country's telecom regulator—said it is reviewing the Deutsche Telekom proposal to see if it is in violation of network-neutrality protocols that prohibit service providers from discriminating against classes of customers by charging different rates.[13]

The struggle over network neutrality is, at its core, a battle of paradigms. The Second Industrial Revolution telecom giants are anxious to gain control of the new communications medium and force on it a centralized command and control that will allow them to enclose the content and the traffic, boost their margins, and secure a monopoly by dint of their ownership of the "pipes." End users are equally determined to keep the Internet an open Commons and find new apps that will advance network collaboration and a push to near zero marginal costs and near free services.

Governments seem to be caught in the middle attempting to serve two masters, one dedicated to a capitalist model and the other to a Commons model. While the FCC had previously championed network neutrality, in 2010 the agency published an open Internet order laying out three cardinal rules to ensure an open and free Internet that seemed to alter its long-standing, ironclad commitment to do just that. The first two rules called for transparency in management practices and forbade the blocking of applications and services. The third rule, however, gave network providers a ray of hope that they might re-seize the initiative and bring the Internet into their web of enclosure. The rule states that "fixed broadband providers may not unreasonably discriminate in transmitting lawful network traffic."[14]

The third principle raised more than a few eyebrows. Some see the rule as a "coming to their senses" and others as a "capitulation." Brett Frischmann's wry comment that "what is (un)reasonable remains to be seen" seems to capture everyone's second-guessing of what the FCC really intended.[15]

And it's not just the big bad telecoms and cable guys that are muscling in from the outside, attempting to enclose the Internet. It's coming from the inside as well. Some of the best-known social media sites on the Web are revving up to find new ways to enclose, commercialize, and monopolize the new communications medium. And their bite is potentially far bigger than the companies managing the pipes.

In a November 2010 article in *Scientific American*, Tim Berners-Lee, inventor of the World Wide Web, issued a damning missive on the twentieth anniversary of the day the Web first went live. He was concerned about what was happening to the Internet.

Berners-Lee's invention was simple in design and acute in impact. The Web allows anyone, anytime, anywhere to share information with anyone else without having to ask for permission or pay a royalty fee. The Web is designed to be open, universally accessible, and distributed.

Unfortunately, some of the biggest applications on the Web, like Google, Facebook, and Twitter, are cashing in on the very rules of engagement that made them so successful and selling the masses of transmitted Big Data that comes their way to commercial bidders and businesses that use it for targeted advertising and marketing campaigns, research efforts, the development of new goods and services, and a host of other commercial propositions. They are, in effect, exploiting the Commons for commercial ends. In his article, Berners-Lee warns that "large social networking sites are walling off information posted by their users from the rest of the Web" and creating enclosed commercial spaces.[16]

While the Internet is a commons, the applications on the Web are a hybrid of nonprofit organizations, generally operated as Commons, and commercial enterprises with an eye to the market. Wikipedia and Linux line up in the first category and Google and Facebook in the second category.

Although users of Web applications on the Internet are aware that sites like Amazon are purely commercial, they are less likely to feel so about sites like Google and Facebook, because the apps provide them with opportunities to link up to a range of free services, from the world's premiere search engine to inclusion in the largest family album on Earth. The smattering of ads at the margins of the screens are a small inconvenience to bear for connectivity. Behind the scenes however, Google, Facebook, Twitter, and scores of other social networking sites are sequestering Big Data coming into their system, either to provide value-added services on their sites or to sell the data to third parties.

Berners-Lee explains that the key to capturing your data for their exclusive use is understanding what happens to the user's universal resource locator (URL) when he or she enters a social media site. Each user's URL allows the user to follow any link on the Web, becoming part of the flow in an interconnected Commons information space. But when someone connects to commercially driven social media sites, unbeknownst to them, at least until recently, their vital information is immediately captured, siloed, enclosed, and commodified.[17]

Berners-Lee describes how a user's data is enclosed:

> Facebook, LinkedIn, Friendster and others typically provide value
> by capturing information as you enter it: your birthday, your e-mail
> address, your likes, and links indicating who is friends with whom

and who is in which photograph. The sites assemble these bits of data into brilliant databases and reuse the information to provide value-added services—but only within their sites. Once you enter your data into one of these services, you cannot easily use them on another site. Each site is a silo, walled off from the others. Yes, your site's pages are on the Web, but your data are not. You can access a Web page about a list of people you have created in one site, but you cannot send that list, or items from it, to another site. The isolation occurs because each piece of information does not have a URL. Connections among data exist only within a site. So the more you enter, the more you become locked in. Your social-networking sites become a central platform—a closed silo of content, and one that does not give you full control over your information in it.[18]

Should we worry about social media sites sharing everything they know about us with third-party commercial interests? Of course, no one wants to be pestered by targeted advertising. More sinister, however, is the prospect of health insurance companies learning whether you had been Googling research on specific illnesses or prospective employers prying into your personal social history by analyzing your data trail on the Web to spot potential quirks, idiosyncrasies, or even possible antisocial behavior.

Of course, not all social media sites are commercial. Many, like Wikipedia, are nonprofit and remain true to a purely Commons governance. For social media sites operated by commercial firms, however, the business model Berners-Lee describes is the standard operating procedure. He continues: "The more this kind of architecture gains widespread use, the more the Web becomes fragmented, and the less we enjoy a single, universal information space."[19]

Berners-Lee is hinting at a darker force at work. Is it possible that the very operational features of the Internet itself—its distributed, collaborative, peer-to-peer, laterally scaled architecture—are providing a treasure trove of valuable personal data that is being mined, rebundled, and sold to profit-making firms for targeted commercial leveraging? Worse, is this newest form of commercial exploitation creating corporate monopolies in virtual space that are every bit as centralizing and proprietary as the Second Industrial Revolution companies they are dislodging from power?

By 2012, Google was fielding "3 billion queries every day from users in 180 or more countries."[20] In 2010, Google enjoyed a market share of 65.8 percent among search engines in the United States, 97.09 percent in Germany, 92.77 percent in the United Kingdom, 95.59 percent in France, and 95.55 percent in Australia.[21] The company's revenue topped $50 billion in 2012.[22]

Facebook has gobbled up 72.4 percent of the global market share of social networks, and as of March 2013, boasted over 1.1 billion active users—that's about one out of every seven human beings living on Earth.[23] When it comes to measuring how many minutes per month visitors spend on the most popular social media sites, Facebook breaks away from the pack. Its visitors spend an average of 405 minutes a month on the site: that's the number of minutes of the next six most popular sites combined—Tumblr (89), Pinterest (89), Twitter (21), LinkedIn (21), Myspace (8), and Google+ (3).[24] Facebook's revenue in 2012 was $5 billion.[25]

In 2012 Twitter had 500 million registered users, of which 200 million are active tweeters.[26] The rest prefer to be listeners. The company is expected to make more than $1 billion in revenue in 2014.[27]

The overtly commercial sites, like Amazon and eBay, that include Collaborative Commons features, are also quickly becoming online monopolies. According to a study conducted by Forrester Research, one out of every three online users starts their product searches on Amazon.com, "compared to 13 percent who started their search from a traditional search site."[28] Amazon has "over 152 million active Amazon customer accounts," "over 2 million active seller accounts," and a worldwide logistical network that serves 178 countries.[29] By 2008, eBay had grabbed 99 percent of the market for online auctions in the United States, with a similar track record in most other industrialized countries.[30] EBay's revenue in 2012 was $14.1 billion.[31]

The dominance of new social media sites is now so pervasive that users are rarely even aware of how often they reference them. Case in point: a recent ruling by the French government forbids broadcasters from mentioning Facebook or Twitter on air unless the stories pertain directly to the companies. The decision itself inspired a few tweets from media pundits and a not-unexpected poke at French bureaucrats for butting in. Still, the government made a valid point, arguing that by continually referring to Facebook and Twitter, for example, in their news and entertainment reporting, broadcasters were providing a form of free advertising, favoring market leaders at the expense of ignoring wannabes among their distant competitors.[32]

Tim Wu, a professor of law at Colombia University and a senior adviser to the U.S. Federal Trade Commission, raises an interesting question about the new corporate giants that are colonizing large swaths of virtual space. He asks, "how hard would it be to go a week without Google? Or, to up the ante, without Facebook, Amazon, Skype, Twitter, Apple, eBay, and Google?"[33] Wu is putting his finger on a disquieting new reality—that the new communication medium a younger generation gravitated to because of its promise of openness, transparency, and deep social collaboration masks another persona more concerned with ringing up profit by advancing a networked Commons. Wu writes:

> Most of the major sectors [on the Internet] today are controlled by one dominant company or an oligopoly. Google "owns" search; Facebook, social networking; eBay rules auctions; Apple dominates online content delivery; Amazon, retail; and so on.

Wu asks why the Internet looks "increasingly like a Monopoly board."[34]

If there were any lingering doubts about the intentions of these new corporate players, argue some of the critics, a search of recent patent acquisitions should put the qualms to rest. In just 2 years—2011 and 2012—new patent acquisitions were enough to take the breath away from even the most seasoned intellectual property attorneys. In 2011, Apple, Microsoft and other companies won Nortel networks' 6,000 patents worth $4.5 billion—in auction; Google purchased Motorola for $12.5 billion, acquiring 17,000 patents; Microsoft purchased 925 patents from AOL for $1.1 billion; and Facebook bought 650 patents from Microsoft for 550 million.[35]

A growing number of communications-industry analysts, antitrust attorneys, and Free Culture Movement advocates are asking whether these new heavyweights in virtual space are really "natural monopolies" like AT&T and the power and utility companies of the twentieth century and therefore either legitimate candidates for antitrust action or for regulation as public utilities. They argue that if one or both of these courses is not rigorously pursued, the great promise of the Internet as a shared, networked global Commons is going to be irretrievably lost and, with it, the hopes and aspirations of a generation that has put such store on a peer-to-peer collaboratist ethos.

Commons advocates contend that when a search engine like Google becomes an "essential facility," because it provides a universal service that everyone needs and alternative search engines pale in comparative performance, there is really nowhere else to go. In such circumstances, Google begins to look and feel like a natural monopoly. Some voices are beginning to call for "search neutrality" and clamoring for regulations not dissimilar from those imposed by governments to assure network neutrality. They warn that a dominant search engine in the private sector might be tempted to manipulate search results, either for commercial or political reasons.

Others are concerned that social media sites like Twitter might be tempted to manipulate rankings, one of the more popular features used to engage their members. For example, Twitter hosts a feature called Twitter Trends, which identifies hot topics and issues of current interest that are "trending." Questions have been raised about whether the algorithms companies use to spot and rank trends might be programmed to reflect the biases of the management that oversees them, consciously or otherwise. Julian Assange's supporters suspected that Twitter deliberately finagled the trending during the WikiLeaks scandal.[36] Industry watchers are beginning to ask, how we can maintain "algorithm neutrality"?

Tarleton Gillespie, a professor of communications at Cornell University, says that algorithm manipulation is not entirely out of the question, especially when the algorithms are created by commercial players who might see a pecuniary or ideological rationale for tampering with the data. He writes:

> The debate about tools like Twitter Trends is, I believe, a debate we will be having more and more often. As more and more of our online public discourse takes place on a select set of private content platforms and communication networks, and these providers turn to complex algorithms to manage, curate, and organize these massive collections. . . . [We] must . . . recognize that these algorithms are not neutral, and that they encode political choices, and that they frame information in a particular way.[37]

Gillespie says that as the public relies more on algorithms to sort, rank, and prioritize information, we will have to find some way to build in protocols and regulations to assure transparency and objectivity, especially when mostly commercial players control both the data and the algorithms.[38] Not to do so and just hope that corporate goodwill will be sufficient to preserve the integrity of the process is at best naïve and at worst foolhardy.

The dilemma is that, as enterprises like Google, Facebook, and Twitter continue to grow, the increasing number of users in their networks benefits everyone using the network. But because the networks are commercial enterprises, their interest is in maximizing profits by being able to sell information about their users to third parties, while their users' interest is optimizing their social connections. In other words, the problem is that companies are operating a social Commons as a commercial venture. Zeynep Tufekci, a sociology professor at the University of North Carolina, calls this practice "the corporatization of the social Commons."[39]

Not everyone worries that a handful of companies will monopolize the Internet. Some legal scholars argue that firms operating social media sites are not comparable to telecom companies or power and utility companies, whose huge up-front capital investments in physical infrastructure guarantee their natural monopoly. New entrants to the utility space, they argue, would find it difficult—if not impossible—to compete with an already established firm with a mature physical infrastructure in place and a captive user-base secured. On the other hand, new entrants in social media have far smaller up-front costs to contend with. Writing code and coming up with new apps can be done at a fraction of the cost of setting up a utility, allowing new players to come in and quickly gain dominance or, at least, competitive advantage. As proof, they point to social media market leaders like Myspace and Friendster, whose dominance looked invincible just a few years ago only to be nearly wiped off the map by upstarts like Facebook and Twitter.

Free-market advocates also warn that the very act of anointing companies like Google, Facebook, and Twitter as "social utilities" and regulating them as a natural monopolies makes them, in fact, just that—protecting them in perpetuity from potential competition. That is exactly what happened with AT&T after World War I. As mentioned in chapter 3, the federal government granted the phone company giant a natural monopoly status, regulated by federal law, virtually guaranteeing it an unchallengeable control of the telecommunications market for most of the twentieth century.

Finally, the opponents of regulating social media giants as social utilities contend, somewhat justifiably, that regulated utilities tend to be risk adverse and shy away from innovations without competition nipping at their heels. With a guaranteed rate of return and fixed prices built in, what possible incentives would they have to introduce new technologies and business models?

These counterarguments resonate. It's also the case, however, that corporate giants like Google, Facebook, Twitter, eBay, and Amazon have each spent billions of dollars securing global markets whose user bases are many times larger than anything from the past we might want to measure them against. What does it mean when the collective knowledge of much of human history is controlled by the Google search engine? Or when Facebook becomes the sole overseer of a virtual public square, connecting the social lives of 1 billion people? Or when Twitter becomes the exclusive gossip line for the human race? Or when eBay becomes the only ring master for the global auction market? Or when Amazon becomes the go-to virtual marketplace for nearly everyone's purchases online? There is nothing comparable to these monopolies in the history of the brick-and-mortar world of commerce.

The reality is that while these companies got in near the ground floor of the Internet, could leverage a good idea, and depose market leaders with very little capital investment, it's far more difficult to do so today. Google, Facebook, Twitter, eBay, Amazon, et al. are investing billions of dollars in expanding their user base while simultaneously creating impenetrable enclosures, protected by layer upon layer of intellectual property, all designed to profit from the global social Commons they helped create.

It's highly unlikely that the companies capturing these vast social spheres will escape some kind of regulatory restriction by way of either antitrust action or treating them as global social utilities with appropriate regulatory oversight. The nature and extent of the oversight is still very much an open question.

What's not in question is the need to address the worrisome commercial enclosure of a communications medium whose very existence is predicated on the premise of providing a universal Commons in which all of humanity can collaborate and create value across every sector of social life at near zero marginal cost.

THE ENERGY COMMONS

Assuring that the Internet remains an open global Commons to optimize the vast social and economic benefits of its laterally scaled architecture is a formidable challenge. Harnessing the new communications media to the management of laterally scaled renewable energies and assuring that the Energy Internet also remains an open global Commons is no less challenging. Already, the creation of an Energy Internet Commons across locales, regions, countries, and continents is coming up against entrenched commercial interests every bit as formidable as those the Communications Internet is facing with the telecommunications and cable companies.

Global energy companies and power and utility companies are, in some cases, blocking the creation of an Energy Internet altogether. In other instances, they are attempting to force a centralized architecture on the smart grid, to enable the commercial enclosure of the new energies.

The European Union, the world's largest economy, has taken steps to keep the Energy Internet an open architecture by requiring that conventional power and utility companies unbundle their power generation from their transmission of electricity. The unbundling regulations came about because of growing complaints by millions of small, new energy producers that the big power and utility companies were making it difficult for them to connect their local micropower plants to the main transmission grid. The companies were also accused of discriminatory practices that favored speedy connectivity for green electricity generated by affiliated business partners and of imposing bureaucratic delays and even refusing to accept green electricity from others.

Electric utilities are also fighting on a second front, with behind-the-scenes maneuvers to design a smart grid that is centralized, proprietary, and closed, and in which all transmission data flows only in one direction, from prosumers to headquarters. The objective is to withhold vital information from the millions of new prosumers on moment-to-moment changes in the price of electricity as well as to prevent them from controlling when to upload their electricity onto the grid to take advantage of peak electricity prices at various times of the day.

These efforts by the electricity transmission companies appear to be losing steam as countries all over the world introduce green feed-in tariffs to encourage millions of end users to produce their own green electricity and share it across an Energy Internet. A growing number of electricity-transmission companies are coming to grips with the new reality of energy prosumers and are changing their business model to accommodate the new Energy Internet. In the future, their income will increasingly rely on managing their customers' energy use, reducing their energy needs, increasing their energy efficiencies and productivity, and sharing a percentage of the increased productivity and savings. Transmission companies will profit more from managing energy use more efficiently and selling less rather than more electricity.

At this early stage of the Energy Internet, questions are being raised about the best approach to manage distributed electricity generation. A new Commons model is just beginning to take form, and interestingly enough, it is an outgrowth of an older Commons model for managing electricity that arose in the 1930s to bring electricity to the rural areas of the United States.

THE NEW DEAL'S GREATEST SUCCESS

Our story begins by revisiting Harold Hotelling's speech of 1937 in which he suggested that the nation's electricity transmission grid be paid for by the government. He argued that since the electricity grid is a public good that everyone needs, the general welfare would be best optimized by paying for it with federal monies rather than allowing it to remain in the hands of private utilities. Because consumers would not be paying "rent" to private utilities for their electricity, the price of electricity would not exceed the marginal cost, which would head toward zero, once the transmission grid was erected.

What I did not tell you in chapter 8 is that Hotelling used an example of a then new government program to illustrate the superiority of his idea. The project was the Tennessee Valley Authority (TVA), a massive public works project—the biggest ever conceived up to that time. On May 18, 1933, President Franklin Delano Roosevelt signed into law the Tennessee Valley Authority Act. The plan called for building 12 dams and a steam plant between 1933 and 1944, employing 28,000 workers in the Tennessee Valley, which covered parts of seven of the poorest states—Tennessee, Kentucky, Virginia, North Carolina, Georgia, Alabama, and Mississippi. Construction was on a gigantic scale, equivalent to erecting 20 Empire State Buildings.[40]

The federal government would harness the hydropower and produce cheap electricity for many of the poorest communities in the nation, in the hope of stimulating long-term economic growth. Hotelling explained that bringing cheap hydroelectric power to the Tennessee Valley would "raise the whole level of economic existence, and so of culture and intelligence, in that region, and that the benefits enjoyed by the local population will be such as to exceed greatly in money value the cost of development, taking account of interest."[41] "But," he warned, "if the government demands for the electricity generated a price sufficiently high to repay the investment, or even the interest on it, the benefits will be reduced to an extent far exceeding the revenue thus obtained by the government."[42] Therefore he concluded that "it appears to be good public policy to make the investment, and to sell electricity energy at marginal cost, which is extremely small."[43]

Hotelling acknowledged that the cost of the TVA project would have to be paid for by taxpayers in the rest of the country, but suggested that the improved economic conditions in the Tennessee Valley would indirectly benefit other parts of the country by reducing the costs of agricultural exports from the region.[44] An increase in income and the standard of living in the region would also mean greater consumption of products made in other parts of the country. Finally, he suggested that the success of the TVA project would spur similar public works programs in other parts of the country. He reasoned that

> a government willing to undertake such an enterprise is, for the same reasons, ready to build other dams in other and widely scattered places, and to construct a great variety of public works. Each of these entails benefits which are diffused widely among all classes. A rough randomness in distribution should be ample to ensure such a distribution of benefits that most persons in every part of the country would be better off by reason of the program as a whole.[45]

Ronald Coase didn't buy Hotelling's arguments. Recall that Coase, a free-market advocate, didn't think government was a good prognosticator of consumer demand, even in the case where the public good or service in question was undeniably something everybody needed. He wrote, "I do not myself believe that a government could make accurate estimates of individual demand in a regime in which all prices were based on marginal costs."[46]

Coase's first argument, on closer scrutiny, appears rather spurious. One wonders whether consumers would turn down cleaner tap water provided as a public good at marginal cost in favor of well water; or whether they would turn their backs on using public highways in favor of unpaved roads; or, for that matter, whether they would reject public electric lighting in favor of torches, when they could enjoy such conveniences at prices that reflected their marginal cost.

As to the contagion effect, Coase dismissed the argument that a successful public works venture like the TVA would stimulate copy-cat projects in other parts of the country, arguing that even if the project proved successful, there is no way to assume that roughly the same preexisting conditions would prevail in other regions, thereby favoring a similar result.

Coase wrote his rejoinder to Hotelling in 1946, when returning GIs and their families were anxious to make up for lost time during the war by using their pent-up savings to buy all the things they went without during the war years. The marketplace became the engine that would fuel consumer society. Understandably, after 15 years of economic depression, a world war, and government rationing of goods, millions of people were ready to embrace the marketplace and make their own individual decisions on how their income ought to be spent.

Coase caught the tenor of the times. Most other economists followed his lead. Henceforth, the conventional economic wisdom was that the market, not the government, is the better arbiter for picking winners over losers in the economic life of the country—although it should be pointed out that the American public was more than willing to make substantial exceptions when it came to the public financing of the interstate highways, college loans for veterans, and government-subsidized Federal Housing Authority (FHA) home mortgages.

But hold on. Few scholars have been interested enough in the history of the period to see whether Hotelling's contentions and best-case example turned out to be correct. Had they done so, they would have seen that, in his rush to dismiss Hotelling's thesis and his use of the TVA as an example of the merits of his argument, Coase's rejoinder utterly flunked the test of time.

Buried in that history is the emergence of a novel new mechanism for Commons management of electricity that would fundamentally alter the course of economic development in America in the twentieth century and provide the essential Commons business model for organizing the Energy Internet in the twenty-first century.

The federal government got into the business of producing electricity in the first place because private utilities were not interested in extending transmission lines into rural areas, arguing that the households were too few, too spread out, and without sufficient purchasing power to afford the service.

By the 1930s, 90 percent of urban dwellings had electricity, compared to only 10 percent of rural dwellings.[47] The lack of electrification kept a sizable portion of the American population in dire poverty with little expectation of bettering their lot. The Depression years only deepened the divide.

The TVA was meant to bring a backward rural region into the twentieth century and, by its example, extend the program to other rural regions across the country. The power and utility companies shot back. Although they were not interested in the rural market, they were enraged that the federal government was rushing headlong into the power market and that the TVA was authorized to provide farmers and rural communities "preference" in the sale of electricity at an affordable rate. Despite the companies' opposition, by 1941 the TVA was the single largest producer of electrical energy in the United States—and the electricity was generated from hydropower, a renewable resource.[48]

The private-utility industry, backed up by conservative business interests, charged that the TVA was the stalking horse for a wholesale government effort to turn the United States into a socialist society. A *Chicago Tribune* editorial accused the TVA of establishing "a little red Russia in the Tennessee Valley."[49] The utility companies asserted that the Constitution did not allow for the federal government to usurp the authority to produce power, and they took their case all the way to the Supreme Court, where they lost the battle as the court reaffirmed the constitutionality of the law.

In addition to generating power, the TVA had also been authorized to build transmission lines to local communities to advance rural electrification. So, in 1935, Roosevelt signed an executive order establishing the Rural Electric Administration (REA), with the mission of getting transmission wires to every rural household in America. "In 1936 and 1937 the new agency constructed 73,000 miles of electrical lines, reaching more than 300,000 farms."[50]

The REA's achievement was impressive. It became clear, however, that the agency couldn't possibly muster the in-house technical expertise and workforce to build its own transmission lines across all of rural America. With private power utilities stubbornly refusing to lend a hand, the REA took up the unorthodox and, at the time, radical idea of encouraging farmers to band together in local communities and establish electrical cooperatives. (A few rural electric cooperatives were already operating in the TVA region, Pennsylvania, and the Pacific Northwest, and were proving successful.)

Under the new plan, the REA would provide low-interest federal loans to local farming communities for the construction of the lines and offer technical and legal assistance. The vision was to foster a decentralized approach to electrification that would allow local rural electric cooperatives to install their lines and connect with each other, creating regional transmission grids. The cooperatives would function as nonprofit, self-managed Commons, with their boards of directors democratically elected from their membership.

The REA lines cost, on average, $750 a mile to construct, 40 percent below the estimates of the private electric utilities.[51] Expenses were often kept low by allowing local farmers to devote their time to work on the installation of the transmission lines to pay back money they owed the cooperative. By 1942, 40 percent of all the farms in the country were electrified, and by 1946 half of American farms were electrified.[52] Four years later, the other half of American rural households were electrified—a momentous feat, accomplished mostly at the hands of farmers who picked up the necessary skills to both manage their own electric cooperatives and assist in the build-out.

The economic benefit to rural communities from the Tennessee Valley to California was inestimable. Electrification lengthened the productive workday, eased the burden of heavy lifting on the farm, dramatically increased farm productivity, and improved the health and well-being of millions of rural families. In the first five years of the REA program, more than 12,000 rural schools were electrified.[53] Having electricity and lighting allowed students to extend their learning day with homework assignments that could be done in the evenings after their daily chores.

Rural electrification had a major impact on the manufacturing and retailing of appliances. The REA convinced General Electric and Westinghouse to manufacture cheaper appliances that would sell at half the usual price to stimulate the equipping of millions of rural households with the latest electrical conveniences.[54] The acquisition of new appliances by rural households accounted for an amazing 20 percent increase in appliance sales during the worst years of the Depression, helping to keep a flagging economy afloat.[55]

Rural electrification also increased property values across rural America and provided the electrical-transmission infrastructure for the mass migration from urban to rural areas in the 1950s to the 1980s, with the build-out of the interstate highway system and the construction of millions of new suburban homes, offices, and shopping malls off of the highway exits. The suburbanization of America also brought new commercial opportunities to rural areas, and with it, millions of new jobs, marking the most prosperous economic period in U.S. history.[56]

Every argument that Hotelling advanced in his paper in favor of federal government financing of the TVA proved to be astonishingly accurate. The only wrinkle, and it's a positive one, is that the electrification of rural America did not require a massive outpouring of tax dollars. Much of the electricity infrastructure was financed by low-interest government loans to rural electricity cooperatives, virtually all of which were paid back.[57] What Hotelling missed is that it was not necessary for government to shoulder the entire burden, but only to facilitate and underwrite the process.

Finally, although rural electric cooperatives continue to receive federal government subsidies, "electric cooperatives receive the smallest federal subsidy per consumer" of all electric utilities—a fact that might surprise taxpayers.[58]

If Coase was obsessed with the superiority of the capitalist market and Hotelling with the superiority of government management, what unfolded instead was a third approach to optimizing the general welfare. The government threw its support to a distributed, collaborative, laterally scaled economic institution—the cooperative—as the best vehicle for electrifying and transforming rural America. This Commons form of self-management accomplished in just 13 years what private enterprise and government could not have done in twice that time at anywhere near the low cost.

Today, 900 nonprofit rural electric cooperatives serve 42 million customers over 2.5 million miles in 47 states. Rural electric cooperatives account for 42 percent of the nation's electricity distribution lines. The transmission lines cover 75 percent of the nation's landmass and deliver 11 percent of the total kilowatts sold in the United States. The combined assets of rural electric cooperatives total more than $140 billion.[59]

Most important of all, 70,000 employees of the nation's rural electric cooperatives provide "at cost" electric service to their customers. Being cooperatives, they are not structured to make a profit.[60]

THE COOPERATIVES' RENAISSANCE

The first thing to understand about cooperatives is that they are designed to operate as a Commons, while private companies are structured to operate as profit-making ventures. Cooperatives are structured to fulfill a very different set of goals than private companies.

The International Cooperative Alliance (ICA)—an association representing all the world's cooperatives—defines a cooperative as

> an autonomous association of persons united voluntarily to meet
> their common economic, social, and cultural needs and aspirations
> through a jointly-owned and democratically controlled enterprise.[61]

Cooperatives are driven by cooperation rather than competition and by broad social commitments rather than narrow economic self-interests. Their field of operations is on the Commons rather than in the market. The ICA explains that

> cooperatives are based on the values of self-help, self-responsibility, democracy, equality, equity, and solidarity. . . . Cooperative

members believe in the ethical values of honesty, openness, social responsibility, and caring for others.[62]

While cooperative business arrangements extend far back in history, the modern cooperative business structure began in England in 1844 when 28 textile workers formed a cooperative that they called the Rochdale Society of Equitable Pioneers. The weavers pooled their finances, allowing them to buy quality supplies for their trade at cost. Their first cooperative store bought and sold food products, including flour and sugar, to its members.

The Rochdale Society established seven rules for Commons management that became the standard protocol for cooperatives. Those rules, which have been revised and formally ratified as the governance model for cooperatives by the ICA, epitomize the vision and practice of Commons management:

> First, any individual is welcome to become a member of a cooperative regardless of race, religion, ethnicity, gender, or social or political affiliation.
>
> Second, cooperatives are democratically run associations in which each member enjoys a single vote. Elected representatives, drawn from the membership, are responsible for management of the association and accountable to the membership.
>
> Third, members contribute equitably and democratically to the capital of their cooperative. Part of that capital becomes the common property of the cooperative. Members jointly decide on how their funds ought to be used in the development and day-to-day operations of the cooperative.
>
> Fourth, cooperatives are autonomous, self-help associations. Although they can and do enter into various business arrangements with other organizations, they do so in a manner that ensures their democratic control of the cooperative and its autonomy.
>
> Fifth, cooperatives provide education and ongoing training for their members, managers, and employees to encourage their full participation in the programs, projects, and initiatives of the association.

Sixth, cooperatives are expected to broaden the networked Commons by providing an ever-expanding and ever-integrating space for collaboration and cooperation across regions and the world.

Seventh, cooperatives are tasked with the mission of promoting sustainable development within the communities they serve through the policies and programs they engage in.[63]

In a world dominated by the capitalist market and its accompanying utilitarian ethos—which views human behavior as competitive and self-interested—the very idea that human beings might be drawn to a cooperative business model based on collaboration, equity, and sustainability seems hopelessly impractical. Yet much of humanity is already organizing at least some parts of its economic life in cooperative associations operating in Commons. It's just that we never hear about it. The year 2012 was officially recognized by the United Nations as the International Year of Cooperatives, but a quick Google search shows barely a blip of news about the year-long celebrations. Perhaps it's because the global media are concentrated in the hands of a few giant for-profit media companies that decide what is news.

The fact is, more than 1 billion people are currently members of cooperatives—that's one out of every seven human beings on Earth. More than 100 million people are employed by cooperatives, or 20 percent more employees than in multinational companies. The 300 largest cooperatives would be equivalent in population to the tenth-largest country in the world. In the United States and Germany, one out of every four people is a member of a cooperative. In Canada, four out of every ten people are members of cooperatives. In India and China, 400 million people belong to cooperatives. In Japan, one out of every three families are members of cooperatives and in France, 32 million people participate in cooperatives.[64] In June 2011, Paul Hazen, CEO of the National Cooperative Business Association, noted that

in the U.S., there are 29,000 cooperatives, with 120 million members, operating in 73,000 places of business throughout our nation. Overall, U.S. cooperatives account for more than $3 trillion in assets, over $500 billion in annual revenue, $25 billion in wages and benefits, and nearly 2 million jobs.[65]

U.S. cooperatives operate in virtually every economic sector, including agriculture and food production, retail, health care, insurance, credit unions, energy, electricity generation and transmission, and telecommunications. The next time you drop into an Ace Hardware store, you are doing business in a cooperative. "Americans hold over 350 million cooperative memberships."[66]

Hundreds of millions of people around the world buy their food from cooperatives, live in cooperative housing, and do their banking with cooperative financial institutions. Most Americans are unaware that "about 30 percent of farmers' products and supplies in the U.S. are marketed through 3,000 farmer-owned cooperatives."[67] Land O'Lakes butter and Welch's grape juice are just a few of the recognizable brand names of food products on grocery store shelves that are marketed by agricultural cooperatives.[68]

Ten million dwellings, or 12 percent of all the households in the European Union, are cooperative housing.[69] In Egypt, nearly one-third of the population belongs to a housing cooperative.[70] Even in the United States, which boasts the largest percentage of private home-owners, more than 1.2 million dwellings are cooperatives.[71] In Pakistan, 12 percent of the housing is cooperative.[72]

Banking cooperatives are also major players in the financial community. In six European countries—Germany, France, Italy, the Netherlands, Austria, and Finland—cooperatives account for about 32 percent of all deposits and nearly 28 percent of all domestic loans.[73] In Asia, 45.3 million people are members of credit unions, which are member-owned financial cooperatives.[74] In France, 60 percent of the retail banking is done through cooperatives.[75]

In the United States, credit unions, which claim over 90 million members—the most of any country in the world—have enjoyed a renaissance since the collapse of the financial market in 2008.[76] Deposits in credit unions have risen by 43 percent, compared to 31 percent at the nation's biggest banks.[77] U.S. credit unions now have assets of nearly $1 trillion.[78]

Despite the cooperative's venerable track record, it remained a secondary player to profit-making enterprises throughout the First and Second Industrial Revolutions. The substantial capital requirements brought on by centralized communication and energy matrices tipped the game in favor of private companies that could amass sufficient sums in the stock and bond markets. The vertical integration and scaling of manufacturing and services ensured that private enterprises, operating in capitalist markets, would dominate the previous two industrial eras.

Cooperatives were a way for small- and medium-sized businesses to survive by pooling their financial resources in order to purchase raw materials and goods from suppliers upstream at significant discounts while cutting their costs downstream by sharing marketing, logistics, and distribution channels. By operating as nonprofit enterprises in a shared Commons, outside the market, they could move goods and services to their members at low marginal cost because they were operating through a nonprofit business model.

Now the tables have suddenly turned. As mentioned in previous chapters, the Internet of Things gives the advantage to hundreds of thousands of small enterprises, but only if they are able to join together in producer cooperatives and take advantage of the lateral power made possible by the new distributed and collaborative communications and energy configuration.

The prospect of a new economic infrastructure and paradigm that can reduce marginal costs to near zero makes the private firm, whose very existence depends on sufficient margins to make a profit, less viable. Cooperatives are the only business model that will work in a near zero marginal cost society.

Thousands of green energy and electricity cooperatives are springing up in communities around the world, establishing a bottom-up Commons foundation for peer-to-peer sharing of electricity across regional and continental transmission grids.

In the European Union, where more people invest in cooperatives than in the stock market—a striking fact—cooperative banks are taking the lead in financing green electricity cooperatives. Dirk Vansintjan, founding director of the Belgian cooperative Ecopower, says that, for the most part, cooperative banks are the first to jump in and finance wind and solar projects. In the spirit of one of the seven governing principles of cooperatives—that they cooperate with each other when possible—cooperative banks are increasingly financing green electricity cooperatives like Ecopower with members' funds. Ecopower, which started with 30 members in 1990, had 43,000 members in 2013, and already provides 1.2 percent of Flemish households with green electricity generated by its renewable wind and hydropower energy installations.[79]

In Germany, green energy cooperatives are sprouting all over the country. In 2011 alone, 167 new green energy cooperatives were created.[80] The Horb Ecumenical Energy Cooperative in Stuttgart, Germany, is a typical example of the clout cooperatives can bring to bear in transforming energy generation and use patterns in local communities. The cooperative has already installed several solar power plants in the region, with more scheduled. As already mentioned, Germany is currently producing more than 23 percent of its electricity with renewable energy, much of it generated by local cooperatives.[81] Bernhard Bok, a prime mover of the Stuttgart renewable-energy cooperative, says it is not so surprising given that "we are in a country of cooperatives."[82]

Denmark is also at the forefront of transforming its society by installing an IoT infrastructure, and has relied heavily on the bottom-up cooperative model to establish a sustainable economic paradigm. When I fly into Copenhagen, I always look down on the harbor during the approach, admiring the 20 or so wind turbines, half of which are owned by cooperatives.[83]

The Danes have found that the key to effective implementation of the new infrastructure is buy-in by local communities, and that cooperatives provide the best vehicle for building public trust and gaining local support for the new energy infrastructure. They are particularly proud of their lighthouse project on the tiny island of Samsø—a community of around 4,000 inhabitants—where the local households and businesses were able to transform their region from nearly 100 percent reliance on imported electricity, mainly from coal power plants, to 100 percent renewable energy in just ten years.[84]

At a time when installation of wind farms by major corporate developers has faced opposition from local communities, Samsø countered the backlash by vesting ownership of the new energy among its own citizens. The island followed the lead of the rest of the country, where 80 percent of the installed wind energy capacity is owned either by cooperatives or individuals.[85]

Local residents explain to the island's visitors, who are anxious to understand how they were able to achieve such a success, that it all boils down to democratic participation and community ownership. The green-energy cooperatives provided a Commons that any resident could join, with an equal voice in the decisions governing development and management of the wind turbines on the island and just offshore. Residents became part owners as well, allowing them to benefit from the cheaper prices of the new green electricity.

The cooperatives also afforded the inhabitants of the island the opportunity to become part of something bigger than themselves. Active participation in the decision making and management of the green energy cooperatives built social capital, trust, and good will.

In the United States, rural electric cooperatives have been at the forefront of the movement to green electricity. The National Rural Electric Cooperatives Association has set a goal of producing 25 percent of members' electricity from renewable resources by 2025.[86] In 2009 a North Dakota rural electric cooperative, Basin Electric, put online a $240 million 115-megawatt wind farm, the nation's largest.[87] The project was completed in a record time of four months, rivaling the largest renewable-energy projects in the world. The cooperative, which serves 2.8 million rural consumers in nine Western states, has begun the process of transforming its energy generation from fossil fuels to renewables. In 2005, 94 percent of the company's electricity was derived from coal and less than 1 percent from wind. Today more than 20 percent of its electricity is green and generated from wind farms.[88]

Rural electric cooperatives have also outperformed private and municipally owned utilities in the build-out of the new Energy Internet. Over 40 percent of all electric cooperatives have installed advanced meters at industrial, commercial, and residential locations.[89]

Green electricity cooperatives are also taking hold in urban and suburban neighborhoods, as well as in rural areas, in many regions of the world. A study done in Germany on the future role of urban electricity cooperatives found, contrary to earlier assumptions, that green electricity cooperatives are not more likely to develop in rural areas. It appears that urban green cooperatives are developing as fast if not faster than their rural counterparts. In the German study, 80 percent of the members of one of the nation's biggest green energy cooperative live in towns or large cities. When asked about their rationale for becoming members of a green electricity Commons, most respondents mentioned "political motivation," by which they meant their desire to be actively involved in planning their own and their community's energy future.[90]

The generation that grew up on the Internet and that takes for granted its right to create value in distributed, collaborative, peer-to-peer networks has little hesitation about generating their own green electricity and sharing it on an Energy Internet. They find themselves living through a deepening global economic crisis and an even more terrifying shift in Earth's climate, caused by an economic system reliant on fossil fuel energy and managed by centralized, top-down command and control systems. If they fault the giant telecommunications, media, and entertainment companies for blocking their right to collaborate freely with their peers in an open Information Commons, they are no less critical of the world's giant energy, power, and utility companies, which they blame, in part, for the high price of energy, a declining economy, and looming environmental crisis.

For a growing number of young people, the conventional energy and utility companies represent the very archetype of centralized power and all the ills that it has forced on the world. The prospect that those ills can be cured by joining together in open, collaborative, and democratically managed cooperatives to produce and share clean, green energy is empowering. It is inspiring a generation to rally under the banner of sustainability. The call for free access to communication is now being joined by the demands for free, green energy.

THE LOGISTICS COMMONS

There is one remaining sphere that needs to be brought into the matrix to create a Commons infrastructure. Internet communication, which is beginning to manage laterally scaled green electricity, is now being used to create a Transportation Internet that will automate logistics networks around the world. The coming together of the Communications Internet, the Energy Internet, and the Transportation Internet in an integrated Internet of Things operating on a Commons paves the way to the Collaborative Age.

While roads are by and large treated as public goods all over the world, the modes of transport we use to travel on them and to ship materials and goods are a mix of public and private enterprises. Hundreds of millions of human beings each day use public transportation to commute to and from work and for social mobility.[91] Commuter trains, light rail, and buses provide services at just above cost, subsidized by taxes. Hundreds of millions of other people depend on private cars for their economic and social mobility. Others use a combination of public transport, private cars, bicycling, and walking.

Most shipments of commercial goods across roads are done by private carriers. Large vertically integrated Second Industrial Revolution companies rely on their own internal car and truck fleets or outsource to other private carriers to store and move materials, components, and other supplies as well as finished goods across the value chain. Going it alone, however, has its drawbacks. Although maintaining an internal, top-down, centralized command over logistics and transport gives private firms a strong measure of control over their production, storage, and distribution channels, that control comes with a high cost of lost efficiencies and productivity and increased carbon dioxide emissions.

A recent global study revealed several different ways that privately managed logistics contribute to lost efficiencies and productivity and increased carbon dioxide emissions. First, in the United States alone, trailer trucks are on average only 60 percent full when on the road. Global transport does even less well and is estimated to be lower than 10 percent efficient.[92] While trucks often leave their docks loaded, they become less and less full after each drop and often return empty. In the United States in 2002, trucks were, on average, empty of cargo for 20 percent of the miles driven and spent many more miles with their trailers nearly empty.[93] Second, manufacturers, wholesalers, distributors, and retailers are storing products in warehouses for long periods of time, often far away from where they will ultimately be shipped, at a high cost. As of March 2013, U.S. business inventories were estimated at $1.6 trillion.[94] These inventories represent goods sitting idle and taking up huge overhead costs. Warehouses are underutilized during certain periods of the year and overextended at others because of the seasonal nature of the product lines. Third, many time-sensitive products like food and clothes go unsold because distributors aren't able to deliver them in a timely manner due to logistical inefficiencies. These time-sensitive losses are only compounded in developing countries where the transport and logistics infrastructure is weak, unreliable, and subject to breakdown. Fourth, products are often shipped in circuitous routes rather than the fastest routes, in large part because of reliance on giant centralized warehouses and distribution centers that serve large terrains. Fifth, in a global logistics system dominated by hundreds of thousands of private carriers, there is a lack of common standards and protocols that would allow firms to collaborate with each other, using the newest IT and Internet technology apps, and share logistical resources in a way that would increase efficiencies and productivity and reduce operating costs.[95]

Free-market economists would argue that a capitalist system wedded to private exchange of goods and services in the marketplace and driven by the profit motive is the most efficient means of allocating scarce resources for productive ends. However, when it comes to logistics—the means by which these goods and services are stored and delivered to customers—the process is so grossly inefficient and unproductive that it should at least give economists pause. Rethinking the way we store and ship materials and goods is especially important now, with the cost of energy careening to higher peaks, placing an ever-heavier burden on a logistics system that is already redundant and inefficient. The inefficiencies rack up a huge carbon dioxide bill. In 2006, U.S. trucks traveled 263 billion miles on billions of gallons of fuel, sending record amounts of carbon dioxide emissions into the atmosphere.[96]

If logistics were just a minor part of the economy, it might not matter so much. But logistics is the driver of the whole system—the process by which suppliers and buyers connect and conduct business at every step of the value chain. In 2009, transportation represented "10% of the U.S. Gross Domestic Product, or roughly $1.4T (trillion)." Expenditures on freight transportation came in at $500 billion, packaging rang up at $125 billion, and warehousing accounted for $33 billion.[97]

Now, a new generation of academics and logistics professionals is looking to the distributed, collaborative, laterally scaled Internet communication system, with its open-systems architecture and Commons-style management, as a model for radically transforming global logistics in the twenty-first century. The irony of applying Internet lessons and metaphors to logistics is not lost on industry leaders as they recall that the IT and telecommunications industry borrowed metaphors from logistics to conceptualize their first forays into the Internet communication revolution. Soon after the World Wide Web went on line, vice president of the United States Al Gore talked about the need to create "an information superhighway," noting that the creation of the interstate highway system a generation earlier had connected road transportation, with spillover effects that included suburban development, the geographic dispersal of manufacturing and retailing, and the growth in tourism—all of which gave the United States the period of greatest economic prosperity in its 200-year history.[98] The open architecture of an interconnected interstate highway system—on which a car could travel coast to coast without a single stoplight—inspired techies to conceptualize an interconnected communication medium that would allow packets of information to travel effortlessly across various networks in a distributed system.

Today, the logistics industry is using Internet metaphors to rethink its own sector. Benoit Montreuil of the University Research Center on Enterprise Networks, Logistics, and Transport (CIRRELT) in Montreal, Canada, explains that just as the digital world took up the superhighway metaphor, now the logistics industry ought to take up the open-architecture metaphor of distributed Internet communication to remodel global logistics.[99]

Montreuil describes the essential features of a Transportation/Logistics Internet, noting that many of the components are already in play but not yet connected in a single, transparent, open system. To begin with, a packet of information transmitted over the Internet contains information on both its identity and routing to its destination. The data packet is structured independently from the equipment, allowing the packet to be processed through different systems and networks, including copper wires, fiber-optic wires, routers, local area networks, wide area networks, etc. Similarly, with a Transportation/Logistics Internet, all physical products would need to be embedded in standardized modular containers that could be transported across all the logistics networks. The containers would need to be equipped with smart tags and sensors for identification and sorting. The entire system, from warehousing to transport to end users, would need to operate by the same standard technical protocols to assure easy passage from one point to another.

On the Transportation/Logistics Internet, conventional point-to-point and hub-and-spoke transport would give way to distributed, multisegment, intermodal transport. Instead of one driver handling the entire load from the production center to the drop off and then heading to the nearest location to pick up a shipment designated for delivery on the way back home, the delivery would be distributed. The first driver might deliver the shipment to a hub close by and then pick up another trailer and shipment and head back home. A second driver would pick up the shipment and deliver it to the next hub down the line, whether it be at a truck port, railyard, or airport, until the entire shipment arrived at the destination.

Montreuil explains that in the current system, a driver would travel from Quebec to Los Angeles and back on a 10,000-kilometer round-trip, racking up at least 240 hours, with the container reaching Los Angeles after 120 hours. In the distributed system, 17 different drivers would each drive an average of about three hours to the drop-off point and return home the same day. The hand-off system would get the container to Los Angeles in approximately 60 hours, or half the time of the traditional point-to-point system. Internet tracking of the container would assure quick relay at every distribution point, making sure there was no time lost in the handover.[100]

In the current logistics system, most private companies own one or a few warehouses or distribution centers, but rarely more than 20. Most independent warehouses or distribution centers usually contract exclusively with one private enterprise, but rarely handle the logistics of more than ten enterprises. This means that private firms have available to them only a few warehouses or distribution centers, limiting their operations in storing and moving goods across continents.

But what if any enterprise could use all of the 535,000 currently used warehouses and distribution centers in the United States?[101] If those centers were connected in an open supply web managed by sophisticated analytics and algorithms, companies could use the system to store items and route shipments in the most efficient manner possible at any given moment of time. The improved energy efficiencies and productivity would be dramatic, as would the savings in fuel and the reduction in carbon dioxide emissions for every firm using the network.[102]

Montreuil points out that an open supply network allows firms to reduce their lead time to near zero if their stock is distributed among some of the hundreds of distribution centers that are located near their final buyer market. Moreover, as 3D printing advances, firms can transmit the code for the product to local 3D printers who can then print out the item and store it in a nearby distribution center for delivery to regional wholesalers and retailers.

The technology is already available. What's needed is the acceptance of universal standards and protocols and a business model to manage a regional, continental, and global logistics system.

Only by joining together in logistics cooperatives or other forms of Commons management could each private firm reap the cost benefits that flow from being part of a larger network. Integrated transport service providers already exist and will likely increasingly take on the task of clustering clients in cooperatives to realize the potential of a Transportation/Logistics Internet that facilitates lateral economies of scale. An open logistics infrastructure will give integrated transport service providers a universal playing field—made up of thousands of warehouses and distribution centers linked into a single cooperative network—that they can access to optimize each client's logistical requirements.

MANAGING TEMPORAL RESOURCES ON THE THREE INTERNET COMMONS

All three of the critical infrastructures that make up the Internet of Things share a similar management task. Unlike most traditional Commons, where the primary self-policing concern is stewarding common physical resources to prevent a depletion of stock, the three infrastructure Commons of the collaborative era need to steward temporal resources to prevent congestion. The Communications Internet has to self-police against data congestion in the transmission of information across radio bands. The Energy Internet has to prevent congestion in the management of peak and base-load electricity and maintain a proper balance between storage of energy and transmission of electricity to avoid power surges, brownouts, and blackouts. The Transportation Internet has to coordinate logistical flows and balance storage and transport of physical material and goods to prevent traffic congestion and optimize delivery schedules on the roads, rails, waterways, and air corridors. In all three instances, the more players in the networked Commons, the more benefits that accrue to each Commons member, but also the greater need to guard against congestion.

The capitalist model of private ownership, in which each firm is an island unto itself and attempts to gather economic activity vertically under one roof to achieve economies of scale, is incapable, by dint of its very operational features, to manage activities that require the active collaboration of thousands of players in laterally scaled operations. In lieu of Commons management, each private firm will attempt to optimize its own temporal flow at the expense of others, leading only to greater congestion in the network and a loss in operability, affecting every company in the system and resulting in a tragedy that goes with an unmanaged Commons.

The kinds of cost benefits that come with the Communications Internet, the Energy Internet, and the Transportation Internet are simply not realizable in a purely market economy, where each company goes it alone. No company, regardless of how ambitious, could hope to engage in sufficient mergers and acquisitions to achieve the efficiencies and productivity gains available by being part of a laterally scaled networked Commons.

AS BRIEFLY TOUCHED ON in chapter 1, to function, every society requires a means of communication, a source of energy, and a form of mobility. The coming together of the Communications Internet, the Energy Internet, and the Logistics Internet in an Internet of Things provides the cognitive nervous system and physical means to integrate all of humanity in an interconnected global Commons that extends across the entirety of society. This is what we mean when we talk about smart cities, smart regions, smart continents, and a smart planet.

The linking up of every human activity in an intelligent global network is giving birth to a wholly new economic being. The old being of the First and Second Industrial Revolutions relied on a communication/energy/transportation infrastructure that required huge sums of capital, and therefore had to be organized in vertically integrated enterprises under centralized command and control to achieve economies of scale. The capitalist system and the market mechanism proved to be the best institutional tools to advance the paradigm.

The new being of the Third Industrial Revolution, however, is of a very different nature. It requires less finance capital and more social capital, scales laterally rather than vertically, and is best implemented by a Commons management rather than by a strictly capitalist market mechanism. This means that the capitalist market's continued survival will depend on its ability to find value in a world where the new efficiencies and productivity lie in a society that is increasingly designed to be more distributed, open, collaborative, and networked.

If the old system favored autonomous self-interest in the capitalist market, the new system that is emerging favors deep collaboration in networked Commons. In the coming era, the long-standing partnership between government and the private sector to organize the economic life of society will give way to a tripartite partnership with Commons management playing an ever-greater role, complemented by government and market forces.

PART IV
SOCIAL CAPITAL AND THE SHARING ECONOMY

CHAPTER THIRTEEN

THE TRANSFORMATION FROM OWNERSHIP TO ACCESS

I f private property is the defining characteristic of a capitalist system, then the privately owned automobile is the signature item. In many regions of the world, more people own automobiles than own homes. It's often people's most valuable piece of private property. Automobile ownership has long been considered a rite of passage into the world of property relationships.

The very term *auto mobile* conveys the classical economic idea that human nature is driven by the quest for *auto*nomy and *mobil*ity, with every person desiring to be sovereign over his or her own domain. Americans have long associated the idea of freedom with autonomy and mobility. Nowhere is one's sense of autonomy more keenly felt than when behind the wheel in an enclosed vehicle capable of amplifying one's physical prowess by a magnitude of raw horsepower. To be autonomous is to be the master of one's fate, to be self-sufficient, and not to be dependent on or beholden to others—in other words, to be free. The automobile represents the ultimate enclosure. The privately owned car reflects the desire to be an island to oneself, to be self-contained, and unencumbered. We also equate freedom with unobstructed mobility. The ability to travel anywhere without restriction has become intimately bound up with our sense of physical freedom.

Every young person of my generation experienced the exhilaration of this kind of freedom the first time they took the wheel in their own automobile and headed out on the open road. In the capitalist era, we came to define freedom in negative terms as the right to exclude. The automobile became the symbol of our conventional notion of freedom.

The Internet generation, however, has come to think of freedom not in the negative sense—the right to exclude others—but rather in the positive sense of the right to be included with others. For them, freedom means the ability to optimize one's life, and the optimal life is realized by the diversity of one's experiences and the distributed reach of one's relationships in the various communities to which one affiliates over a lifetime. Freedom is measured more by access to others in networks than ownership of property in markets. The deeper and more inclusive one's relationships, the more freedom one enjoys. Having continuous access to others in social spaces like Facebook and Twitter gives one's life meaning. Freedom for an Internet generation is the ability to collaborate with others, without restriction, in a peer-to-peer world.

For the doubters who question the generational shift in thinking regarding the nature of freedom—from the right to own and exclude to the right to have access and be included—consider the following eye-opening statistics. In a recent survey of drivers between the ages of 18 and 24, 46 percent said they would choose Internet access over owning a car. Equally revealing, "in 2008, 46.3 percent of potential drivers 19 years old and younger had drivers' licenses, compared with 64.4 percent in 1998." When 3,000 millennial consumers born between 1981 and 2000 were asked which of 31 brands they preferred, not a single car made it in the top ten, which mainly consisted of Internet companies like Google.[1]

THE CAR AS METAPHOR

A generation of young people are transforming their relationship to the automobile, preferring access over ownership. Car sharing has become popular among millennials all over the world. An increasing number of young people belong to car-sharing clubs in which they pay a small membership fee and, in return, are provided access to automobiles when they need them. Their membership comes with smart cards giving them access to vehicles scattered in various car parks across cities. Members reserve cars in advance over the Web or with a smart-phone app. While some of the operations, like Zipcar and Chicago's I-Go, are privately owned, many more are operated by nonprofit orga-nizations, like Philly Car Share, City CarShare in San Francisco, and HourCar in Minneapolis.

In 2012, 800,000 people in the United States belonged to car-sharing services. Globally, 1.7 million people are car sharing in 27 countries.[2] A recent study by Frost and Sullivan Consultants forecasts more than 200 car-sharing operations across the European Union by 2020, with a car-sharing vehicle fleet expected to increase from 21,000 to 240,000 vehicles. Car-sharing membership is projected to grow from 700,000 to 15 million in less than seven years, with rev-enue reaching €2.6 billion. Car-sharing revenue is expected to grow even faster in North America, topping $3 billion by 2016.[3]

As car-sharing networks expand, the number of vehicles owned by members drops. A study of 11 leading car-sharing enterprises found that 80 percent of the members sampled who owned a car before car sharing sold it after joining the network. Of those households that still owned cars, the number of vehicles owned dropped from 0.47 vehicles per household to 0.24 vehicles per household after joining a car-share club.[4]

Car sharing not only reduces the number of cars on the road, but it also lowers carbon emissions. In 2009, each car-share vehicle elimi-nated 15 personally owned cars. In addition, car-share members drove 31 percent less than when they owned a vehicle. These changes in car-traveling behavior reduced CO_2 emissions in the United States by 482,170 tons.[5]

Car-sharing behavior also has significant crossover effects. Ac-cording to a study done in 2011, once people car share they tend to change their other mobility behavior, increasing bicycling, walking, and the use of public transportation.[6] Bike sharing, in particular, has taken off over the past five years, thanks in part to technological ad-vances like smart cards, touchscreen kiosks for easy check in and de-ployment, and GPS tracking on the bicycle that allows the rider to integrate bike sharing with car sharing and public transit. The newest innovation, solar-powered electric bicycles, has generated rave reviews from a younger generation. As of 2012, there were 19 bike-sharing programs in North America with over 215,000 users.[7] Globally, there are over 100 bike-sharing operations with 139,300 bicycles in service.[8]

In the United States and Canada, 58 percent of the new IT-based public bike-sharing operations are run by nonprofit organizations, 21 percent are privately owned, and 16 percent are publicly owned and contractor operated. The nonprofit operations are the heavy hitters, accounting for 82 percent of the membership and 66 percent of the bicycles used.[9]

Bike-sharing memberships can be taken out on an annual, monthly, or daily basis, or even be paid for on a trip-by-trip basis. Riders gain access to bikes by swiping membership cards or credit cards, or by checking in via their smartphones.

Bike sharing has become very popular in congested metropolitan areas where car traffic is often at a standstill during peak rush hours. In surveys conducted by Vélib' bike sharing in Paris and Capital Bikeshare in Washington, D.C., the overwhelming majority of bike sharers said that traveling by bike was faster and more convenient. Bike sharing also saves money that would have gone into operating a car.[10]

Car sharing also saves households money. In the United States, the average car costs hundreds of dollars a month to own and operate and eats up 20 percent of household income, making it the second-most-expensive cost after housing. The steep rise in gasoline prices has only exacerbated the expense of car ownership. With car sharing, the user is freed from ownership costs as well as from the fixed operating costs, including maintenance, insurance, licenses, taxes, etc.

The average vehicle in the United States is idle 92 percent of the time, making it an extremely inefficient fixed asset.[11] For that reason, young people are far more comfortable paying for mobility in time segments rather than in ownership.[12]

Car-sharing services are also pioneering the transition to electric vehicles. In 2013, the city government of Paris joined in a car-sharing collaboration with 46 neighborhood municipalities, making 1,750 electric vehicles (EVs) available at 750 charging stations throughout Paris and the suburbs.[13] Autolib' is one of a growing number of new car-sharing operations offering electric vehicles at zero carbon emissions to a user base that is increasingly committed to practicing sustainable mobility. Frost and Sullivan estimates that one in five new car-shared vehicles and one in ten total shared vehicles will be EVs by 2016.[14]

In peer-to-peer car-sharing practice, individual owners of cars register their vehicle online for free in networks like RelayRides and share them with users. The lender can set the price per hour and the hours available for renting, as well as screen any prospective users. RelayRides does background checks on the user and covers the insurance. The user covers the gasoline and road repair. The owner of the car gets 60 percent of what the user pays and RelayRides gets the other 40 percent. The lender is responsible for servicing and maintaining the automobile but because all new vehicles and many used vehicles come with free servicing and warranties for most of the basic systems maintenance, the lender is only paying for the fixed overhead of the car. Owners can earn between $2,300 and $7,400 annually based on car rentals that average $5 to $12 per hour. Since the average car owner spends around $715 a month on his or her vehicle, by peer-to-peer sharing, he or she can significantly reduce the cost of owning and keeping a car.[15]

Car-share clubs are increasingly using Integrated Transportation Provider Services (ITPS) to help their members switch from one mode of transport to another en route. A member might be routed by a car share and dropped off at a light-rail station where she will climb aboard the train. Several stops later, she will disembark at a bike-share rack where she will pick up a bike and pedal to another bike-share rack within blocks of her final destination. An ITPS app on the user's smartphone will keep her from getting lost. If she wants to stop somewhere on route and change course, she programs the request and the app charts a new course in seconds, taking into consideration current traffic flows and congestion bottlenecks along the route.

Some of the big auto manufacturers have jumped onboard the car-sharing bandwagon. GM has teamed up with RelayRides. General Motors Ventures has provided the peer-to-peer car-sharing network with financial support and has made its Onstar system available so that users can gain easy access to any GM vehicles with their mobile phones. GM's vice chairman, Stephen Girsky, says that the company is becoming involved in car sharing because the "goal is to find ways to broaden our customer reach, reduce traffic congestion in America's largest cities and address urban mobility concerns."[16]

GM and the other automakers find themselves in the same untenable position that capitalist firms are facing in other sectors of the economy. The emergence of a networked Commons is driving down the cost of mobility. In the short run, no single automaker can afford to stay on the sidelines, for fear its competitors will jump in—which they are—and attempt to grab at least a part of the action in the new car sharing Commons. But any value the automakers reap by embracing car sharing has to be weighed against the fewer cars they will be selling. Recall that 80 percent of the members of car-sharing clubs who owned a car prior to car sharing sold it after joining the network and that each car-sharing vehicle eliminates 15 personally owned cars from the road. With car companies already experiencing razor-thin margins, and with little wiggle room to stay in the game, they can't afford not to be in the car-sharing business even though the game itself is only going to reduce their car sales and diminish their already-slim margins.

Lawrence D. Burns, the corporate vice president of research, development, and planning at General Motors until 2009 and currently professor of engineering at the University of Michigan, gets to the nub of the contradiction facing the automobile industry. Burns did his calculations and concluded that

> for a citizen of a city like Ann Arbor [Michigan], such a service [car sharing] could be more than 70% cheaper and would require residents to invest less than one-fifth of the amount needed to own their cars.[17]

Incredibly, Burns admits that "about 80% fewer shared, coordinated vehicles would be needed than personally owned vehicles to provide the same level of mobility, with less investment."[18] Yet he recognizes that from an efficiency perspective, shared vehicles providing comparable mobility at 20 percent of the cost of owning a vehicle optimizes the general welfare and is simply too good of a deal to pass up, even though it is likely to eliminate 80 percent of the vehicles manufactured and sold. Still, the former GM heavyweight enthusiastically supports the shift from car ownership in markets to car sharing in Collaborative Commons, knowing that it will result in a dramatic shrinkage in the number of vehicles on the road.

The privately owned automobile, the centerpiece of the capitalist marketplace during the Second Industrial Revolution, is falling victim to the distributed, laterally scaled opportunities of car sharing on a rising Collaborative Commons better suited to optimize the general welfare of society. Rather than the market taming the Commons, it is the Commons taming the market—a reality that has yet to be fully grasped by those who continue to labor under the assumption that a sharing economy is a market opportunity rather than a devourer of capitalism.

The shift in personal mobility from ownership to access and from markets to shared Commons is likely to quicken in the years ahead with the introduction of driverless vehicles. In 2012, Governor Jerry Brown of California signed a law making it legal for driverless vehicles to operate on California roads. Nevada and Florida have also authorized driverless vehicles on their roadways. In signing the new law, Governor Brown declared that "today, we're looking at science fiction becoming tomorrow's reality."[19]

Google, which lobbied heavily for the new law, has already racked up 300,000 miles of testing driverless vehicles.[20] General Motors, Mercedes, BMW, Audi, Volvo, and Volkswagen are also testing driverless vehicles. The Google vehicle is a refitted Toyota Prius that drives itself using cameras, radar sensors, and a laser range finder and detailed Google maps connected to a GPS navigation system.[21]

Some car enthusiasts worry about the safety of driverless vehicles. Automotive engineers, however, point out that 90 percent of automobile accidents are caused by human error.[22] Unlike human drivers, automated vehicles don't get distracted, don't get intoxicated, and don't fall asleep at the wheel, opening up the prospect of saving the lives of many of the tens of thousands of people each year who die from car accidents in the United States alone.[23] According to a J.D. Power and Associates research survey, 30 percent of drivers aged 18 to 37 say they would definitely or possibly buy a driverless vehicle, demonstrating the tremendous potential of this revolutionary change in road transport.[24]

Traditionalists argue that a majority of drivers will likely opt out, preferring the thrill—not to mention the control—of steering their own vehicle. Maybe the older generation will, but I doubt it for the Internet generation. For millennials, who are already distracted behind the wheel using their smartphones, it's unlikely that they would be more interested in driving a car than being driven by one. In the Collaborative Age, when time is the scarce commodity and attention is at a premium, freeing oneself from driving an automobile several hours a day is significant extra time to attend to more interesting activities in virtual space.

Sergey Brin, cofounder of Google, looks to a day not too far off when millions of car-share members summon cars electronically. After dropping off the members at their destinations, the driverless vehicles will be automatically dispatched to their next pick up or proceed back to the nearest car-share lot to charge their electric batteries and await the next summons.

In May 2013, Mercedes introduced its new S-Class automobile that can already partially drive itself and even park itself. The automobile, with a price tag of $100,000, can even hold itself in the middle of a lane and keep its distance from the car ahead. Dieter Zetsche, Daimler's CEO, says that Mercedes's newest vehicle "marks the beginning of autonomous driving."[25]

Industry analysts estimate that driverless vehicles will be commercially available in eight years or so. Brin is more optimistic, suggesting that a completely driverless automobile is not more than five years away.[16]

Why would anyone want to "own" and maintain an automobile when they could "access" a driverless vehicle from a car-sharing service at a moment's notice from their cell phone and have it ferry them effortlessly with GPS guidance to their destination, paying only for the precise time they are using the vehicle?

If ever proof were needed that the capitalist era, wedded to the exchange of property in markets, is ceding ground to the access of services in the Collaborative Commons, the changing relationship to the automobile is prima facie evidence of the great transformation at hand.

LETTING GO OF OWNERSHIP

In 2000, I published a book entitled *The Age of Access*. The book was released on the eve of the dot-com bubble burst. Ten years after the advent of the World Wide Web, the Internet was coming of age. Hundreds of millions of people were connecting and exploring a new virtual world every bit as expansive with opportunities as the discovery of the new world 500 years earlier. There was a manic rush to map the new territory of cyberspace and exploit a virgin domain that was virtually limitless and without boundaries. New social media spaces were coming alive every day, and an entire generation seemed awed by the possibilities of creating entirely new ways to collaborate and share their lives with one another.

Beneath all the surface hyperbole that went along with the colonization of cyberspace, scholars and activists alike were beginning to ask the question of how this new virtual public square—one that is capable of connecting the entire human race for the very first time in history—might change the fundamentals of how society is organized. What consequences would flow from a social space where everyone could reach everyone else, connect, collaborate, and create new ways to interact with one another on a planetary scale—something never before imaginable?

I started thinking about writing the book in 1998. I was teaching at the time in the advanced management program at the Wharton School at the University of Pennsylvania. CEOs from around the world were beginning to sniff around the Internet, attempting to figure out whether it posed a threat, an opportunity, or both to their way of doing business. It was then that I began to ponder some questions. What might happen if millions of Internet users began bypassing the traditional commercial channels of the market? What if they created their own virtual meeting places and began to use the distributed, collaborative nature of the Internet to create lateral economies of scale and start sharing ideas, information, and even things with one another on a Commons, skipping all the middle men, markups, and margins on the traditional capitalist value chain, and by doing so, bring the marginal cost of producing additional units to near zero? Amazon and eBay had already been around for three or four years and offered a taste of the potential commercial gains in collapsing the cost spread along the value stream to just a few players separating the seller from the buyer.

More importantly, Napster had just formed in 1999 and was taking that possibility to the next level. Napster was a peer-to-peer Internet file-sharing network that allowed millions of people to share music with one another for free on the Commons. Suddenly a new economic model opened up. Within a few years, other Internet file-sharing networks would follow, bringing the music industry to its knees.

Napster changed the rules of the economic game. Many sellers and buyers disappeared, replaced by providers and users. Ownership of CDs gave way to access to music libraries online. Markets succumbed to networked Commons. A vertically integrated industry controlled by a handful of giant recording companies buckled under the collective weight of millions of buyers turned peer-to-peer collaborators.

Could the contagion spread? Might it touch every company and industry represented in my management classes? I asked my corporate executives, but they weren't sure.

In *The Age of Access*, I acknowledged that

the very thought of leaving markets and the exchange of property behind—of advancing a conceptual change in the structuring of human relationships away from ownership and toward access—is as inconceivable to many people today as enclosure and privatization of land and labor into property relationships must have been more than a half a millennium ago. [However,] it is likely that for a growing number of enterprises and consumers, the very idea of ownership will seem limited, even old fashioned, 25 years from now.[27]

In the ten years that followed the publication of the book, I continued to put the same question to corporate leaders in my Wharton classes. The "not sure" responses fell in number as the growing thirst for access over ownership spread to every quarter of commercial culture. Global companies are beginning to adjust to the generational shift from ownership to access by deemphasizing the sale of things and refocusing their business practices on managing every aspect of their client's value chain—what they call being a "solution provider." They are trying to find relevance in a fast changing economic environment where margins are quickly disappearing. Today there are few industries unaffected by the shift from ownership to access and from markets to networked Commons as a younger generation flexes its collaborative muscle in pursuit of a near zero marginal cost society.

Millions of people are sharing not only automobiles and bicycles, but also their homes, clothes, tools, toys, and skills in networked Commons. The sharing economy is arising for a combination of reasons. The global collapse of the Second Industrial Revolution economy in the summer of 2008 was a wake-up call. In America and elsewhere, hundreds of millions of families found themselves awash in "stuff" they barely used and buried in debt to finance it. The sober reality is that when crude oil hit $147 per barrel on world markets, purchasing power tumbled, and the economy tanked, sending millions of employees home with pink slips. There was real worry of another Great Depression—we settled for calling it the Great Recession. Without a paycheck and with few prospects, millions of families looked to their savings and found they had none. What they did find was astronomical debt built up over nearly 20 years of profligate consumption in the biggest buying spree in history. Try this on: total American household debt topped out at $13.9 trillion in 2008.[28] Coming out from under that would take decades, and economists were cautioning that, even then, today's youth would not likely enjoy anywhere near the standard of living of their parents' and grandparents' generations.

For the first time, millions of families began to look over all the stuff they didn't need and hadn't even fully paid for and asked not just "why me?" but "why?" It was a collective existential question—a soul-searching reevaluation of the nature of modern life. "What was I thinking?" became the unspoken litany of the so-called "consumer society." Some began to question the value of accumulating more and more possessions that added little or nothing to their sense of happiness and well-being.

At the same time, parents were being bombarded by dire warnings of catastrophic climate change as a result of two centuries of industrial activity that had created untold prosperity—the average upper-middle-class person's wealth exceeding that of emperors and kings just four centuries earlier—at the expense of Earth's ecological endowment. Was their wealth saddling their children and grandchildren with an even bigger environmental debt that might never be paid back?

Families began to realize they had been sold a bill of goods, that they had been sucked into a debilitating addiction fed by billions of dollars of corporate advertising that had left them at the doorstep of ruin and despair. It was a collective "ah ha" moment when large numbers of people stopped dead in their tracks and began to reverse course. The way out was to turn the entire economic system on its head—buy less, save more, and share what one has with others. Runaway consumption would be replaced by a shareable economy.

A powerful new economic movement took off overnight, in large part because a younger generation had a tool at its disposal that enabled it to scale quickly and effectively and share its personal bounty on a global Commons. The distributed, collaborative nature of the Internet allowed millions of people to find the right match-ups to share whatever they could spare with what others could use. The sharing economy was born. This is a different kind of economy—one far more dependent on social capital than market capital. And it's an economy that lives more on social trust rather than on anonymous market forces.

Rachel Botsman, an Oxford- and Harvard-educated former consultant to GE and IBM who abandoned her career to join the new sharing economy, describes the path that led up to collaborative consumption. She notes that the social Web has passed through three phases—the first enabled programmers to freely share code; Facebook and Twitter allowed people to share their lives; and YouTube and Flickr allowed people to share their creative content. "Now we're going into the fourth phase," Botsman says, "where people are saying, 'I can apply the same technology to share all kinds of assets offline, from the real world.'"[29]

Let me add an amplifier at this juncture: while the Communications Internet is an enabler, as it merges with the Energy Internet and the Transportation Internet in the years ahead, establishing an integrated and sharable communication, energy, and transportation infrastructure—an Internet of Things—that can operate at near zero marginal cost, it dramatically boosts the potential of the other sharable sectors, including rentals, redistribution networks, cultural exchanges, and exchanges of professional and technical skills. When that happens, collaborative production and exchange will scale up from a niche sector to the dominant paradigm and capitalism will be reactive to the Commons, not the other way around.

Botsman captures the physiology of the new economic paradigm growing up in our midst. She writes:

Every day people are using Collaborative Consumption—traditional sharing, bartering, lending, trading, renting, gifting, and swapping, redefined through technology and peer communities. Collaborative Consumption is enabling people to realize the enormous benefits of access to products and services over ownership, and at the same time save money, space, and time; make new friends; and become active citizens once again. . . . These systems provide significant environmental benefits by increasing use efficiency, reducing waste, encouraging the development of better products, and mopping up the surplus created by over-production and -consumption.[30]

SHARING EVERYTHING

Much of what we own goes unused some of the time. Sharing spare rooms or even couches has become a big-ticket item among enthusiasts. Airbnb and HomeAway are among the many start-ups that are connecting millions of people who have homes to rent with prospective users. Airbnb, which went online in 2008, boasted 110,000 available rooms listed on its site just three years later and was expanding its available listings by an astounding 1,000 rooms every day.[31] To date, 3 million Airbnb guests booked 10 million nights in 33,000 cities, spanning 192 countries.[32] In 2012 bookings were growing at a blistering pace of 500 percent a year, an exponential curve that would bring envy, if not terror, to any global hotel chain.[33] Airbnb is expected to pass the venerable Hilton and InterContinental hotel chains—the world's largest hotel operations—in 2014 by filling up more rooms per night across the globe.[34]

Like other shareable brokers, Airbnb gets only a small cut from the renter and owner for bringing them together. It can charge such low fees because it has very low fixed costs and each additional rental brokered approaches near zero marginal cost. Like all the new sharable sites, the lateral scaling potential on the Internet is so dramatic that start-ups like Airbnb can take off, catch up to, and even surpass the older, global hotel chains in just a few short years.

Airbnb is a private firm operating in a shared Internet Commons. Couchsurfing, Airbnb's major competition, is of a different mold. It started as a nonprofit organization and remained so until 2011. During that time, it picked up 5.5 million members in 97,000 cities in 207 countries.[35] (Although it switched nominally to a profit-making operation in 2012, it continues as a free service, but users can pay a one-time $25 membership fee if they so choose.)[36] Its members provide free lodging to each other.

Couchsurfing also differentiates itself from its more commercial competitor, Airbnb, by viewing its mission more broadly as social rather than commercial in nature. Members are encouraged to socialize with each other during their stays and develop bonds of friendship that continue after their visits. The goal is to help "couchsurfers share their lives with the people they encounter, fostering cultural exchange and mutual respect."[37] More than 99 percent of the members say they have had positive experiences couch surfing.[38] Members report more than 19.1 million friendships arising from their visits. Members also participate in more than 40,000 different couch-sharing interest groups.[39]

Toy rentals have also enjoyed success as sharable items. Baby Plays, Rent That Toy!, and Spark Box Toys are typical. For a small subscription of between $25 and $60 per month, the services ship between four and ten toys each month to the member's home. The toys are sanitized after each shipment to assure that they meet appropriate health safeguards. Any parent knows that children generally tire of new toys quite quickly, after which they remain in a toy chest, closet, or box in the attic, sometimes for years, gathering dust. With sharable toys, toddlers come to learn early on that a toy is not a possession to own, but rather a short-term experience to enjoy, changing the very way they think about the physical things they use.

Even clothes, the most personal of all physical items, are metamorphosing from a possession to a service. Ties, of all things, are now being rented. Tie Society, a start-up in Washington, D.C., stocks more than 300 designer ties—each of which, if bought, would cost an arm and a leg. For a monthly fee of $11, subscribers receive a box of sanitized ties to use, and they can change their tie selection monthly.[40]

For women there's Rent The Runway, I-Ella, MakeupAlley, Avelle, and scores of other sites that connect providers and users across the retail-fashion industry. Women who have purchased designer dresses, handbags, and jewelry connect with users who rent the apparel and accessories for a fraction of their retail purchase price.

While rentables are booming, so too are redistribution networks. It's not surprising that a younger generation that grew up recycling plastics, glass, and paper would turn next to recycling the items they own. The notion of optimizing the lifecycle of items in order to reduce the need to produce more partially used goods has become second nature to young people for whom sustainability is the new frugality.

The Freecycle Network (TFN) was an early Commons leader in shareable recyclables. The nonprofit organization, with 9 million members in 85 countries, is organized into 5,000 local groups whose members post unwanted items that are available for free to other members in the community. The founders of TFN boast that their recyclable Commons model is "changing the world one gift at a time."[41]

ThredUP is another popular redistribution organization. The online consignment shop, which has 400,000 members, started by recycling toddlers' and children's clothes and has recently moved into women's apparel.[42] ThredUp points out that the average child outgrows more than 1,360 articles of clothing by age 17.[43] When children outgrow their clothes, their parents fill a ThredUP bag and put it on the front porch. ThredUP then retrieves it and pays for the shipping. Every time ThredUP finds another home for the clothing item, the provider receives a credit in the ThredUP store that can be used to obtain "new" old clothes for their growing youngster. The sharable consignment boutique sells used clothes for up to a 75 percent discount, allowing the items to be handed around (rather than down) and enjoy multiple lives. ThredUP owes its success to the Web's ability to bring together hundreds of thousands of providers and users in a distributed, laterally scaled network. Its members can browse over thousands of items on the website racks, finding just the right match for their children. ThredUP draws approximately 385,000 visits a month and sold over 350,000 items in 2012, and orders are growing by a whopping 51 percent a month.[44]

Who could be opposed to the idea of collaborative consumption and a sharing economy? These new economic models seem so benign. Sharing represents the best part of human nature. Reducing addictive consumption, optimizing frugality, and fostering a more sustainable way of life is not only laudable, but essential if we are to ensure our survival.

But even here, there are winners and losers. The still-dominant capitalist system believes it can find value in the collaborative economy by leveraging aspects of the sharing culture toward new revenue-generating streams. Still, whatever profit it can squeeze out of the growing networked Commons will pale in comparison to the ground it loses.

Although hotels will continue to book, they are already seeing their markets decline as millions of young people migrate to Airbnb and Couchsurfing. How does a huge hotel chain, with its high fixed costs, compete with literally millions of privately owned spaces that can be shared at low and even near zero marginal costs?

Retailers of all kinds, already on the ropes with disappearing profit margins, are going to be equally disadvantaged by a sharable economy where clothes, appliances, toys, tools, and thousands of other items are continually in use through rental and redistribution networks. Extending the lifecycle of stuff by passing it on from user to user significantly cuts into new sales.

The retailers' dilemma struck me when I heard about a new sharable site called Yerdle that came online in 2012. The founders are veterans of the sustainability movement with close ties to the business community: Adam Werbach was formerly president of the Sierra Club, and Andy Ruben was formerly the chief sustainability officer at Walmart. Yerdle matches up Facebook friends who have unused items they'd like to either give away or sell. Besides clothes, Yerdle members can exchange just about anything: cell phones, computers, sports equipment, kitchen appliances, pet accessories . . . you name it.

For now, Yerdle communities are locally based. Facebook friends can come together and create a sharable space if they have at least 50 items to share. Some networks have several thousand items inventoried, providing a one-stop shopping experience for things a "friend" might want to share. Yerdle doesn't charge for each sharing transaction, but friends usually have to cover the shipping expenses. As Yerdle grows, it will allow its local networks to expand geographically, so items can be sold to strangers as well as to friends. Yerdle plans on taking a small transaction fee to cover its operational costs.

The Yerdle plan, like so many others, helps advance the idea of a circular economy in which everything is recycled and reused and nothing is sent to the landfill before its time. The sustainable business logic makes perfect sense, but gets muddled when the founders try to make the case for the retailer's buy-in. Werbach says that "if you can borrow that chain saw from the person next door, the retailer's job is to help you with what you're trying to do, not just sell you another chain saw."[45] Maybe . . . but likely?

Werbach and Ruben tout the idea that "sharing is more fun than shopping," which an increasing number of people seem to agree with. But Walmart? Doubtful! Still, determined to find at least a niche commercial opportunity for the big-box chain stores that might draw them in, Werbach and Ruben propose some scenarios in which they might benefit from a movement hinged on sharing rather than shopping. If, for example, a Yerdle member wanted to go camping for the first time but didn't want to lay out $500 or more for expensive equipment before he knew whether he would even enjoy the experience, he might start by using camping equipment made available on Yerdle. If commercial retailers were sponsors or friends on Yerdle, the smitten camper might trade up along the line, for the latest camping paraphernalia, bringing him or her into the bosom of commerce. Again, this is the hope of so many of the young social entrepreneurs who walk the line between capitalist markets and the social Commons. The central question is: Where does one's loyalty lie? Is the near zero marginal cost Commons seen mainly as a new commercial opportunity for the market to exploit, as Chris Anderson and others have argued, or is it an end unto itself—a new economic paradigm—with spillover applications that can draw some market engagement? I have no doubt that most social entrepreneurs line up in the second category, but are anxious to at least find a responsible way to engage the conventional capitalist system in the newly forming networked Commons.

Neal Gorenflo, the cofounder and editor of *Shareable* magazine, a nonprofit online media publication that reports on new developments in the collaborative consumption economy, notes that while U.S. retail sales in 2011 were $4.7 trillion, collaborative consumption represented nearly $100 billion in turnover that year. Gorenflo asked what retailers can do to leverage their formidable commercial power and quickly take collaborative consumption mainstream.[46]

Gorenflo outlines a tracking system that would allow a retailer to continue to capture part of the income stream of each item it sold, as it moved from user to user across the sharable economy. The point of purchase at the retailer would be "a gateway to a collaborative marketplace that manages a product through its lifecycle including multiple owners and users."[47] Each item would have all the product and transaction data automatically encoded on it and a unique identifier providing a chronicle of its journey from one user to another. The big retailers could establish a mega–online marketplace that allows each purchaser to list his or her resharable items for rent or swap. Gorenflo says that such a plan would allow him to control how he manages his assets and give him the biggest marketplace in the world to share his stuff. He adds that "I'd be happy to pay a small fee for each transaction for this service."[48] In this scenario, says Gorenflo, everyone wins.[49] Retailers continue to capture revenue through the product's lifecycle. They might also be encouraged to market some of their products as a fee-based service, putting them at the center of the resharable economy. Exacting value through the entire lifecycle of a good would also encourage retailers to upgrade the quality and durability of their products. The user benefits from the lower cost of short-term access versus long-term ownership and also comes to feel like part of a larger sharing economy that is less wasteful and more sustainable.

Interesting idea. Certainly it provides retailers with a piece of the action—but it's more like throwing them a bone than handing them a golden opportunity. Whatever small transaction fees they receive in the remaining lifecycle of a product they initially sold are insignificant compared to the losses they incur as millions of people share more and buy fewer new items. Again, it's not that the capitalist market can't find value on the Commons, but it will continue to shrink into ever more restricted niche spaces as the social economy comes to eclipse the market economy.

Even backyard gardens are being shared. SharedEarth was founded by Adam Dell, an Internet entrepreneur. Dell wanted a vegetable garden in his yard in Austin, Texas, but had neither the time nor skills to do it himself. So he posted an ad on Craigslist in 2010 that read: "I'll provide the land, water, and materials if you'll provide the work. We can share the produce 50–50." He made the deal with a woman who loved gardening but who lived in an apartment.[50]

Like most Internet-savvy professionals, Dell saw the potential opportunity of laterally scaling his experience by taking it to the Web. Within four months, SharedEarth went from 800,000 square feet to 25,000,000 square feet of shared space. Dell envisions millions of acres of unused backyards being transformed into vegetable garden Commons:

> I think SharedEarth is something that can be meaningful in its impact, and that is my hope. Just imagine if we had 10 million acres of producing land. That would produce a lot of oxygen, consume a lot of CO_2 and produce a lot of food. [51]

SharedEarth is not yet a serious threat to conventional agriculture. Undeterred, Dell believes that if large numbers of wannabe gardeners were connected with unused land they could produce high-quality, local, organic food. He hopes that such efforts will encourage a trend away from vertically scaled centralized farming, with produce shipped over long distances, to distributed, laterally scaled regional farming for local consumption—with the efficiency gains that go with it.

Dell adds that "we are a free service. We have no business model!" A correction: SharedEarth does have a business model—it's called the Commons.[52]

While gardeners are beginning to share harvests on microplots, a younger generation of farmers is sharing harvests on an agricultural scale with urban consumers. Community supported agriculture (CSA) began inauspiciously in Europe and Japan in the 1960s and accelerated rapidly in the United States and other countries in the 1990s with the rise of the Internet. Urban consumers pledge a fixed amount of money to local farmers in advance of the growing season to pay for the up-front cost of growing the crops. The consumers become, in effect, shareholders. In return, the consumers are provided with the bounty from the harvest delivered to their door or to nearby distribution centers throughout the growing season. If the farmers' crops are plentiful, the shareholders are awarded with the additional yield. Likewise, if yields are down because of adverse weather or other conditions, the shareholders share in the losses with the delivery of less produce.

The sharing of risk between consumers and farmers creates a bond of mutual trust and fosters social capital. Moreover, eliminating all the middlemen in the conventional, vertically integrated agribusiness operations dramatically reduces the costs of the produce for the end user.

Many CSA operations use ecological agricultural practices and organic farming techniques, eliminating the high costs and environmental damage caused by the use of petrochemical fertilizers and pesticides. Energy and environmental costs are further reduced by eliminating plastic packaging and the long-haul transport of produce.

The Internet has been a great facilitator of CSA by making it easier for farmers and consumers to connect in peer-to-peer networks. Local CSA websites also allow farmers and customers to stay in constant contact, sharing up-to-date information on crop performance and delivery schedules. CSAs replace sellers and buyers in the conventional market with providers and users exchanging produce on a social Commons. In a sense, consumers become prosumers by financing the means of production that deliver the end products they will consume. There are thousands of CSA enterprises scattered around the world, and their numbers are growing as a younger generation becomes increasingly comfortable with the idea of exercising more of its commercial options in a social economy on the Commons.

PATIENT-DRIVEN HEALTH CARE

If sharing couches, clothes, and food touches on the more personal aspects of people's daily lives, sharing medical data reaches down into the most intimate domain uploaded on the Commons. Millions of people are open sourcing the personal details of their medical history and current conditions, sharing information on symptoms, diagnoses, and treatments; collaborating in research to find cures; joining in support groups to provide solace, comfort, and encouragement to one another; and spearheading advocacy groups to push governments, insurance companies, and the medical community to rethink medical-health assumptions and protocols across every aspect of the health-care field. In the United States, where health-care costs represent 17.9 percent of GDP, patients are becoming their own advocates on a giant health Commons that's paralleling the market economy and shaking up the theory and practice of medicine.[53]

Health care, which was traditionally a private relationship between doctor and patient—in which the physician prescribed and a passive patient followed the physician's instructions—has suddenly been transformed into a distributed, laterally scaled, peer-to-peer relationship in which patients, doctors, researchers, and other health-care providers collaborate in open-networked Commons to advance patient care and the health of society.

Patient-driven health care began randomly as increasing numbers of people started to search for their symptoms on the Internet to pinpoint a diagnosis of their medical condition. In the process, they came across others on the Web who had similar conditions and began sharing notes. Those who had already been diagnosed began to share their personal histories of a disease or illness on various health-care websites in hopes of eliciting feedback from individuals with similar case histories. Still others, unhappy with the treatment prescribed by their physicians, began searching for like-minded individuals who had similar misgivings in hopes of learning about alternative treatments. Individuals also began comparing notes on the side effects they were experiencing in taking certain drugs, especially if they were being taken in tandem with other drugs. People with chronic or life-threatening illnesses for which existing treatments were either inadequate or nonexistent began to band together in search of potential cures. The more activist inclined started groups to lend each other emotional and practical support and launched advocacy organizations to bring public attention to their disease and push for more public funds to find a cure.

Today there are numerous social media websites where millions of people are engaging, supporting, and aiding each other in the pursuit of advances in medical care and public health. Some of the most popular sites include PatientsLikeMe, ACOR, the LAM Foundation, Cure Together, the Life Raft Group, the Organization for Autism Research, the Chordoma Foundation, and LMSarcoma Direct Research.

Many of the patient-driven health-care sites are the outgrowths of very personal stories, often dealing with rare diseases that have received little attention and even less research into treatment and cures. Lymphangioleiomyomatosis (LAM) is a rare and fatal disease that is caused by a defect in a cellular pathway that regulates cell growth. The defect, which destroys young women's lungs, has been associated with a number of cancers including melanoma and breast cancer.

In 2005, Amy Farber, then a student and now a member of the faculty of the Harvard Medical School, was diagnosed with LAM and was warned that a pregnancy might risk accelerating the disease. Anxious to find a treatment or cure, Farber reached out to the conventional research establishment and found that very little work was being done on this rare disease, and even then, the efforts were isolated and disjointed, with little or no attempt at collaboration. Frustrated at the lack of progress in dealing with the disease, she contacted Dr. George Demetri, a professor and cancer researcher at Harvard Medical School who had been interested in using the Internet to link patients all around the world with the aim of tapping into their experiences and insights with rare cancers. Demetri hoped that the data might reveal a "collective wisdom" of sorts about the nature and course of such diseases that could be drawn upon to find treatment protocols and cures. The two subsequently joined forces with Frank Moss, director of the MIT Media Lab, and out of that collaboration came thelamfoundation.org, a website that allows patients to report on their health. The data in the reports are aggregated and analyzed to aid researchers in mapping out new research scenarios. This crowd-sourcing approach to research differs substantially from traditional randomized controlled trials used in conventional research, which are expensive and time consuming and conceived of and carried out by researchers from the top down, with patients serving as passive subjects. The LAM site, like other research efforts on the health-care Commons, starts with the patients' collective wisdom, which helps determine the research protocols. Moss explains that "we're really turning patients into scientists and changing the balance of power between clinicians and scientists and patients."[54]

The Association of Cancer Online Resources (ACOR), founded by Gilles Frydman, has taken the idea of patient-driven health care a step further by creating a more comprehensive health Commons where over 600,000 patients and caregivers are actively engaged in 163 public online communities. Where the LAM Treatment Alliance relied on patients reporting on their own condition and researchers creating protocols, ACOR patients and caregivers share scientific information and are co-involved in "organizing and developing new methodologies of data collection and aggregation—with the ultimate goal of guiding the research on their disease."[55] They also raise funds for scientific research. These e-patients are developing what Frydman calls a "participatory-medicine model," which brings all the various players together in a Commons—patients, researchers, doctors, payers, medical-device companies, caregivers, drug companies, and medical professionals—where they collaborate to optimize the care of patients.

Patient-driven research (PDR) is even beginning to penetrate the inner sanctum of science. Some e-patient online communities have erected tissue and specimen banks. Others have created cell lines for testing. Still others have set up patient registries and formed clinical-trial networks.[56]

PatientsLikeMe, a patient-driven health-care network of more than 200,000 patients that tracks 1,800 diseases, published the first patient-initiated observational study refuting the findings of a conventional study that found that the drug lithium carbonate could slow the progression of the neurodegenerative disease amyotrophic lateral sclerosis (ALS).[57] The organization reports that it "developed a novel algorithm designed to match patients who reported taking lithium with a number of other ALS patients that had similar disease courses."[58] PatientsLikeMe tracked 348 ALS patients using off-label lithium, and found that "lithium was not having an observable effect on the disease progression of these patients."[59]

Although the patient-directed trial might not quite compare to the double-blind, controlled clinical study, its speed and reduced cost make it a powerful new player in the research arena. Norman Scherzer of the Life Raft Group, a health-care Commons that deals with gastro-intestinal stromal tumors, explains why many patients are migrating to the new Commons approach to research.

> One of the great benefits of PDR is its speed. We can get lifesaving information out to the people who need it right away, much faster than professional researchers, who must go though many time-consuming steps. . . . This can take several years. So professional research has a built-in lethal lag time—a period of delay between the time some people know about an important medical breakthrough and the time everyone knows.[60]

While double-blind, controlled clinical studies are extremely expensive, patient-initiated observational studies using Big Data and algorithms to discover health patterns and impacts can be undertaken at near zero marginal cost.

Still in its infancy, this open-source approach to research often suffers from a lack of verification that the slower, time-tested professional review process brings to conventional randomized control trials. Advocates are aware of these shortcomings but are confident that patient-directed research can begin to build in the appropriate checks, much like Wikipedia does in the shakeout process of verifying and validating articles on its websites. Today, Wikipedia has 19 million contributors. Thousands of users fact check and refine articles, assuring that the open-source website's accuracy is competitive with other encyclopedias. Wikipedia is now the world's eighth-most-visited website, drawing millions of viewers to the encyclopedia of the world's knowledge.[61]

Patient-driven health Commons advocates remind us that when Wikipedia first came online, academics argued that the democratization of scholarly research would severely compromise the high academic standards that went into compiling encyclopedias. Their fears turned out to be unjustified. The champions of patient-directed open-source Commons health research ask why crowdsourcing of research, with rigorous scientific protocols in place, should fare any worse.

EVERYONE'S A DOCTOR

There are also signs that a younger generation of doctors is beginning to align with the new patient-driven health Commons movement. Dan Hoch, a neurologist who specializes in epilepsy at Massachusetts General Hospital, penned an insightful piece on his own conversion to the new e-patient online Commons movement. He acknowledged that there had always been an "unspoken prohibition" within the medical profession on patients getting together for fear that it might undermine the authority of physicians. He wrote, "I had the uncomfortable sense that by promoting interactions between patients and de-emphasizing the central role of the physician, I might be violating some deep taboo."[62]

Hoch threw caution to the wind and decided to look into an online epilepsy support group called BrainTalk Communities—a nonprofit website community established by a colleague at Mass General, John Lester. At the time, BrainTalk hosted more than 300 free online groups for a range of neurological conditions, including Alzheimer's, multiple sclerosis, Parkinson's, Huntington's, and epilepsy. More than 200,000 individuals around the world visit the BrainTalk website regularly.

Hoch was surprised to find that, contrary to his suspicion, only 30 percent of the postings were related to emotional support, while the remaining 70 percent were taken up with group members educating each other about the disease, treatment options, management protocols, side effects, and learning to cope with the disease from day to day. Of particular interest was the finding that members were continuously fact-checking each other in a process of self-correction, challenging unfounded or dubious information. Hoch said that what surprised him most of all was the realization "that an online group like the BrainTalk Communities epilepsy group is not only much smarter than any single patient, but is also smarter, or at least more comprehensive, than many physicians—even medical specialists."[63]

Hoch concluded with a stunning admission:

> I had been taught to believe that patients could only be "empowered" by their clinicians . . . it now seems quite clear that growing numbers of patients are perfectly capable of empowering themselves, with or without their clinician's blessing.[64]

There are currently hundreds of open-source health Commons online. That number is likely to increase dramatically in the years ahead as nations begin to use electronic health records to streamline the delivery of health-care services. In 2009, the U.S. government awarded $1.2 billion in grants to assist health-care providers in implementing electronic health-care records.[65] The Big Data that will be potentially available in the United States and other countries will provide a pool of information that, if used by open-source patient-driven health Commons, with the appropriate privacy guarantees put in place, could revolutionize the health-care field.

The potential of using Big Data to address health issues became apparent in the winter of 2013 when a serious flu epidemic spread quickly around the world. Google was able to pinpoint the locations where the flu was breaking out and the intensity of the epidemic, as well as track where it was spreading in real time, by analyzing data of people's searches for flu-related topics on Google. While subsequent analysis showed that Google had overestimated the intensity of the epidemic, in part because of widespread media coverage—especially in social media—that drew more people to flu-related searches, its tracking was sufficiently reliable as an early-warning mechanism that the U.S. Centers for Disease Control and Prevention subsequently made Google an official partner in their surveillance programs.[66]

With epidemics, tracking the spread of breakouts in real time is critical to controlling the disease. Being able to mobilize local health-care services, ensure that flu shots are available and quickly administered where needed, and alert the public makes a big difference in the severity of the outbreak. In the traditional surveillance system, it can take between one and two weeks to collect data from doctors around the country based on patients' visits. By that time the flu virus could have peaked or even run its course. Google tracks peoples' first response when they search the Web to see if their symptoms match those of the disease, often days before they call or visit their physician.

Twitter is also being looked to as a tracker. Twitter users send more than 500 million tweets per day. People who are not feeling well will often tweet their condition to friends, hours before the flu has disabled them, again providing an up-to-the-moment account of how the virus is spreading.

Epidemiologists, at present, assert that these early-warning tracking tools are complementary, or even supplementary, to the tried-and-true surveillance models. Yet there is a growing consensus that refining the algorithms to screen out noise and establish a more accurate reading of the data will make Google and Twitter surveillance and tracking more robust and the systems themselves more critical to the monitoring and containment of viral epidemics.[67] Using Big Data to track global epidemics and blunt contagions will save billions of dollars in health-care costs while the surveillance and reporting system heads to near zero marginal cost.

As researchers discover more about the links between genetic abnormalities and environmental triggers in the new field of genomic medicine, they're learning that while illness can be broadly categorized—for example, breast cancer, leukemia, and lung disease—each individual's illness is unique, even if diagnosed as part of a generally defined illness. Genetic medicine is at the forefront of a new customized approach to illness that treats each individual's affliction as an "orphan" disease.

The diminishing cost of DNA sequencing is making available a library of Big Data that can be used by individuals to begin connecting with others who share a similar DNA profile. In the future, as DNA databases expand and the full sequence of human DNA becomes available for testing, millions of people will be able to match up with those who share common inherited genetic traits in customized patient-driven health networks, and compare notes on illnesses and collaborate to find cures. These more customized patient-directed health Commons will also be able to create sufficient lateral scale to bring public attention to their disease cluster and encourage increased government, academic, and corporate research into their illnesses as well as raise funds for their own research, clinical trials, and treatment.

These DNA clusters of biologically matched individuals will also be able to use Big Data to cross-reference each other's lifestyles—eating habits, smoking and drinking, exercise regimens, and work environments—to further correlate the relationship between genetic predispositions and various environmental triggers. Because the matched human clusters will include a chronology of life histories from in utero to old age and death, algorithms will undoubtedly be developed to pinpoint potential disease risks at various stages of one's life as well as effective treatments.

By midcentury or earlier, I suspect that any individual will be able to access a global health Commons search engine, register their genetic makeup, find a matching cluster of similar genomes, and receive a detailed account of their health risks over a lifetime as well as a rundown of the most effective customized medical treatments to make them well and keep them well, at near zero marginal cost.

Organ transplants are among the most expensive medical procedures. Even here, new medical breakthroughs are opening up the possibility of significantly lowering the costs of organ replacements. If replacement tissues and organs are necessary, they will be able to be printed on a 3D printer, again at low or near zero marginal cost, in the not-too-distant future. Three-dimensional printing of human body parts is already well along. The Wake Forest Institute for Regenerative Medicine in North Carolina has recently printed a prototype human kidney using living cells.[68] Organovo, a San Diego-based Life Science company, has used 3D bioprinting to print a functioning section of human liver tissue.[69] Researchers at the ARC Centre of Excellence for Electromaterials Science at the University of Wollongong in Australia are experimenting using 3D processes to print muscle and nerve cells into living tissue. Cameron Ferris, a researcher at the ARC Centre, explains how bioprinting works: "We use the same technology as ink-jet printers, however instead of ink we are using cell types."[70] Using the cells from a patient's own body to reproduce the tissue, rather than implanting donor tissue, avoids rejection of the implant.

The 3D bioprinting of supplemental tissues, including heart patches, nerve grafts, blood vessel segments, and cartilage for degenerating joints, is expected to be in widespread use within the next ten years. The 3D bioprinting of complete organs will take a little longer.

Stuart Williams, a scientist at the Cardiovascular Innovation Institute in Louisville, Kentucky, is experimenting with taking fat-derived cells extracted during liposuction and mixing them with glue to print a heart. Williams believes that a 3D-printed "bioficial" heart may be possible in ten years.[71] Gordon Wallace of the ARC Centre says that "by 2025, it is feasible that we will be able to fabricate complete functional organs, tailored for an individual patient."[72] The brave new world of 3D bioprinted spare body parts will likely be a reality in the next several decades. As with other forms of 3D printing, the cost of replicating biological spare parts will plummet as the new technology scales up.

Today's high-cost health care—much of which is primitive, ill-informed, and costly—will be a thing of the past in a Big Data culture and a near zero marginal cost society.

Like the democratizing of information on the Internet, the democratization of electricity on the Energy Internet, the democratization of manufacturing with open-source 3D printing, the democratization of higher education with MOOCs, and the democratization of exchange in the sharable economy, the potential democratization of health care on the Web adds one more layer to the social economy, making the Collaborative Commons an ever more prominent force in the affairs of society.

THE END OF ADVERTISING

The shareable economy on the Commons is already forcing a fundamental restructuring of one of the key components of the traditional market-exchange economy. From the very beginning, advertising has been the driving force of the capitalist system. In the precapitalist era, when economic activity looked more like a flat line than an upward curve, human beings were conditioned to work just enough hours to secure their daily survival. Savings were virtually nonexistent. The onset of the Industrial Revolution brought with it a dramatic increase in material output and an accompanying increase in wages. Ensuring that those wages were quickly turned around and spent on consuming the goods workers produced became the mission of advertising. If there ever was an invisible hand, it is surely advertising's ability to keep demand at pace with increasing supply. No small task.

Recall that until the early twentieth century, "consumption" had a negative connotation. It was the lay term for tuberculosis and the early dictionary definition of consumption was "to waste, pillage and exhaust." It was only in the 1920s, with the advent of modern advertising, that consumption was given a makeover, turning it from a scourge to a social aspiration. The advertising industry reoriented the popular psyche, casting out an age-old tradition of frugality in favor of a new ethos that lauded the spendthrift over the skinflint. To be a consumer became the very mark of success and the epitome of what it meant to be thoroughly modern. By the second half of the century, consumer society began to overtake civil society as the primary community to which people owed their allegiance and forged their social identity. It's no mistake that immediately after the attack on the World Trade Center and the Pentagon on 9/11, President George W. Bush's public response to a terrified nation was to announce that "the American economy will be open for business." The president urged consumers to visit Disney World.[73]

In 2012, the U.S. advertising industry brought in revenues totaling $153 billion. Global advertising revenues that same year totaled $479.9 billion.[74] While the advertising industry appears to be thriving, insiders are worried. What they see is millions of people shifting from passive consumers to peer-to-peer prosumers of their own news, knowledge, entertainment, and energy. (And soon, their own 3D manufacturing.) The same multitudes are minimizing their purchases in the marketplace by sharing already-bought items with others in the collaborative economy. They are choosing access over ownership and using everything from cars to sports equipment on a "just-in-time" basis. And virtually all this activity is being negotiated on an open Internet Commons where the marginal cost of exchanging information is nearly zero. A younger generation is quietly disengaging from the traditional capitalist market. It's not yet a tidal wave, but the curve is exponential and likely irreversible.

This means that there is a diminishing consumer market for advertisers to exploit. And because the evolving social economy on the Commons is distributed, collaborative, and peer-to-peer, economic decisions are determined less by the sway of corporate advertising campaigns and more by recommendations, reviews, word of mouth, and likes and dislikes exchanged by "friends" and cohorts on Facebook, Twitter, YouTube, and hundreds of other social media sites online.

A spate of recent surveys reports that consumers place as much trust in consumer-generated reviews online as on recommendations from friends and family when it comes to purchasing decisions. Some 66.3 percent of consumers in one national survey say they rely "heavily" on user-generated content reviews and recommendations when making purchasing decisions.[75] In the Local Consumer Review Survey in 2012, "72% of consumers said they trust online reviews as much as personal recommendations."[76] Another survey found that 87 percent of consumers said a favorable online consumer-generated review sealed their decision to buy a product.[77] Even more revealing, "65% of consumers trust word of mouth on the Internet more than content produced by advertisers."[78] Consumer-generated reviews are potentially important when people are deciding on which local business to use, with 52 percent saying that positive online reviews influence their decision.[79]

Review websites abound on the Internet. Yelp, Angie's List, Citysearch, TripAdvisor, Travelocity, Judy's Book, and Local are among the hundreds of review sites where consumers check in to track other consumers' experiences—positive and negative—with goods and services. Now these reviews can be viewed on location when consumers are actually handling a product in the store. Consumr Reviews is a smartphone application that connects the phone directly with reviews of specific products. The user simply scans the barcode on the product into his or her cell phone and instantly accesses reviews of the item. Some of the new apps are even tied to the consumer's own ethical value preferences. GoodGuide is a cell phone application that allows the consumer to scan the barcode and scroll down reviews on the screen to see how others rated the product on safety, health, ethical considerations, and general sustainability.[80] The increasing use of mobile apps will allow consumers to post their reviews of products and services online in real time, making them available to others within seconds after they have used the product or service.

When asked why they trust consumer-generated reviews over advertiser content, respondents in a survey conducted by SurveyMonkey cited lack of bias versus vested interest in comparing the trustworthiness of consumers versus advertisers. In a typical response, a respondent said he trusted customer-generated reviews over advertisers "because producers of most products tend to be really promotional in their product descriptions, and consumers have no vested interest in the sales of the product, so their reviews are inherently more trustworthy."[81]

Although it's not uncommon for firms to game the system by posting anonymous favorable reviews of their own products and services or for competitors to post unfavorable reviews to hurt their rivals, they are the exception. Review sites are increasing their surveillance and monitoring devices and using ever more refined algorithms to weed out the fakes to protect their good name among consumers.[82]

Traditional advertising is being whacked from every direction. Consider one of the mainstays of advertising—classified ads in newspapers and magazines. Craigslist was founded in 1995 by Craig Newmark to list local classifieds and forums online, largely for free. Craigslist is still listed online as a dot-org rather than a dot-com to reflect what the organization says is its "relatively noncommercial nature, public-service mission, and noncorporate culture." More than 60 million people in the United States, along with millions more in 70 countries, use Craigslist each month—the website is in 13 languages— to search for jobs, housing, romance, and goods and services of all kinds. Craigslist users post 1 million classified ads each month, and its discussion forums attract 200 million people. Its entire operation is financed by tiny posting fees for jobs in 28 areas, and broker fees on New York City apartments.[83]

It's estimated that Craigslist single-handedly wiped out $10 billion in classified ad revenues in print publications annually, replacing it with $100 million in online revenues, with operating costs representing a fraction of the cost incurred by newspapers and magazines, which long relied on classified ads to stay afloat.[84] Craigslist's global online bulletin board is managed by a staff of just 30 people in its office in San Francisco.[85]

A 2012 study by IBM Global Business Services with the provocative title "The End of Advertising as We Know It" acknowledges that the Internet social Commons "puts at risk the revenue base of incumbent, traditional content distributors and aggregators."[86] The problem for the advertisers is that their business model is predicated on financing much of the delivery of newspapers, magazines, television, and radio content. The content is generated by professional journalists, television producers, writers, performers, and artists. In the past, passive consumers were willing to put up with advertisements in return for receiving the content it financed. But with the Internet, an increasing amount of the content is generated by the users themselves and shared with millions of others for free on sites like YouTube, Flickr, Facebook, etc. When consumers become prosumers and exchange content for free with one another in a sharable economy, what added value is corporate advertising bringing to the table? Advertisers could elect to finance the delivery of professional content online but it would likely fail because what brings millions of people to the Internet is the participatory nature of the medium. It's a Commons that operates in large part in a social economy governed by interactive peer-to-peer engagement.

While passive users of television might not be overly irritated by its scheduled advertising breaks, active and engaged online participants on the Internet are less tolerant of ads suddenly popping up in the middle of the screen blocking copy or interrupting their activity. The blast is seen as rude and intrusive. And Internet players are increasingly mistrustful of website search engines that sell access to advertisers by putting corporate sponsors at the front of the queue when users are looking for a particular resource or service.

Corporate advertising on a peer-to-peer medium is so strangely out of place that it is treated more like an interloper than a mere distraction and nuisance. Eric Clemons, a professor of operations and information management at the Wharton School, says that the very social nature of the Internet puts it out of bounds for commercial exploitation. He explains that the Internet "is participatory, like swapping stories around a campfire or attending a renaissance fair. It is not meant solely to push content, in one direction, to a captive audience, the way movies or traditional network television did."[87]

So when we tack on the proviso that the majority of Internet users mistrust advertising messages and instead look to other users' peer reviews of products as the most reliable source of information on what to buy, and that much of the content on the Internet is generated by the users themselves and not corporate advertisers, it's difficult to imagine how the advertising industry will survive the shift to a peer-to-peer communications medium except in a very reduced role. Clemons believes that paid advertising "will fail as a major revenue source for most Internet sites" for all the reasons mentioned above. His conclusion is that "the Internet is not replacing advertising but shattering it."[88] Even *The Economist* reluctantly agrees. In a sober editorial on "The End of the Free Lunch," it takes umbrage at what it regards as a faulty assumption that if social media sites can aggregate millions of users by providing them with free content, advertisers will be anxious to target ads on the medium, in the hope of capturing a percentage of the "long tail." But what if the users aren't listening, aren't watching, and are looking to their peers for product recommendations and validation? The *Economist* concludes that "the number of companies that can be sustained by revenues from internet advertising turns out to be much smaller than many people thought, and Silicon Valley seems to be entering another 'nuclear winter.'"[89]

Advertising revenues are beginning to reflect the pessimism. Internet advertising accounted for $36.6 billion in 2012, while, as mentioned, total U.S. advertising revenue came in at $153 billion, bringing the Internet share of the U.S. advertising market to only around 24 percent.[90] The growth in Internet advertising spending, however, appears to be slowing, indicating that the early euphoria about corporate advertising paying the bill for all the free content given away on profit-driven social media sites has softened. The rate of growth in Internet advertising declined from 23 percent between 2010 and 2011 to only 14 percent between 2011 and 2012.[91] GM's decision to yank ads from Facebook in 2012, saying they had "little impact on consumers' car purchases" reflects a growing sentiment among some corporations about the real value of advertising on the Internet.

The rate of growth of Internet advertising revenue is likely to continue to fall as millions of users switch from computers to mobile devices. Google, the leader in Internet advertising revenue, is already beginning to see ad revenue dry up in this changeover. While clicks on Google using laptop and desktop computers were flat in the third quarter of 2013, clicks on mobile phones doubled and clicks on tablets were up by 63 percent.[92] The problem is that mobile ads only cost one half to two-thirds as much as desktop ads and, worse still, they only lead to purchases of products and services a quarter to a third of the frequency of desktop ads, and there is no sign that this trajectory is going to significantly change. The reality is that Google's primary revenue stream is weakening. The *New York Times* reports that

> the price that advertisers pay [Google] each time someone clicks on
> an ad decreased for the eighth quarter in a row. It fell 8 percent
> from the period last year, largely because mobile ads cost less than
> desktop ones.[93]

With Internet users migrating quickly to mobile devices, the growth rate in advertising revenue is likely to continue to slow. The big question being asked in the C-suites of all the major for-profit social media enterprises is what the impact will be on their future growth potential.

Like other segments of the capitalist market, advertising will not altogether disappear with the rise of the Collaborative Commons. It will adjust and eventually settle into a niche within a maturing social economy. The reconditioning of the capitalist market to accommodate the social economy is a new phenomenon and difficult to accept in a world where for so long the social economy was the weak adjunct to market forces. In some instances, the market and the Commons will find potential synergies and even enjoy a symbiotic relationship that advances both. In others, like advertising, whose very thrust is at such odds with the collaborative peer-to-peer nature of the social Commons, efforts to find an accommodation will be more like trying to mix oil and water.

ALL THE VARIOUS ENTERPRISES CHRONICLED in the preceding pages are collaborative in nature, sharable in design, and take advantage of a distributed, laterally scaled IoT architecture. Some of the commerce is shareable in the sense of gift giving, like Couchsurfing. Others are mixed, combining gift giving and exchanges with some form of compensation. Still others are purely profit-seeking enterprises like eBay. If we think of a collaborative economy as both gift giving as well as redistribution and recycling with or without compensation, everyone is covered.

Recent surveys underscore the broad economic potential of the Collaborative Commons. A 2012 study by Campbell Mithun, a Minneapolis ad agency, in partnership with Carbonview Research, found that 62 percent of Gen Xers and millennials are attracted to the notion of sharing goods, services, and experiences in Collaborative Commons. These two generations differ significantly from the baby boomers and World War II generation in favoring access over ownership. When asked to rank the rational benefits of a sharing economy, respondents to the survey listed saving money at the top of the list, followed by impact on the environment, lifestyle flexibility, the practicality of sharing, and easy access to goods and services. As for the emotional benefits, respondents ranked generosity first, followed by a feeling of being a valued part of a community, being smart, being more responsible, and being a part of a movement.[94]

The public-opinion surveys show a profound change in thinking about the nature of economic activity among the younger generation. The shift from ownership to access, which I first identified back in 2000 in *The Age of Access*, is demonstrable and growing. Collaborative peer-to-peer economic activity is already robust, with a trend line that is only going to become more pronounced with the phasing in of the IoT.

How likely is it that the collaborative economy will disrupt the conventional business model? According to an opinion survey conducted by Latitude Research in 2010, "75% of respondents predicted their sharing of physical objects and spaces will increase in the next five years. . . . 78% of participants felt their online interactions with people have made them more open to the idea of sharing with strangers." And "85% of participants believe that Web and mobile technologies will play a critical role in building large-scale sharing communities in the future."[95] Many industry analysts agree with these optimistic forecasts. In 2011, *Time* magazine declared collaborative consumption to be one of its "10 ideas that will change the world."[96]

The Collaborative Commons has the potential to massively undermine the conventional capitalist market much sooner than many economists expect, because of the 10 percent effect. Umair Haque, author of *The New Capitalist Manifesto* and a contributing writer to the *Harvard Business Review*, sees the collaborative economy as having a "lethally disruptive" impact at a much lower threshold of buy-in than normally expected because of its ability to undercut already dangerously low profit margins across many sectors of the economy. He writes:

> If the people formally known as consumers begin consuming 10% less and peering 10% more, the effect on margins of traditional corporations is going to be disproportionately greater. . . . Which means certain industries have to rewire themselves, or prepare to sink into the quicksand of the past.[97]

The low threshold effect has already decimated the music industry, newspaper publishing, and the brick-and-mortar book trade. In publishing, e-books accounted for 22.6 percent of U.S. publishing in 2012.[98] The diminishing marginal cost of producing and delivering e-books has reduced retail prices significantly and forced smaller publishers and many retail book sellers out of business. Even the cheaper e-books are facing ever stiffer competition from copyleft publications that are distributed for free or nearly free.

We observed this same low threshold effect in chapter 5 in the disruptive impact renewable energy is having in Germany, where the generation of just 22 percent green electricity is already making it cost-prohibitive for power and utility companies to bring on line new backup fossil fuel power plants.[99] The amount of time these plants would need to be used would be less because of the surges of solar and wind electricity being fed into the grid by millions of prosumers, making the companies' payback time to cover their fixed costs too long and unpredictable to warrant the up-front costs of building them.

What's becoming apparent is that a growing number of giant capitalist enterprises across a range of commercial sectors that are already facing plummeting profit margins will not be able to survive for very long against the rising tide of near zero marginal costs in the production and delivery of goods and services. Although the thousand or so highly integrated, vertically scaled megacorporations that currently account for much of the world's commerce are imposing and seemingly invincible, they are, in fact, highly vulnerable to a collaborative economy that is quickly eating away at their already precariously low profit margins.

It's not unreasonable to expect a significant die-off of the vertically integrated global companies of the Second Industrial Revolution when the Collaborative Commons accounts for between 10 and 30 percent of the economic activity in any given sector. At the very least, we can say that conventional capitalist markets will increasingly lose their dominant hold over global commerce and trade as near zero marginal costs push an ever greater share of economic activity onto the Collaborative Commons in the years ahead.

CHAPTER FOURTEEN

CROWDFUNDING SOCIAL CAPITAL, DEMOCRATIZING CURRENCY, HUMANIZING ENTREPRENEURSHIP, AND RETHINKING WORK

The near collapse of the global banking system in 2008 terrified millions of people. Lending froze and the U.S. government was forced to bail out the biggest financial institutions in the country with the rationale that they were just "too big to fail." The American public was enraged that $700 billion in tax revenue was handed over to banks, rewarding them for financial recklessness, while millions of Americans were losing their homes because they couldn't pay off their mortgages. In other words, they were "too small to matter."[1]

PEER-TO-PEER SOCIAL LENDING

In the aftermath of the banking debacle, a new kind of lending institution emerged on the Internet. It's called peer-to-peer lending or social lending. Online banking platforms like Zopa, Lending Club, and Prosper lend money directly to individuals and projects. These online financing mechanisms are becoming popular alternative lending vehicles to traditional banks because they eliminate the middlemen and the high fixed costs of large financial institutions that are passed on to lenders in the form of higher interest rates.

Web-facilitated scaling of financing brings the marginal cost of lending to borrowers to near zero, which translates to lower interest rates and fees. Zopa, the U.K.'s first peer-to-peer lender, has processed loans of more than £414 million.[2] Peer-to-peer social lenders brokered $1.8 billion in loans by the end of 2012, forcing the big banks to take notice.[3]

A more recent offshoot of peer-to-peer social lending is something called crowdfunding. Kickstarter, the leading crowdfunding enterprise, was launched in April 2009. Here's how it works. Kickstarter goes around conventional investment vehicles and raises finance capital from the general public on the Internet. Originators of a project put their plan up on a site and pick a deadline by which the necessary funds have to be raised. If the goal is not reached by this deadline, no funds are collected. This provision ensures that the project has enough financing to at least make a go of the venture. The money pledged by donors is collected by Amazon payments. Kickstarter collects 5 percent of the funds raised and Amazon charges, on average, an additional 3 to 5 percent.[4] Kickstarter, unlike traditional lenders, has no ownership in the ventures. It's merely a facilitator.

By November 2013, Kickstarter had fostered 51,000 projects with a 44 percent success rate. The projects had raised more than $871 million. Kickstarter limits the project funding to 13 categories—art, dance, design, fashion, films and video, food, games, music, photography, publishing, technology, and theater.[5]

Various crowdfunding platforms offer different forms of compensation. Donors can either pledge funds as gifts or receive the comparable value of the funds extended to the borrower in the form of goods or services once the project is up and running, or provide funds as a straight loan with interest, or invest in the project in return for equal shares.

Although still a small player in the financial sector, crowdsourcing funders are playing an important supporting role in the creation of many of the new start-ups in the IoT infrastructure build-out. Mosaic, mentioned earlier, used crowdfunding to raise $1.1 million for a dozen solar projects. Mosaic posted its first solar investment project offering a 4.5 percent return to investors who could pony up as little as $25 to participate. Billy Parish, the company's cofounder, expected to raise the initial $313,000 in a month if all went well. He was taken by surprise, however, when 435 people crowdfunded with all the necessary funds in less than 24 hours. The company had 10,000 investors in its portfolio in 2013, ready to make loans to get its solar projects built.[6]

One of Mosaic's solar systems, partially financed by crowdfunding, along with government and private investment funds, has been installed in a 26,000-square-foot building in Oakland, California, created by the nonprofit Youth Employment Partnership (YEP). The solar system cost $265,000. Mosaic leases the system to YEP. The 85 percent drop in utility bills is a significant cost saver, allowing YEP to use the funds for its vital programs. The deal is made even more enticing with the option for YEP to buy the system from Mosaic after ten years, giving it nearly free power from then on.[7]

The demand for solar technology is expected to surge in the coming decade. Bloomberg New Energy Finance estimates that more than $62 billion in financing will be required. Social lending, and especially crowdfunding, is expected to carry some of the load, allowing millions of small players to finance each other's micropower installations—another example of the lateral power of peer-to-peer collaboration.[8]

Lest the cynics doubt whether millions of small players can phase in an energy revolution via laterally scaled collaborative efforts, recall, as mentioned in chapter 8, that in Germany, the world leader in renewable energy, 51 percent of the installed renewable energy is owned by small businesses and individuals while the nation's giant utilities own a mere 7 percent of green energy production.[9]

Crowdfunding platforms like Indiegogo, Early Shares, Crowdfunder, Fundable, and Crowdcube are appearing everywhere on the Web, thanks, in part, to the passage of the Jumpstart Our Business Start Ups Act in 2012, which allows small businesses to raise as much as $1 million in investments annually from the general public via crowdfunding platforms.[10]

Crowdfunding enthusiasts emphasize that it's not about the money. They enjoy being intimately involved with helping others pursue their dreams and feel that their small contribution packs a wallop—that it really counts in moving a project forward. The Gartner Group estimates that peer-to-peer financial lending will top $5 billion by the end of 2013.[11]

The sharing economy, in all its various incarnations, is a hybrid creature, part market economy and part social economy. While the market economy is regulated by laws and by the inherent rules that underlie the capitalist system, the social economy, being a Commons, follows a different regulatory path. Although some of the oversight and regulation is government directed, much of the rest lies with the self-governing norms that millions of players agree to voluntarily as a condition for their participation on the Commons.

REPUTATION RANKINGS AND COMMONS CURRENCIES

Social trust, rather than "let the buyer beware," guides the social economy. And like more traditional Commons, the new Collaborative Commons has experimented with a range of protocols to maintain the high level of social trust necessary to ensure sufficient social capital to build a collaborative ethos, including sanctions to punish and even weed out free riders and spoilers. Virtually all the major collaborative social networks have instituted reputation systems to rank the trustworthiness of their members. Unlike conventional credit-rating systems that rank one's credit worthiness in a market economy, reputation systems are designed to rank one's social capital in a Commons.

ThredUP operates by what it calls its "golden ThredUp rule," that asks its members to only send the "quality of apparel" they would expect to receive in return. ThredUP ranks the "quality" of each members' items on a four-star scale. A second rating, called "style points," which goes from 0 to 10, ranks the items on their "stylishness." The final ranking is a measure of the "punctuality" of their members' shipments.

The online collaborative consignment shop has a zero-tolerance policy with regard to parents who send clothes that are frayed or torn.

First-time offenders are identified and second-time offenders are removed from the Commons.[12] Members with consistently high ratings are matched with each other to encourage all members to ratchet up the quality of their contributions.

Reputation services on the Internet Commons, similar to credit-rating services in the market economy, are becoming an important mechanism for regulating activity, ensuring compliance with agreed-upon norms and building social trust. TrustCloud is among a new crop of reputation services. TrustCloud "measures your virtuous behavior and transactions online then turns it into a portable TrustScore you can use anywhere within the Sharing Economy." Each member is ranked from 1 to 1,000 (the latter being a perfect score) for his or her truthfulness.[13] Rankings take into consideration a person's consistency, generosity, and transparency, based on past activity on the Internet. TrustCloud algorithms search for behaviors like responsiveness and longevity in drawing up its trustworthiness profiles. Members then receive a TrustCloud badge with the ranking, all at no cost.

Couchsurfing has its own rating system. Opening up one's home to a stranger to stay in, for free, is a bit harrowing. Then, adding to the angst, both host and guest are expected to socialize and share their respective cultures with one another. After each stay, both the host and guest rate each other and provide a reference. Couchsurfing's gold standard is called vouching. Users are allowed to vouch for other members, if at least three other couch surfers have actually met them and vouched for them previously.[14]

With the sharable Commons already estimated to be worth more than $100 billion and growing by leaps and bounds and the social economy becoming an ever more important part of people's everyday lives, expect social-capital ratings to become as important to millions of participants on the Collaborative Commons as credit ratings were to consumers in the capitalist marketplace.[15]

The collaborative economy is coming on strong. Just before sitting down today to write, I happened to read this week's cover story on the sharing economy in *The Economist*—the editors and contributors extolling its virtues and arguing about its potential impacts on the traditional market economy. Many observers are wondering how the entrenched capitalist system and the upstart Collaborative Commons will adjust to each other. A tantalizing clue might be found in the new kinds of exchange currencies that are being established to differentiate the way people do business on the Commons versus how they do business in the market.

The currency a society uses to enable its members to trade goods and services with one another is a good marker of the underlying values held by the community. In his masterful book *The Philosophy of Money*, the nineteenth-century sociologist Georg Simmel reminds us of the critical role that money has played throughout history in extending and deepening human social interaction. Simmel points out that coins are promissory notes, backed by an unstated collective trust among strangers that guarantees that at some future date the token passed on in an earlier exchange will be honored by a third party in a subsequent exchange.

While currencies have been backed up by all sorts of valuable metals, the most favored over time being silver and gold, anthropologists observe that behind these assets lies a deeper asset—social capital—without which currency as a medium of exchange would be valueless. The Trobiand Islanders in New Guinea, for example, engaged in an elaborate exchange of native shells, often canoeing long distances to pass the tokens back and forth, as a way of establishing bonds of mutual trust. The exchange of social currency built up sufficient social capital to enable trade to flourish.

Until the collapse of the global economy in 2008, which exposed the hollow innards of a dysfunctional, and even criminal, global financial system, most people took for granted that the world's currency system was reliable, if occasionally volatile. And even if the currency was in trouble, we assumed the government would guarantee our bank savings—in the United States up to $250,000—if a bank were to fail. Behind the banks, the Federal Reserve System, at least, would be there to rescue the dollar.[16] It's only when economists began to suggest that if the currency system were to plunge to the very bottom, we would be saved from the abyss because the U.S. Treasury could always print more dollars and put them into circulation, that millions of people became very scared. We began to realize that behind all the rules, regulations, and firewalls lay an empty chasm.

The global financial collapse exposed the longstanding myth that commercial exchange is a primary institution. There are no examples in history where people created commercial markets and exchange before creating a culture. We have mistakenly come to believe that commerce precedes and makes possible the development of culture when in fact it's the other way around. As mentioned in chapter 1, culture is the sphere where we socialize ourselves. It's where we create the social narratives that allow us to extend our empathic sensibility and cohere in larger fictional families. Our shared sense of identity builds bonds of social trust, allowing us to accumulate a sufficient reserve of social capital to function as an integrated whole. Our shared identity is what allows us to create various symbolic tokens that serve as promissory notes, assuring us that we can trust each other to honor both past commercial commitments and future transactions.

We too often forget that commerce has always existed as an extension of culture. Commerce feeds off of society's accumulated social capital. On those occasions in history when commercial institutions, and specifically financial institutions, have compromised society's social trust and depleted its social capital, as they did in 2008, it's not surprising that people have come to fear the currency mechanisms and begun to search for alternatives.

In 2008, millions of people turned to gold—sending its value to record highs in the world market—hoping that it might provide a degree of security in unpredictable times. Others began to question the value of holding on to a metal brick that, for all intents and purposes, was just another symbolic token whose worth was not a measure of any intrinsic value of the metal but, rather, a measure of the paranoia and fear brought on by financial institutions that had rapidly depleted the social capital and trust and, with it, people's faith in conventional currency.

More and more people began to experiment with a different type of currency, built on deep collaboration and backed up by new layers of social capital. Alternative currencies, often referred to as community currencies, local exchange trading systems (LETS), or microcurrencies, began to take hold in locales around the world after the economic collapse of 2008. While they had existed before in scattered places, most notably during the Great Depression, their impact was marginal. This newest reincarnation, however, is potentially of far greater consequence to society because it comes at a time when the social economy is enjoying a renaissance, with hundreds of millions of human beings spending an increasing amount of their daily lives engaged in collaborative activities—be it social or economic—on a Collaborative Commons.

The so-called alternative currencies are really social currencies that enable the collaborative exchange of goods and services to flourish in the Commons. As in other areas of the collaborative economy, people are bypassing the middlemen, the fixed overhead costs of big financial institutions, the markups, and the high interest rates imposed by credit card companies, and exchanging their labor time directly with one another. But what makes this different from old-fashioned, one-on-one bartering of services is that Web-generated apps provide individuals with a mechanism to store and use points, represented by comparable labor time, for the exchange of all kinds of goods and services, in both the social economy and market economy.

There are more than 4,000 microcurrencies in circulation around the world.[17] Many of them are based on the labor time one person gives to another in making a good, repairing an item, or performing a service. The hours are stored in a time bank, just like cash, and exchanged for other hours of goods and services. Edgar Cahn, a law professor at the University of the District of Columbia, developed the idea of a time bank. He said it was inspired by people giving blood at a blood bank. The concept is based on a core principle that underlies the social economy—reciprocity. A neighbor helps another neighbor with the expectation that someone down the line will reciprocate in kind.

Cahn's time bank does not distinguish between different types of labor time. A car mechanic's hour is worth the same as a physician's. The notion is that everyone's time is to be regarded as equally valuable and not subject to tiering based on professional or technical skill sets. Other time banks allow hours accumulated to be calculated by skill. A tax accountant would earn more hours than a car washer. Time banks are operating around the world.[18]

The Hour Exchange Portland, in Maine, for example, assists people in paying for health care. TrueNorth, a nonprofit health clinic, has entered into an agreement with the Hour Exchange Portland by which its physicians accept time dollars as payments from patients who have accrued the currency for services they provided to others in the community.[19] Those time dollars can be used by the physicians to secure services from others through the time bank.

Other community currencies traded in LETS are designed to facilitate the exchange of goods. The WIR currency in Switzerland credits sales against future purchases for its members. When a seller receives credit for an item sold, it can be spent buying another item from another WIR member.[20]

Community currencies are also employed, in part, to prevent wealth from leaking out of the community. BerkShares, in the Berkshire region of Massachusetts, is one of a number of social currencies that is designed to encourage local buying. Members purchase Berk-Shares from any of the six banks in the region at the same exchange rate as the dollar, with a little extra bonus. If a member deposits $95, he or she is given $100 worth of BerkShares from the bank, making the exchange a net gain for the member.[21] He or she then uses the shares to purchase goods and services in local business establishments, which ensures that the money continues to circulate in the local economy. By using a nonprofit bank as the intermediary, members avoid the additional expense that would be incurred were they to use a credit card or pay by a commercial bank check.[22] The BerkShare was introduced in 2006, and in the following five years, more than three million BerkShares went into circulation—a hefty sum for the local economy.[23]

Alternative currencies have mushroomed in some of the regions of Europe hardest hit by the Great Recession. In Greece and Spain, community currency networks are proliferating.[24] In regions where unemployment is high, nonprofits are setting up online sites to connect individuals who have skills to render with those in need of them—creating a distributed, collaborative, laterally scaled microsocial economy inside a centralized market economy that is increasingly inoperable. Microcurrencies have become the new mechanism of exchange, putting at least some workers back to work.

While social currencies cued to locales are proliferating, global alternative currencies that bypass national boundaries are scaling in on the Internet. Bitcoin is a peer-to-peer currency network with millions of bitcoins in circulation. The bitcoin is tradable with other world currencies, and as of November 2013, it was selling around 400 U.S. dollars per bitcoin.[25] Amir Taaki and Donald Norman, co-founders of Bitcoin Consultancy, say they became interested in the bitcoin phenomenon when they were in Amsterdam, and a friend from the United

Kingdom asked them to wire some emergency funds. Their only two options were Western Union and MoneyGram, both of which took a usurious 20 to 25 percent of the transfer in fees. They saw the value of using bitcoin, an Internet currency, to bypass the fee gouging.[26]

Futurist Heather Schelgel, who advises the world's leading banks on transaction standards, doesn't believe that global, Internet-based currencies will replace traditional currencies, but adds that "as communities begin to realize the possibility of expressing themselves through money, I expect you'll see hundreds of BitCoin [sic], or something similar—or something we haven't even thought of yet."[27]

Others are even more bullish. Jean-Francois Noubel, a cofounder of AOL France, believes it is shortsighted to think that the same disruptive power of a distributed, collaborative, and latterly scaled Internet that gave rise to eBay, Facebook, Amazon, Etsy, and thousands of other ventures wouldn't make its way into the financial domain. Noubel says he wouldn't be surprised to see "millions of free currencies circulating on the Net and through our cell phones" in the years ahead.[28]

SOCIAL ENTREPRENEURSHIP

New business models are beginning to emerge alongside new funding vehicles and social currencies to accommodate the requisites of two very different economies—one, a capitalist economy operating in the market, and the other a social economy operating on the Commons. The new business models are an attempt to find value in the spaces where the two economies enjoy symbiotic relationships. We already discussed cooperatives. From the perspective of their architectural design and operating protocols, they are best positioned to bridge the gap between the two economies and find value at the edges where potential synergies arise.

In the United States, the "benefit corporation" is an interesting new business model that's attempting a makeover of the conventional capitalist corporation to allow it to be more agile and able to maneuver in the hybrid world of markets and Commons. Patagonia, the California-based global sports clothier, with annual sales around $540 million, is the most prominent company to date to make the switch to a benefit corporation.[29]

Benefit corporations, which are now recognized and regulated as legal entities in 18 U.S. states, offer entrepreneurs a form of legal protection against outside investors who might force them to give up their social or environmental commitments in return for new financing.[30] Although benefit corporations operate as capitalist companies and are responsible to their shareholders, their new legal status enables them to put their social and environmental mandates up front without risking the wrath of investors interested only in optimizing shareholder value.

The benefit corporation is part of a larger wave loosely defined under the rubric of social entrepreneurialism that's captured the imagination of a younger generation coming out of business schools around the world. Social entrepreneurialism casts a wide net from the nonprofits that are the mainstay of the Commons to the traditional shareholding companies that are the dominant enterprises in the marketplace. The two models—nonprofit organizations and profit-directed corporations—are not only interacting at the edges where the social and market economies meet, but are also taking on some of each other's attributes, blurring the distinction between nonprofit and profit-seeking enterprises. Social entrepreneurship is the big tent where the profit-making and nonprofit worlds are creating all sorts of new business arrangements and protocols to accommodate a dual-tier commercial space made up of both the market economy and the Collaborative Commons.

Social entrepreneurialism has its roots in the nonprofit community. The paring down of the welfare state in the United States, the United Kingdom, and elsewhere in the 1980s and 1990s created a crisis and an opportunity for the nonprofit sector. The shrinking of government programs to aid the needy left disadvantaged communities at risk. Private philanthropy attempted to fill the vacuum by financing nonprofit initiatives, but the available revenue to communities paled in comparison to the lost revenue stream when the government began to exit. Caught with an expanding social burden and less revenue to meet critical community needs, nonprofit organizations began to look to new business models that could mesh with their primary mission and provide a supplemental source of revenue to continue operating and expand their services. Countless nonprofit organizations established a fee-for-services component into their playbook. Nonprofits—whose managers were previously skilled in seeking government grants and philanthropic contributions from foundations to administer programs ranging from the arts and recreation to food kitchens and health clinics—began recruiting a new type of leader versed in entrepreneurialism but committed to using his or her skills to advance the social well-being of the communities being served.

With government disengagement, new for-profit startups also began to eye promising business opportunities in the social sector and came in from the market side to fill the vacuum. Peter Drucker, the management guru, talked up the idea of doing good and doing well. He made the argument that the problems of chronic poverty, poor education, environmental deterioration, and a host of other societal ills were best addressed by letting loose the creative juices of entrepreneurialism. Schools, day-care centers, low-income housing projects, and scores of other activities and services traditionally embedded in the governmental domain became fair game for commercial exploitation.

Meanwhile, as described in chapter 7, in the 1990s, a new generation in the United States—the first to be exposed to service learning in high schools and colleges—began to enter the economy. Service learning's pivotal role in creating the mindset for the new social entrepreneurialism has never been fully recognized or acknowledged. Young people weaned on participating in and contributing to nonprofit projects and initiatives in communities at risk got a taste of a new way to find meaning and self-worth, beyond the strictly commercial opportunities offered up by the marketplace. Their enthusiasm translated into a new career path, at least for a significant minority. Social entrepreneurship was born.

Defining social entrepreneurialism can be a slippery business. While profit-making enterprises emphasize what they call the triple bottom line of "people, planet, and profit," a term coined by John Elkington in 1994, nonprofit organizations prefer "people and planet before profit."[31] An in-depth survey of 80 social entrepreneurs, from both the profit and nonprofit sectors, highlights some of the subtle differences in how they approach the same set of circumstances. To begin with, the profit-making social entrepreneurs are motivated by the prospect of commercial opportunity, while the nonprofit social entrepreneurs are more focused on addressing unmet social needs. Second, both entrepreneurs are risk takers, but of a different kind.

The former bundles risks in terms of return on investment. The latter rarely risks their own funds. For them, risk is bound up in their social "reputation" in the community. Third, while both profit-seeking and nonprofit-directed social entrepreneurs believe in the centrality of their role, the study found that nonprofit "social entrepreneurs more clearly must include and, indeed, must share credit for success with a collective of volunteers and beneficiaries."[32]

Whatever the differences, it is interesting to observe the various ways that the profit-seeking and nonprofit-directed social entrepreneurs are edging closer together, especially among millennials, who are feeling their way toward new business models that combine attributes long associated with each respective domain. *The Economist,* in an editorial titled "Capital Markets with a Conscience" described the evolution of social entrepreneurialism.

> The notion of social capital markets can seem incoherent because it brings together such a diverse group of people and institutions. Yet there is a continuum that connects purely charitable capital at one extreme and for-profit capital at the other, with various trade-offs between risk, return and social impact in between. Much of the discussion . . . is expected to focus on that continuum and to figure out, for any given social goal, which sort of social capital, or mix of different sorts of it, is most likely to succeed.[33]

For example, while the benefit corporation is an attempt to modify the profit-making drive of capitalist firms to edge closer to the social and environmental priorities of nonprofits in the social Commons, nonprofit organizations are making their own modifications, edging closer to the profit orientation of capitalist firms. Nine states in the United States—Illinois, Maine, Rhode Island, Michigan, Louisiana, Wyoming, North Carolina, Vermont, and Utah—have enacted what are called L3C laws. These are variations of the laws governing limited liability companies that allow nonprofits to make a "low profit" as long as their primary objective is social goals. The L3Cs provide a legal means for nonprofits to have access to capital, which is becoming ever more important as they become more oriented to social-entrepreneurial ventures, while retaining their status as charitable organizations.[34]

Social entrepreneurship has become the hot item at scores of universities around the world. The Harvard curriculum includes courses with titles such as "Managing Social Enterprise" and "Introduction to Social Entrepreneurship."[35] The sociology department has an entrepreneurship "collaboratory" to immerse students in the sociological aspects of the new social economy. The President's Challenge, another university initiative, distributes $150,000 to student teams engaged in academic and field work to find "solutions to global problems, from education to health to clean water and air."[36]

Global networks like Ashoka, the Skoll Foundation, the Acumen Fund, and Duke University's Center for the Advancement of Social Entrepreneurship serve as think tanks, trade associations, and funding agents to advance social entrepreneurship around the world. Bill Drayton, a leading figure in the social-entrepreneurial movement, is the founder of Ashoka. The organization runs competitions that draw social entrepreneurs from every corner of the world to collaborate on issues ranging from human trafficking to conflict resolution. Social entrepreneurs are encouraged to post their projects on Ashoka's Changemakers website, where others can log in and collaborate to enhance their initiatives. Ashoka currently supports the work of more than 3,000 social-entrepreneur fellows in more than 70 countries.[37]

The Skoll Foundation, another key player in social entrepreneurship, founded in 1999, has awarded more than $358 million in grants to 97 social entrepreneurs and 80 organizations on five continents that are involved in advancing social entrepreneurship.[38]

Success for social entrepreneurs is measured more by the improvement in the well-being of the communities served than on return on investment. Social capital is the critical asset and it, in turn, is a reflection of the bonds of solidarity and trust forged by the collaborative partnership between the social enterprise and the community. In this regard, nonprofit social entrepreneurs generally enjoy an advantage over profit-seeking social entrepreneurs, although not always, because the primary motivation is "doing good" rather than "doing well."

There are several hundred thousand social enterprises in the United States that employ over 10 million people and that have revenues of $500 billion per year. These enterprises represented approximately 3.5 percent of the nation's GDP in 2012. Some 35 percent of social enterprises are nonprofit organizations, and 31 percent are corporations or limited liability companies. Social enterprises have experienced a spectacular growth curve. Sixty percent of all U.S. social enterprises were created in 2006 or after, and 29 percent of them were created in 2011 and 2012.[39]

In the United Kingdom there were 62,000 social enterprises employing a workforce of 800,000 people and contributing £24 billion to the U.K. economy in 2010. Peter Holbrook, chief executive of the U.K. Social Enterprise Coalition (SEC), foresees a threefold increase in the social enterprises' contribution to the nation's GDP by 2020. The SEC is also lobbying for the government to formally recognize the social-enterprise sector as an entity distinct from the volunteer and private sectors, with accompanying tax incentives and other support.[40]

In Australia there were an estimated 20,000 social enterprises in 2010. In the nonprofit arena, 29 percent of the organizations had a business venture and 58 percent of the organizations provided fees for services.[41]

Social entrepreneurship, which today is rather equally balanced between for-profit and nonprofit businesses, is likely to increasingly gravitate to the latter in the coming decades as the social economy embedded on the Collaborative Commons continues to gain ground on the capitalist marketplace.

NEW KINDS OF EMPLOYMENT

Social entrepreneurs are not the only ones in the workforce who are beginning to pass from the capitalist market economy to the Collaborative Commons. Millions of others have already done so. As discussed in chapter 8, the marginal cost of labor is heading toward near zero in the capitalist marketplace, as IT, Big Data, advanced analytics, AI, and robotics replace millions of workers across the manufacturing and service industries and the knowledge and entertainment sectors.

The reality is the IoT is both a job killer and a source of employment. In the long run, the smart IoT infrastructure—the Communications Internet, the Energy Internet, and the Transportation Internet—is going to carry on much of the economic activity of civilization with a small supervisory and professional work force.

In the short and mid terms, however, the massive build-out of the IoT infrastructure in every locality and region of the world is going to give rise to one last surge of mass wage and salaried labor that will run for 40 years, spanning two generations. Transforming the global energy regime from fossil fuels and nuclear power to renewable energies is extremely labor intensive and will require millions of workers and spawn thousands of new businesses. Retrofitting and converting hundreds of millions of existing buildings into green micropower plants and erecting millions of new positive micropower buildings will likewise require tens of millions of workers and open up new entrepreneurial opportunities for energy-saving companies (ESCOs), smart-construction companies, and green-appliance producers. Installing hydrogen and other storage technologies across the entire economic infrastructure to manage the flow of green electricity will generate comparable mass employment and new businesses as well. The reconfiguration of the world's electricity grid into an Energy Internet will generate millions of installation jobs and give birth to thousands of clean Web app start-up companies. And finally, rebooting the transport sector from the internal-combustion engine to electric and fuel-cell vehicles will necessitate the makeover of the nation's road system and fueling infrastructure. Installing millions of plug-in electric fueling outlets along roads and in every parking space is labor-intensive work that will employ a sizable workforce.

In the mid to long term, an increasing amount of employment is going to migrate from the market sector to the Commons. While fewer human beings will be required to produce goods and services in the market economy, machine surrogates will play a smaller role on the Commons for the evident reason that deep social engagement and the amassing of social capital is an inherently human enterprise. The very idea that machines might someday create social capital is not entertained by even the most ardent technophiles.

The nonprofit sphere is already the fastest-growing employment sector in many of the advanced industrial economies of the world. Aside from the millions of volunteers who freely give of their time, millions of others are actively employed. In the 42 countries surveyed by the Johns Hopkins University Center for Civil Society Studies, 56 million full-time workers are currently employed in the nonprofit sector. In some countries, employment in the nonprofit arena makes up more than 10 percent of the workforce. In the Netherlands, nonprofits account for 15.9 percent of paid employment. In Belgium, 13.1 percent of the workforce is in the nonprofit sector. In the United Kingdom, nonprofit employment represents 11 percent of the workforce, while in Ireland it's 10.9 percent. In the United States, nonprofit employment accounts for 9.2 percent of the workforce, and in Canada it's 12.3 percent. These percentages will likely rise steadily in the coming decades as employment switches from a highly automated market economy to a highly labor-intensive social economy.[42]

Despite the dramatic growth curve in Commons employment, many economists look at it askance, with the rejoinder that the nonprofit sector is not an independent economic force but rather largely dependent on government-procurement contracts and private philanthropy. One could say the same about the enormous government procurements, subsidies, and incentives meted out to the private sector. But this aside, the Johns Hopkins study of 42 countries revealed that contrary to the view of many economists, approximately 50 percent of the aggregate revenue of the nonprofit sector operating on the Commons already comes from fees for services, while government support accounts for only 36 percent of the revenues, and private philanthropy for only 14 percent.[43]

I expect that by midcentury, if not much sooner, a majority of the employed around the world will be in the nonprofit sector on the Collaborative Commons, busily engaged in advancing the social economy, and purchasing at least some of their goods and services in the conventional marketplace. The traditional capitalist economy will be managed by intelligent technology attended by small professional and technical workforces.

John Maynard Keynes's futurist essay, written more than 80 years ago for his grandchildren and alluded to in chapter 1, envisioned a world where machines have freed up human beings from toil in the marketplace to engage in deep cultural play on the Commons in the pursuit of more lofty and transcendent goals. It might prove to be his most accurate economic forecast.

The business at hand will be to provide both retraining for the existing workforce and the appropriate skill development for students coming into the labor market to ease the transition into the new job categories and business opportunities that come with a massive build-out of an Internet of Things infrastructure around the world. At the same time, students will need to be educated for the new professional skills that come with the job opportunities opening up in the Collaborative Commons. Although a herculean effort will be required, the human race has shown itself capable of similar efforts in the past—particularly in the rapid shift from an agricultural to an industrial way of life between 1890 and 1940.

IT'S UNDERSTANDABLE THAT IN A SOCIETY where the market imperative and capitalist mystique are so firmly entrenched in popular lore, not to mention in government subsidies, that the slew of new economic initiatives and institutional arrangements flooding onto the Collaborative Commons are still being treated as mere supplements to the main economic currents. Few are suggesting that the quickening pace to near zero marginal cost that is beginning to impact the media, entertainment, and publishing industries; renewable energies; 3D printing of manufactured products; and open-source online higher education are any more than variations that can be fit comfortably within the existing economic paradigm. Even fewer are suggesting that the replacement of the global workforce with AI and automated technology, the shift from ownership to access, the transformation from markets to networks, and the emergence of a sharing economy represents a fundamental assault on the system itself. Even when confronted with the crowdfunding of capital, the democratization of currency, and the rapid spread of social entrepreneurialism, there is little worry that they pose any kind of significant threat to capitalism. Yet one can't help but be awed by how these new models fundamentally diverge from the standard way we have organized economic life over the past two centuries.

These new approaches are so radically different from the existing economic paradigm, in both their overarching narrative and operating assumptions, that it is difficult to imagine how they might be absorbed, in total, into the current regime. It is more probable that as these various departures mesh and begin to feed off each other, they are likely to outgrow their capitalist context and at some point rupture the existing paradigm, giving birth to a new economic order whose life force is as different from market capitalism as the latter was from the feudal and medieval systems from which it emerged.

PART V
THE ECONOMY OF ABUNDANCE

CHAPTER FIFTEEN
THE SUSTAINABLE CORNUCOPIA

Classical and neoclassical economic theory is mute once a society's productive economic activity approaches near zero marginal cost. When marginal costs shrink to near zero, profits disappear because goods and services have been liberated from market pricing. They become essentially free. When most things become nearly free, the whole operating rationale of capitalism as an organizing mechanism to produce and distribute goods and services becomes meaningless. That's because capitalism's dynamism feeds off scarcity. If resources, goods, and services are scarce, they have exchange value and can be priced in the marketplace beyond what they cost to bring them there. But when the marginal cost of producing those goods and services approaches zero and the price becomes nearly free, the capitalist system loses its hold over scarcity and the ability to profit from another's dependency. *Free* implies free in two senses of the term: free in price and free from scarcity. When the marginal cost of producing additional units of a good or service is nearly zero, it means that scarcity has been replaced by abundance. Exchange value becomes useless because everyone can secure much of what they need without having to pay for it. The products and services have use and share value but no longer have exchange value.

The notion of organizing economic life around abundance and use and share value rather than scarcity and exchange value is so alien to the way we conceive of economic theory and practice that we are unable to envision it. But that is what is just beginning to emerge in wide sectors of the economy as new technologies make possible efficiencies and productivity that all but eliminate the cost of producing additional units and services—that is, excluding the initial investment and overhead costs.

DEFINING ABUNDANCE

Abundance is a slippery word. Traditionally the term meant sufficient access to resources to ensure a flourishing life. Biologists tell us that the average human being requires around 2,000 to 2,500 calories a day to maintain his or her physical well-being.[1] Today more than 2 billion human beings live on less than that and a billion of them are classified as undernourished.[2] With the human population expected to increase by 35 percent, or 2.5 billion people, by 2050, the United Nations Food and Agriculture Organization says that food production alone would have to increase by 70 percent to provide the nourishment needed to "adequately" ensure every individual's well-being.[3]

The average American, by contrast, consumes 3,747 calories of energy a day.[4] If all 7 billion people living on the planet today were to "sustain" their lives by consuming a comparable amount of resources as the average American, it would require four to five more Earths. The human race, rich and poor, is currently gobbling up the equivalent resources of 1.5 Earths—in other words it takes approximately one and a half years to regenerate what we consume in a single year. The United Nations projects that if population growth and consumption trends continue, even without an appreciable change in the quality of life of the world's poor, by 2030 we will need the equivalent of two Earths to support our resource appropriations.[5]

Abundance, then, is in the eye of the beholder. The sustainability of the planet, however, is not. When it comes to reconciling abundance and sustainability, Gandhi's observation, cited in chapter 6, that the "Earth provides enough to satisfy every man's need but not for every man's greed" remains the gold standard.[6]

Gandhi had an instinctual understanding of sustainability. Today, however, we can actively measure it with sophisticated metrics. It is called ecological footprint. Sustainability is defined as the relative steady state in which the use of resources to sustain the human population does not exceed the ability of nature to recycle the waste and replenish the stock. Ecological footprint is a direct measure of the demand human activity puts on the biosphere. More precisely, it measures the amount of biologically productive land and water that is required to produce all the resources an individual or population consumes and to absorb the waste they generate, given prevailing technology and resource-management practices. This area can then be compared with biological capacity (biocapacity)—that is, the amount of productive area that is available to generate these resources and to absorb the waste.[7]

The enlargement of humanity's ecological footprint over the past half century is unprecedented. In 1961, our species' footprint was approximately half of the planet's biocapacity—which means, in ecological accounting terms, we were still drawing off of the ecological interest but had not yet eaten into the principal. By 2008, however, the ecological footprint of 6.7 billion human beings alive at the time was equivalent to 18.2 billion global hectares (a hectare is equivalent to 2.47 acres), with an average footprint of 2.7 hectares per person, on a planet with only 12 billion global hectares of biocapacity available, or 1.8 hectares available per person. We were consuming Earth's biocapacity faster than it could be recycled and replenished. The United States alone, with only 4 percent of the world's population, was using 21 percent of Earth's available biocapacity and the ecological footprint of the average American was a whopping 10 hectares of biocapacity.[8]

The statistics on ecological footprint become even more pronounced when the high-income population of the world is compared to the low-income population. The 1 billion wealthiest consumers—with a gross national income of $12,196 or more per person—are using up the equivalent of 3.06 hectares of biocapacity per person while the 1.3 billion poorest human beings—with a gross national income of $995 or less per person—are using the equivalent of 1.08 hectares of biocapacity per person.[9]

If abundance is tied to sustainability and measured by living only on the interest but not the principal of Earth's biocapacity, the question is, how many human beings can live comfortably without destroying the biosphere's ability to continually replenish the ecological resources necessary to maintain the health and well-being of each individual and our species as a whole?

Lester Brown, founder of the World Watch Institute—an organization that tracks the human impact on global resources—says that the answer depends on which diet we choose. If we look to the U.S. diet as a baseline—the average person takes in 800 kilograms (a kilogram is equivalent to 2.2 pounds) of grain per year in the form of food and feed. If everyone in the world had an equivalent diet, then the 2 billion metric tons annual world harvest of grain could support a global population of only 2.5 billion people. If, however, the Italian/Mediterranean diet of 400 kilograms of grain per person per year was used as the baseline, the annual world harvest could sustain a population of 5 billion people. Finally, if we were to use the Indian diet of 200 kilograms of grain consumed per person per year, the planet could sustain a maximum of 10 billion people.

Brown makes the point that populations that live too high or too low on the food chain do not live as long as those who eat near the middle of the food chain. Those engaged at the top suffer from diseases of affluence—including diabetes, cancers, heart disease, and strokes—while those at the bottom suffer from malnutrition and die of diseases of poverty—including rickets, scurvy, beriberi, pellagra, anemia, and xerophthalmia. Study after study indicates that people who eat a Mediterranean diet—consisting of meat, fish, cheese, and vegetables—live healthier, longer lives.[10]

To bring our human population in line with the biocapacity of the planet and transform our society from scarcity to sustainable abundance, we will need to address the great disparity in ecological footprint between the rich and poor, while simultaneously lowering the overall human population on Earth.

WHAT MAKES US HAPPY?

While the notion of ecological footprint provides a compelling scientific metric for reducing human impact on the biosphere's carrying capacity, the spate of studies and surveys in recent years reporting on what makes people happy provides an equally compelling sociological and psychological rationale for equalizing the ecological footprint.

Virtually every scientific study on happiness concludes that it appreciates then depreciates along a classic bell curve. The more than 40 percent of the human race that lives on two dollars per day or less in dire poverty and barely surviving from week to week, are understandably deeply unhappy.[11] Lacking the bare essentials of life, and unable to even feed and clothe their own children and provide the rudiments of shelter, they live in a despondent state, their lives sapped of vigor and hope. As the poor are lifted out of poverty, they begin to experience happiness. Each advance in income, wealth, and security makes them happier. But here's where it becomes surprising. When individuals reach an income level that provides the basic comforts and securities of life, their level of happiness begins to plateau. Additional increases of wealth and accompanying consumption triggers diminishing marginal returns in overall happiness, until a point is reached, after which happiness actually reverses course and individuals become less happy. The studies show that the accumulation of wealth becomes an albatross and that profligate consumption becomes an addiction with fewer and shorter-lived psychological rewards. The possessions end up possessing the owners.

A closer examination into the reasons why increasing wealth beyond the comfort level leads to malaise and despair shows that relationships with others become increasingly mediated by status and are driven by envy and jealousy. Individuals report that their relationships become superficial and valued only by what can be gained and lost in a strictly material sense.

Yet even when confronted with their own increasing unhappiness, materialistic individuals are far more likely to rev up their pursuit of material gain in the belief that the problem is not with their preoccupation with wealth, but rather, with not having enough. They reason that if only they can gain a bit more material success that their elevated status will earn them the abiding admiration of others and the pleasures they hope will come with indulging in even more consumptive behavior—what psychologists refer to as the hedonistic treadmill. Instead, each additional foray into this hedonistic fantasy brings them more unhappiness, pulling them ever downward in a vicious cycle of addiction from which there is no escape, until they get off the treadmill and pursue an alternative path to happiness.

Studies conducted around the world have shown a close correlation between materialist values, depression, and substance abuse. Materialists are more likely than others to exhibit possessiveness and to be less generous and trusting. Materialists also have more difficulty reining in impulses and are more aggressive toward others.

Psychology professor Tim Kasser, author of *The High Price of Materialism*, sums up the overwhelming evidence accumulated in years of studies on materialistic behavior. What virtually every study shows, he says, is that

> people who strongly value the pursuit of wealth and possessions report lower psychological well-being than those who are less concerned with such aims. . . . The more materialistic values are at the center of our lives, the more our quality of life is diminished.[12]

Several years ago, I had the opportunity of visiting with the British economist Richard Layard, whose book *Happiness: Lessons from a New Science* caused a bit of a stir among economists. Layard was one of my faculty hosts for a lecture I gave at the London School of Economics. He took me back to his office and shared with me some interesting data he had collected on the increasing wealth of a society and the population's sense of their happiness over time. I was quite interested in seeing the data on the United States. It turns out that while Americans today enjoy twice the income they did in 1957, the percentage of "very happy" had dropped from 35 to 30 percent.[13]

Nor is the United States an exception. Studies conducted in other industrialized countries tell pretty much the same story. Layard's research shows that individual happiness rises until the average individual income hits about $20,000 per year—the minimum comfort level—after which additional increases of income result in diminishing returns in the level of happiness.[14]

Studies also show that the level of happiness of a society closely tracks with the income disparity of the population. The United States, which boasted the most robust middle class in the world in 1960, descended over the subsequent 50 years, with the top 1 percent becoming richer while the ranks of the middle class thinned and the number of people in poverty thickened. By 2012, the United States had the ignominious distinction of being ranked 28 out of 30 Organization for Economic Cooperation and Development (OECD) countries in income disparity—the gap between the rich and the poor—bettering only Mexico and Turkey.[15]

It's not surprising that the increasing disparity in income has led to a drop in the overall happiness of society. Happiness studies show that countries that have the smallest gap between rich and poor score higher in their sense of collective happiness and well-being. Part of the reason lies in the fact that increased poverty breeds unhappiness. But equally important, the gap between the haves and the have-nots is a breeding ground for mistrust. It creates a mental garrison with those on the top increasingly fearful of reprisal from the impoverished masses and more protective of their wealth and possessions.

I remember a moment my wife and I experienced in Mexico City nearly 20 years ago. We were riding in the back seat of an armored car that was ferrying us from a lecture presentation I had just given before an audience of distinguished business leaders to a dinner party at the home of one of Mexico's wealthiest families. My host, a leading social reformer in Mexico who had dedicated much of his life to improving the lot of Mexico's poor, was sitting in the front seat across from an armed driver. As we worked our way out of some of the city's worst slums, with police on every corner, into a posh, fortresslike gated community protected by security guards, where the rich huddled together, he noted the irony, remarking that Mexico was a nation increasingly made up of imprisoned communities for the rich and the poor, with each fearful and mistrusting of the other's intentions. As the United States has become more like Mexico, mistrust has risen as well. In the 1960s, 56 percent of Americans said that most people can be trusted. Today, less than one-third still do.[16]

What makes materialism so toxic is that it robs the individual of the primary drive that animates our species—our empathic nature. We are learning from evolutionary biologists and neuroscientists that human nature is not what we've been told over the past several hundred years. Our Enlightenment philosophers, at the very beginning of the modern era, painted a picture of human nature as rational, self-interested, materialistic, utilitarian, and driven by a need for autonomy—all of which predisposes us to accumulate more property and become an island unto ourselves. The new scientific studies tell a different story. Human beings are the most social of creatures. We yearn for companionship and crave social embeddedness. Much of that sociability is soft wired into our neural circuitry and either nourished or extinguished by our culturalization.

In the 1990s, scientists stumbled upon mirror neurons in human beings—popularly dubbed empathy neurons. Several of our primate relatives and elephants have empathy neurons—we are still not sure of other species. Mirror neurons and other parts of our neural makeup allow us to experience another being's feelings as our own—not just intellectually, but physiologically and emotionally. For example, if I'm observing a spider travel up another person's arm, I'm likely to feel the same creepy feeling in my neural circuitry as if it was climbing up my limb. We take these everyday feelings for granted but are just beginning to understand that it is this physiological ability to experience the other as one's self—to feel their joy, shame, disgust, suffering, and fears—that makes us the social creatures we are. The empathic sensibility is what allows us to respond to one another as an extended self, embedded in a deeply integrated society. When we hear of individuals who lack all sense of empathy, whose behavior shows no sensitivity to or concern for others, we think of them as inhuman. The sociopath is the ultimate pariah.

Studies repeatedly show a close correlation between materialistic behavior and the suppression or extinction of the empathic drive. Children who grow up with parents who are cold, arbitrary, sadistic, and uncaring, and who experience emotional abuse and the inflicting of corporal punishment, often become either aggressive and exploitive or withdrawn loners as adults. Their empathic drive is squashed and replaced by fear, mistrust, and a sense of abandonment. By contrast, parents who are affectionate and responsive and able to nurture an infant, and who provide him or her with a secure environment that encourages the development of selfhood, bring out the social trust that is so essential for empathy to flourish.

Children who never experienced empathy growing up are less likely to be able to express it to others as adults. Unable to connect with their fellow human beings at the most basic level, they become for all intents and purposes isolated and alone. Their materialism becomes a pale substitute for their sense of loss. Their attachment to things becomes a surrogate for a loss of attachment to people. Their obsession with material success, fame, and recognition also becomes a means to win social acceptance.

As their materialism comes to define their lives, it also shapes their relationships with others. In a world driven by material success, every relationship becomes a means to advance that end. Others are treated expediently and become reduced to instruments to accumulate more wealth. The sought-for prize of human warmth and affection becomes ever more elusive as the world of the materialist becomes divided into two realms—mine versus thine. The miserly Ebenezer Scrooge in Charles Dickens's *A Christmas Carol* is both despised and pitied, and treated as an outcast by society.

For the materialist, advertising becomes the powerful drug that feeds the addiction. Advertising prays on one's sense of inadequacy and loneliness. It promises that products and services will enhance a person's personality and identity and make him or her more appealing, attractive, and acceptable to others. The German philosopher Georg Friedrich Hegel defined the new materialist man and woman coming of age at the dawn of the capitalist ethos. He argued that beyond its utilitarian and material value, property is an expression of one's persona. It's by forcing one's will into objects that one projects his unique persona on the world and creates a presence among his fellow human beings. One's very personality, then, is present in all the objects one claims as one's own. Our property becomes indistinguishable from our personality. Everything that is mine enlarges my unique presence and sphere of influence and becomes the means by which others know me.

The philosopher William James described the consumer personality in terms that are uncomfortably recognizable to most of us living in a highly charged materialist culture. He wrote:

> It is clear that between what a man calls *me* and what he simply calls *mine* the line is difficult to draw. We feel and act about certain things that are ours very much as we feel and act about ourselves. Our fame, our children, the work of our hands, may be as dear to us as our bodies are, and arouse the same feelings and the same acts of reprisal if attacked. . . . *In its widest possible sense*, however, *a man's Self is the sum total of all that he* CAN *call his*, not only his body and his psychic powers, but his clothes and his house, his wife and children, his ancestors and friends, his reputation and works, his lands and horses, and yacht and bank-account. All these things give him the same emotions. If they wax and prosper, he feels triumphant; if they dwindle and die away, he feels cast down . . . a great part of our feeling about what is ours is due to the fact that we *live closer* to our own things, and so feel them more thoroughly and deeply.[17]

Advertising plays off the idea that property is the measure of a human being and pushes products and services as essential to the creation of an individual's identity in the world. For much of the twentieth century, advertising pitched the idea that property is an extension of one's personality and made deep inroads in reorienting each successive generation to a materialist culture. The Boston College sociologist Juliet Schor notes that by the 1990s, children spent "as much time shopping as visiting, twice as much time shopping as reading or going to church, and five times as much as playing outdoors."[18] Even more disturbing, youngsters said that they "would rather spend time buying things than doing almost anything else" and more than half believe that "when you grow up, the more money you have, the happier you are."[19]

It's been 15 years since these surveys were conducted. In the interim, a Millennial Generation has come of age, and the evidence is contradictory on the question of how the young line up on the spectrum running from empathy to materialism. Psychologists, sociologists, political scientists, and anthropologists are publishing reports and studies that are deeply at odds with one another.

A massive study of 14,000 college students conducted between 1979 and 2009 by the Institute for Social Research at the University of Michigan concluded that "college kids today are about 40 percent lower in empathy than their counterparts of 20 or 30 years ago, as measured by standard tests of this personality trait."[20] Sarah Konrath, a University of Michigan researcher who conducted the meta-analysis study, which combined the results of 72 studies of American college students over the 30-year period, says that today's college students are less likely to agree with statements such as, "I sometimes tried to understand my friends better by imagining how things look from their perspective" and "I often have tender, concerned feelings for people less fortunate than me."[21]

Other studies on the Millennial Generation, however, appear to show the opposite trend. Unlike the Gen Xers, millennials are "much more likely to feel empathy for others in their group and to seek to understand each person's perspective."[22] Studies also show that the Millennial Generation is more likely to give others' opinions in their peer group equal weight, prefer to work collaboratively, and seek group consensus, all of which require an empathic mindfulness.

On the question of trusting others, which is so essential to fostering empathy, while millennials are far more distrustful of government, the business community, and experts of all kinds, they are far more trusting of their fellow collaborators on the Internet and, as mentioned earlier, more willing to put their trust in opinions, reviews, and rankings of their peers and in the combined wisdom of crowds.

Studies also indicate that millennials are the least prejudiced and most empathic of any generation in history in championing the legal and social rights of previously marginalized groups of the population, including women, people of color, gays and lesbians, and the disabled. They are also less xenophobic. About 23 percent of American college students have studied abroad, and 73 percent of millennials favor liberal immigration policies compared to only 39 to 57 percent of the rest of the adult population.[23]

My sense is that the Millennial Generation is not a monolith, but rather a mix of contradictions. While there is evidence of their famed narcissism and materialism, there is also evidence of an increase in empathic engagement. I also suspect that the narcissistic and materialistic inclination is of waning influence in the aftermath of the Great Recession. A spate of new studies concur. In December 2013, *The New York Times* ran a lead article in its "Sunday Review" section reporting new findings by researchers that suggest that the millennial generation, deeply affected by the Great Recession and a stagnant global economy, has begun to shift its psychic priorities from material success to living a meaningful existence. A report commissioned by the Career Advisory Board found that among millenials between the ages of 21 and 31, having a meaningful career took precedence over making lots of money. A longitudinal study carried out by Jennifer L. Aaker, a professor of marketing at the Stanford Graduate School of Business, and her colleagues, followed several hundred Americans for a month to assess what the subjects meant by "meaningful." What they discovered is that young millennials who said they have a meaningful life "saw themselves as more other-oriented—by being more specifically a 'giver.'" People who said that doing things for others was important to them reported having "more meaning in their lives."[24]

Even more telling, in a 2013 survey of 9,000 high school high achievers conducted by the National Society of High School Scholars, students were asked to pick a place they would like to work for in a list of over 200 enterprises, and health care, hospitals, and government accounted for 14 of the top 25 choices. St. Jude Children's Research Hospital was the top choice of the best and brightest high school students in the country. James W. Lewis, the CEO of the National Society of High School Scholars, summed up the findings, saying that "the focus on helping others is what millennials are responding to."[25]

As noted, less empathic individuals tend to be more materialistic. If millennials are more empathic than previous generations, then we should pick up the trend in their changing views on materialism over the past decade. That's beginning to happen. In a study published in the summer of 2013 in the journal *Social Psychological and Personality Science*, researchers examined surveys that tracked the attitudes of hundreds of thousands of high school seniors over nearly 40 years and found a startling reversal in values with the onset of the Great Recession in 2008. While empathy for others had been decreasing and materialism was becoming more rampant with each passing year, the trend suddenly turned around after 2008 among young millennials, who reported "more concern for others and less interest in material goods."[26] The new studies find that millennials are less interested in keeping up with materialistic trends and less invested in obsessive consumerism as a way of life.

These findings dovetail with the sharp rise of collaborative consumption and the sharing economy. All over the world, a younger generation is sharing bikes, automobiles, homes, clothes, and countless other items and opting for access over ownership. A growing number of millennials are eschewing designer brands in favor of generics and cause-oriented brands and are far more interested in the use value of material things than their exchange value or status. A sharing economy of collaborative prosumers is, by its very nature, a more empathic and less materialistic one.

The waning of the materialistic ethos is also reflected in the increasing commitment to sustainability and environmental stewardship. It's not surprising that materialists display less empathy not only to their fellow human beings, but also to their fellow creatures and the larger natural environment. They view nature in a purely instrumental manner as a resource to exploit rather than a community to preserve. For them, the environment, like their relationships with others, is valued only for its utility and market value and never for its intrinsic value.

At the University of Rochester, researchers tested 80 students to ascertain how materialistic values affected the way they chose to use natural resources. The students were categorized as holding either highly materialistic values or nonmaterialistic values. They were then invited to play a game in which they were the head of a timber company in competition with other companies bidding to log 200 hectares of national forest. Each could bid to cut up to a maximum of ten hectares per year, with the understanding that whatever remained would grow back at 10 percent a year. If the group bid to cut only a few hectares, profits would be low. But if they bid to cut a huge number of acres, profits would be high but the forest would be depleted in short order.

Not surprisingly, the materialists bid to harvest far more of the forest than the nonmaterialists, giving them a quick profit but at the expense of an equally quick depletion of the forest. They consistently focused on short-term financial gain over long-term conservation practices. The nonmaterialists enjoyed greater profit in the long run because the forest lasted longer.[27]

The kind of value orientation demonstrated in this experiment is showing up in the real world. Millennials are not only less materialistic but also far more supportive of environmental stewardship than older generations. According to a 2009 survey conducted by the Center for American Progress, a think tank based in Washington, D.C., 75 percent of the Millennial Generation favors a shift out of fossil fuels and into renewable energies—surpassing all the other adult generations.[28] A Gallup poll conducted several years ago is even more dramatic. Some 58 percent of young people between the ages of 18 and 29 said that environmental protection should be a national priority in the United States "even at the risk of curbing economic growth."[29]

So what do all these experiments, studies, and surveys show us? First, that money doesn't buy happiness. While poverty breeds despair, increasing wealth, after a modicum of comfort is reached, also breeds increasing despair. Second, rampant materialism, far from making people happier, makes them increasingly alienated, fearful, mistrusting, and lonely.

Third, the primary human drive is not insatiable material wants, as the economists would have us believe, but rather the quest for sociability. What makes us happy, after our minimum requirements for material comfort are met, is affection and companionship. We seek to belong, not to possess and devour—all of which puts into doubt the two governing assumptions of economics: that the things we want most in life are scarce, and that our wants are unlimited. In reality, the things we want most are not scarce but infinitely abundant—love, acceptance, and recognition of our humanity. The advertising industry understands this even if the economists do not. Hundreds of billions of advertising dollars are spent each year appealing to these deeper drives, suggesting, in a twisted way, that they can best be met by buying, hoarding, and consuming more material things, knowing full well that in reality these fabricated wants only pull us further away from our search for community. Imagine how quickly human behavior would change were the advertising industry to suddenly disappear from our daily lives. The obsession with materialism would quickly fade, allowing us the breathing room to rediscover our yearning for one another rather than for things.

But what about the argument that in a near zero marginal cost society, where everyone can have many of the things they desire, whenever they want, for nearly free, human beings will likely gobble up Earth's remaining resources even more quickly, bringing ruin to the planet? Not likely. It's scarcity that breeds overconsumption, not abundance. In a world where everyone's material needs are met, the fear of going without is extinguished. The insatiable need to hoard and overindulge loses much of its currency. So too does the need to grab what one can from others. Moreover, in a world where everyone's needs are more or less met, social distinctions based on material status become less relevant. Society is no longer solely divided up on the basis of "mine versus thine." Nor is everyone's worth determined by what they have.

That's not to argue that an era of abundance takes the human race to utopia. No one is naïve enough to believe that the dark side of human nature will suddenly vanish from our cultural DNA. It's only to say that when abundance replaces scarcity, the human disposition is likely to be far less consumed with the relentless drive to have more and more for fear of what tomorrow might bring. Although, at first glance, the very notion of replacing an economy of scarcity with an economy of abundance might conjure up the prospect of runaway consumption of the planet's remaining largesse, in fact it is likely, for all the reasons mentioned above, to be the only effective path to securing a sustainable future for our species on Earth.

At least a portion of the younger generation growing up in a new world mediated by distributed, collaborative, peer-to-peer networks is starting to break out of the materialist syndrome that characterized much of the economic life of the capitalist era. They are creating a shareable economy that is less materialistic and more sustainable, less expedient and more empathic. Their lives are being lived out more on a global Commons and less in a capitalist market. The new ethos of sharing is just beginning to have a measurable impact on the ecological footprint of a younger generation in the advanced industrialized economies.

This shift from materialism to a sustainable quality of life opens up the prospect of dramatically reducing the ecological footprint of the wealthiest human beings on the planet, making available more of Earth's abundance so the world's poorest human beings can lift themselves out of poverty, raise their standard of living, and enjoy the happiness that comes from meeting their basic needs and comforts. Whether these two forces can come together and meet at the gateway of comfort where the whole of humanity can live off Earth's ecological interest rather than its capital in a sustainable quality of life is an open question.

I'm quite sure that at this point many readers are asking, is this enough? Even if the richest 40 percent of the human race narrows its ecological footprint, it will be of little solace if the poorest 40 percent increases its numbers and expands its ecological footprint. Agreed. We not only have to narrow the ecological footprint of the rich, but also reduce the rising tide of population of the poor if we are all to enjoy the fruits that an abundant planet can provide.

Handing out condoms and counseling families on limiting births is a futile exercise as long as they are mired in poverty. We know that in the poorest countries of the world, large families serve as a de facto insurance policy, guaranteeing that additional bodies will be available to take on the work should some siblings die prematurely. Women and children in impoverished communities in the developing world are the beasts of burden. In particular, they are the mules that marshal much of the scant resources to assure their families' survival. So how do we encourage smaller families?

We are beginning to learn that the key to population stabilization on Earth is access to electricity. That's why Ban Ki-moon, secretary general of the United Nations, has made the universal access to electricity the centerpiece of his administration's economic development agenda.

It was electricity that freed women in Europe, the Americas, and certain other countries in the twentieth century. Electricity liberated women from the yolk of household chores that chained them to the hearth as little more than indentured servants. Electricity allowed young girls, as well as boys, enough time to pursue an education and better their lot in life. As women became more independent as well as breadwinners, their lives became more secure and the number of births dramatically declined. Today, with few exceptions, the fertility rate in industrialized countries has fallen to 2.1 children per woman, the rate at which children replace parents. Population has fallen precipitously across the wealthiest nations of the world.[30]

Still, more than 20 percent of the human race is without electricity, and an additional 20 percent has only marginal and unreliable access to electricity. These are the very countries where population is rising the fastest. The United Nations Industrial Development Organization (UNIDO) has made a commitment to help empower local populations to lay down a Third Industrial Revolution (TIR) infrastructure that can bring green electricity to 1.5 billion impoverished people. In 2011, I joined Dr. Kandeh Yumkella, director general of UNIDO and the head of U.N. Energy, at the organization's global conference in support of the TIR build-out in developing nations. Yumkella declared that "we believe we are at the beginning of a third industrial revolution and I wanted all member countries of UNIDO to hear the message and ask them the key question: How can we be part of this revolution?"[31] The goal is to make electricity universally available by 2030. The electrification of every community on Earth will provide the impetus to lift the world's poor out of poverty and toward the zone of comfort that can sustain a decent quality of life for every human being.

As the movement for universal access to electricity unfolds, the population surge in the poorest countries will very likely diminish as it has in every other country where electrification has brought people out of abject poverty. By midcentury, the falling fertility rate is likely to approach 2.1 children per family across the world, marking the beginning of a slow decline in human population, eventually bringing it down to 5 billion people—the number that will secure our ability to live off of nature's ecological interest and enjoy an economy of abundance.

THE TWO WILD CARDS OF THE APOCALYPSE

Reducing the ecological footprint of the wealthy, bringing 40 percent of the human race up out of poverty, and stabilizing and shrinking the human population to allow our species to live off the interest rather than the principal of Earth's biocapacity are challenging but not impossible endeavors. These tasks, however, are made more problematic by two wild cards that could undermine our best efforts to replenish the planet and replace scarcity with abundance.

Industrial-induced climate change is now compromising our ecosystems and imperiling our species' survival as well as the survival of our fellow creatures. If that weren't enough to contend with, the same IT and Internet technologies that are connecting the human race in a sharable economy of abundance are increasingly being used by cyberterrorists to wreak havoc on the evolving Internet of Things infrastructure, with potentially catastrophic impacts that could result in the collapse of modern civilization and the deaths of hundreds of millions of people.

A WARMING PLANET

Climate scientists report that the global atmospheric concentration of carbon, which ranged from a 180 to 300 parts per million (ppm) for the past 650,000 years, has risen from 280 ppm just before the outset of the industrial era to 400 ppm in 2013.[32] The atmospheric concentrations of methane and nitrous oxide, the other two powerful global warming gases, are showing similar steep trajectories.[33]

At the Copenhagen global climate summit in December 2009, the European Union proposed that the nations of the world not exceed carbon dioxide emissions of 450 ppm by 2050, with the hope that if we were able to do so, we might limit the rise in Earth's temperature to 3.5°F (2°C). Even a 3.5°F rise, however, would take us back to the temperature on Earth several million years ago, in the Pliocene epoch, with devastating consequences to ecosystems and human life.[34]

The EU proposal went ignored. Now, four years later, the steep rise in the use of carbon-based fuels has pushed up the atmospheric levels of carbon dioxide (CO_2) far more quickly than earlier models had projected, making it likely that the temperature on Earth will rush past the 3.5° target and could top off at 8.1°F (4.5°C) or more by 2100—temperatures not seen on Earth for millions of years.[35] (Remember, anatomically modern human beings—the youngest species—have only inhabited the planet for 175,000 years or so.)

What makes these dramatic spikes in the Earth's temperature so terrifying is that the increase in heat radically shifts the planet's hydrological cycle. We are a watery planet. The Earth's diverse ecosystems have evolved over geological time in direct relationship to precipitation patterns. Each rise in temperature of 1°C results in a 7 percent increase in the moisture-holding capacity of the atmosphere.[36] This causes a radical change in the way water is distributed, with more intense precipitation but a reduction in duration and frequency. The consequences are already being felt in ecosystems around the world. We are experiencing more bitter winter snows, more dramatic spring storms and floods, more prolonged summer droughts, more wildfires, more intense hurricanes (category 3, 4, and 5), a melting of the ice caps on the great mountain ranges, and a rise in sea levels.

The Earth's ecosystems cannot readjust to a disruptive change in the planet's water cycle in such a brief moment in time and are under increasing stress, with some on the verge of collapse. The destabilization of ecosystem dynamics around the world has now pushed the biosphere into the sixth extinction event of the past 450 million years of life on Earth. In each of the five previous extinctions, Earth's climate reached a critical tipping point, throwing the ecosystems into a positive feedback loop, leading to a quick wipe-out of the planet's biodiversity. On average, it took upward of 10 million years to recover the lost biodiversity. Biologists tell us that we could see the extinction of half the Earth's species by the end of the current century, resulting in a barren new era that could last for millions of years.[37]

James Hansen, former head of the NASA Goddard Institute for Space Studies and the chief climatologist for the U.S. government, forecasts a 6°C rise in the Earth's temperature between now and the turn of the century—and with it, the end of human civilization as we've come to know it. The only hope, according to Hansen, is to reduce the current concentration of carbon in the atmosphere from 385 ppm to 350 ppm or less—something no government, not even the European Union, is currently proposing.[38]

Here, the wild card is the impact that climate change and the shift in the hydrological cycle is likely to have on agricultural production and infrastructure. The dramatic rise in floods and droughts are wreaking devastation on large swaths of agricultural land around the world. Typhoon Haiyan, one of the most powerful storms ever recorded, ravaged the agriculture fields of the Philippines at the onset of the rice planting season in November 2013, destroying hundreds of thousands of hectares of plantable land, decimating the rice production in that country. Just a month earlier, cyclone Phailin stormed across east India with nearly equal destructive force. In the regions of Odisha and Bihar alone, crop losses were estimated at $45 billion.[39] In June 2013, torrential rainfall across Central Europe caused rivers to overflow their banks, flooding agricultural fields. In Passau, Germany, where the Danube, Inn, and Ilz rivers come together, flood waters peaked at 42.3 feet, topping the worst flood ever recorded in the region back in 1501.[40] I saw the devastation firsthand while traveling from the Frankfurt airport to the historic city of Weimar. Cropland along the route was underwater. Damage to agriculture production is expected to exceed $16.5 billion.[41]

Mojib Latif, a climate scientist at the Helmholtz Center for Ocean Research in the German city of Kiel, warned that more extreme storms and floods, like the ones Europe experienced in 2002 and 2013, are the new normal as rising world temperatures, caused by climate change, intensify precipitation events. Latif noted that powerful storms and flooding "such as the one[s] we're seeing now are occurring about twice as often as they did a century ago."[42]

Droughts are also proliferating everywhere in the world, further reducing agricultural production. Recurring drought in the western

United States over the past several years has dramatically reduced agricultural output. With the 17 western states accounting for 40 percent of the nation's net farm income, concern is mounting that climate change might turn the most bountiful farming region in the world into a desert in the coming decades. In 2012, more than 15,000 counties—half of the counties in the United States—experienced such extreme drought that they were declared national disaster areas. These agricultural regions have been experiencing temperatures of 10–20 degrees higher than the long-term averages for several years. In 2013, temperatures reached 105°F, or ten degrees higher than the threshold for most temperate-zone crops. The western United States is quickly losing surface and ground water and having to pump water in from other areas of the country, increasing its already high energy costs.[43] According to a 2011 study by the U.S. National Center for Atmospheric Research, climate change is likely to induce droughts in the United States more severe than those that caused the great dust bowl in the 1930s.[44]

Climate change-induced droughts are also proliferating in other regions around the world, further reducing agricultural yield. A recent study projects a twofold increased in the frequency of droughts worldwide by the mid-twenty-first century, and a threefold increase by the end of the century.[45]

A 2009 International Food Policy Research Institute report on the impact of climate change on agriculture in the developing world was sobering—even more so because its forecasts were based on earlier estimates of an increase in temperature of only 3°C. South Asia is likely to be the hardest hit by 2050, with an estimated decline from the level of the year 2000 of 50 percent in wheat yields, 17 percent in rice outputs, and 6 percent in maize yields because of the impact of climate change. In East Asia and the Pacific, rice production will decrease by 20 percent, soybeans by 13 percent, wheat by 16 percent, and maize by 4 percent by 2050. The average calorie availability is forecasted to plunge by 15 percent, and cereal consumption is projected to decline by 24 percent by 2050 because of climate change. The number of malnourished children is expected to rise to 59 million in South Asia and to 14 million in East Asia and the Pacific.[46]

Sub-Saharan Africa, already the poorest region of the world, is expected to face equally devastating declines in food production because of its reliance on rainfall agriculture. By 2050 average rice yields will decline by 14 percent, wheat by 22 percent, and maize by 5 percent. In a subcontinent already plagued by malnutrition, forecasts project an additional drop of 500 calories per person per day by 2050 because of climate change, which amounts to a 21 percent decline in food consumption per person. The number of malnourished children is expected to increase from 33 to 42 million in the next 38 years. The number increases to 52 million when accounting for climate change.[47]

The impact on agriculture in the Middle East and North Africa over the next four decades because of climate change is equally alarming. Rice yields will decline by 30 percent, maize by 47 percent, and wheat by 20 percent. As with Sub-Saharan Africa, the average person will see their food intake reduced by 500 calories per day, resulting in over 2 million malnourished children by 2050.[48]

Latin America and the Caribbean fare somewhat better, with rice yields declining by 6.4 percent, maize by 3 percent, soybeans by 3 percent, and wheat by 6 percent. Average food consumption will diminish by 300 calories per day or a 12 percent decline overall, with 6.4 million malnourished children in the region by 2050.[49]

Agricultural output in the industrialized countries of the North will also be negatively impacted by climate change. Corn and soy yields in the United States are expected to decline by 30 to 46 percent in a low carbon-dioxide-emissions scenario, and a decline of 63 to 82 percent in a high carbon-dioxide-emissions scenario by the end of the century. The higher emissions scenarios take on added significance with new scientific data suggesting their greater likelihood. These projected declines in the nation's corn and soy yields—of 80 percent or more—are potentially catastrophic, especially when we consider the fact that the United States is the leading grain exporter in the world.[50]

Unless we can dramatically reduce global warming emissions to the levels Hansen and other climatologists say is required to slow the course of climate change, any hope of creating an economy of abundance, especially when it comes to food, is likely to escape us in the coming century and for centuries, if not millennia, to come.

Climate change will have no less of a dramatic impact on human infrastructure in the twenty-first century. Category 3, 4, and 5 hurricanes and torrential storms producing flash floods and the overflow of rivers are increasing at an alarming rate, with devastating impacts on infrastructure. Hurricane Katrina, a category 3 storm that slammed into New Orleans and the Gulf Coast in 2005, caused $148 billion in damages to the region's infrastructure and economy and the loss of 1,833 lives. The storm destroyed more than 126,000 homes and damaged an additional 1.2 million dwellings. Three million people in eight states were without power, some for weeks, and 600,000 families were homeless, some for months.[51]

Sandy, also a category 3 hurricane, which roared up the East Coast in 2012, destroyed vital infrastructure from New Jersey and New York into New England. Though less severe than Katrina, it sowed a path of destruction that will take years to repair. Some 8.51 million people lost power, 305,000 homes were damaged or destroyed, and public transport came to a near halt in New York City. The estimated damage in New York and New Jersey alone exceeded $71 billion.[52]

The power grid, transportation arteries, telecommunications, and water and sewage systems that were never designed to withstand the fury of a runaway hydrological cycle are being crippled in regions around the world. The energy infrastructure is particularly vulnerable. Power stations near rivers and coast lines are often defenseless against storm surges. The tsunami that slammed into the east coast of Japan in 2011 tore the Fukushima nuclear facility apart, resulting in the meltdown of four of its six nuclear reactors and the spread of nuclear radiation across the island, making a 62-square-mile radius around the plant uninhabitable for decades, perhaps even centuries.[53] Flooding is also disabling offshore oil rigs, leading to shutdowns and spills. Oil pipelines on land are also being adversely affected by extreme-weather-related events.[54]

Droughts are increasingly threatening the supply of cooling water to power stations. In France, 43 percent of all fresh water consumed each year goes to cooling nuclear reactors. When the heated water is returned, it dries out already drought-ridden ecosystems, affecting agricultural yields. At the front end, when the water becomes too hot because of extreme heat induced by climate change, it can no longer be used to cool nuclear reactors, forcing a slowdown or shutdown of nuclear power plants. In the summer of 2009, a heat wave across France led to a shortage in cooling waters, forcing one-third of the nuclear power plants in the country to shut down.[55] With nuclear power accounting for 28 percent of the electricity supply of the EU, increasing temperatures, brought on by climate change, are expected to cause significant disruptions to the continent's power generation in the years ahead.[56]

Extreme storms are also damaging power and transmission lines, resulting in frequent disruptions in electrical service and a record number of brownouts and blackouts. Loss of electrical power also has a cascading effect on other parts of the infrastructure since electricity is needed to maintain communication, water treatment plants, pumping stations, ICT equipment, gasoline pumps, etc.

High-intensity water-related events also damage roads, bringing freight and commuter traffic to a standstill, with severe impacts on the economy. Rail transport is also affected by washed-out rail lines. Subways are vulnerable to flooding, as was the case in New York when Hurricane Sandy swept down into the tunnels, filling them with water across lower Manhattan. Some subway service was out for days and weeks.[57]

Extreme wind and storms are also increasingly shutting down airports and backing up air traffic over connecting regions. Seaports and inland waterways are likewise experiencing downtime from an increase in floods, more droughts, and even more dense fog.

The water infrastructure is acutely vulnerable to changes in the hydrological cycle. Changes in rainfall patterns have multiple effects, including drought, which diminishes the available water in reservoirs. Changes in precipitation also stress drainage systems, causing backups and floods. Higher mean water temperatures can also negatively impact biological treatment processes and the quality of drinking water.[58]

Total public spending on infrastructure in the United States alone exceeds $300 billion per year.[59] That figure is expected to rise dramatically in the decades ahead as a result of the increasing damage inflicted on infrastructure by extreme weather events. Some economists are even beginning to suggest that the price tag for maintaining human civilization could become prohibitive—forcing the human race into a new world that we can scarcely imagine.

Shoring up the existing fossil fuel infrastructure to withstand more severe weather is likely to be a futile exercise as long as our industrial society continues to emit massive amounts of carbon dioxide into the atmosphere. It's simply foolish to believe that we can get ahead of the extreme weather and effectively arrest its escalating assaults by patching up a carbon-based regime.

Rather, the primary focus of our efforts should be on transitioning out of a carbon-based configuration. The IoT infrastructure offers a realistic hope of quickly replacing fossil fuel energies with renewable energies and slowing climate change. The question becomes whether the new infrastructure can be deployed around the world fast enough to significantly reduce carbon dioxide emissions and other greenhouse gas emissions before climate change so disrupts the planet's hydrological system that it becomes too late to make a difference.

THE CYBERTERRORISTS ARE OUT THERE

A second wild card that could undermine efforts to transition into a sustainable economy of abundance is cyberterrorism. Governments and businesses around the world are becoming increasingly alarmed over the escalation of cyberterrorist attacks aimed at infrastructure and are voicing growing concern over the possibility that they might cripple and even shut down many of the vital services necessary to operate society, leading to a high-tech Armageddon and the collapse of civilization.

In 2009, hackers deep inside North Korea succeeded in shutting down websites at the U.S. Treasury Department, the Secret Service, and the Federal Trade Commission. That same year it was discovered that hackers had inserted sophisticated software into the U.S. electricity grid that would allow them to disrupt the system at a later date of their own choosing.[60]

Other cyberattacks aimed at governments, businesses, and infrastructure have been proliferating ever since, with greater ability to disrupt and inflict damage. Hacking has graduated from pranks to terrorist activity, creating a new mass fear not unlike the terror people felt with the spread of nuclear weaponry in the latter half of the twentieth century.

Cyberterrorists employ software programs to do damage in both virtual and physical space. The Center for Strategic and International Studies defines cyberterror as "the use of computer network tools to shut down critical national infrastructures (such as energy, transportation, government operations) or to coerce or intimidate a government or civilian population."[61]

In March 2013, American Express card members attempting to access online accounts found instead a blank screen. The site was down for more than two hours. The American Express cyberattack was just one in a series of highly choreographed assaults that began six months earlier and had taken down, if only temporarily, some of the world's leading financial institutions, including Bank of America, JPMorgan Chase, and Wells Fargo. A group calling itself Izz ad-Din al-Qassam Cyber Fighters claimed responsibility for the cyberattacks, saying that they were a reprisal for an anti-Islamic video on YouTube. The group was suspected of being a front for the Iranian government. In the same vein, the United States and Israel were successful in using online hacking to disable much of Iran's nuclear enrichment plants. In retaliation, Iran announced the establishment of its own state-run initiative, which it dubbed Cyber Corps, to retaliate.[62]

The mounting concern over cyberattacks has spawned a massive cyber-security industry. The global cyber-security market, already at $61.1 billion in 2012, is expected to top $100 billion by 2030, according to a study done by Morgan Stanley.[63]

Governments are most worried about attacks aimed at the electrical power grid. A U.S. government commission report noted that

electrical power is necessary to support other critical infrastructures, including supply and distribution of water, food, fuel, communications, transport, financial transactions, emergency services, governments services, and all other infrastructures supporting the national economy and welfare.[64]

If a cyberattack were to target key components of the power grid and disable them, the country could be without electrical power for several months, or even a year or longer. Without electricity, virtually everything in modern society shuts down—the water system, gas pipelines, sewage, transport, heat, and light. Studies show that within weeks of a massive power outage, society would be thrown into chaos. Millions would die from lack of food, water, and other basic services. Government would cease to function, and the military would be helpless to intervene and restore order. Those that survive would have to flee to the countryside and attempt to eke out a subsistence survival, throwing humanity back into a preindustrial era.

The commission report concluded that, "should significant parts of the electrical power infrastructure be lost for any substantial period of time, . . . the consequences are likely to be devastating, and many people may ultimately die for lack of the basic elements necessary to sustain life in dense urban and suburban communities."[65]

HOW VULNERABLE IS THE NATION'S ELECTRICITY TRANSMISSION GRID?

If cyberattacks were to knock out the 2,000 or so custom-built transformers in the United States that are responsible for revving up the high-voltage electricity for bulk transmission and reducing the voltage for distribution to end users, it would be devastating because most of them are built overseas.[66]

Building 2,000 transformers, shipping them to the United States, and installing them could take a year or more—and this assumes that the cyberattack only targeted U.S. transformers and not those in Europe or elsewhere. Try to imagine the entire U.S. society without electricity and basic government and commercial services for upward of a year. By that time, the United States as we know it will have long since ceased to exist.

In June 2012, some of America's leading security experts, including former homeland security secretary Michael Chertoff and General Michael Hayden, former head of the National Security Agency, called on the Senate to pass a cybersecurity bill to protect vulnerable U.S. infrastructure. They pointed out that 9/11 might have been prevented with the better use of existing intelligence and cautioned that "we do not want to be in the same position again when 'cyber 9/11' hits." They concluded with a warning that "it is not a question of 'whether' this will happen; it is a question of 'when.'"[67]

The U.S. National Academy of Sciences flagged the potential cyberthreat to the nation's electrical grid in a detailed report issued in 2012, paying close attention to the vulnerability of electrical transformers. In March 2012, technicians conducted an emergency-preparedness drill, shipping three transformers from St. Louis to Houston and installing them to assess their ability to respond quickly to a cyberattack on the country's transformers.[68] Richard J. Lordan of the Electrical Power Research Institute (EPRI) said that the nation's power sector is beginning to ask how many transformers need to be stockpiled and stored and how best to transport and deploy them to critically exposed regions in the aftermath of a concerted cyberattack on the nation's power grid.[69]

Although the Congress, EPRI, the National Academy of Sciences, governmental commissions, and private sector groups are to be praised for drawing attention to the level of the threats, their responses come up short because their various "what if" scenarios continue to assume a business-as-usual power grid that relies on fossil fuels and nuclear power to generate electricity that is then distributed across power lines that are designed to transmit it only from a centralized power station to millions of end users. If a centralized smart grid were brought on-line, it would only exacerbate the potential vulnerability to a cyberattack on the grid.

Unfortunately, the United States is playing directly into the hands of cyberterrorists by championing a centralized smart grid. The European Union and other governments, by contrast, are deploying a distributed smart grid—or Energy Internet—that lessens the potential threat and damage that can be inflicted by a massive cyberattack. Even if the electrical transformers were to flame out, if a fully functioning Energy Internet were operational across every region of the country, local communities could go off-grid and continue to generate their own green electricity, sharing it with their neighbors and businesses on microgrids, keeping the power and lights on, at least long enough to keep society functioning.

Interestingly, a similar concern about the vulnerability of America's communications network inspired, at least in part, the creation of the Internet. In the 1960s, Paul Baran and other researchers at the Rand Corporation began to ponder the question of how to ensure the continued operability of the nation's communications network in the event of a nuclear attack. Baran and his colleagues began to envision a distributed network of host computers, without a central switchboard, that could continue to function even if a nuclear attack was to cripple part of the nation's communications system. The idea was to build a communications system in which data could travel several different routes to get to its destination so that no one part was totally dependent on the functioning of another. An experimental network was funded by the Advanced Research Projects Agency (ARPA) of the

Department of Defense and was called the ARPAnet. It connected a handful of computers at major universities and eventually metamorphosed into the Internet.[70]

The distributed architecture of the Energy Internet builds in a similar ability to withstand cyberattacks. The problem is that in many locales, not only in the United States, but also in the European Union and elsewhere, installed micropower in the form of solar installations, wind, etc., is shackled to the main grid, forcing locally generated power to feed only into the larger system. When the main system goes down, the micropower shuts off as well, making it useless on-site. The reason this is done is so power and utility operators can control how the power is dispersed along the grid. They worry that with dynamic pricing monitoring meters available at every micropower site—alerting the owner about moment-to-moment changes in the price of electricity—small generators of electricity might program their system to only sell to the main grid when the price is high and go off-grid and use their electricity when they choose.

The shortcomings of this system became apparent in the aftermath of Hurricane Sandy, when electrical power on Long Island and in the New Jersey coastal towns went out. Many homes and offices with installed solar panels on their roofs were unable to deploy them. Ed Antonio, a homeowner in Queens, equipped his home with a $70,000 solar system powered by 42 solar panels; it went unused, as did similar green micropower systems in the region. Homes like Antonio's "feed electricity from the roof array through an inverter and into the home's electrical panel, sending the excess to the broader electric grid."[71] But when the power goes out, the inverter shuts down to ensure that no electricity is flowing into the grid while utility company workers are patching up the line.

New systems are now available, however, that would allow micropower plants to continue to operate even after a power failure on the transmission lines. A separate electrical panel and more sophisticated inverter can be installed that transfers the electricity flow to the house alone, allowing it to operate essential appliances, light, and heat, and even power an electric vehicle.

The U.S. military is pioneering much of the research, development, and deployment of microgrid technology. Worried that a massive power shutdown would incapacitate the nation's military, the

Department of Defense and the Department of Energy have initiated a $30 million project called Smart Power Infrastructure Demonstration for Energy Reliability and Security (SPIDERS). The green microgrid power infrastructure is being installed in three military installations— Camp H. M. Smith in Hawaii, Fort Carson in Colorado, and the Joint Base Pearl Harbor–Hickam in Hawaii. SPIDERS will enable the military bases to operate all critical functions, even if a cyberattack takes down the main power grid, by relying on locally generated green electricity.[72]

As with global warming impacts on agriculture and infrastructure, where a race is on between an escalating change in Earth's temperature, forcing potentially catastrophic damage on its ecosystems, and the quick deployment of a collaborative IoT infrastructure that can wean society off carbon before reaching a tipping point, a similar race is pitting increasingly sophisticated cyberterrorists against the champions of distributed power generation. The question is whether an Energy Internet can be brought online quickly enough to allow hundreds of millions of local micropower generators to operate off the main grid—when necessary—to keep the economy operating, and effectively counter cyberattacks aimed at the nation's electrical transmission system.

WITH BOTH OF THESE WILD CARDS—climate change and cyberterrorism—humanity faces a formidable threat to its security and an equally challenging opportunity to pass into a more sustainable and equitable post-carbon era. Turning the threat to an opportunity, however, will require more than a workable economic plan. We have the architecture of that plan as well as the technological know-how to implement it. Both will be for naught, however, without a fundamental change in human consciousness. We will need to leave behind the parochialisms of the past and begin to think and act as a single extended family living in a common biosphere. What's urgently called for now is a new way of living on Earth if our species is to survive and flourish.

CHAPTER SIXTEEN
A BIOSPHERE LIFESTYLE

Most conventional economists are still betting that the extreme productivity unleashed by the emerging Internet of Things—even if it speeds the economy ever closer to near zero marginal costs and the swift rise of the Collaborative Commons—will ultimately be absorbabe by the capitalist system. But the reverse is much more likely. That is, the two economies will become accustomed to functioning in more of a hybrid partnership, with the Collaborative Commons increasingly becoming dominant by the mid-twenty-first century and the capitalist economy settling into a more supplementary role.

My sense is that with an unswerving commitment, no costly mistakes or setbacks, and a little luck, the race to a new economic paradigm can be achieved. My reasons for saying so are not based merely on intuition or wishful thinking, but rather on historical comparisons and present trajectories. The incipient infrastructure of both the First and Second Industrial Revolutions in America and Europe was put in place in 30 years, and matured in another 20 years.

The Third Industrial Revolution is following an even faster timeline. The World Wide Web went online in 1990 and matured by 2014, connecting much of the human race across a communications medium that operates at near zero marginal costs. The same exponential curve that enabled the Communications Internet to build out in less than 25 years is moving the Energy Internet forward on a similar timeline, with the prospect of approaching near universal generation of green electricity in many countries at near zero marginal cost in 25 years.

The Transportation Internet, although still in its infancy, is likely to run apace. As for 3D printing, it is already experiencing a faster growth trajectory than the Communications Internet at a comparable stage of development.

We've also seen how the evolution of the social economy on the Commons speeds up even more dramatically when prosumers proliferate and peer production accellerates exponentially across the Internet of Things, reducing the costs of producing, marketing, and delivering goods and services. Already, prosumers and social entrepreneurial firms are grabbing a significant share of economic activity, shrinking already paper-thin profit margins of existing Second Industrial Revolution companies and forcing many of them out of business.

I am also guardedly hopeful that a near zero marginal cost society can take the human race from an economy of scarcity to an economy of sustainable abundance over the course of the first half of the twenty-first century. My hope rests not with technology alone, but with the history of the human narrative. Here's why.

HOMO EMPATHICUS

The great economic paradigm shifts in human history not only bring together communication revolutions and energy regimes in powerful new configurations that change the economic life of society. Each new communication/energy/transportation matrix also transforms human consciousness by extending the empathic drive across wider temporal and spatial domains, bringing human beings together in larger metaphoric families and more interdependent societies.

In early forager/hunter societies, the source of energy was the human body itself—we had not yet domesticated animals as energy carriers or harvested the wind and water currents. Every forager/hunter society created some form of oral language to coordinate foraging and hunting and carry on social life. And every forager/hunter society—even those few still remaining today—had "mythological consciousness." The empathic drive in forager/hunter societies only extended to blood ties and tribal bonds. Studies of forager/hunter societies reveal that the largest social units that could maintain a cohesive community rarely exceeded 500 people—the number of blood-related, extended family members with whom social relations could be regularly maintained and social trust secured, with some degree of familiarity.[1] Other tribes that occasionally intruded into a band's migratory region were thought of as nonhuman or even demons.

The advent of the great hydraulic civilizations in the Middle East around 3500 B.C., in the Yangtze Valley of China in 3950 B.C., and in the Indus Valley of South Asia in 2500 B.C. brought a new communication/energy/transportation matrix. Building and maintaining a centralized, canal-irrigated agricultural system required both mass labor and technical skills.[2] The energy regime—stored grain—gave rise to urban life and spawned granaries, road systems, coinage, markets, and long-distance trade. Governing bureaucracies were established to manage the production, storage, and distribution of grain. Centralized management of these far-flung hydraulic enterprises only became possible with the invention of a new form of communication called writing.

The coming together of writing and hydraulic agricultural production shifted the human psyche from mythological to "theological consciousness." Several great world religions were formed during the period called the Axial Age (about 800 B.C. to 100 A.D.): Judaism and Christianity in the Middle East, Buddhism in India, and Confucianism (a spiritual quest) in China.

The shift from mythological to theological consciousness was accompanied by a vast extension of the empathic drive from blood ties to new fictional families based on religious identity. Although not blood related, Jews began to identify with other Jews as a fictional family. So did Buddhists. In first-century Rome, early converts to Christianity would kiss each other on the cheeks and greet one another as brother or sister—a concept completely alien to previous generations for whom the family was always limited to blood ties.

The great axial religions all spawned the golden rule, "do unto others as you would have others do unto you." This extension of empathic sensibility to extended fictional families based on religious affiliation allowed large numbers of people to create social bonds across the more expansive temporal and spatial reach of the new civilizations born of the coming together of writing and hydraulic agriculture production.

In the nineteenth century, the convergence of coal-powered steam printing and the new coal-powered factory and rail transport system gave rise to "ideological consciousness." The new communication/energy/transportation matrix made possible the expansion of commerce and trade from local to national markets and solidified the nation-state as the governing mode to manage the new economic paradigm. Individuals began to see themselves as citizens and to regard their fellow citizens as an extended family. Each nation created its own historical narrative—much of it fictional—complete with an accounting of great events, historic struggles, collective commemorations, and national celebrations, all designed to stretch empathic sensibility beyond blood and religious ties to include national ties. French men and women began to think of each other as brothers and sisters, and empathized with one another as an extended family that stretched across the new temporal/spatial reach of national markets and national political borders that made up the communication/energy/transportation matrix of French industrial society. The Germans, Italians, British, Americans, and others likewise extended the empathic drive to encompass their own national boundaries.

In the twentieth century, the coming together of centralized electrification, oil, and automobile transport, and the rise of a mass consumer society, marked still another cognitive passage, from ideological to "psychological consciousness." We are so accustomed to thinking introspectively and therapeutically and of living simultaneously in both an inner and outer world that continuously mediates the way we interact and carry on life that we forget that our great-grandparents and all of the generations that preceded them were unable to think psychologically—that is, with a few notable exceptions through history. My grandparents were able to think ideologically, theologically, and even mythologically, but simply unable to think psychologically.

Psychological consciousness extended the empathic drive across political boundaries to include associational ties. Human beings began to empathize in a larger fictional family based on professional and technical affiliations, cultural preferences, and a range of other attributes that stretched the boundaries of social trust beyond the nation to include affinity with like-minded others in a world where the communication/energy/transportation matrix and markets were becoming global.

New communication/energy/transportation matrices and accompanying economic paradigms don't cast aside previous periods of consciousness and empathic extension. Those remain, but they become part of a larger empathic domain. Mythological consciousness, theological consciousness, ideological consciousness, and psychological consciousness all still exist and coexist in ensembles embedded in each individual psyche and in various proportions and degrees in every culture. There are tiny pockets in the world where forager/hunters still live with mythological consciousness. Other societies are exclusively bound to theological consciousness. Still others have migrated to ideological consciousness and now even psychological consciousness.

Nonetheless, there is a detectable pattern to human evolution, captured in the spotty but unmistakable transformation of human consciousness and the accompanying extension of the human empathic drive to larger fictional families cohering in ever more complex and interdependent communication/energy/transportation matrices and economic paradigms.

If this journey appears a revelation, it's only because historians have, for the most part, chronicled the pathological events that punctuate the human saga—the great social upheavals, wars, genocides, natural catastrophes, power struggles, redress of social grievances, etc. Their preoccupation with the dark side of the human journey is understandable. These exceptional, extraordinary events get our attention. They imprint an indelible stamp on our collective memory for the simple reason that they are so unusual and destabilizing to our everyday life.

But if much of human history was made up of primarily pathological episodes and disruptive events, and our true nature as a species was predatory, violent, aggressive, volatile, and even monstrous, we would have perished as a species long before now.

I recall reading a comment by Georg Wilhelm Friedrich Hegel more than 30 years ago on the nature of human history that struck me and inspired some of my own thinking in the writing of *The Empathic Civilization*. Hegel observed that "the periods of happiness . . . are the blank pages of history" because they are "periods of harmony."[3]

There is, indeed, another side of the human historical narrative—the evolution of human consciousness and the extension of the human empathic drive to ever larger and more inclusive domains. The unwritten side of human history includes the periods of happiness and harmony brought about by the human impulse to continually transcend ourselves and find identity in ever more evolved social frames. These frames become our vehicles to create social capital, explore the meaning of the human journey, and find our place in the grand scheme of things. To empathize is to civilize . . . to civilize is to empathize. They are, in fact, inseparable.

The history of the human journey suggests that happiness is not to be found in materialism, but, rather, in empathic engagement. When we look back at our own personal histories at the sunset of our lives, the experiences that stand out in our memory are rarely about material gain, fame, or fortune. The moments that touch the core of our being are the empathic encounters—the transcendent feeling of coming out of ourselves and experiencing the fullness of another's struggle to flourish as if it were our own.

Often, people mistake empathic consciousness with utopianism when, in fact, it is the very opposite. When you and I feel empathy toward another being—be it another human being or one of our fellow creatures—it's tinged with the whiff of their eventual death and the celebration of their existing life. In experiencing their joy, sorrow, hopes, and fears I am constantly reminded of the precarious nature of each of our lives. To empathize with another is to recognize their one and only life as I do my own—to understand that each of their moments, like my own, are irreversible and unrepeatable and that life is fragile and imperfect and challenging, whether it be a human being's journey in civilization or a deer's journey in the woods. When I empathize, I feel the frailty and the transitory nature of another's existence. To empathize is to root for the other to flourish and experience the full potential of their short abide. Compassion is our way of celebrating each other's existence, acknowledging our common bond as fellow travelers here on Earth.

There is no need of empathy in heaven and no place for it in utopia because in these otherworldly realms there is no pain and suffering, no frailties and flaws, but only perfection and immortality. To live among our fellows in an empathic civilization is to come to each other's aid and, through our compassion, acknowledge the reality of our temporary existence, by continually celebrating each other's struggle to thrive in an imperfect world. Does anyone doubt for a moment that the happiest moments are always and unequivocally our most empathic ones?

BIOSPHERE CONSCIOUSNESS

All of which gets us back to the question of advancing the individual and collective happiness of our species. For those who have lost hope in the future prospects of humanity and even our ability to survive as a species—much less secure some measure of collective happiness to boot—let me ask this question: Why would we stop here and put an end to a journey that has taken us into ever more inclusive domains of empathic engagement and collective stewardship? If we have passed from mythological consciousness to theological consciousness to ideological consciousness to psychological consciousness and have extended our empathic drive from blood ties to religious affiliations to national identities and associational communities, is it not possible to imagine the next leap in the human journey—a crossover into biosphere consciousness and an expansion of empathy to include the whole of the human race as our family, as well as our fellow creatures as an extension of our evolutionary family?

A new smart infrastructure, made up of interactive Communications, Energy, and Transportation Internets, is beginning to spread nodally, like Wi-Fi, from region to region, crossing continents and connecting society in a vast global neural network. Connecting every thing with every being—the Internet of Things—is a transformational event in human history, allowing our species to empathize and socialize as a single extended human family for the first time in history. A younger generation is studying in global classrooms via Skype; socializing with cohorts around the world on Facebook; gossiping with hundreds of millions of peers on Twitter; sharing homes, clothes, and just about everything else online in the Communications Internet; generating and sharing green electricity across continents over the Energy Internet; sharing cars, bikes, and public transport on the evolving Transportation Internet; and, in the process, shifting the human journey from an unswerving allegiance to unlimited and unrestrained material growth to a species' commitment to sustainable economic development. This transformation is being accompanied by a change in the human psyche—the leap to biosphere consciousness and the Collaborative Age.

The collaborative sensibility is an acknowledgement that our individual lives are intimately intertwined and that our personal well-being ultimately depends on the well-being of the larger communities in which we dwell. That collaborative spirit is now beginning to extend to the biosphere. Children all over the world are learning about their "ecological footprint." They are coming to understand that everything we human beings do—and for that matter every other creature—leaves an ecological footprint that affects the well-being of some other human being or creature in some other part of Earth's biosphere. They are connecting the dots and realizing that every creature is embedded in myriad symbiotic and synergetic relationships in ecosystems across the biosphere and that the proper functioning of the whole system depends on the sustainable relationships of each of the parts. A younger generation is learning that the biosphere is our planetary community, whose health and well-being determines our own.

Today's youth, connecting with one another across virtual and physical space, is quickly eliminating the remaining ideological, cultural, and commercial boundaries that have long separated "mine" from "thine" in a capitalist system mediated by private property relations, market exchanges, and national borders. "Open source" has become the mantra for a generation that views power relationships in a fundamentally different fashion than their parents and grandparents did. In a geopolitical world, the conversation cues from right to left and hones in on the question of who should own and control the means of production, with some favoring capitalism and others socialism. The Millennial Generation rarely speaks of right versus left or capitalism versus socialism. When millennials judge political behavior they have a very different political spectrum in mind. They ask whether the institutional behavior, be it in the form of a government, political party, business, or educational system, is centralized, top down, patriarchal, closed and proprietary, or distributed, collaborative, open, transparent, peer-to-peer, and an expression of lateral power. Young people are going beyond the capitalist market even as they continue to use it. They are comfortable conducting much of their economic life on a networked Collaborative Commons and engaging each other in the social economy as much as in the market economy.

Their newfound openness is tearing down the walls that have long divided people by gender, class, race, ethnicity, and sexual orientation. Empathic sensitivity is expanding laterally as quickly as global networks are connecting everyone together. Hundreds of millions of human beings—I suspect even several billion—are beginning to experience "the other" as "one's self," as empathy becomes the ultimate litmus test of a truly democratic society. Millions of individuals, especially young people, are also beginning to extend their empathic drive, although less pronounced, to include our fellow creatures, from the penguins and polar bears adrift on the poles to the other endangered species inhabiting the few remaining pristine, wild ecosystems. The young are just beginning to glimpse the opportunity of forging an empathic civilization tucked inside a biosphere community. At this stage, much of the anticipation is more hope than expectation. Still, there is an unmistakable feeling of possibility in the air.

AFTERWORD
A PERSONAL NOTE

I have mixed feelings about the passing of the capitalist era. I look hopefully to the coming of the Collaborative Commons and am convinced that it offers the best vehicle to heal the planet and advance a sustainable economy of abundance. Still there are features of the capitalist system that I deeply admire while other aspects I equally abhor. (I suspect this is also true for many others—no less the men and women at the helm of the capitalist system who have experienced, up close, both its creative dynamism and its destructive excesses.)

I grew up in an entrepreneurial home. My father, Milton Rifkin, was a lifelong entrepreneur. After a brief but unsuccessful stint as an actor in early films in Hollywood in the late 1920s, my dad turned entrepreneur, a vocation that consumed the rest of his life. Not too surprising. In many ways, entrepreneurs are artists of the marketplace, continually in search of creative new commercial narratives that can capture an audience, tell a compelling story, and bring people into the universe they've invented—think Steve Jobs. Entrepreneurs from Thomas Edison to Sergey Brin and Larry Page have thrilled the multitudes with innovative inventions that have transformed their daily lives.

My own father was one of the early pioneers in the plastics revolution. And, before the snickers, I will tell you that when Mr. McGuire turned to a young Ben in the film *The Graduate* and whispered just one word to him, "Plastics," I shrank down in my chair in the movie theater, half amused and half embarrassed, thinking that was my dad whispering to me. My father would corral me over the years, attempting to entice me into the family plastics business, regaling me with the bright future that awaited the human race in a society wrapped in plastic—the miracle material.

My father was, to my knowledge, among the very first manufacturers to convert polyethylene into plastic bags in the early 1950s. While young people today can't possibly comprehend a world without plastic, in those early years it was a novelty. Packaging was usually in the form of paper bags, cardboard, burlap, or metal, glass, and wood containers.

I remember my father sitting the family down around our tiny kitchen table each night entertaining us with new ideas about how plastic bags might be used. Why not package groceries in plastic bags, laundry from the cleaners, appliances from the department store. We may have been the first family to wrap all of our furniture in plastic. I can still recall the sticky feeling of the plastic covers on a hot summer day when I plopped down on the couch in my shorts.

My dad's excitement was contagious. Every bit the performer, he drew prospective buyers into his storyline and they became converts and players in the plastic makeover of the world.

During his nearly 25 years as an entrepreneur in the plastics industry, I never heard my father talk about the financial rewards of his work. While I'm sure it was always in the back of his mind, he was far more concerned with the entrepreneurial game itself. He saw his efforts in creative terms as more art than industry. He wanted to make a difference in people's lives by giving something of himself that could make their lives a little better. Although his efforts were on a very small scale compared to some of the great entrepreneurial giants that created the capitalist economy, biographical accounts of other inventors and innovators follow pretty much the same script.

That is not to say that pecuniary interests are not at play, but many entrepreneurs I've met over the years are far more driven by the creative act than the almighty dollar. The pecuniary fetish generally comes later when entrepreneurial enterprises mature, become publicly traded in the market, and take on shareholders whose interest is in the return on their investment. There are countless tales of entrepreneurs driven out of their own companies by professional management brought in to transform the enterprise from a creative performance to a sober, "financially responsible" business, a euphemism that means focusing more attention on the bottom line.

Of course, my father could never have imagined in the early years that the millions of plastic bags he was selling would end up in landfills and pollute the environment. Nor could he have foreseen that the petrochemicals used to extrude the polyethylene would emit carbon dioxide and play a key role in altering the climate of the planet.

Reflecting on my own father's career, it is clear to me that the invisible hand that Adam Smith alluded to 237 years ago in *The Wealth of Nations* is really not all that invisible. It's the entrepreneurial spirit that drove my dad and countless other entrepreneurs to innovate, reduce marginal costs, bring cheaper products and services to the market, and spur economic growth. That entrepreneurial spirit is now taking us to near zero marginal costs and into a new economic era of history where more goods and services will be nearly free and shared on a Collaborative Commons.

For those who were long skeptical of the operating assumptions of the invisible hand of supply and demand, the approach of a near zero marginal cost society—the optimum efficient state—is "visible" proof that the system first described by Smith did indeed work, in part, although I would add four caveats. First, the invisible hand was often slowed or blocked altogether for long periods of time by the inevitable concentration of monopoly power that continually thwarted innovation in virtually every commercial sector. Second, the invisible hand did little to ensure that the increase in productivity and profits was shared with the workforce that jointly created the largesse. The workers had to fight management at every step of the journey by organizing themselves into trade unions and political lobbies to ensure a fair return on their labor. Third, while capitalism dramatically improved the lives of everyone inside the system, its track record at the margins of the system, where human resources were, more often than not, ruthlessly exploited to benefit those cocooned inside, was horrendous by any reasonable standard. And fourth, the operating logic of the invisible hand of supply and demand never extended beyond the confines of the market mechanism itself and was, therefore, never able to account for the damage that the capitalist system inflicted on the larger environment from which it drew its raw materials and where it dumped its wastes.

Still, Smith's invisible hand proved to be a formidable social force, but not for the philosophical reasons he put forth. Smith's theory revolves around the notion that in a market economy each individual pursues his or her own self-interest in the acquisition and exchange of property, without any intention of promoting the public interest, and by doing so, "inadvertently" advances the general well-being of society as a whole.

Here are Smith's exact words:

> Every individual necessarily labors to render the annual revenue of the society as great as he can. He generally, indeed, neither intends to promote the public interest, nor knows how much he is promoting it . . . he intends only his own gain, and he is in this, as in many other cases, led by an invisible hand to promote an end which was no part of his intention. Nor is it always the worse for the society that it was no part of it. By pursuing his own interest he frequently promotes that of the society more effectually than when he really intends to promote it. I have never known much good done by those who affected to trade for the public good.[1]

By suggesting that each individual does not have others' interest in mind, Smith strangely misunderstood the dynamic of one of the key tenets of classical economic theory—the sellers' unswerving search of new innovations to increase productivity, which enables them to lower operating costs and the price of their products and services in order to win over prospective buyers, improve their profit margins, and increase their market share. Somehow, Smith completely missed the critical element between seller and buyer that brings them together into a mutually reciprocal relationship and makes the invisible hand work. That is the seller's role in tending to the personal welfare of the buyer by continually providing better products and services at lesser prices. It is by being continuously mindful of the needs, desires, and wants of buyers and servicing them that capitalist entrepreneurs thrive. An entrepreneur or firm that is not looking out for the welfare of prospective customers is not going to stay in business for very long.

In other words, it's in an entrepreneur's self-interest to be sensitive to the well-being of others if he wants to succeed. Henry Ford understood that and made it his life's mission to provide a cheap, durable automobile that could put millions of working people behind the wheel and ease their lives. Steve Jobs understood this as well. Servicing the needs and aspirations of a highly mobile, globally connected human population by providing cutting-edge communication technologies was his all-consuming passion. It is this dual role of pursuing one's entrepreneurial self-interest by promoting the welfare of others in the marketplace that has moved us ever closer to a near zero marginal cost society.

The march toward near zero marginal costs and nearly free goods and services has not only partially validated the operating logic of the invisible hand but also, interestingly enough, the utilitarian arguments offered up by David Hume, Jeremy Bentham, and others in defense of market capitalism. Recall that Hume and Bentham argued that private property exchanged in the market is a purely human convention with no basis in natural law and is justified because it is the best mechanism to "promote the general welfare." Were they right?

Since the market mechanism has helped take us to near zero marginal costs and the promise of nearly free goods and services, which is considered to be the optimally efficient state for promoting the general welfare, Hume and Bentham's claim that private property, exchanged in markets, is the best means of promoting the general welfare has proven its utilitarian worth. The irony is that when near zero marginal cost is reached, goods and services become nearly free, profit margins evaporate, and private property exchanged in markets loses its reason for existing. The market mechanism becomes increasingly unnecessary in a world of nearly free goods and services organized around an economy of abundance, and capitalism shrinks to a niche economic realm.

So we would have to say that Hume and Bentham's particular brand of utilitarianism, wedded to the exchange and accumulation of private property in the capitalism marketplace, was never meant to be an eternal verity but only a specific description of the particular economic forces at work that would come to span the First and Second Industrial Revolutions of the nineteenth and twentieth centuries. No doubt, the nineteenth-century utilitarian economists and their twentieth-century progenies would be aghast at the prospect that the very theory they espoused would eventually run its course, but not before taking society to the cusp of a new economic order where promoting the general welfare is best achieved through collaborative pursuits operating in vast networked Commons in an evolving social economy.

Admittedly, the very idea that an economic system that is organized around scarcity and profit could lead to an economy of nearly free goods and services and abundance is so counterintuitive that it is difficult to accept. Nonetheless, this is exactly what is unfolding.

Passing judgment on the capitalist system at the end of its reign is not an easy matter. The capitalist market was not the savior its zealous supporters claimed. Nor was it the devil incarnate that its vocal critics claimed. Rather, it was the most agile and efficient mechanism at the time to organize an economy whose energy and communication matrices, and accompanying industries, required large concentrations of financial capital to support vertically integrated enterprises and accompanying economies of scale.

So, while I celebrate, with qualifications, the entrepreneurial spirit that drove my father and so many others, I don't mourn the passing of capitalism. The new social entrepreneurialism that animates a generation embedded in collaborative networks on the Commons—although as passionately embraced as commercial entrepreneurialism embedded in markets—is of a different kind. The new spirit is less autonomous and more interactive; less concerned with the pursuit of pecuniary interests and more committed to promoting quality of life; less consumed with accumulating market capital and more with accumulating social capital; less preoccupied with owning and having and more desirous of accessing and sharing; less exploitive of nature and more dedicated to sustainability and stewardship of the Earth's ecology. The new social entrepreneurs are less driven by the invisible hand and more by the helping hand. They are far less utilitarian and far more empathically engaged.

While the inherent logic of the invisible hand and the market mechanism helped get us to this critical crossroad of a near zero marginal cost society and the possibility of transforming the human journey from an economy of scarcity to an economy of sustainable abundance, it needs to be said that the entrepreneurs didn't do it alone. Rather, they must share the credit with visionaries wedded to the idea of a social economy on the Commons. The exponential curve in computing that helped bring the marginal cost of producing and sending information to near zero was primarily driven by global companies. On the other hand, recall that the Internet was invented by government scientists and university academics, and the World Wide Web was the creation of a computer scientist interested in promoting the Commons. GPS, touchscreen displays, and voice activated personal assistants (e.g., Siri)—the key technologies that make the celebrated iPhone "smart"— were the result of government funded research. Linux, Wikipedia, and MOOCs are inspirations that come largely from the social economy while Facebook and Twitter are commercial ventures whose success depends on building social Commons in the hopes of reaping financial gain. Breakthroughs in renewable energy have come from government and university laboratories as well as from private companies working the marketplace. Similarly, the 3D printing revolution is being spurred by both nonprofit Fab Labs and commercial developers.

The point is that while the entrepreneurial spirit of the marketplace is helping drive the economy to near zero marginal cost and near free goods and services, it's doing so on an enabling infrastructure made possible by the creative content of all three sectors—the government, the social economy on the Commons, and the market. The contributions from players in all three sectors suggest that the new economic paradigm will likewise continue to be a hybrid venture of the government, the market, and the Commons, although by mid-century the Collaborative Commons is likely to define much of the economic life of society.

I'd like to address my final remarks to those ensconced in the heart of the capitalist system who fear that an approaching society of nearly zero marginal cost will spell their own ruin. Economies are never static. They continually evolve and occasionally metamorphose into entirely new forms. Likewise, business enterprises come and go as economies change. Peter Senge of the MIT Sloan School of Management points out that the average life span of a Fortune 500 Company is only around 30 years. Indeed, only 71 companies that appeared in the original Fortune 500 list of biggest companies in 1955 were still on the list in 2012.[2]

It's not that we wake up one day and suddenly the old economic order has been routed and a new regime has slipped into place. Recall that the Second Industrial Revolution emerged in the 1890s while the First Industrial Revolution was in full throttle and ran parallel to it for another half century until it eventually became the dominant economic force. During the long transition, many First Industrial Revolution industries and companies withered and died—but not all. Those that survived reinvented themselves along the way and found the right balancing act that allowed them to be in two industrial eras simultaneously, while carefully retiring the old model and easing into the new one. Many more start-up companies seized hold of the new opportunities that the Second Industrial Revolution made possible and quickly filled up the remaining playing field.

Similarly, today many Second Industrial Revolution companies are faced with a comparable opportunity, and a choice. Some are already making the leap into the Third Industrial Revolution, incorporating the new business models and services into their existing portfolios and developing transitional strategies to keep pace with the paradigm shift into a hybrid economy made up of both the Collaborative Commons and conventional capitalist marketplace.

The powerful social forces unleashed by the coming zero marginal cost society are both disruptive and liberating. They are unlikely to be curtailed or reversed. The transition from the capitalist era to the Collaborative Age is gaining momentum in every region in the world—hopefully, in time to heal the biosphere and create a more just, humane, and sustainable global economy for every human being on Earth in the first half of the twenty-first century.

NOTES

CHAPTER 1

1. Jean-Baptiste Say, *A Treatise on Political Economy* (Philadelphia: Grigg & Elliot, 1843), 134–35.

2. Dale Dougherty, "How Many People Will Own 3-D Printers?," *Make* [Blog], April 5, 2013, http://makezine.com/2013/04/05/how-many-people-will-own-3d-printers/ (accessed July 1, 2013).

3. Chris Anderson, "Free! Why $0.00 Is the Future of Business," *Wired*, February 25, 2008, http://www.wired.com/techbiz/it/magazine/16-03/ff_free?currentPage=all (accessed March 7, 2013).

4. Oskar Lange, "On the Economic Theory of Socialism: Part Two," *Review of Economic Studies* 4(2) (1937): 129.

5. Ibid., 129–30.

6. Ibid., 130.

7. John Maynard Keynes, *Essays in Persuasion* (Project Gutenberg eBook, 2011), 358–74, http://gutenberg.ca/ebooks/keynes-essaysinpersuasion/keynes-essaysinpersuasion-00-h .html (accessed January 23, 2013).

8. Ibid.

9. J. Bradford Delong and Lawrence H. Summers, "The 'New Economy': Background, Historical Perspective, Questions and Speculations," *Economic Policy for the Informational Economy* (2001): 16.

10. Ibid., 35.

11. Ibid.

12. Ibid., 16.

13. Ibid.

14. Ibid.

15. Ibid.

16. Ibid., 16, 38.

17. Thomas S. Kuhn, *The Structure of Scientific Revolutions* (Chicago: University of Chicago Press, 1962).

18. Isaac Asimov, "In the Game of Energy and Thermodynamics You Can't Even Break Even," *Smithsonian*, August 1970, 9.

19. Viktor Mayer-Schönberger and Kenneth Cukier, *Big Data: A Revolution That Will Transform How We Live, Work, and Think* (Boston: Houghton Mifflin Harcourt, 2013) 59.

20. Ibid., 89.

21. Steve Lohr, "The Internet Gets Physical," *The New York Times*, December 17, 2011, http://www.nytimes.com/2011/12/18/sunday-review/the-internet-gets-physical.html?page wanted=all&_r=0 (accessed November 19, 2013).

22. Ibid.

23. Ibid.

24. Ibid.

25. Lester Salamon, "Putting the Civil Society Sector on the Economic Map of the World," *Annals of Public and Cooperative Economics* 81(2) (2010): 198, http://ccss.jhu.edu/wp-content/uploads/downloads/2011/10/Annals-June-2010.pdf (accessed August 8, 2013); "A Global Assembly on Measuring Civil Society and Volunteering," Johns Hopkins Center for Civil Society Studies, September 26, 2007, 6, http://ccss.jhu.edu/wp-content/uploads/downloads/2011/10/UNHB_GlobalAssemblyMeeting_2007.pdf (accessed July 8, 2013).

26. Salamon, "Putting the Civil Society Sector," 198.

27. "Collaborative [1800–2000], English," Google Books NGram Viewer, http://books.google.com/ngrams/ (accessed June 12, 2013); "Google Books Ngram Viewer," University at Buffalo, http://libweb.lib.buffalo.edu/pdp/index.asp?ID=497 (accessed December 16, 2013).

28. "The World's Top 50 Economies: 44 Countries, Six Firms," Democratic Leadership Council, July 14, 2010, http://www.dlc.org/ndol_cie5ae.html?kaid=10 (accessed May 19, 2013); "Fortune Magazine Releases Its Annual Fortune Global 500 List of Companies Winning Top Rankings by Making Money and Marketing Well," *PRWeb*, July 10, 2012, http://www.prweb.com/releases/fortune-global-500/money-and-marketing/prweb9684625.htm (accessed May 18, 2013); "2011 Economic Statistics and Indicators," Economy Watch, http://www.economywatch.com/economic-statistics/year/2011/ (accessed May 21, 2013).

CHAPTER 2

1. T. W. Schultz, "New Evidence on Farmer Responses to Economic Opportunities from the Early Agrarian History of Western Europe," *Subsistence Agriculture and Economic Development*, ed. Clifton R Wharton, Jr. (New Brunswick, NJ: Transaction Publishers, 1969), 108.

2. Richard Schlatter, *Private Property: The History of an Idea* (New York: Russell & Russell, 1973), 64.

3. Gilbert Slater, *The English Peasantry and the Enclosure of the Commons* (New York: A. M. Kelley, 1968), 1.

4. Karl Polanyi, *The Great Transformation: The Political and Economic Origins of Our Time* (Boston: Beacon Press, 1944), 35; Richard L. Rubenstein, *The Age of Triage: Fear and Hope in an Overcrowded World* (Boston: Beacon Press, 1983), 10.

5. Rubenstein, *The Age of Triage*, 43; Slater, *The English Peasantry*, 6.

6. Thomas More, *Utopia* (Rockville, MD: Arc Manor, 2008), 20.

7. Rubenstein, *The Age of Triage*, 46.

8. Lynn White, *Medieval Technology and Social Change* (London: Oxford University Press, 1962), 129.

9. Karl Marx, *The Poverty of Philosophy* (Chicago: Charles H. Kerr, 1920), 119.

10. Karl Marx, "Division of Labour and Mechanical Workshop: Tool and Machinery," in *Marx and Engels, Collected Works* (New York: International Publishers, 1991), 33: 387–477, http://www.marxists.org/archive/marx/works/1861/economic/ch35.htm (accessed August 8, 2013).

11. Jean-Claude Debeir, Jean-Paul Deléage, and Daniel Hémery, *In the Servitude of Power: Energy and Civilization through the Ages* (London: Zed Books, 1992), 75.

12. Ibid., 76.

13. White, *Medieval Technology and Social Change*, 87.

14. Debeir, Deléage, and Hémery, *In the Servitude of Power*, 79.

15. Jean Gimpel, *The Medieval Machine: The Industrial Revolution of the Middle Ages* (London: Penguin, 1977), 16.

16. E. M. Carus-Wilson, "An Industrial Revolution of the Thirteenth Century," *Economic History Review* 11 (1941): 39.

17. E. M. Carus-Wilson, "The Woollen Industry," in *The Cambridge Economic History*, vol. 2: *Trade and Industry in the Middle Ages*, ed. M. Postan and E. E. Rich (Cambridge: Cambridge University Press, 1952), 409.

18. Debeir, Deléage, and Hémery, *In the Servitude of Power*, 90.

19. White, *Medieval Technology*, 128–29.

20. Michael Clapham, "Printing," in *A History of Technology*, vol. 3: *From the Renaissance to the Industrial Revolution*, ed. Charles Singer, E. G. Holmyard, A. R. Hall, and Trevor Williams (Oxford: Oxford University Press, 1957), 37.

21. Robert L. Heilbroner, *The Making of Economic Society* (Englewood Cliffs, NJ: Prentice-Hall, 1962), 36–38, 50.

22. S. R. Epstein and Maarten Prak, *Guilds, Innovation, and the European Economy, 1400–1800* (Cambridge: Cambridge University Press, 2008) 31.

23. Ibid., 44.

CHAPTER 3

1. Yujiro Hayami and Yoshihisa Godo, *Development Economics: From the Poverty to the Wealth of Nations* (New York: Oxford University Press, 2005), 341.

2. Maurice Dobb, *Studies in the Development of Capitalism* (New York: International Publishers, 1947), 143.

3. Adam Smith, *An Inquiry into the Nature and Causes of the Wealth of Nations* (Edinburgh: Thomas Nelson, 1843), 20.

4. Ibid.

5. Ibid., 21.

6. Ibid., 22.

7. Carl Lira, "Biography of James Watt," May 21, 2013, http://www.egr.msu.edu/~lira/supp/steam/wattbio.html (accessed January 7, 2014).

8. Jean-Claude Debeir, Jean-Paul Deléage, and Daniel Hémery, *In the Servitude of Power: Energy and Civilization through the Ages* (London: Zed Books, 1992), 101–104.

9. Eric J. Hobsbawm, *The Age of Capital, 1848–1875* (New York: Charles Scribner's Sons, 1975), 40.

10. Eric J. Hobsbawm, *The Age of Revolution, 1789–1848* (New York: Vintage Books, 1996), 298.

11. Alfred D. Chandler Jr., *The Visible Hand: The Managerial Revolution in American Business* (Cambridge, MA: Belknap Press of Harvard University Press, 1977), 83.

12. Ibid., 86.

13. Ibid., 90.

14. Ibid., 88.

15. A. Hyma, *The Dutch in the Far East* (Ann Arbor, MI: George Wahr, 1953).

16. Chandler, *The Visible Hand*, 153; "Our History," Canadian Pacific, http://www.cpr.ca/en/about-cp/our-past-present-and-future/Pages/our-history.aspx (accessed June 13, 2013).

17. Chandler, *The Visible Hand*, 120.

18. Randall Collins, "Weber's Last Theory of Capitalism: A Systematization,' *American Sociological Review* 45(6) (1980): 932.

19. Angela E. Davis, *Art and Work: A Social History of Labour in the Canadian Graphic Arts Industry in the 1940s* (Montreal: McGill–Queen's University Press, 1995), 21.

20. "Printing Yesterday and Today," Harry Ransom Center, University of Texas at Austin, http://www.hrc.utexas.edu/educator/modules/gutenberg/books/printing/ (accessed on October 16, 2013).

21. Aileen Fyfe, *Steam-Powered Knowledge: William Chambers and the Business of Publishing, 1820–1860* (Chicago: University of Chicago Press, 2012), 64.

22. Yochai Benkler, *The Wealth of Networks: How Social Production Transforms Markets and Freedom* (New Haven: Yale University Press, 2006), 188.

23. Paul F. Gehl, "Printing," *Encyclopedia of Chicago,* http://www.encyclopedia.chicagohistory.org/pages/1010.html (accessed June 12, 2013).

24. "R. R. Donnelley & Sons Company," *International Directory of Company Histories,* 2001, Encyclopedia.com http://www.encyclopedia.com/doc/1G2-2844200093.html (accessed June 12, 2013).

25. Chandler, *The Visible Hand,* 230.

26. Ibid., 232.

27. Ibid., 245.

28. Paul Lewis, "Ambitious Plans for Iraqi Oil," *New York Times,* July 30, 1994, http://www.nytimes.com/1994/07/30/business/ambitious-plans-for-iraqi-oil.html (accessed June 30, 2013).

29. "Energizing America: Facts for Addressing Energy Policy," API (June 2012): 17, http://www.api.org/~/media/files/statistics/energizing_america_facts.ashx (accessed April 19, 2013).

30. Robert Anderson, *Fundamentals of the Petroleum Industry* (Norman: University of Oklahoma Press, 1984), 279, 286, 289.

31. Ibid., 19, 20, 22.

32. Venu Gadde, "U.S. Oil & Gas Exploration & Production (E&P)," Henry Fund Research, February 8, 2012, 3, https://tippie.uiowa.edu/henry/reports12/oil_gas.pdf (accessed January 13, 2013).

33. Narayan Mandayam and Richard Frenkiel, "AT&T History," Rutgers University, http://www.winlab.rutgers.edu/~narayan/Course/Wireless_Revolution/LL1-%20Lecture%20 1%20reading-%20ATT%20History.doc (accessed on October 16, 2013).

34. Adam Thierer, "Unnatural Monopoly: Critical Moments in the Development of the Bell System Monopoly," *Cato Journal* 14(2) (1994): 270.

35. Ibid., 272.

36. "Milestones in AT&T History," AT&T, http://www.corp.att.com/history/milestones.html.

37. Thierer, "Unnatural Monopoly," 274.

38. Richard H. K. Vietor, *Contrived Competition: Regulation and Deregulation in America* (Cambridge, MA: Harvard University Press, 1994), 171–72.

39. Noobar Retheos Danielian, *AT&T: The Story of Industrial Conquest* (New York: Vanguard Press, 1939), 252.

40. Gerald W. Brock, *The Telecommunications Industry: The Dynamics of Market Structure* (Cambridge, MA: Harvard University Press, 1981), 161.

41. "Wireline Local Market Concentration," The Columbia Institute for Tele-Information, http://www4.gsb.columbia.edu/filemgr?file_id=739241 (accessed June 19, 2013).

42. Carolyn Marvin, *When Old Technologies Were New: Thinking about Electric Communication in the Late Nineteenth Century* (New York: Oxford University Press, 1988), 164.

43. David E. Nye, *Electrifying America: Social Meanings of a New Technology, 1880–1940* (Cambridge, MA: MIT Press, 1991), 239.

44. Ibid., 186.

45. Henry Ford and Samuel Crowther, *Edison as I Know Him* (New York: Cosmopolitan Books, 1930), 30.

46. Nye, *Electrifying America*, 186.

47. Daniel Yergen, *The Prize* (New York: Simon and Schuster, 1992), 208.

48. Q. A. Mowbray, *Road to Ruin* (Philadelphia: Lippincott, 1969), 15.

49. Kenneth R. Schneider, *Autokind vs. Mankind* (Lincoln, NE: Authors Choice Press, 2005), 123.

50. "The Dramatic Story of Oil's Influence on the World," *Oregon Focus* (January 1993): 10–11.

51. New Housing Units: Completed, United States Census Bureau, 2012, http://www.census. gov/construction/nrc/historical_data/ (accessed October 30, 2013); Shopping Centers: Numbers and Gross Leasable Area, United States Census Bureau, http://www.census.gov /compendia/statab/2012/tables/12s1061.pdf (accessed October 30, 2013).

52. "Electric Generation Ownership, Market Concentration, and Auction Size" (Washington, DC: U.S. Environmental Protection Agency, Office of Air and Radiation), July 2010, 4, http://www.epa.gov/airtransport/pdfs/TSD_Ownership_and_Market_Concentration_7 -6-10.pdf (accessed April 7, 2013).

53. "What's Moving: U.S. Auto Sales," *Wall Street Journal,* May 1, 2013, http://online.wsj .com/mdc/public/page/2_3022-autosales.html.

54. Erick Schonfeld, "What Media Company Gained the Most Market Share in 2007? (Hint: It Starts with a G)," *TechCrunch,* March 14, 2008, http://techcrunch.com/2008/03/14/what -media-company-gained-the-most-market-share-in-2007-hint-it-starts-with-a-g/ (accessed June 8, 2013).

55. Andrea Alegria, Agata Kaczanowska, and Lauren Setar, "Highly Concentrated: Companies That Dominate Their Industries," *IBIS World,* February 2012, 1–2, 4, http://www.ibis world.com/Common/MediaCenter/Highly%20Concentrated%20Industries.pdf (accessed February 22, 2013).

56. "Global IB Revenue Ranking—01 Jan-10 Jun 2013," Dealogic, http://fn.dealogic.com/fn /IBRank.htm (accessed June 14, 2013).

57. "The World's Top 50 Economies: 44 Countries, Six Firms," Democratic Leadership Council, http://www.dlc.org/ndol_cie5ae.html?kaid=10 (accessed 14 July 2010).

CHAPTER 4

1. Robert S. Hoyt, *Europe in the Middle Ages,* 2nd ed. (New York: Harcourt, Brace & World, 1966), 300.

2. Max Weber, *The Protestant Ethic and the Spirit of Capitalism* (1930; reprint, London: Routledge, 2005).

3. John Locke, *Two Treatises of Government* (London: Printed for Whitmore and Fenn, Charing Cross; and C. Brown, Duke Street, Lincoln's-Inn-Fields, 1821), §27.

4. Ibid.

5. Ibid., §37.

6. Adam Smith, *An Inquiry into the Nature and Causes of the Wealth of Nations,* ed. Edwin Cannan (London: Methuen, 1961), 1:475.

7. R. H. Tawney, *The Acquisitive Society* (New York: Harcourt, Brace, 1920), 13, 18.

8. Max Weber, *From Max Weber: Essays in Sociology,* eds. and trans. H. H. Gerth and C. Wright Mills (New York: Oxford University Press, 1946), 51.

9. Richard Schlatter, *Private Property: The History of an Idea* (New Brunswick, NJ: Rutgers University Press, 1951), 185.

10. David Hume, *An Enquiry Concerning the Principles of Morals* (London: Printed for A. Millar, 1751).

11. Schlatter, *Private Property,* 242.

12. Jeremy Bentham, "Pannomial Fragments," in *The Works of Jeremy Bentham, Now First Collected; Under the Superintendence of His Executor, John Bowring—Part IX*, ed. John Bowring (Edinburgh: William Tait, 1839), 221; Jeremy Bentham, "Principles of the Civil Code," in *The Works of Jeremy Bentham, Now First Collected; Under the Superintendence of His Executor, John Bowring—Part II*, ed. John Bowring (Edinburgh: William Tait, 1839), 309.

13. Charles Darwin, *The Descent of Man: And Selection in Relation to Sex*, Project Gutenberg, 1999, http://www.gutenberg.org/cache/epub/2300/pg2300.html (accessed June 20, 2013).

14. Ibid.

15. Herbert Spencer, *The Principles of Biology* (London: Williams and Norgate, 1864), 1:444–45.

16. Charles Darwin, *The Variation of Animals and Plants under Domestication* (London: John Murray, 1899), 1:6.

17. Stephen Jay Gould, "Darwin's Untimely Burial," in *Philosophy of Biology*, ed. Michael Ruse (New York: Prometheus Books, 1998), 93–98.

18. Janet Browne, *Charles Darwin: The Power of Place* (Princeton, NJ: Princeton University Press, 2002), 2:186.

19. Thomas Paine, "Rights of Man: Being an Answer to Mr. Burke's Attack on the French Revolution," in *The Political Works of Thomas Paine* (New York: C. Blanchard, 1860).

CHAPTER 5

1. "Solar 101: Solar Economics," States Advancing Solar, http://www.statesadvancingsolar.org/solar-101/solar-economics (accessed January 31, 2014); "Wind Energy Payback Period Workbook," National Renewable Energy Laboratory, April 1, 2001, www.nrel.gov/wind/docs/spread_sheet_Final.xls (accessed October 22, 2013).

2. "Productivity," Merriam-Webster, http://www.merriam-webster.com/dictionary/productivity.

3. Moses Abramovitz, *Thinking about Growth: And Other Essays on Economic Growth and Welfare* (Cambridge: Cambridge University Press, 1989), 133.

4. Robert U. Ayres and Edward H. Ayres, *Crossing the Energy Divide: Moving from Fossil Fuel Dependence to a Clean-Energy Future* (Upper Saddle River, NJ: Wharton School Publishing, 2010), 14.

5. Rachael Larimore, "Why 'You Didn't Build That' Isn't Going Away," *Slate*, August 30, 2012, http://www.slate.com/articles/news_and_politics/politics/2012/08/_you_didn_t_build_that_it_doesn_t_matter_what_obama_meant_to_say_but_what_people_heard_.html (accessed July 13, 2013).

6. Robert U. Ayres and Benjamin Warr, *The Economic Growth Engine: How Energy and Work Drive Material Prosperity* (Northampton, MA: Edward Elgar Publishing, 2009), 334–37.

7. John A. "Skip" Laitner, Steven Nadel, R. Neal Elliott, Harvey Sachs, and A Siddiq Khan, "The Long-Term Energy Efficiency Potential: What the Evidence Suggests," American Council for an Energy-Efficient Economy, January 2012, http://www.garrisoninstitute.org/downloads/ecology/cmb/Laitner_Long-Term_E_E_Potential.pdf, 2 (accessed September 21, 2013).

8. Ibid., 66.

9. "How Many Smart Meters are Installed in the US and Who Has Them?," *US Energy Information Administration*, last modified January 10, 2013, http://www.eia.gov/tools/faqs/faq.cfm?id=108&t=3 (accessed October 12, 2013).

10. Brian Merchant, "With a Trillion Sensors, the Internet of Things Would Be the 'Biggest Business in the History of Electronics,'" Motherboard, November 2013, http://mother

board.vice.com/blog/the-internet-of-things-could-be-the-biggest-business-in-the-history
-of-electronics (accessed November 14, 2013).

11. "Data, Data Everywhere," *Economist*, February 25, 2012, http://www.economist.com/node
/15557443 (accessed September 18, 2013); Joe Hellerstein, "Parallel Programming in the
Age of Big Data," *GigaOM,* November 9, 2008, http://gigaom.com/2008/11/09/mapre
duce-leads-the-way-for-parallel-programming/ (accessed September 18, 2013).

12. S. Mitchell, N. Villa, M.S. Weeks, and A. Lange, "The Internet of Everything for Cities,"
Cisco, 2013, http://www.cisco.com/web/about/ac79/docs/ps/motm/IoE-Smart-City_PoV
.pdf (accessed on October 31, 2013).

13. Peter C. Evans and Marco Annunziata, "Industrial Internet: Pushing the Boundaries of
Minds and Machines," General Electric, November 26, 2012, http://www.ge.com/sites
/default/files/Industrial_Internet.pdf, 4 (accessed January 5, 2013).

14. Ibid., 24.

15. "The Internet of Things Business Index: A Quiet Revolution Gathers Pace," *The Economist
Intelligence Unit* (2013), 10, http://www.arm.com/files/pdf/EIU_Internet_Business_Index
_WEB.PDF (accessed October 29, 2013).

16. Ibid.

17. "The Difference Engine: Chattering Objects," *Economist* (August 13, 2010), http://www
.economist.com/blogs/babbage/2010/08/internet_things (accessed September 5, 2013).

18. Ibid.

19. Ibid.

20. Ibid.

21. "Conclusions of the Internet of Things Public Consultation," Digital Agenda for Europe,
A Europe 2020 Initiative, February 28, 2013, http://ec.europa.eu/digital-agenda/en/news
/conclusions-internet-things-public-consultation (accessed March 21, 2013).

22. "Internet of Things Factsheet Privacy and Security: IoT Privacy, Data Protection, Information Security," Digital Agenda for Europe, A Europe 2020 Initiative (February 28, 2013):
1, http://ec.europa.eu/digital-agenda/en/news/conclusions-internet-things-public-consulta
tion (accessed March 21. 2013).

23. Ibid., 5.

24. Ibid., 7.

25. "The Internet of Things Business Index," 11.

26. Ibid.

27. Ibid., 14, 16.

28. Gordon E. Moore, "Cramming More Components onto Integrated Circuits," *Electronics*
38(8) (April 19, 1965): 115.

29. Michio Kaku, "Tweaking Moore's Law: Computers of the Post-Silicon Era," *Big Think,*
March 7, 2012, http://bigthink.com/videos/tweaking-moores-law-computers-of-the-post
-silicon-era-2 (October 1, 2013).

30. Gail Robinson, "Speeding Net Traffic with Tiny Mirrors," *EE Times,* September 26, 2000,
http://www.eetimes.com/document.asp?doc_id=1142186 (accessed November 6, 2013).

31. "Early Computers 1960's," *Pimall,* 2006, http://www.pimall.com/nais/pivintage/burrou
ghscomputer.html (accessed November 7, 2013); "Study: Number of Smartphone Users
Tops 1 Billion," *CBS News,* October 17, 2012, http://www.cbsnews.com/8301-205_162-57
534583/ (accessed November 7, 2013).

32. Robert D. Atkinson et al., "The Internet Economy 25 Years After.Com," *The Information
Technology & Innovation Foundation,* March 2010, 9, http://www.itif.org/files/2010-25
-years.pdf (accessed August 13, 2013).

33. Fred Kaplan, *1959: The Year Everything Changed* (Hoboken, NJ: John Wiley, 2009),
82; Mark W. Greenia, *History of Computing: An Encyclopedia of the People and Machines that Made Computer History,* Lexikon Services, January 1, 1998; "Reference/

FAQ/Products and Services," IBM, http://www-03.ibm.com/ibm/history/reference/faq_00 00000011.html (accessed November 7, 2013).

34. "The Raspberry Pi in Scientific Research," *Raspberry Pi*, April 25, 2013, http://www.rasp berrypi.org/archives/tag/research (accessed September 19, 2013).

35. "Cray 1-A: 1977–1989," Computer and Information Systems Laboratory, 2009, http:// www.cisl.ucar.edu/computers/gallery/cray/cray1.jsp (accessed March 7, 2013).

36. Ramez Naam, "Smaller, Cheaper, Faster: Does Moore's Law Apply to Solar Cells?," *Scientific American* (blog), March 16, 2011, http://blogs.scientificamerican.com/guest -blog/2011/03/16/smaller-cheaper-faster-does-moores-law-apply-to-solar-cells (accessed June 19, 2013).

37. "Sunshot Vision Study—February 2012," U.S. Department of Energy, February 2012, www1.eere.energy.gov/solar/pdfs/47927.pdf, 74 (accessed April 8, 2013); Eric Wesoff, "First Solar Surprised with Big 2013 Guidance, 40 Cents per Watt," *GreenTechMedia*, April 9, 2013, http://www.greentechmedia.com/articles/read/First-Solar-Surprises-With -Big-2013-Guidance-40-Cents-Per-Watt-Cost-by-201 (May 6, 2013).

38. Hariklia Deligianni, Shafaat Ahmed, and Lubomyr Romankiw, "The Next Frontier: Elec-trodeposition for Solar Cell Fabrication," Electrochemical Society (summer 2011): 47.

39. Naam, "Smaller, Cheaper, Faster."

40. Peter Hockenos, "Germany's Grid and the Market: 100 Percent Renewable by 2050?," *Re-newable Energy World*, November 21, 2012, http://www.renewableenergyworld.com/rea /blog/post/2012/11/ppriorities-germanys-grid-and-the-market (November 1, 2013); Je-evan Vasagar, "German Farmers Reap Benefits of Harvesting Renewable Energy," *Finan-cial Times*, December 2, 2013, http://www.ft.com/intl/cms/s/0/f2bc3958-58f4-11e3-9798 -00144feabdc0.html#axzz2nMj6ILk2 (accessed December 13, 2013).

41. Josiah Neeley, "Texas Windpower: Will Negative Pricing Blow Out the Lights? (PTC vs. Reliable New Capacity)," *MasterResource*, November 27, 2012, http://www.masterre source.org/2012/11/texas-negative-pricing-ptc/ (accessed August 2, 2013).

42. Rachel Morison, "Renewables Make German Power Market Design Defunct, Utility Says," *Bloomberg*, June 26, 2012, http://www.bloomberg.com/news/2012-06-26/renewables-ma ke-german-power-market-design-defunct-utility-says.html (accessed April 29, 2013).

43. Nic Brisbourne, "Solar Power—A Case Study in Exponential Growth," *The Equity Kicker*, September 25, 2012, http://www.theequitykicker.com/2012/09/25/solar-powera-case-stu dy-in-exponential-growth/ (accessed May 27, 2013).

44. Max Miller, "Ray Kurzweil: Solar Will Power the World in 16 Years," *Big Think*, March 17, 2011, http://bigthink.com/think-tank/ray-kurzweil-solar-will-power-the-world-in-16 -years (accessed June 1, 2013).

45. Eric Wesoff, "Mainstream Media Discovers Solar Power and Moore's Law," *Greentech Media*, November 8, 2011, http://www.greentechmedia.com/articles /read/Mainstream -Media-Discovers-Solar-Power-and-Moores-Law (accessed October 9, 2013).

46. Cristina L. Archer and Mark Z. Jacobson, "Evaluation of Global Wind Power," *Jour-nal of Geophysical Research* 110, June 30, 2005, http://www.stanford.edu/group/efmh /winds/2004jd005462.pdf (accessed March 3, 2013).

47. Rudolf Rechsteiner, "Wind Power in Context—A Clean Revolution in the Energy Sec-tor," EnergyWatchGroup, December 2008, http://www.energywatchgroup.org/fileadmin /global/pdf/2009-01_Wind_Power_Report.pdf (accessed November 4, 2013).

48. "Wind Power Experiencing Exponential Growth Globally," *Renewable Energy World-wide*, January 30, 2009, http://www.renewableenergyworld.com/rea/news/article/2009 /01/wind-power-experiencing-exponential-growth-globally-54631 (accessed January 9, 2013).

49. Miller, "Ray Kurzweil."

50. Greg Price, "How Much Does the Internet Cost to Run?," *Forbes*, March, 14, 2012, http://www.forbes.com/sites/quora/2012/03/14/how-much-does-the-internet-cost-to-run/ (accessed July 18, 2013).

51. "UN Projects 40% of World Will Be Online By Year End, 4.4 Billion Will Remain Unconnected," UN News Centre, October 7, 2013, http://www.un.org/apps/news/story.asp?NewsID=46207&Cr=internet&Cr1# (accessed November 7, 2013).

52. "The Hidden Expense of Energy—Print Is Costly, Online Isn't Free," *Scholarly Kitchen*, January 19, 2012, http://scholarlykitchen.sspnet.org/2012/01/19/the-hidden-expense-of-energy-costs-print-is-costly-online-isnt-free/ (accessed August 21, 2013).

53. Jonathan Koomey, "Growth in Data Center Electricity Use 2005 to 2010," *Analytics Press* (2011): iii; Gerad Hoyt, "The Power Hungry Internet," *Energy Manager Today*, last modified November 21, 2012, http://www.energymanagertoday.com/the-power-hungry-internet-087256/ (accessed October 4, 2013).

54. "The Hidden Expense of Energy."

55. "Report to Congress on Server and Data Center Energy Efficiency," U.S. Environmental Protection Agency ENERGY STAR Program, August 2, 2007, 5, http://www.energystar.gov/ia/partners/prod_development/downloads/EPA_Datacenter_Report_Congress_Final1.pdf (accessed October 16, 2013).

56. James Glanz, "Power, Pollution and the Internet," *New York Times*, September 22, 2012, http://www.nytimes.com/2012/09/23/technology/data-centers-waste-vast-amounts-of-energy-belying-industry-image.html?pagewanted=all (accessed November 3, 2013).

57. Rich Miller, "How Many Data Centers? Emerson Says 500,000," *Data Center Knowledge*, December 14, 2011, http://www.datacenterknowledge.com/archives/2011/12/14/how-many-data-centers-emerson-says-500000/ (accessed November 3, 2013).

58. "Report to Congress on Server and Data Center Energy Efficiency," 7.

59. Glanz, "Power, Pollution and the Internet."

60. Krishna Kant, "Challenges in Distributed Energy Adaptive Computing," *ACM SIGMETRICS Performance Evaluation Review* 37(3) (January 2010): 3–7.

61. "Apple Facilities: Environment Footprint Report," Apple, 2012, 8, http://images.apple.com/environment/reports/docs/Apple_Facilitates_Report_2013.pdf (accessed November 10, 2013).

62. "McGraw-Hill and NJR Clean Energy Ventures Announce Largest Solar Energy Site of Its Kind in the Western Hemisphere," *McGraw-Hill Financial*, June 13, 2011, http://investor.mcgraw-hill.com/phoenix.zhtml?c=96562&p=RssLanding&cat=news&id=1573196 (accessed October 25, 2013).

63. "Apple Facilities Environment Footprint Report," 7.

64. Nick Goldman, Paul Bertone, Siyuan Chen, Christophe Dessimoz, Emily M. LeProust, Botond Sipos, and Ewan Birney, "Towards Practical, High-Capacity, Low-Maintenance Information Storage in Synthesized DNA," *Nature* 494 (February 7, 2013): 77–80.

65. Malcolm Ritter, "Study: Digital Information can be Stored in DNA," *Huffington Post*, January 23, 2013, http://www.huffingtonpost.com/huff-wires/20130123/us-sci-dna-data/# (accessed November 6, 2013).

66. Derik Andreoli, "The Bakken Boom—A Modern-Day Gold Rush," Oil Drum, December 12, 2011, http://www.theoildrum.com/node/8697 (October 30, 2013); A. E. Berman, "After the Gold Rush: A Perspective on Future U.S. Natural Gas Supply and Price," Oil Drum, February 8, 2012, http://www.theoildrum.com/node/8914 (accessed October 30, 2013).

67. Ajay Makan and Javier Blas, "Oil Guru Says US Shale Revolution is 'Temporary,'" *Financial Times*, May 29, 2013, www.ft.com/cms/s/0/281b118e-c870-11e2-acc6-00144feab7de.html#axzz2UbJC9Zz1 (accessed October 17, 2013).

68. Matthew L. Wald, "Shale's Effect on Oil Supply Is Forecast to Be Brief," *The New York Times*, November 12, 2013, http://www.nytimes.com/2013/11/13/business/energy-envi

ronment/shales-effect-on-oil-supply-is-not-expected-to-last.html?_r=0, (accessed November 13, 2013).

CHAPTER 6

1. Mark Richardson and Bradley Haylock, "Designer/Maker: The Rise of Additive Manufacturing, Domestic-Scale: Production and the Possible Implications for the Automotive Industry," *Computer Aided Design and Applications* (2012): 35.

2. Ashlee Vance, "3-D Printers: Make Whatever You Want," *Bloomberg Businessweek,* April 26, 2012, http://www.businessweek.com/articles/2012-04-26/3d-printers-make-whatever -you-want (accessed August 23, 2013).

3. "Wohlers Associates Publishes 2012 Report on Additive Manufacturing and 3-D Printing: Industry Study Shows Annual Growth of Nearly 30%," Wohlers Associates, May 15, 2012, http://wohlersassociates.com/press56.htm (accessed August 16, 2013).

4. Richardson and Haylock, "Designer/Maker."

5. Irene Chapple, "Dickerson: Etsy Is Disrupting Global Supply Chains," CNN, June 5, 2013, http://edition.cnn.com/2013/06/05/business/etsy-leweb-craft-disrupting (accessed June 28, 2013).

6. "A Brief History of 3D Printing," T. Rowe Price, December 2011, http://individual.trowe price.com/staticFiles/Retail/Shared/PDFs/3-D_Printing_Infographic_FINAL.pdf (accessed November 2, 2013).

7. "Definition: Hacker," Search Security, October 2006, http://searchsecurity.techtarget. com/definition/hacker (accessed October 15, 2013).

8. Chris Anderson, "In the Next Industrial Revolution, Atoms Are the New Bits," *Wired,* January 25, 2010, http://www.wired.com/magazine/2010/01/ff_newrevolution/ (accessed August 8, 2013).

9. J. M. Pearce, C. Morris Blair, K. J. Laciak, R. Andrews, A. Nosrat, and I. Zelenika-Zovko, "3-D Printing of Open Source Appropriate Technologies for Self-Directed Sustainable Development," *Journal of Sustainable Development* 3(4) (2010): 18.

10. "Fab Lab FAQ," MIT Center for Bits and Atoms, http://fablab.cba.mit.edu/about/faq/ (accessed June 27, 2013).

11. "MIT Fab Lab: The New Technology Revolution," Cardiff School of Art and Design, August 27, 2013, http://cardiff-school-of-art-and-design.org/magazine/mit-fab-lab-the -new-technology-revolution/ (accessed November 14, 2013); Alison DeNisco, "Fab Lab Beginnings," District Administration (December 2012), http://www.districtadministration .com/article/fab-lab-beginnings (accessed November 14, 2013); "FabLab," Fab Education Bremen, http://www.fabeducation.net/en/fablab-2.html (accessed November 14, 2013).

12. Katherine Ling, "'Fab Labs' Out Front in U.S. Push to Make Manufacturing Cool," Environment & Energy Publishing, September 18, 2013, http://www.eenews.net/stories /1059987450 (accessed November 14, 2013).

13. Andy Greenberg, "The Fab Life," *Forbes,* August 13, 2008, http://www.forbes.com/20 08/08/13/diy-innovation-gershenfeld-tech-egang08-cx_ag_0813gershenfeld.html (accessed April 1, 2013).

14. Cory Doctorow, story in *Over Clocked: Stories of the Future Present* (New York: Thunder's Mouth Press, 2007), 4.

15. Chris Waldo, "Will We 3-D Print Renewable Energy?," *3d Printer,* June 5, 2012, http:// www.3dprinter.net/3d-printing-renewable-energy (accessed July 30, 2013).

16. "Print Me the Head of Alfredo Garcia," *Economist,* August 10, 2013, http://www .economist.com/news/science-and-technology/21583238-new-low-cost-way-making-thi ngs-print-me-head-alfredo-garcia (accessed August 18, 2013).

17. Markus Kayser, "Solar Sinter," MarkusKayser, 2011, http://www.markuskayser.com/wo rk/solarsinter/ (accessed January 11, 2013).

18. "Plastic, Fantastic! 3-D Printers Could Recycle Old Bottles," *Tech News Daily*, January 18, 2012, http://www.technewsdaily.com/5446-filabot-3d-printing-material-recycled-plastic .html (accessed February 2, 2013); "Filabot Wee Kit Order Form," Filabot: the Personal Filament Maker, http://www.filabot.com/collections/filabot-systems/products/filabot-wee -kit-welded (accessed February 2, 2013).

19. David J. Hill, "3-D Printing Robot Produces Chairs and Tables from Recycled Waste," *Singularity Hub*, April 23, 2012, http://singularityhub.com/2012/04/23/3d-printing-robot -produces-chairs-and-tables-from-recycled-waste/ (accessed April 4, 2013).

20. Jason Dorrier, "3-D Printed Homes? Here's the Scoop," Singularity Hub, August 22, 2012, http://singularityhub.com/2012/08/22/3d-printers-may-someday-construct-homes-in -less-than-a-day/ (accessed April 30, 2013).

21. Jordan Cook, "The World's First 3-D-Printed Building Will Arrive in 2014 (and It Looks Awesome)," *TechCrunch*, January 20, 2013, http://techcrunch.com/2013/01/20/the-wor lds-first-3d-printed-building-will-arrive-in-2014-and-it-looks-awesome/ (accessed January 26, 2013).

22. "Dutch Architect to Build 'Endless' House With 3-D Printer," *3ders*, January 15, 2013, http:// www.3ders.org/articles/20130115-dutch-architect-to-build-endless-house-with-3d-pr inter.html (accessed January 26, 2013).

23. "Foster + Partners Works with European Space Agency to 3-D Print Structures on the Moon," Foster and Partners press release, January 31, 2013, http://www.fosterandpart ners.com/news/foster-+-partners-works-with-european-space-agency-to-3d-print-structur es-on-the-moon/ (accessed February 18, 2013).

24. Ibid.; "Building a Lunar Base with 3-D Printing," European Space Agency, January 31, 2013, http://www.esa.int/Our_Activities/Technology/Building_a_lunar_base_with_3-D _printing (accessed February 18, 2013).

25. Edwin Kee, "Urbee 2 to Cross Country on Just 10 Gallons of Ethanol," *Ubergizmo*, March 1 2013, http://www.ubergizmo.com/2013/03/urbee-2-to-cross-country-on-just-10-gallons -of-ethanol/ (accessed September 4, 2013).

26. "Automotive Case Studies: Prototyping Is the Driving Force behind Great Cars," *Stratasys*, http://www.stratasys.com/resources/case-studies/automotive/urbee (accessed June 27, 2013).

27. Henry Ford and Samuel Crowther, *My Life and Work* (Garden City, NY: Garden City Publishing, 1922), 72.

28. Alexander George, "3-D Printed Car Is as Strong as Steel, Half the Weight, and Nearing Production," *Wired*, February 27, 2013, http://www.wired.com/autopia/2013/02/3d -printed-car/ (accessed June 2, 2013).

29. Mary Beth Griggs, "3-D Printers Spit Out Fancy Food, Green Cars, and Replacement Bones," *Discover Magazine*, March 26, 2012, http://discovermagazine.com/2012/mar/31 -3-d-printers-spit-out-fancy-food-and-green-cars#.UnvIBPmkoSU (accessed November 7, 2013).

30. "Manitoba's Kor Ecologic Debuts Hybrid Urbee," *Canadian Manufacturing*, November 2, 2012, http://www.canadianmanufacturing.com/designengineering/news/manitobas-kor -ecologic-debuts-hybrid-urbee-11992 (accessed November 1, 2013).

31. Stewart Brand and Matt Herron, "Keep Designing—How the Information Economy Is Being Created and Shaped by the Hacker Ethic," *Whole Earth Review* (May, 1985): 44.

32. Deborah Desrochers-Jacques, "Green Energy Use Jumps in Germany," *Der Spiegel*, August 30, 2011, http://www.spiegel.de/international/crossing-the-20-percent-mark-green-energy -use-jumps-in-germany-a-783314.html (accessed August 7, 2013); Berlin and Niebull,

"Germany's Energy Transformation: Eneriewende," *Economist,* July 28, 2012, http://www.economist.com/node/21559667 (accessed October 1, 2013).

33. "The Strategic Cooperation between Daimler and the Renault-Nissan Alliance Forms Agreement with Ford," Daimler, January 28, 2013, http://www.daimler.com/dccom/0-5 -7153-1-1569733-1-0-0-0-0-0-16694-0-0-0-0-0-0-0-0.html (accessed March 31, 2013).

34. Marcel Rosenbach and Thomas Schulz, "3-D Printing: Technology May Bring New Industrial Revolution," *Der Spiegel,* January 4, 2013, http://www.spiegel.de/international /business/3d-printing-technology-poised-for-new-industrial-revolution-a-874833.html (accessed August 5, 2013).

35. Goli Mohammadi, "Open Source Ecology: Interview with Founder Marcin Jakubowski," *Makezine,* February 11, 2011, http://blog.makezine.com/2011/02/11/open-source-ecology -interview-with-founder-marcin-jakubowski/ (accessed June 17, 2013).

36. Rohan Pearce, "Open Source Ecology: Can Open Source Save the Planet?," *Computerworld Techworld,* December 15, 2011, http://www.techworld.com.au/article/410193/open _source_ecology_can_open_source_save_planet_/ (accessed September 9, 2013).

37. "Marcin Jakubowski: Open-Sourced Blueprints For Civilization," *Huffington Post,* December 19, 2011, http://www.huffingtonpost.com/2011/12/19/wiki-diy-civilization_n_11 57895.html?view=print&comm_ref=false (accessed September 12, 2013).

38. Helen Pidd, "Indian Blackout Held No Fear for Small Hamlet Where the Power Stayed On," *Guardian,* September 10, 2012, http://www.guardian.co.uk/world/2012/sep/10/india -hamlet-where-power-stayed-on (accessed September 29, 2013).

39. Ibid.

40. Peerzada Abrar, "Gram Power: Yashraj Khaitan's 'Smart Microgrid' Produces, Stores Renewable Energy on Location," *Economic Times,* July 6, 2012, http://articles.econo mictimes.indiatimes.com/2012-07-06/news/32566187_1_renewable-energy-innovation -pilferage (accessed September 29, 2013).

41. Pidd, "Indian Blackout Held No Fear."

42. "From Micro-Grids to Smart Grids," *Kidela,* November 20, 2012, http://www.kidela.com /resources/blackout-from-micro-grids-to-smart-grids/ (accessed September 30, 2013).

43. Ibid.

44. "Mahatma Gandhi on Mass Production," interview, May 16, 1936, http://www.tinytech india.com/gandhiji2.html (accessed April 21, 2013).

45. Surur Hoda, *Gandhi and the Contemporary World* (Indo-British Historical Society, 1997).

46. "Mahatma Gandhi on Mass Production."

47. Ibid.

48. Ibid.

49. Hoda, *Gandhi and the Contemporary World.*

50. "Mahatma Gandhi on Mass Production."

51. Hoda, *Gandhi and the Contemporary World.*

52. *The Collected Works of Mahatma Gandhi,* vol. 83, June 7, 1942–January 26, 1944 (New Delhi: Publications Division of the Government of India, 1999), 113, http://www.gandhi serve.org/cwmg/VOL083.PDF (accessed November 14, 2013).

53. Mahatma Gandhi, *The Mind of Mahatma Gandhi: Encyclopedia of Ghandi's Thoughts,* ed. R. K. Prabhu and U. R. Rao (Ahmedabad, India: Jitendra T Desai Navajivan Mudrana-laya, 1966), 243–44.

54. Adam Smith, *An Inquiry into the Nature and Causes of the Wealth of Nations,* ed. Edwin Cannan (London: Methuen, 1961), 1: 475.

55. "Mahatma Gandhi's Views," TinyTech Plants, http://www.tinytechindia.com/gandhi4 .htm (accessed June 14, 2013).

56. Prarelal, *Mahatma Gandhi: Poornahuti,* vol. 10: *The Last Phase,* part 2 (Ahmedabad, India: Navajivan Trust, 1956), 522.

CHAPTER 7

1. "Skype in the Classroom," Skype, 2013, https://education.skype.com/ (accessed November 6, 2013); Sarah Kessler, "Skype CEO: Our Goal Is to Connect 1 Million Classrooms," Mashable, September 21, 2011, http://mashable.com/2011/09/21/skype-in-the-classroom -tony-bates/ (accessed November 12, 2013).

2. "Curriki at a Glance," Curriki homepage, April 2012, http://www.curriki.org/welcome /wp-content/uploads/2012/06/Curriki-At-a-Glance-04.04.12-update.pdf (accessed April 23, 2013).

3. "Einstein Middle School, 8th Grade," *Facing the Future,* http://www.facingthefuture.org /TakeAction/StudentsTakingAction/EinsteinMiddleSchool/tabid/165/Default.aspx#.Ubj 2AaIkLE1 (accessed April 18, 2013).

4. Jennifer Rebecca Kelly and Troy D. Abel, "Fostering Ecological Citizenship: The Case of Environmental Service-Learning in Costa Rica," *International Journal for the Scholarship of Teaching and Learning* 6(2) (2012), http://digitalcommons.georgiasouthern.edu /cgi/viewcontent.cgi?article=1330&context=int_jtl (accessed November 8, 2013).

5. "Study Finds Environmental Education Programs Leads to Cleaner Air," Air Quality Partnership, April 13, 2009, http://www.airqualityaction.org/news.php?newsid=84 (April 11, 2013).

6. Kelly and Abel, "Fostering Ecological Citizenship."

7. "Campus Compact Annual Membership Survey Results," Campus Compact, 2011, http:// www.compact.org/wp-content/uploads/2008/11/2010-Annual-Survey-Exec-Summary-4 -8.pdf (accessed May 5, 2013).

8. William Morgan, "Standardized Test Scores Improve with Service-Learning," National Service-Learning Clearinghouse, 2000, http://www.servicelearning.org/library/resource /4752 (accessed May 1, 2013).

9. Andrew Martin and Andrew W. Lehren, "A Generation Hobbled by the Soaring Cost of College," *New York Times,* May 12, 2012, http://www.nytimes.com/2012/05/13/business /student-loans-weighing-down-a-generation-with-heavy-debt.html?pagewanted=all&_r=0 (accessed May 19, 2013).

10. Carole Cadwalladr, "Do Online Courses Spell the End for the Traditional University?," *Guardian,* November 10, 2012, http://www.theguardian.com/education/2012/nov/11/on line-free-learning-end-of-university (accessed November 1, 2013).

11. Tamar Lewin, "College of Future Could Be Come One, Come All," *New York Times,* November 19, 2012, http://www.nytimes.com/2012/11/20/education/colleges-turn-to-crowd -sourcing-courses.html?pagewanted=all (accessed November 1, 2013).

12. Richard Pérez-Peña, "Harvard Asks Graduates to Donate Time to Free Online Humanities Class," *New York Times,* March 25, 2013, http://www.nytimes.com/2013/03/26/educa tion/harvard-asks-alumni-to-donate-time-to-free-online-course.html?_r=0 (accessed November 1, 2013).

13. Kathryn Ware, "Coursera Co-founder Reports on First 10 Months of Educational Revolution," *UVA Today,* February 21, 2013, http://curry.virginia.edu/articles/coursera-co -founder-reports-on-first-10-months-of-educational-revolution (accessed November 8, 2013); "Courses," Coursera, 2013, https://www.coursera.org/courses, (accessed November 12, 2013).

14. Cindy Atoji Keene, "A Classroom for the Whole World," *Boston Globe,* May 19, 2013, http://www.bostonglobe.com/business/specials/globe-100/2013/05/18/edx-president-an ant-agarwal-aims-reach-billion-students-around-world/Kv5DZOiB0ABh84F4oM8luN /story.html (accessed October 30, 2013); Thomas L. Friedman, "Revolution Hits the Universities," *New York Times,* January 26, 2013, http://www.nytimes.com/2013/01/27/opini on/sunday/friedman-revolution-hits-the-universities.html?_r=0 (accessed October 31, 2013).

15. Cadwalladr, "Do Online Courses Spell the End."
16. Ibid.
17. Josh Catone, "In the Future, The Cost of Education Will Be Zero," *Mashable,* July 24, 2013, http://mashable.com/2009/07/24/education-social-media/ (accessed August 6, 2013).
18. Tamar Lewin, "Universities Team with Online Course Provider," *New York Times,* May 30, 2013, http://www.nytimes.com/2013/05/30/education/universities-team-with-online-course-provider.html (accessed November 1, 2013).
19. "Costs for University of Maryland College Park," CollegeCalc, http://www.collegecalc.org/colleges/maryland/university-of-maryland-college-park/ (accessed June 28, 2013).
20. Geoffrey A. Fowler, "An Early Report Card on Massive Open Online Courses," *Wall Street Journal,* October 8, 2013, http://online.wsj.com/news/articles/SB10001424052702303759604579093400834738972 (accessed November 25, 2013).
21. Tamar Lewin, "Universities Reshaping Education on the Web," *New York Times,* July 17, 2012, http://www.nytimes.com/2012/07/17/education/consortium-of-colleges-takes-online-education-to-new-level.html?pagewanted=all (accessed October 28, 2013).
22. Kevin Carey, "Into the Future with MOOC's," *Chronicle of Higher Education,* September 3, 2012, http://chronicle.com/article/Into-the-Future-With-MOOCs/134080/ (accessed October 28, 2013).

CHAPTER 8

1. Jeremy Rifkin, *The End of Work* (New York: G. P. Putnam's Sons, 1995), xv.
2. Jacob Goldstein and Lam Thuy Vo, "22 Million Americans Are Unemployed Or Underemployed," NPR, April 4, 2013, httpwww.npr.orgblogsmoney2013040417569781323-million-americans-are-unemployed-or-underemployed (accessed November 12, 2013).
3. Jenny Marlar, "Global Unemployment at 8% in 2011," Gallup World, April 17, 2012, http://www.gallup.com/poll/153884/global-unemployment-2011.aspx (accessed October 15, 2013).
4. "Global Employment Trends 2013," International Labor Organization, 2013, 10, http://www.ilo.org/wcmsp5/groups/public/—dgreports/—dcomm/—publ/documents/publication/wcms_202326.pdf (accessed July 7, 2013).
5. "Difference Engine: Luddite Legacy," *Economist,* November 4, 2011, http://www.economist.com/blogs/babbage/2011/11/artificial-intelligence (accessed July 9, 2013).
6. Ibid.
7. Michaela D. Platzer and Glennon J. Harrison, "The U.S. Automotive Industry: National and State Trends in Manufacturing Employment," Cornell University ILR School, August 2009, 8, http://digitalcommons.ilr.cornell.edu/cgi/viewcontent.cgi?article=1671&context=key_workplace (accessed July 7, 2013).
8. James Sherk,"Technology Explains Drop in Manufacturing Jobs," Heritage Foundation, October 12, 2010, http://www.heritage.org/research/reports/2010/10/technology-explains-drop-in-manufacturing-jobs (accessed August 10, 2013).
9. Mark J. Perry, "The US Economy Is Now Producing 2.2% More Output than before the Recession, but with 3.84 Million Fewer Workers," American Enterprise Institute, November 6,2012, http://www.aei-ideas.org/2012/11/the-us-economy-is-now-producing-2-2-more-output-than-before-the-recession-but-with-3-84-million-fewer-workers/ (accessed September 3, 2013).
10. Boerje Langefors, "Automated Design," in Robert Colborn, *Modern Science and Technology* (Princeton, NJ: Princeton University Press, 1965), 699.
11. *Management Report on Numerically Controlled Machine Tools* (Chicago: Cox and Cox Consulting, 1958).

12. Alan A. Smith to J. O. McDonough, September 18, 1952, N/C Project Files, MIT Archives.

13. Peter Joseph, Roxanne Meadows, and Jacque Fresco, "The Zeitgeist Movement: Observations and Responses," *Zeitgeist Movement*, February 2009 http://www.bibliotecapley ades.net/sociopolitica/zeitgeist08.htm (accessed June 13, 2013).

14. Caroline Baum, "So Who's Stealing China's Manufacturing Jobs?," *Bloomberg*, October 14 2003, http://www.bloomberg.com/apps/news?pid=newsarchive&sid=aRI4bAft7Xw4 (accessed July 1, 2013).

15. John Markoff, "Skilled Work, without the Worker," *New York Times*, August 18, 2012, http://www.nytimes.com/2012/08/19/business/new-wave-of-adept-robots-is-changing -global-industry.html?pagewanted=all&_r=0 (accessed July 1, 2013).

16. Ibid.

17. "World Robotics 2012 Industrial Robots," International Federation of Robotics, http://www.ifr.org/industrial-robots/statistics/ (accessed May 26, 2013).

18. Russell Roberts, "Obama vs. ATMs: Why Technology Doesn't Destroy Jobs," *Wall Street Journal*, June 22, 2011, http://online.wsj.com/article/SB1000142405270230407010457639 99704275939640.html (accessed May 26, 2013).

19. Katie Drummond, "Clothes Will Sew Themselves in Darpa's Sweat-Free Sweatshops," *Wired*, June 8, 2012, http://www.wired.com/dangerroom/2012/06/darpa-sweatshop/ (accessed June 1, 2013).

20. Bernard Condon, "Millions of Middle-Class Jobs Killed by Machines in Great Recession's Wake," *Huffington Post*, January 23, 2013, http://www.huffingtonpost.com/2013/01/23 /middle-class-jobs-machines_n_2532639.html?view=print&comm_ref=false (accessed July 21, 2013).

21. Joseph G. Carson, "US Economic and Investment Perspectives—Manufacturing Payrolls Declining Globally: The Untold Story (Part 2)," *AllianceBernstein* (October 2003).

22. "Postal Service Flexes Its Workforce Flexibility," USPS Office of Inspector General, June 10, 2013, http://www.uspsoig.gov/blog/postal-service-flexes-its-workforce-flexibility/, (accessed June 13, 2013).

23. "Occupational Employment and Wages News Release," U.S. Bureau of Labor Statistics, March 29, 2013, http://www.bls.gov/news.release/ocwage.htm (accessed August 3, 2013).

24. Condon, "Millions of Middle-Class Jobs Killed by Machines in Great Recession's Wake."

25. Alana Semuels, "Retail Jobs Are Disappearing as Shoppers Adjust to Self-Service," *Los Angeles Times*, March 4, 2011, http://articles.latimes.com/print/2011/mar/04/business/la -fi-robot-retail-20110304 (accessed July 13, 2013).

26. Bill Siwicki, "Wal-Mart expands Self-Checkout in Stores via Its iPhone App," *Internet Retailer*, February 20, 2013, http://www.internetretailer.com/2013/02/20/wal-mart-exp ands-self-checkout-stores-its-iphone-app (accessed November 3, 2013).

27. Ricardo Sanchez, "Brick and Mortar vs. Online Retailers, A Decade Later . . . ," *On Techies*, January 31, 2012, http://ontechies.com/2012/01/31/brick-and-mortar-vs-online -retailers-a-decade-later/ (accessed June 17, 2013).

28. Ibid.

29. Sun Joo Kim, "How Will Brick and Mortar Stores Survive?," *Smart Planet*, October 19, 2012, http://www.smartplanet.com/blog/bulletin/how-will-brick-and-mortar-stores-surv ive/3122 (accessed June 19, 2013).

30. Barney Jopson, "Shoes Stores Sock It to Online Buyers," *Financial Times*, May 5, 2013, http://www.ft.com/cms/s/0/42893492-b385-11e2-b5a5-00144feabdc0.html#axzz2W 1rGveQo (accessed November 7, 2013).

31. Campbell Phillips, "'Fit-lifters' Give Showrooming Shoe Browsers a Bad Name," *Power Retail*, May 6, 2013, http://www.powerretail.com.au/multichannel/fit-lifters-give-show rooming-a-bad-name/ (accessed July 6, 2013).

32. Jason Perlow, "In the Battle of Clicks versus Bricks, Retail Must Transform or Die," *ZD-Net,* December 8, 2011, http://www.zdnet.com/blog/perlow/in-the-battle-of-clicks-versus -bricks-retail-must-transform-or-die/19418 (accessed August 3, 2013).

33. "Occupational Employment and Wages News Release," U.S. Bureau of Labor Statistics, March 29, 2013, http://www.bls.gov/news.release/ocwage.htm (accessed June 8, 2013).

34. John Markoff, "Armies of Expensive Lawyers, Replaced by Cheaper Software," *New York Times,* March 4, 2011, http://www.nytimes.com/2011/03/05/science/05legal.html?p agewanted=all (accessed October 20, 2013).

35. Ibid.

36. Christopher Steiner, "Automatons Get Creative," *New York Times,* August 17, 2012, http://online.wsj.com/news/articles/SB1000087239639044437510457759130427722953 4#printprin (accessed June 30, 2013).

37. Ibid.

38. "IBM Watson: Ushering in a New Era of Computing," IBM, http://www-03.ibm.com/in novation/us/watson/ (accessed October 22, 2013).

39. Brian T. Horowitz, "IBM, Nuance to Tune Watson Supercomputer for Use in Health Care," *EWeek,* February 17, 2011, http://www.eweek.com/c/a/Health-Care-IT/IBM-Nuance -to-Tune-Watson-Supercomputer-for-Use-in-Health-Care-493127/ (accessed October 22, 2013).

40. Associated Press, "Watson's Medical Expertise Offered Commercially," *Telegram,* February 8 2013, http://www.telegram.com/article/20130208/NEWS/102089640/0 (accessed October 22, 2013).

41. "Lionbridge Language Solution Provider Expands Opportunities with Translation Technology," Microsoft Case Studies, July 9, 2013, http://www.microsoft.com/casestudies /Bing/Lionbridge/Language-Solution-Provider-Expands-Opportunities-with-Translation -Technology/710000001102 (accessed September 4, 2013).

42. Niko Papula, "Are Translators Losing Their Jobs Because of Machine Translation?," Multilizer Translation Blog, April 13, 2011, http://translation-blog.multilizer.com/are-transla tors-losing-their-jobs-because-of-machine-translation/ (accessed September 6, 2013).

CHAPTER 9

1. Harold Hotelling, "The General Welfare in Relation to Problems of Taxation and of Railway and Utility Rates," *Econometrica* 6(3) (July, 1938): 242.

2. Ibid., 258.

3. Ibid., 260–61.

4. Ibid., 242.

5. Ronald H. Coase, "The Marginal Cost Controversy," *Economica* 13(51) (August, 1946): 180.

6. Ibid., 173

7. John F. Duffy, "The Marginal Cost Controversy in Intellectual Property," *University of Chicago Law Review* 71(1) (2004): 38.

8. Robert S. McIntyre, Matthew Gardner, Rebecca J. Wilkins, and Richard Phillips, "Corporate Taxpayers & Corporate Tax Dodgers 2008–10," Citizens for Tax Justice and the Institute on Taxation and Economic Policy, November, 2011, http://www.ctj.org/corpor atetaxdodgers/CorporateTaxDodgersReport.pdf (accessed October 7, 2013).

9. "ICT Facts and Figures: The World in 2013," ICT Data and Statistics Division of the International Telecommunication Union, February 2013, 2, http://www.itu.int/en/ITU-D /Statistics/Documents/facts/ICTFactsFigures2013.pdf (accessed October 2, 2013).

10. United Nations Environment Programme, "Feed in Tariffs as a Policy Instrument for Promoting Renewable Energies and Green Economies in Developing Countries," ed. Wilson

Rickerson, Chad Laurent, David Jacobs, Christina Dietrich and Christina Hanley, 2012, 4, http://www.unep.org/pdf/UNEP_FIT_Report_2012F.pdf (accessed October 21, 2013).

11. Ibid.

12. Geert De Clercq, "Renewables Turn Utilities into Dinosaurs of the Energy World," Reuters, March 8, 2013, http://www.reuters.com/article/2013/03/08/us-utilities-threat-idUS BRE92709E20130308 (accessed August 30, 2013).

13. Dave Toke, "Community Wind Power in Europe and in UK," *Wind Engineering* 29(3) (2005).

14. De Clercq, "Renewables Turn Utilities into Dinosaurs."

15. Ibid.

16. Ibid.

17. "Smart Grid Investment Grant Program: Progress Report," U.S. Department of Energy, July, 2012, ii, http://www.smartgrid.gov/sites/default/files/doc/files/sgig-progress-report -final-submitted-07-16-12.pdf (accessed February 3, 2014).

18. Litos Strategic Communication, "The Smart Grid: An Introduction," U.S. Department of Energy, 2008, 5, http://energy.gov/sites/prod/files/oeprod/DocumentsandMedia/DOE_SG _Book_Single_Pages.pdf (accessed September 3, 2013).

19. "Technology," Transphorm, Inc., http://www.transphormusa.com/technology (accessed June 6, 2013).

20. "Estimating the Costs and Benefits of the Smart Grid: A Preliminary Estimate of the Investment Requirements and the Resultant Benefits of a Fully Functioning Smart Grid," Electric Power Research Institute, March 2011, 4, http://ipu.msu.edu/programs/MIGrid2011/pre sentations/pdfs/Reference Material - Estimating the Costs and Benefits of the Smart Grid. pdf (accessed February 3, 2014).

21. Michael Bame, "USS Gerald Ford Aircraft Carrier," About.com, 2013, http://defense. about.com/od/Navy/a/Uss-Gerald-Ford-Aircraft-Carrier.htm (accessed June 17, 2013); "Building an Energy Future: Annual Report," Royal Dutch Shell, December 31, 2012: 10, http://reports.shell.com/annual-review/2012/servicepages/downloads/files/entire_shell_re view_12.pdf (accessed February 3, 2014).

22. Vaclav Smil, "Moore's Curse and the Great Energy Delusion," *American,* November 19, 2008, http://www.american.com/archive/2008/november-december-magazine/moore201 9s-curse-and-the-great-energy-delusion (accessed June 6, 2013).

23. Scott DiSavino, "U.S. Smart Grid to Cost Billions, Save Trillions," Reuters, May 24, 2011, http://www.reuters.com/article/2011/05/24/us-utilities-smartgrid-epri-idUSTRE74N 7O420110524 (accessed June 7, 2013); "Estimating the Costs and Benefits of the Smart Grid: A Preliminary Estimate." Electric Power Research Institute, March 2011, 21.

24. "Growing International Co-Operation Driving the Spread of Smart Grids," *GlobalData* (June, 2012): 1–7.

25. Katie Fehrenbacher, "For the Smart Grid, the Wireless Debates Are Over," *Gigaom,* January 23, 2012, http://gigaom.com/2012/01/23/for-the-smart-grid-the-wireless-debates-are -over/ (accessed July 5, 2013).

26. Dave Karpinski, "Making the 'Smart Grid' Smarter with Broadband Wireless Networks and the Internet," *Crain's Cleveland Business,* September 11, 2012, http://www.crains cleveland.com/article/20120911/BLOGS05/309119999 (accessed July 7, 2013).

27. Ibid.

28. Sunil Paul and Nick Allen, "Inventing the Cleanweb," *MIT Technology Review,* April 2, 2012, http://www.technologyreview.com/news/427382/inventing-the-cleanweb/ (accessed August 17, 2013).

29. Paul Boutin, "The Law of Online Sharing," *MIT Technology Review,* January/February 2012.

30. Yuliya Chernova, "New York's Cleanweb Hackathon Sparks Green Ideas Where Clean-tech and IT Intersect," *Wall Street Journal*, October 2, 2012, http://blogs.wsj.com/venture capital/2012/10/02/new-yorks-cleanweb-hackathon-sparks-green-ideas-where-clean-tech-and-it-intersect/ (accessed September 3, 2013); Martin LaMonica, "Cleanweb Hackers Get Busy with Energy Data," *CNET*, January 23, 2012, http://news.cnet.com/8301-11128_3-5 7363873-54/cleanweb-hackers-get-busy-with-energy-data/ (accessed September 3, 2013).

31. Paul and Allen, "Inventing the Cleanweb."

32. "Green Button Data: More Power to You," U.S. Department of Energy, May 18, 2012, http://energy.gov/articles/green-button-data-more-power-you (accessed September 10, 2013).

33. "Statements of Support for Green Button Initiative," White Houe Office of Science and Technology Policy, last modified March 22, 2012, http://www.whitehouse.gov/administra tion/eop/ostp/pressroom/03222012-support (accessed August 22, 2013).

34. "Check Out the Social Energy App by Facebook, NRDC, Opower," *Alliance to Save Energy*, last modified March 20, 2012, http://www.ase.org/efficiencynews/preview-social -energy-app-facebook-nrdc-opower (accessed July 19, 2013).

35. Dominic Basulto, "The Cleanweb: Green Energy Meets Moore's Law," *Big Think*, May 15, 2012, http://bigthink.com/endless-innovation/the-cleanweb-green-energy-meets-moores -law (accessed July 19, 2013).

36. Cecilia Kang, "Tech, Telecom Giants Take Sides as FCC Proposes Public Wi-Fi Networks," *Cullman Times*, February 4, 2013, http://www.cullmantimes.com/local/x1303538507 /Tech-Telecom-Giants-Take-Sides-as-FCC-Proposes-Public-Wi-Fi-Networks (accessed No-vember 3, 2013).

37. Ibid.

38. Ibid.

39. Ibid.

40. Ibid.

41. Ibid.

42. "Radio Act of 1927," United States Early Radio History, February 23, 1927, http://early radiohistory.us/sec023.htm#part090 (accessed October 22, 2013).

43. "The Communications Act of 1934," U.S. Department of Justice, June 19, 1934, http://it .ojp.gov/default.aspx?area=privacy&page=1288#contentTop (accessed October 22, 2013).

44. "Unlicensed Spectrum Subcommittee Report," U.S. Department of Commerce, National Telecommunications and Information Administration, January 6, 2010, 4.

45. Ibid.

46. Ibid.

47. Carmela Aquino and Sarah Radwanick, "2012 Mobile Future in Focus," ComScore, Feb-ruary 2012, http://www.comscore.com/Insights/Presentations_and_Whitepapers/2012/20 12_Mobile_Future_in_Focus (accessed October 23, 2013).

48. "Cisco Visual Networking Index: Global Mobile Data Traffic Forecast Update, 2010–2015," Cisco, February 1, 2011, 10, http://newsroom.cisco.com/ekits/Cisco_VNI_Global _Mobile_Data_Traffic_Forecast_2010_2015.pdf (accessed February 3, 2014).

49. "Cisco Visual Networking Index: Global Mobile Data Traffic Forecast Update, 2012–2017," Cisco, February 6, 2013, 11, http://www.cisco.com/en/US/solutions/collateral /ns341/ns525/ns537/ns705/ns827/white_paper_c11-520862.html (accessed February 3, 2014).

50. Yochai Benkler, "Open Wireless vs. Licensed Spectrum: Evidence from Market Adoption," *Harvard Journal of Law and Technology* 26(1) (2012), http://cyber.law.harvard.edu/publi cations/2012/unlicensed_wireless_v_licensed_spectrum (accessed October 23, 2013).

51. "Auctions," U.S. Federal Communications Commission, http://www.fcc.gov/topic/auc tions (accessed June 4, 2013).

CHAPTER 10

1. Garrett Hardin, "The Tragedy of the Commons," *Science* 162(3859) (December 13, 1968): 1244.

2. Ibid., 1243–48.

3. Garrett Hardin, "Political Requirements for Preserving Our Common Heritage," in *Wildlife and America*, ed. Howard P. Brokaw (Washington, DC: Council on Environmental Quality, 1978), 310–17.

4. Carol Rose, "The Comedy of the Commons," *University of Chicago Law Review* 53(3) (1986): 720.

5. Crawford B. Macpherson, *Democratic Theory* (Oxford: Clarendon Press, 1973), 123–24.

6. Rose, "The Comedy of the Commons," 767.

7. Ibid., 768.

8. Ibid., 774.

9. Ibid.

10. Elinor Ostrom, *Governing the Commons*, (Cambridge University Press, 1990), 58.

11. Hardin, "The Tragedy of the Commons," 1244.

12. Ostrom, *Governing the Commons*, 59.

13. Ibid.

14. Ibid., 61–62.

15. Ibid., 62.

16. Robert McC. Netting, "What Alpine Peasants Have in Common: Observations on the Communal Tenure in a Swiss Village," *Human Ecology* 4(2) (1976): 135–46.

17. Ostrom, *Governing the Commons*, 62.

18. Ibid., 62–63.

19. Netting, "What Alpine Peasants Have in Common."

20. Ostrom, *Governing the Commons*, 64.

21. Ibid., 91–102.

22. Elinor Ostrom, "Beyond Markets and States: Polycentric Governance of Complex Economic Systems," Nobel Prize lecture, Workshop in Political Theory and Policy Analysis from Indiana University, Bloomington, IN, December 8, 2009, 424, 425, http://www.nobelprize.org/nobel_prizes/economic-sciences/laureates/2009/ostrom_lecture.pdf (accessed November 3, 2013).

23. Ibid.

24. Douglas Robinson and Nina Medlock, "*Diamond v. Chakrabarty*: A Retrospective on 25 Years of Biotech Patents," *Intellectual Property and Technology Law Journal* 17(10) (2005): 12.

25. Leonard S. Rubenstein, "Brief on Behalf of the Peoples Business Commission, Amicus Curiae," regarding *Diamond v. Chakrabarty*, no. 79-136, December 13, 1979, http://www.justice.gov/atr/public/workshops/ag2010/015/AGW-14399-a.doc (accessed November 1, 2013).

26. Ibid.

27. "New Forms of Life Can be Patented U.S. Court Rules," *Montreal Gazette* (Associated Press), June 17 1980, http://news.google.com/newspapers?nid=1946&dat=19800617&id=OokxAAAAIBAJ&sjid=dKQFAAAAIBAJ&pg=3169,3065019 (accessed July 20, 2013).

28. "A History of Firsts," Genentech, 2012, http://www.gene.com/media/company-information/chronology (accessed June 19, 2013).

29. Keith Schneider, "Harvard Gets Mouse Patent, A World First," *New York Times*, April 13, 1988, http://www.nytimes.com/1988/04/13/us/harvard-gets-mouse-patent-a-world-first.html?pagewanted=print&src=pm (accessed June 25, 2013).

30. Marcy Darnovsky and Jesse Reynolds, "The Battle to Patent Your Genes," *American Interest,* September/October 2009, http://www.the-american-interest.com/article-bd.cfm ?piece=653 (accessed July 20, 2013).

31. "Porto Alegre Treaty to Share the Genetic Commons," UK Food Group, February 1, 2002, http://www.ukabc.org/genetic_commons_treaty.htm (accessed July 21, 2013).

32. John Roach, "'Doomsday' Vault Will End Crop Extinction, Expert Says," *National Geographic,* December 27, 2007, http://news.nationalgeographic.com/news/2007/12/071227 -seed-vault.html (accessed April 28, 2013).

33. Aaron Saenz, "Costs of DNA Sequencing Falling Fast—Look at these Graphs!," Singularity University, March 5, 2001, http://singularityhub.com/2011/03/05/costs-of-dna -sequencing-falling-fast-look-at-these-graphs/ (accessed June 19, 2013).

34. David Altshuler, John Bell, Todd Golub, et al, "Creating a Global Alliance to Enable Responsible Sharing of Genomic and Clinical Data," *Broad Institute,* June 3 2013, http:// www.broadinstitute.org/files/news/pdfs/GAWhitePaperJune3.pdf (accessed November 8, 2013).

35. Ariana Eunjung Cha, "Glowing Plants Illuminate Regulatory Debate," *Washington Post,* October 4, 2013, http://www.washingtonpost.com/national/health-science/glowing-plant-project-on-kickstarter-sparks-debate-about-regulation-of-dna-modification/2013/10/03/e 01db276-1c78-11e3-82ef-a059e54c49d0_story.html (accessed November 8, 2013).

36. Ibid.

37. Jeremy Rifkin, *The Biotech Century* (New York: Jeremy P. Tarcher/Putnam Books, 1998), 9.

38. Kendall Haven, *One Hundred Greatest Science Discoveries of All Time* (Westport, CT: Libraries Unlimited, 2007), 221.

39. Lydia Nenow, "To Patent or Not to Patent: The European Union's New Biotech Directive," *Houston Journal of International Law* 23(3) (2001): 25, http://www.thefreelibrary.com /To+patent+or+not+to+patent%3A+the+European+Union's+new+biotech . . . -a075908314 (accessed November 7, 2013).

CHAPTER 11

1. William Henry Gates III, "An Open Letter to Hobbyists," February 3, 1976, http://www .blinkenlights.com/classiccmp/gateswhine.html (accessed February 3, 2014).

2. "What Is Free Software?," GNU Project–Free Software Foundation, June 18, 2013, http:// www.gnu.org/philosophy/free-sw.html (accessed June 26, 2013).

3. Ibid.

4. C. Arvind Kumar, *Welcome to the 'Free' World: A Free Software Initiative* (Hyderabad: Indian Universities Press, 2011), 28.

5. Lawrence Lessig, "Code Is Law: On Liberty in Cyberspace," *Harvard Magazine,* January-February 2000, http://harvardmagazine.com/2000/01/code-is-law-html (accessed June 13, 2013).

6. Eben Moglen, "Anarchism Triumphant: Free Software and the Death of Copyright," *First Monday* 4(8) (August 2, 1999), http://pear.accc.uic.edu/ojs/index.php/fm/article/view/684 /594 (June 10, 2013).

7. Steven J. Vaughan-Nichols, "Fast, Faster, Fastest: Linux Rules Supercomputing," *ZD Net,* June 19, 2012, http://www.zdnet.com/blog/open-source/fast-faster-fastest-linux-rules-su percomputing/11263 (accessed June 13, 2013); Roger Parloff, "How Linux Conquered the Fortune 500," CNN Money, May 6, 2013, http://money.cnn.com/2013/05/06/technology /linux-500.pr.fortune/ (accessed November 13, 2013).

8. Moglen, "Anarchism Triumphant."

9. Ibid.

10. "History of the OSI," Open Source Initiative, September 2012, http://opensource.org/history (accessed June 13, 2013).

11. Richard Stallman, "Why 'Open Source' Misses the Point of Free Software," *Communications of the ACM* 52(6) (2009): 31.

12. Ibid.

13. Ibid., 33.

14. Eric Steven Raymond, "The Cathedral and the Bazaar," UnderStone.net, August 22, 2001 http://www.unterstein.net/su/docs/CathBaz.pdf (accessed June 13, 2013).

15. Jeremy Rifkin, *The Empathic Civilization* (New York: Penguin Books, 2009), 266.

16. Elizabeth L. Eisenstein, *The Printing Revolution in Early Modern Europe* (Cambridge: Cambridge University Press, 1983), 95.

17. Lawrence Lessig, "Culture Wars: Getting to Peace," in *Copyright Future Copyright Freedom: Marking the 40th Anniversary of the Commencement of Australia's Copyright Act of 1968,* ed. Brian Fitzgerald and Benedict Atkinson (Sydney: Sydney University Press, 2011), 116.

18. "ICT Facts and Figures: The World in 2013," ICT Data and Statistics Division of the International Telecommunication Union, February 2013, http://www.itu.int/en/ITU-D/Statistics/Documents/facts/ICTFactsFigures2013.pdf (accessed June 20, 2013).

19. Lawrence Lessig, "Getting Our Values around Copyright Rights," *Educause Review* 45(2) (March/April 2010): 36.

20. Ibid.

21. "History," Creative Commons, June 2013, http://creativecommons.org/about/history, (accessed June 13, 2013).

22. "200 Million Creative Commons Photos and Counting!," Flickr, October 5, 2011, http://blog.flickr.net/en/2011/10/05/200-million-creative-commons-photos-and-counting (accessed June 26, 2013).

23. Dara Kerr, "YouTube breaks records with 4M Creative Commons Videos," CNET, July 25, 2012, http://news.cnet.com/8301-1023_3-57480300-93/youtube-breaks-records-with-4m-creative-commons-videos/ (accessed June 23, 2013).

24. "History," Creative Commons.

25. "Personal Genome Project—Homepage," Personal Genome Project, 2013, http://www.personalgenomes.org/ (accessed June 23, 2013).

26. Ibid.; David Ewing Duncan, "On a Mission to Sequence the Genomes of 100,000 People," *New York Times,* June 7, 2010, http://www.nytimes.com/2010/06/08/science/08church.html (accessed November 13, 2013).

27. "Sharing Policies," Personal Genome Project, 2013, http://www.personalgenomes.org/sharing (accessed June 23, 2013).

28. Lessig, "Getting Our Values around Copyright Rights," 42.

29. James Boyle, "The Second Enclosure Movement and the Construction of the Public Domain," *Law and Contemporary Problems* 66(33) (2003): 37.

30. Ibid., 40

31. Ibid., 48.

32. Nicholas Polunin and Jacques Grinevald, "Vernadsky and Biosphere Ecology," *Environmental Conservation* 15(2) (Summer 1988): 117–122.

33. Ibid.

34. James E. Lovelock and Lynn Margulis, "Atmospheric Homeostasis By and For the Biosphere: The Gaia Hypothesis," *Tellus* 26 (1–2) (1974): 2–10.

35. Geoffrey Lean, "Focus: Trade Wars–The Hidden Tentacles of the World's Most Secret Body," *Independent,* July 18, 1999, http://www.independent.co.uk/life-style/focus-trade-wars—the-hidden-tentacles-of-the-worlds-most-secret—body-1107215.html (accessed July 1, 2013).

36. Kim Murphy and Lynn Marshall, "WTO Protesters Return to Seattle without the Violence of Last Year," *Los Angeles Times,* December 1, 2000, http://articles.latimes.com/2000 /dec/01/news/mn-59763 (accessed October 22, 2013).

37. Sonny Bono Copyright Term Extension Act, PL 105–298, 105th Congress, 2nd Session, October 27, 1998, http://www.gpo.gov/fdsys/pkg/PLAW-105publ298/pdf/PLAW-1 05publ298.pdf (accessed June 13, 2013).

38. Digital Millennium Copyright Act, PL 105–304, 105th Congress, 2nd Session, October 28, 1998, http://www.gpo.gov/fdsys/pkg/PLAW-105publ304/pdf/PLAW-105publ304.pdf (accessed June 13, 2013).

39. Jay Walljasper, "From Middle East to Wall Street, Justice Depends on Public Spaces," *Commons Magazine,* June 25, 2012, http://onthecommons.org/magazine/middle-east -wall-street-justice-depends-public-spaces (accessed November 7, 2013).

40. Ibid.

41. Jonathan Rowe, "The Hidden Commons," *Yes! Magazine,* June 30, 2001, http://www .yesmagazine.org/issues/reclaiming-the-commons/the-hidden-commons (accessed June 16, 2013).

42. Mike Bergan, "The American Commons," 10,000 Birds, August 6, 2007, http://10000birds .com/the-american-commons.htm (accessed July 2, 2013).

43. Yochai Benkler, "Coase's Penguin, or, Linux and *The Nature of the Firm,*" *Yale Law Journal* 112(369) v.04.3 (August 2002): 1–2, http://www.benkler.org/CoasesPenguin.PDF (accessed June 26, 2013).

44. Peter Barnes, *Capitalism 3.0: A Guide to Reclaiming the Commons* (San Francisco: Berrett-Koehler Publishers, 2006), xiv.

CHAPTER 12

1. Yochai Benkler, *The Wealth of Networks: How Social Production Transforms Markets and Freedom* (New Haven, CT: Yale University Press, 2006), 470.

2. Brett M. Frischmann, "Cultural Environmentalism and *The Wealth of Networks,*" *University of Chicago Law Review* 74(1083) (2001): 1132.

3. Ibid., 1133.

4. "Internet Corporations for Assigned Names and Numbers: Board of Directors," ICANN, 2013, http://www.icann.org/en/groups/board (accessed June 13, 2013).

5. "Who Governs the Internet," Global Partners and Associates, 3, http://www.global-part ners.co.uk/wp-content/uploads/who-governs-internet_web2.pdf (accessed June 13, 2013).

6. Ibid.

7. Chengetai Masango, "About the Internet Governance Forum," Internet Governance Forum, October 17, 2011, http://www.intgovforum.org/cms/aboutigf (accessed June 13, 2013).

8. "Who Governs the Internet," 4.

9. Ibid., 7.

10. Ibid., 8.

11. Patricia O'Connell, ed. "OnlineExtra: At SBC, It's All about Scale and Scope," *Bloomberg Businessweek,* November 6, 2005, http://www.businessweek.com/stories/2005-11-06/online -extra-at-sbc-its-all-about-scale-and-scope.

12. Kevin O'Brien, "Limiting Data Use in Germany," *New York Times,* May 12, 2013, http:// www.nytimes.com/2013/05/13/technology/deutsche-telekom-data-use-and-net-neutrality .html.

13. Ibid.

14. "Open Internet," Federal Communications Commission, http://www.fcc.gov/openinternet #rules.

15. Brett Frischmann, *Infrastructure: The Social Value of Shared Resources* (New York: Oxford University Press, 2013), 349.

16. Tim Berners-Lee, "Long Live the Web: A Call for Continued Open Standards and Neutrality," *Scientific American,* November 22, 2010, http://www.scientificamerican.com/article.cfm?id=long-live-the-web&print=true.

17. Ibid.

18. Ibid.

19. Ibid.

20. Matt Beswick, "Google Search Queries by the Numbers," *STAT,* July 27, 2012, http://getstat.com/blog/google-search-queries-the-numbers/.

21. "Internet and Search Engine Usage by Country," Globalization Partners International, 2011, http://ptgmedia.pearsoncmg.com/images/9780789747884/supplements/9780789747884_appC.pdf (accessed June 13, 2013).

22. Glenn Chapman, "Google 2012 Revenue Hits $50 Billion, Profits Up," *Dawn,* January 23, 2013, http://beta.dawn.com/news/780915/google-2012-revenue-hits-50-billion-profits-up.

23. "Social Media Market Share," KarmaSnack, 2013, http://www.karmasnack.com/about/social-media-market-share/ (accessed June 14, 2013); "Number of Active Users at Facebook Over the Years," *Yahoo! News* (Associated Press), May 1, 2013, http://news.yahoo.com/number-active-users-facebook-over-230449748.html.

24. Alexis C. Madrigal, "The Case for Facebook," *Atlantic,* May 29, 2012, http://www.theatlantic.com/technology/archive/2012/05/the-case-for-facebook/257767/.

25. Robert Hof, "Poof! $1 Billion Slashed from 2012 Facebook Revenue Forecast," *Forbes,* August 30, 2012, http://www.forbes.com/sites/roberthof/2012/08/30/poof-1-billion-slashed-from-2012-facebook-revenue-forecast/.

26. Lisa O'Carroll, "Twitter Active Users Pass 200 Million," *Guardian,* December 18, 2012, http://www.guardian.co.uk/technology/2012/dec/18/twitter-users-pass-200-million.

27. Jonathan Erlichman and Brian Womack, "Twitter Said to Expect $1 Billion in Ad Revenue in 2014," *Bloomberg,* June 2, 2012, http://www.bloomberg.com/news/2012-06-01/twitter-said-to-expect-1-billion-in-sales-in-2014-on-ad-growth.html.

28. Hal Singer, "Who Competes with Google Search? Just Amazon, Apple, and Facebook," *Forbes,* September 18, 2012, http://www.forbes.com/sites/halsinger/2012/09/18/who-competes-with-google-in-search-just-amazon-apple-and-facebook/.

29. "Inside Amazon," Amazon.com, http://india.amazon.com/InsideAmazon.html (accessed June 28, 2013).

30. Justus Haucap and Ulrich Heimeshoff, "Google, Facebook, Amazon, eBay: Is the Internet Driving Competition or Market Monopolization?," Dusseldorf Institute for Competition Economics, no. 83, January 2013.

31. Alex Wilhelm, "eBay Beats Expectations with Q4 Revenues of $3.99 Billion, EPS of $0.70 on Back of Strong PayPal Performance," *TNW,* January 16, 2013, http://thenextweb.com/insider/2013/01/16/ebays-hitsmisses-with-q4-revenue-of-earnings-per-share-of/.

32. Paul Sawers, "Facebook Twitter, iTunes, and Google: The Rise of Digital Monopolies," *TNW,* October 2, 2011, http://thenextweb.com/insider/2011/10/02/facebook-twitter-itunes-and-google-the-rise-of-digital-monopolies/.

33. Tim Wu, "In the Grip of the New Monopolists," *Wall Street Journal,* November 13, 2010, http://online.wsj.com/article/SB10001424052748704635704575604993311538482.html.

34. Ibid.

35. Lam Thuy Vo, "Another Ridiculous Number from the Patent Wars," *NPR Planet Money,* April 27, 2012, http://www.npr.org/blogs/money/2012/04/27/151357127/another-ridiculous-number-from-the-patent-wars.

36. Angus Johnston, "Still More Questions about Why Wikileaks Hasn't Trended on Twitter," *Student Activism*, December 5, 2010, http://studentactivism.net/2010/12/05/wikileaks-twi tter-3/.

37. Tarleton Gillespie, "Can an Algorithm Be Wrong? Twitter Trends, the Specter of Censorship, and Our Faith in the Algorithms around Us," *Social Media Collective,* October 19, 2011, http://socialmediacollective.org/2011/10/19/can-an-algorithm-be-wrong/.

38. Ibid.

39. Zeynep Tufekci, "Google Buzz: The Corporatization of Social Commons," *Technosociology,* February 17, 2010, http://technosociology.org/?p=102.

40. "From the New Deal to a New Century," Tennessee Valley Authority, http://www.tva.com /abouttva/history.htm (accessed June 14, 2013); Phillip F. Schewe, *The Grid* (Washington, DC: Joseph Henry Press, 2007), 101.

41. Harold Hotelling, "The General Welfare in Relation to Problems of Taxation and of Railway and Utility Rates," *Econometrica* 6(3) (July, 1938): 258.

42. Ibid.

43. Ibid.

44. Ibid.

45. Ibid., 258–59.

46. R. H. Coase, "The Marginal Cost Controversey," *Economica*, 13(51) (August 1946): 176.

47. "Rural Electrification Administration," Next New Deal, February 25, 2011, http://www .nextnewdeal.net/rural-electrification-administration.

48. "Tennessee Valley Authority," United States History, http://www.u-s-history.com/pages /h1653.html.

49. "Vote for Republican Congressmen," *Chicago Tribune*, November 4, 1934, 46.

50. David E. Nye, *Electrifying America: Social Meanings of a New Technology, 1880–1940* (Cambridge, MA: MIT Press, 1991), 317.

51. Ibid., 318.

52. Ibid., 320.

53. Ibid., 322.

54. Ronald C. Tobey, *Technology as Freedom: The New Deal and the Electrical Modernization of the American Home* (Berkeley: University of California Press, 1996), 6.

55. Nye, *Electrifying America,* 321.

56. "Path to Prosperity," SEIU, January 2009, 9–10, http://www.seiu.org/images/pdfs/Path_to _Prosperity.pdf.

57. "Rural Energy Savings Program: Frequently Asked Questions," *Assistant Democratic Leader,* http://assistantdemocraticleader.house.gov/index.cfm?a=Files.Serve&File_id=c77 509d5-0838-4371-bc47-d7e20f509375 (accessed October 28, 2013).

58. "Rural Electric," University of Wisconsin Center for Cooperatives, Research on the Economic Impact of Cooperatives, http://reic.uwcc.wisc.edu/electric/.

59. "Co-op Facts & Figures," National Rural Electric Cooperative Association, 2013, http:// www.nreca.coop/members/Co-opFacts/Pages/default.aspx.

60. Ibid.

61. "Cooperative Principles and Values," International Cooperative Alliance, 2011, http:// www.cdi.coop/icaprinciples.html.

62. Ibid.

63. "The Rochdale Principles," Rochdale Pioneers Museum, http://www.rochdalepioneersmu seum.coop/about-us/the-rochdale-principles.

64. "Cooperative Facts and Figures," International Cooperative Alliance, http://ica.coop/en /whats-co-op/co-operative-facts-figures (accessed September 4, 2013); "Cooperatives Around the World," 2012 International Year of Cooperatives, 2012, http://usa2012.coop /about-co-ops/cooperatives-around-world (accessed November 12, 2013).

65. Paul Hazen, "Remarks of Paul Hazen—White House Meeting, June 2, 2011," National Co-operative Business Association, June 2, 2011, http://www.ncba.coop/component/content/article/6-what-we-do/1087-remarks-of-paul-hazen-white-house-meeting-june-2-2011.

66. Joan Sanstadt, "Cooperatives Have Important Worldwide Role," *Agri-View*, October 11, 2012, http://www.agriview.com/news/regional/cooperatives-have-important-worldwide-role/article_09b0b020-13f1-11e2-ae03-001a4bcf887a.html.

67. Ibid.

68. "Welcome to Land O'Lakes, Inc.," Land O'Lakes Inc., 2011, http://www.landolakesinc.com/company/default.aspx (accessed June 19, 2013); "National Grape Cooperative," Welch's International, 2012, http://www.welchsinternational.com/resources/coop.shtml (accessed June 19, 2013).

69. "Profiles of a Movement: Co-operative Housing around the World," CECODHAS Housing Europe, April 2012, http://www.housingeurope.eu/issue/2577.

70. David Rodgers, "Housing Co-Operative: Some Comparative Statistics," Northern Ireland Co-operative Forum, May 9, 2012, nicoop-forum.co.uk/wp-content/ . . . /David-Rodgers -9th-May-20121.ppt.

71. "Profiles of a Movement."

72. Ibid.

73. Hans Groeneveld and August Sjauw-Koen-Fa, "Co-Operative Banks in the New Financial System," Rabobank Group, October 2009, http://www.globalcube.net/clients/eacb/content/medias/publications/external_studies/cb_financial_system_Rabobank_2009.pdf.

74. Giselle Weybrecht, "2012 International Year of Cooperatives and Management Educa-tion–Introduction (part 1)," *Prime Time*, November 27, 2012, http://primetime.unprme .org/2012/11/27/2012-international-year-of-cooperatives-and-management-education-int roduction-part-1/.

75. "International Co-operatives," *Year Book Australia*, 2012, http://www.abs.gov.au/ausstats /abs@.nsf/Lookup/by%20Subject/1301.0~2012~Main%20Features~International%20co -operatives~291.

76. "Statement for the Record of the House Financial Services Committee Hearing on Finan-cial Literacy and Education: The Effectiveness of Governmental and Private Sector Initia-tives," Credit Union National Association, April 15, 2008, http://ow.ly/mdE4I.

77. Catherine New, "Credit Union Deposits Outpaced Banks since WaMu Failure, Study," *Huffington Post*, August 2, 2012, http://www.huffingtonpost.com/2012/08/02/credit-uni on-deposits_n_1733448.html.

78. Credit Union Industry Assets Top $1 Trillion, National Credit Union Administration, March 2012, httpwww.ncua.govNewsPagesNW20120601AssetsTrillion.aspx (accessed November 13, 2013).

79. Clare Taylor, "Renewable Energy Cooperatives: Power to the People," *The Energy Collec-tive*, February 15, 2013, http://theenergycollective.com/claretaylor/186416/power-people -growth-renewable-energy-cooperatives.

80. Bernward Janzing, "Energy Cooperatives Are Booming in Germany," *DW*, July 6, 2012, http://www.dw.de/energy-cooperatives-are-booming-in-germany/a-16076317.

81. Jeevan Vasagar, "German Farmers Reap Benefits of Harvesting Renewable Energy," *Finan-cial Times*, December 2, 2013, http://www.ft.com/intl/cms/s/0/f2bc3958-58f4-11e3-9798 -00144feabdc0.html#axzz2nMj6ILk2 (accessed December 13, 2013).

82. Janzing, "Energy Cooperatives Are Booming in Germany."

83. "About Middelgrunden Wind Cooperative," Middelgrundens Vindmollelaug Windfarm, 2003, http://www.middelgrunden.dk/middelgrunden/?q=en/node/35.

84. Peter Jacob Jørgensen, "Samsø: A Renewable Energy Island," *PlanEnergi* (2007): 7, 50, http://sallan.org/pdf-docs/Samso.pdf.

85. Tildy Bayar, "Community Wind Arrives Stateside," *Renewable Energy World,* July 5, 2012, http://www.renewableenergyworld.com/rea/news/article/2012/07/community-wind-arrives-stateside.

86. Megan McKoy, "Tackling Climate Change: Renewing Innovation," *Rural Missouri,* May 2009, http://www.ruralmissouri.org/NRECAClimateChange/ClimateChange11.html.

87. Susan Kraemer, "Rural Electric Cooperative Completes $240 Million Wind Farm in 4 Months," *Clean Technica,* January 1, 2010, http://cleantechnica.com/2010/01/01/rural-electric-cooperative-completes-240-million-wind-farm-in-4-months/.

88. Ibid.

89. "Electric Cooperatives and Renewable Energy: Our Commitment to America," National Rural Electric Cooperative Association, March 2012, http://www.touchstoneenergy.com/about/Documents/RenewableEnergyBrochure.pdf.

90. Jakob Miller and Jens Rommel, "Is There a Future Role for Urban Electricity Cooperatives? A Case of Greenpeace Energy," University of Berlin, http://academia.edu/603390/IS_THERE_A_FUTURE_ROLE_FOR_URBAN_ELECTRICITY_COOPERATIVES_THE_CASE_OF_GREENPEACE_ENERGY.

91. "Facts at a Glance," Public Transportation Takes Us There, http://www.publictransportation.org/news/facts/Pages/default.aspx; "Statistics," International Association of Public Transport, http://www.uitp.org/knowledge/Statistics.cfm.

92. Benoit Montreuil, "Towards a Physical Internet: Meeting the Global Logistics Sustainability Grand Challenge," CIRRELT, January 2011, 2, https://www.cirrelt.ca/DocumentsTravail/CIRRELT-2011-03.pdf.

93. "Potential for Energy Efficiency Improvement beyond the Light-Duty-Vehicle Sector," Office of Energy Efficiency and Renewable Energy, February 2013, http://www.nrel.gov/docs/fy13osti/55637.pdf, 12, 13.

94. "Manufacturing and Trade Inventories and Sales—April 2013," *U.S. Census Bureau News,* June 13, 2013, http://www.census.gov/mtis/www/data/pdf/mtis_current.pdf.

95. Montreuil, "Towards a Physical Internet," 5.

96. Ibid., 2.

97. Ibid., 2.

98. "Path to Prosperity," SEIU, 4, http://www.seiu.org/images/pdfs/Path_to_Prosperity.pdf.

99. Montreuil, "Towards a Physical Internet," 2–5.

100. Ibid.

101. Ibid., 15.

102. Josie Garthwaite, "Smarter Trucking Saves Fuel over the Long Haul," *National Geographic,* September 23, 2011, http://news.nationalgeographic.com/news/energy/2011/09/110923-fuel-economy-for-trucks/.

CHAPTER 13

1. Amy Chozick, "As Young Lose Interest in Cars, G.M. Turns to MTV for Help," *New York Times,* March 22, 2012, http://www.nytimes.com/2012/03/23/business/media/to-draw-reluctant-young-buyers-gm-turns-to-mtv.html?pagewanted=all (accessed May 29, 2013).

2. Stephanie Steinberg and Bill Vlasic, "Car-Sharing Services Grow, and Expand Options," *New York Times,* January 25, 2013, http://www.nytimes.com/2013/01/26/business/car-sharing-services-grow-and-expand-options.html?_r=0 (accessed May 29, 2013).

3. "Growing Awareness of Peer-to-Peer Car Sharing Will Boost Car Sharing Rentals in Less Populated Areas in Europe, Says Frost & Sullivan," Frost & Sullivan, August 22, 2012, http://www.frost.com/ (accessed May 29, 2013); "Car Sharing—Driving the Way to a Greener Future, Says Frost & Sullivan," Frost & Sullivan, February 18, 2010, http://www

.frost.com/prod/servlet/press-release.pag?Src=RSS&docid=193331843 (accessed May 29, 2013); Danielle Sacks, "The Sharing Economy," *Fast Company*, May 2011, http://www.fastcompany.com/1747551/sharing-economy (accessed March 19, 2013).

4. Elliot Martin and Susan Shaheen, "The Impact of Carsharing on Household Vehicle Ownership," *ACCESS* 38 (Spring 2011): 24.

5. David Zhao, "Carsharing: A Sustainable and Innovative Personal Transport Solution with Great Potential and Huge Opportunities," Frost & Sullivan, January 28, 2010, https://www.frost.com/sublib/display-market-insight.do?id=190795176 (accessed May 29, 2013).

6. Elliot Martin and Susan Shaheen, "The Impact of Carsharing on Public Transit and Non-Motorized Travel: An Exploration of North American Carsharing Survey Data," *Energies* 4 (2011): 2094–2114.

7. Susan A. Shaheen et al., "Public Bikesharing in North America: Early Operator and User Understanding," Mineta Transportation Institute, June 2012, 1.

8. Susan A. Shaheen et al., "Bikesharing in Europe, the Americas, and Asia: Past, Present, and Future," *Transportation Research Record: Journal of the Transportation Research Board* 2143 (October 2010): 159–167.

9. Susan A. Shaheen et al., "Public Bikesharing in North America," 27.

10. Ibid., 16.

11. Anita Hamilton, "Will Car-Sharing Networks Change the Way We Travel?," *Time*, February 7, 2012, http://www.time.com/time/specials/packages/article/0,28804,2094921_2094 923_2106141,00.html (accessed May 29, 2013).

12. Adam Cohen, Susan Shaheen, and Ryan McKenzie, "Carsharing: A Guide for Local Planners," *PAS Memo* (2008), http://pubs.its.ucdavis.edu/download_pdf.php?id=1240 (accessed February 3, 2014).

13. "Autolib' Brings Intelligent Car-Sharing to the Streets of Paris and Suburbs," Microsoft News Center, February 12, 2013, http://www.microsoft.com/en-us/news/Features/2013 /Feb13/02-12autolib.aspx (accessed May 29, 2013).

14. Dave Zhao, "Carsharing: A Sustainable and Innovative Personal Transport Solution with Great Potential and Huge Opportunities," Frost and Sullivan, January 28, 2010, http://www.frost.com/prod/servlet/market-insight-print.pag?docid=190795176 (accessed November 12, 2013).

15. Jeff Cobb, "GM Partners on Ground Floor Opportunity with RelayRides Carsharing," GM-Volt.com, October 10, 2011, http://gm-volt.com/2011/10/10/gm-partners-on-ground -floor-opportunity-with-relayrides-carsharing/ (accessed May 29, 2013).

16. "GM Enters Carsharing Business; Teams Up with RelayRides," GM News, October 5, 2011, http://media.gm.com/media/us/en/gm/news.detail.html/content/Pages/news/us/en/2 011/Oct/1005_relay.html (accessed May 29, 2013).

17. Lawrence Burns, "A Vision of Our Transport Future," *Nature* 497 (May 9, 2013): 181–82.

18. Ibid.

19. Joann Muller, "With Driverless Cars, Once Again It Is California Leading the Way," *Forbes*, September 26, 2012, http://www.forbes.com/sites/joannmuller/2012/09/26/with -driverless-cars-once-again-it-is-california-leading-the-way/ (accessed June 2, 2013).

20. Chris Urmson, "The Self-Driving Car Logs More Miles on New Wheels," *Google Blog*, August 7, 2012, http://googleblog.blogspot.com/2012/08/the-self-driving-car-logs-more -miles-on.html (accessed June 2, 2013).

21. Mary Slosson, "Google Gets First Self-Driven Car License in Nevada," Reuters, May 8, 2012, http://www.reuters.com/article/2012/05/08/uk-usa-nevada-google-idUSLNE84701 320120508 (accessed June 3, 2013).

22. Alex Hudson, "Will Driverless Cars Mean Computer Crashes?," BBC News, October 1, 2012, http://news.bbc.co.uk/2/hi/programmes/9755210.stm (accessed June 2, 2013).

23. John Markoff, "Google Cars Drive Themselves, in Traffic," *New York Times*, October 9, 2010, http://www.nytimes.com/2010/10/10/science/10google.html?pagewanted=all&_r=0 (accessed June 2, 2013).

24. "2012 U.S. Automotive Emerging Technologies Study," J.D. Power and Associates, April 26, 2012, http://autos.jdpower.com/content/press-release/gGOwCnW/2012-u-s-automotive-emerging-technologies-study.htm (accessed June 3, 2013).

25. Jack Ewing, "A Benz with a Virtual Chauffeur," *New York Times*, May 16, 2013, http://www.nytimes.com/2013/05/19/automobiles/a-benz-with-a-virtual-chauffeur.html?pagewanted=all&_r=0 (accessed May 28, 2013).

26. Emi Kolawole, "A Win For Google's Driverless Car: Calif. Governor Signs a Bill Regulating Autonomous Vehicles," *Washington Post*, September 25, 2012, http://www.washingtonpost.com (accessed June 2, 2013).

27. Jeremy Rifkin, *The Age of Access: The New Culture of Hypercapitalism Where All of Life Is a Paid-For Experience* (New York: Tracher/Penguin, 2000), 6, 14.

28. Matthew Ruben, "Forgive Us Our Trespasses? The Rise of Consumer Debt in Modern America," *ProQuest*, February 2009, http://www.csa.com/discoveryguides/debt/review.php (accessed February 3, 2014).

29. Danielle Sacks, "The Sharing Economy," Fast Company, May 2011, http://www.fastcompany.com/1747551/sharing-economy (accessed November 12, 2013).

30. Rachel Botsman and Roo Rogers, *What's Mine Is Yours: The Rise of Collaborative Consumption* (New York: HarperCollins, 2010), xv–xvi.

31. Bruce Upbin, "Airbnb Could Have More Rooms than Hilton by 2012," *Forbes*, June 29, 2011, http://www.forbes.com/sites/bruceupbin/2011/06/29/airbnb-could-have-more-rooms-than-hilton-by-2012/ (accessed June 18, 2013).

32. "Airbnb at a Glance," https://www.airbnb.com/about (accessed June 18, 2013).

33. "Airbnb Global Growth," https://www.airbnb.com/global-growth (accessed June 18, 2013).

34. Andrew Cave, "Airbnb Plans to Be World's Largest Hotelier," *Telegraph*, November 16, 2013, http://www.telegraph.co.uk/finance/newsbysector/retailandconsumer/leisure/10454879/Airbnb-plans-to-be-worlds-larget-hotelier.html (accessed November 26, 2013).

35. "Couchsurfing: Statistics," Couchsurfing, 2013, https://www.couchsurfing.org/statistics (accessed June 19, 2013).

36. Cody Kittle, "Adventures in Couch Surfing: One Sojourner's Truth," *Time*, February 15, 2011, http://www.time.com/time/printout/0,8816,2045092,00.html# (accessed June 19, 2013).

37. "Couchsurfing: Sharing Your Life," Couchsurfing, 2013, https://www.couchsurfing.org/n/about (accessed June 19, 2013).

38. Cody Kittle, "Adventures in Couch Surfing."

39. "Couchsurfing: Statistics."

40. Katherine Boyle, "Why Buy that Dress, Movie, Car or Bike When You Can Rent?" *Washington Post*, March 4, 2012, http://articles.washingtonpost.com/2012-03-04/lifestyle/35449189_1_zipcar-rent-ties (accessed June 15, 2013).

41. "History and Background," The Freecycle Network, http://www.freecycle.org/about/background (accessed June 27, 2013).

42. Sarah Perez, "Kids' Clothing Consignment Service ThredUP Prepares to Take on Threadflip, Poshmark & More with Move into Women's Apparel," TechCrunch, February 20, 2013, http://techcrunch.com/2013/02/20/kids-clothing-consignment-service-thredup-prepares-to-take-on-threadflip-poshmark-more-with-move-into-womens-apparel/ (accessed June 18, 2013).

43. "ThredUP Jobs with Part-Time, Telecommuting, or Flexible Working," FlexJobs, http://www.flexjobs.com/jobs/telecommuting-jobs-at-thredup (accessed June 18, 2013).

44. Sarah Perez, "Kids' Clothing Consignment Service thredUP."

45. Benny Evangelista, "S.F.'s Yerdle: Sharing Not Shopping," *San Francisco Chronicle,* November 24, 2012, http://www.sfgate.com/technology/article/S-F-s-yerdle-sharing-not-sho pping-4063638.php (accessed June 18, 2013).

46. Neal Gorenflo, "How Big Retail Could Mainstream Collaborative Consumption Overnight," *Shareable,* June 6, 2012, http://www.shareable.net/blog/how-big-retail-could-main stream-collaborative-consumption-overnight (accessed June 19, 2013).

47. Ibid.

48. Ibid.

49. Ibid.

50. Alex Pasternack, "SharedEarth.com: A Landshare Grapevine Linking Gardeners with Gardens," TreeHugger, April 29, 2010, http://www.treehugger.com/green-food/sharedea rthcom-a-landshare-grapevine-linking-gardeners-with-gardens.html (accessed June 21, 2013).

51. Ibid.

52. Ibid.

53. Charlotte Howard, "The Temporary Calm," *Economist,* January 9, 2013, http://www .economist.com/blogs/democracyinamerica/2013/01/health-care-spending (accessed June 18, 2013).

54. Sarah Arnquist, "Research Trove: Patients' Online Data," *New York Times,* August 24, 2009, http://www.nytimes.com/2009/08/25/health/25web.html?pagewanted=all&_r=0 (accessed June 18, 2013).

55. Gilles J. Frydman, "Patient-Driven Research: Rich Opportunities and Real Risks," *Journal of Participatory Medicine* 1 (October 2009), http://www.medscape.com/viewarticle/71 3872 (accessed June 19, 2013).

56. Ibid.

57. Bruce Upton, "PatientsLikeMe is Building a Self-Learning Healthcare System," *Forbes,* March 1, 2013, http://www.forbes.com/sites/bruceupbin/2013/03/01/building-a-self-learn ing-healthcare-system-paul-wicks-of-patientslikeme/ (accessed June 19, 2013); Frydman, "Patient-Driven Research."

58. "PatientsLikeMe Social Network Refutes Published Clinical Trial," PatientsLikeMe, April 25, 2011, http://news.patientslikeme.com/press-release/patientslikeme-social-network-refu tes-published-clinical-trial (accessed June 20, 2013).

59. Ibid.

60. Frydman, "Patient-Driven Research."

61. "Wikipedians," Wikipedia, https://en.wikipedia.org/wiki/Wikipedia:Wikipedians (accessed June 18, 2013).

62. Dan Hoch and Tom Ferguson, "What I've Learned from E-Patients," *PLOS Medicine* 2(8) (2005), http://www.plosmedicine.org/article/info:doi/10.1371/journal.pmed.0020206 (accessed June 19, 2013).

63. Ibid.

64. Ibid.

65. "Vice President Biden Announces Availability of Nearly $1.2 Billion in Grants to Help Hospitals and Doctors Use Electronic Health Records," White House Statements and Releases, August 20, 2009, http://www.whitehouse.gov/the-press-office/vice-president -biden-announces-availability-nearly-12-billion-grants-help-hospitals (accessed June 20, 2013).

66. Tim Carmody, "Google and CDC Show US Flu Epidemic among Worst in a Decade," *Verge,* January 10, 2013, http://www.theverge.com/2013/1/10/3861538/google-cdc-show -us-flu-epidemic-among-worst-in-decade (accessed June 19, 2013).

67. Brooke Jarvis, "Twitter Becomes a Tool for Tracking Flu Epidemics and Other Public Health Issues," *Washington Post,* March 4, 2013, http://articles.washingtonpost.com/2013 -03-04/national/37429814_1_twitter-data-tweets-mark-dredze (accessed June 19, 2013).

68. Claire Barrett, "One Day It Will be Possible to 3-D-Print Human Heart," *Dezeen,* May 19, 2013, http://www.dezeen.com/2013/05/19/3d-printing-organs-medicine-print-shift/ (accessed July 12, 2013).

69. Scott Smith, "Coming Soon to a 3-D Printer near You: Human Tissue and Organs," *Quartz,* April 30, 2013, http://qz.com/78877/how-soon-will-we-be-able-to-3-d-print-entire-human -organs-sooner-than-you-think/ (accessed July 11, 2013).

70. Stuart Gray, "3-D Printing Creates Synthetic 'Tissue,'" ABC Science, April 5, 2013, http:// www.abc.net.au/science/articles/2013/04/05/3729985.htm (July 12, 2013).

71. Laura Ungar, "Researchers Closing in on Printing 3-D Hearts," *USA Today,* May 29, 2013, http://www.usatoday.com/story/tech/2013/05/29/health-3d-printing-organ-transpla nt/2370079/ (accessed July 11, 2013).

72. Mikayla Callen, "Scientists Advance 3-D Printing toward Fabrication of Living Tissues and Functional Organs," *Objective Standard,* May 9, 2013, http://www.theobjectivestan dard.com/blog/index.php/2013/05/scientists-advance-3d-printing-toward-fabrication-of -living-tissues-and-functional-organs/ (accessed July 11, 2013).

73. "The Text of President Bush's Address Tuesday Night, after Terrorist Attacks on New York and Washington," CNN, September 11, 2001, http://archives.cnn.com/2001/US/09/11/bush .speech.text.

74. "Magna Global Advertising Forecast 2013," *Magna Global,* http://news.magnaglobal .com/magna-global/press-releases/advertising-growth-2013.print.

75. Katherine A. MacKinnon, "User Generated Content vs. Advertising: Do Consumers Trust the Word of Others over Advertisers?" *Elon Journal of Undergraduate Research in Com- munications* 3 (Spring 2012): 14.

76. Myles Anderson, "Study: 72% of Consumers Trust Online Reviews as Much as Personal Rec- ommendations," *Search Engine Land,* March 12, 2012, http://searchengineland.com/study -72-of-consumers-trust-online-reviews-as-much-as-personal-recommendations-114152.

77. Kate Brown, "Review Websites: Is It a Genuine Review or Advertising in Disguise?," *Choice: The People's Watchdog,* January 23, 2013, http://www.choice.com.au/reviews-and -tests/money/shopping-and legal/shopping/review%20sites.aspx.

78. MacKinnon, "User Generated Content vs. Advertising."

79. Anderson, "Study: 72% of Consumers Trust Online Reviews."

80. "About," Consumr: The People's Product Guide, http://www.consumr.com/about (ac- cessed November 4, 2013); "GoodGuide Delivered to Your Phone," *GoodGuide,* 2011, http://www.goodguide.com/about/mobile (accessed June 19, 2013).

81. MacKinnon, "User Generated Content vs. Advertising," 18.

82. Michael Learmonth, "As Fake Reviews Rise, Yelp, Others Crack Down on Fraudsters," *Advertising Age,* October 30, 2012, http://adage.com/article/digital/fake-reviews-rise-yelp -crack-fraudsters/237486/.

83. "Craigslist Factsheet," Craigslist, updated March 27, 2013, http://www.craigslist.org/abo ut/factsheet.

84. Jeff Jarvis, "When Innovation Yields Efficiency," *BuzzMachine,* June 12, 2009, http://bu zzmachine.com/2009/06/12/when-innovation-yields-efficiency/.

85. "Craigslist Factsheet."

86. Saul J. Berman, Bill Battino, Louisa Shipnuck, and Andreas Neus, "The End of Advertis- ing as We Know It," IBM Global Business Services, 2007, 8, http://www-05.ibm.com/de /media/downloads/end-of-advertising.pdf.

87. Eric Clemons, "Why Advertising Is Failing on the Internet," *Tech Crunch,* March 22, 2009, http://techcrunch.com/2009/03/22/why-advertising-is-failing-on-the-internet/.

88. Ibid.

89. "The End of the Free Lunch—Again," *Economist,* March 19, 2009, http://www.econo mist.com/node/13326158.

90. "Magna Global Advertising Forecast 2013"; "IAB Internet Advertising Revenue Report—2012 Full Year Results," PricewaterhouseCoopers, April 2013, http://www.iab.net /media/file/IAB_PWC_Internet_Advertising_Revenue_Report_FY_2012_Apr_16_2013 .pdf

91. Ki Mae Heussner, "Internet Advertising Still a Growth Business, but Pace Slows," *Gigaom,* October 11, 2012, http://gigaom.com/2012/10/11/internet-advertising-still-a-gro wth-business-but-pace-slows/.

92. Claire Cain Miller, "Google Grapples with Mobile," *International New York Times,* October 19–20, 2013, 14.

93. Ibid.

94. "National Study Quantifies the 'Sharing Economy' Movement," *PRNewswire,* February 8, 2012, http://www.prnewswire.com/news-releases/national-study-quantifies-the-sharing-e conomy-movement-138949069.html (accessed March 19, 2013).

95. Neal Gorenflo, "The New Sharing Economy," *Shareable,* December 24, 2010, http://www .shareable.net/blog/the-new-sharing-economy (accessed March 19, 2013).

96. Bryan Walsh, "10 Ideas that Will Change the World: Today's Smart Choice: Don't Own. Share," *Time,* March 17, 2011, http://www.time.com/time/specials/packages/article/0,28 804,2059521_2059717,00.html (accessed March 19, 2013).

97. Danielle Sacks, "The Sharing Economy," *Fast Company,* April 18, 2011, http://www.fast company.com/1747551/sharing-economy (accessed March 19, 2013).

98. Bob Van Voris, "Apple Battles E-Books Pricing Claims in Antitrust Trial," *Bloomberg,* June 3, 2012, http://www.bloomberg.com/news/2013-06-03/apple-to-fight-e-books-pric ing-claims-in-antitrust-trial.html (accessed June 4, 2013).

99. Geert De Clercq, "Renewables Turn Utilities into Dinosaurs of the Energy World," Reuters, March 8, 2013, http://www.reuters.com/article/2013/03/08/us-utilities-threat-idUS BRE92709E20130308 (accessed August 30, 2013).

CHAPTER 14

1. Matthew Ericson, Elaine He, and Amy Schoenfeld, "Tracking the $700 Billion Bailout," *New York Times,* June 19, 2009, http://www.nytimes.com/packages/html/national /200904_CREDITCRISIS/recipients.html (accessed March 29, 2013).

2. "Peer-to-Peer Lending: How Zopa Works," Zopa, http://uk.zopa.com/about-zopa/peer-to -peer-lending (accessed June 11, 2013).

3. David Bornstein, "Crowdfunding Clean Energy," *New York Times,* March 6, 2013, http:// opinionator.blogs.nytimes.com/2013/03/06/crowd-funding-clean-energy/ (accessed March 6, 2013).

4. "Amazon Payment Fees," Amazon, http://www.kickstarter.com/help/amazon (accessed June 11, 2013); "What Is Kickstarter?" Kickstarter, http://www.kickstarter.com/hello?ref =nav (accessed June 11, 2013).

5. "What Is Kickstarter?"

6. "Re-imagining US Solar Financing," Bloomberg New Energy Finance (June 4, 2012) from David Bornstein, "Crowdfunding Clean Energy," *New York Times* Opinion Pages, March 6, 2013, http://opinionator.blogs.nytimes.com/2013/03/06/crowd-funding-clean -energy/?_r=0 (accessed November 8, 2013).

7. Ibid.

8. Ibid.

9. Geert De Clercq, "Analysis: Renewables Turn Utilities into Dinosaurs of the Energy World," Reuters, March 8, 2013, http://www.reuters.com/article/2013/03/08/us-utilities-threat-idUSBRE92709E20130308 (accessed March 8, 2013).

10. Deborah L. Jacobs, "The Trouble with Crowdfunding," Forbes, April 17, 2013, http://www.forbes.com/sites/deborahljacobs/2013/04/17/the-trouble-with-crowdfunding/ (accessed April 18, 2013).

11. "Manipulating Peer2Peer Marketplaces: Controlling What You Aren't Supposed to Control," TaskUs, November 1, 2012, https://www.taskus.com/white_paper/manipulating-peer2peer-marketplaces-controlling-arent-supposed-control/ (accessed July 8, 2013).

12. Jenna Wortham, "Trading in Your Old Web Threads in the Web," New York Times, October 9 2009, http://bits.blogs.nytimes.com/2009/10/09/tradin-in-your-old-threads-on-the-web/ (accessed May 28, 2013).

13. "FAQ," TrustCloud, https://trustcloud.com/faq (accessed June 11, 2013).

14. Rachel Botsman and Roo Rogers, What's Mine Is Yours: The Rise of Collaborative Consumption (New York: HarperCollins, 2010), 179.

15. Cait Poynor Lamberton and Randall L. Rose, "When Is Ours Better than Mine? A Framework for Understanding and Altering Participation in Commercial Sharing Systems," Journal of Marketing 76(4) (July 1, 2012): 109–25.

16. "Who is the FDIC?," Federal Deposit Insurance Corporation, January 18, 2013, http://fdic.gov/about/learn/symbol/ (accessed June 27, 2013).

17. Ben Block, "Local Currencies Grow During Economic Recession," Worldwide Institute, January 8, 2009, http://www.worldwatch.org/node/5978 (accessed June 4, 2013).

18. Edgar Cahn, "Time Banking: An Idea Whose Time Has Come?," Yes Magazine, November 17, 2011, http://www.yesmagazine.org/new-economy/time-banking-an-idea-whose-time-has-come (accessed November 13, 2013).

19. Eric Garland, "The Next Money: As the Big Economies Falter, Micro-currencies Rise," Atlantic, May 16, 2012, http://www.theatlantic.com/international/archive/2012/05/the-next-money-as-the-big-economies-falter-micro-currencies-rise/257216/ (accessed June 4, 2013).

20. Anthony Migchels, "The Swiss WIR, or: How to Defeat the Money Power," Real Currencies, April 19, 2012, http://realcurrencies.wordpress.com/2012/04/19/the-swiss-wir-or-how-to-defeat-the-money-power/ (accessed November 13, 2013).

21. "US Community Uses Local Currency to Weather Financial Storms," Voice of America, November 6, 2011, http://www.voanews.com/content/us-community-uses-local-currency-to-weather-financial-storms-133374073/163272.html (accessed June 4, 2013).

22. Douglas Rushkoff, "Life Dollars: Finding Currency in Community," Futurist, September–October 2010, http://www.wfs.org/content/life-dollars-finding-currency-community (accessed June 5, 2013).

23. "US Community Uses Local Currency to Weather Financial Storms," VOAvideo, 2:31, November 7, 2011, http://www.youtube.com/watch?v=KRID85f-dmQ (accessed June 4, 2013).

24. Helena Smith, "Euros Discarded as Impoverished Greeks Resort to Bartering," Guardian, January 2, 2013, http://www.guardian.co.uk/world/2013/jan/02/euro-greece-barter-poverty-crisis (accessed January 3, 2013); Ariana Eunjung Cha, "Spain's Crisis Spawns Alternative Economy that Doesn't Rely on the Euro," Guardian, September 4, 2012, http://www.guardian.co.uk/world/2012/sep/04/spain-euro-free-economy (accessed June 4, 2013).

25. Saabira Chaudhuri, "Bitcoin Price Hits New Record High," Wall Street Journal, November 13, 2013, http://online.wsj.com/news/articles/SB10001424052702303789604579195773841529160 (accessed November 13, 2013).

26. Garland, "The Next Money."

27. Ibid.

28. Judith D. Schwartz, "Alternative Currencies Grow in Popularity," *Time*, December 14, 2008, http://www.time.com/time/business/article/0,8599,1865467,00.html (accessed June 5, 2013).

29. Hugo Martin, "Outdoor Retailer Patagonia Puts Environment Ahead of Sales Growth," *Los Angeles Times*, May 24, 2012, http://articles.latimes.com/2012/may/24/business/la-fi -patagonia-20120525 (accessed February 27, 2013).

30. "What are B Corps?—Legislation," B Corporation, April 18, 2013, http://www.bcorpora tion.net/what-are-b-corps/legislation (accessed April 18, 2013).

31. John Elkington, "From the Triple Bottom Line to Zero," JohnElkington.com, http://www .johnelkington.com/activities/ideas.asp (accessed March 4, 2013).

32. Eleanor Shaw and Sara Carter, "Social Entrepreneurship: Theoretical Antecedents and Empirical Analysis of Entrepreneurial Processes and Outcomes," *Journal of Small Business and Enterprise Development* 14(3) (2007): 418–34, http://www.emeraldinsight.com /journals.htm?articleid=1621426&show=abstract (accessed May 3, 2013).

33. "Capital Markets with a Conscious," *Economist*, September 1, 2009, http://www.econo mist.com/node/14347606 (accessed May 3, 2013).

34. "L3Cs—A Hybrid Low Profit Business Entity," Nolo, s.v., http://www.nolo.com/legal-en cyclopedia/l3cs-a-hybrid-low-profit-business-entity.html (accessed May 3, 2013).

35. "Elective Curriculum: Course Descriptions," Harvard Business School, http://www.hbs .edu/coursecatalog/; "Introduction to Social Entrepreneurship," Harvard Law School, http://www.law.harvard.edu/academics/curriculum/catalog/index.html?o=64904 (accessed November 14, 2013).

36. Kate Koch, "The Business of Changing the World," *Harvard Gazette*, February 27, 2012, http://news.harvard.edu/gazette/story/2012/02/the-business-of-world-changing/ (accessed May 3, 2013).

37. "Ashoka: Frequently Asked Questions," Ashoka, https://www.ashoka.org/facts (accessed May 3, 2013); "Ashoka: About Us," Ashoka, https://www.ashoka.org/about (accessed November 13, 2013).

38. "Skoll Foundation: About," Skoll Foundation, www.skollfoundation.org/about/ (accessed May 3, 2013).

39. Ben Thornley, "Facts on U.S. Social Enterprise," *Huffington Post*, November 8, 2012, http://www.huffingtonpost.com/ben-thornley/social-enterprise_b_2090144.html (accessed May 4, 2013).

40. Mark Gould, "Taking Social Enterprise to New Heights," *Guardian*, January 26, 2010, http://www.guardian.co.uk/society/2010/jan/27/peter-holbrook-social-enterprise-coali tion (accessed May 4, 2013).

41. Jo Barraket, Nick Collyer, Matt O'Connor and Heather Anderson, "Finding Australia's Social Enterprise Sector: Final Report," FASES, June 2010, http://www.socialtraders.com .au/finding-australias-social-enterprise-sector-fases-final-report (accessed May 4, 2013).

42. Lester Salamon, "Putting the Civil Society Sector on the Economic Map of the World," *Annals of Public and Cooperative Economics* 81(2) (June 2010): 187–88, http://ccss.jhu.edu /wp-content/uploads/downloads/2011/10/Annals-June-2010.pdf (accessed May 3, 2013).

43. Ibid.

CHAPTER 15

1. Catherine Brahic, "Americans Must Diet to Save Their Economy," *ABC News*, July 25, 2008, http://abcnews.go.com/Technology/story?id=5443470&page=1#.Ua3tYkDqkb0 (accessed June 3, 2013).

2. "Preventing Micronutrient Malnutrition: A Guide to Food-based Approaches," FAO, 1997, http://www.fao.org/docrep/x0245e/x0245e01.htm (accessed November 13, 2013).

3. "How to Feed the World in 2050," UN Food and Agriculture Organization, June 2009, 2, ftp://ftp.fao.org/docrep/fao/012/ak542e/ak542e00.pdf (accessed June 14, 2013).

4. Brahic, "Americans Must Diet to Save Their Economy."

5. Paul R. Ehrlich and Anne H. Ehrlich, "Can a Collapse of Global Civilization Be Avoided?" *Proceedings of the Royal Society B: Biological Sciences* 280 (2013): 2, http://rspb.royal societypublishing.org/content/280/1754/20122845.full.pdf+html (accessed February 8, 2013); Monique Gruten, et al., "Living Planet Report 2012: Biodiversity, Biocapacity, and Better Choices," World Wildlife Fund, 2012, 6, http://awsassets.panda.org/downloads/1_lpr _2012_online_full_size_single_pages_final_120516.pdf (accessed January 17, 2013).

6. Pyarelal, *Mahatma Gandhi*, vol. 10: *The Last Phase*, part 2 (Ahmedabad, India: Navaji-van, 1956), 552.

7. "Ecological Footprint Accounting and Methodology," Global Footprint Network, http://www.footprintnetwork.org/images/uploads/Part_III_Technical_Document.pdf (accessed June 10, 2013).

8. Michael Borucke et al., "National Footprints Accounts, 2011 Edition," Global Footprint Network, 2011, 5, http://www.footprintnetwork.org/images/uploads/NFA_2011_Edition .pdf (accessed June 10, 2013); Tim Radford, "How Many People Can the Earth Support?," *Guardian*, November 11, 2004, http://www.guardian.co.uk/science/2004/nov/11 /thisweekssciencequestions1 (accessed June 4, 2013).

9. Brad Ewing, David Moore, Steven Goldfinger, Anna Oursler, Anders Reed, and Mathis Wackernagel, "Ecological Footprint Atlas 2010," Global Footprint Network, October 13, 2010, http://www.footprintnetwork.org/en/index.php/GFN/page/ecological_footprint_at las_2010 (accessed June 10, 2013).

10. Lester R. Brown, "Improving Food Security by Strategically Reducing Grain Demand," Earth Policy Institute, November 9, 2010, http://www.earth-policy.org/book_bytes/2010 /pb4ch09_ss6 (accessed June 19, 2013); Mary Vanderkooi, M.D., *Village Medical Manual: A Layman's Guide to Healthcare in Developing Countries*, vol. 1 (Pasadena, CA: William Carey Library, 2000), 39.

11. Anup Shah, "Poverty Facts and Stats," *Global Issues,* January 7, 2013, http://www.global issues.org/article/26/poverty-facts-and-stats (accessed January 23, 2013).

12. Tim Kasser, *The High Price of Materialism* (Chester, NJ: Bradford Book, 2002), 5, 14.

13. Alison Grant, "Money = Happiness? That's Rich," *Sun Herald,* January 8, 2005, http://www.unlimitedloveinstitute.org/news/pdf/money_and_happiness.pdf (accessed March 21, 2013).

14. Richard Layard, *Happiness: Lessons from a New Science* (New York: Penguin Press, 2006), 29–30.

15. Peter A. Corning, "The Fair Society: It's Time to Re-Write the Social Contract," *Seattle Journal for Social Justice* 11(1) (July 2012): 205, http://digitalcommons.law.seattleu.edu /sjsj/vol11/iss1/17/ (accessed May 4, 2013).

16. Robert D. Putnam, *Bowling Alone: The Collapse and Revival of American Community* (New York: Simon and Schuster, 2001), 140.

17. William James, *The Principles of Psychology*, vol. 1 (New York: Henry Holt, 1890), 291, 327.

18. Juliet B. Schor, *Born to Buy: The Commercialized Child and the New Consumer Culture* (New York: Scribner, 2004), 31.

19. Ibid., 37.

20. Diane Swanbrow, "Empathy: College Students Don't Have as Much as They Used To," University of Michigan News Service, May 27, 2010, http://ns.umich.edu/new/releases/7724 (accessed April 2, 2013).

21. Swanbrow, "Empathy"; Sara H. Konrath, Edward H. O'Brien, and Courtney Hsing, "Changes in Dispositional Empathy in American College Students over Time: A Meta-Analysis," *Personality and Social Psychology Review* 5(2) (2011): 180–81, http://www .sitemaker.umich.edu/eob/files/konrathetal2011.pdf (accessed April 2, 2013).

22. Morley Winograd and Michael D. Hais, *Millenial Makeover: MySpace, YouTube, and the Future of American Politics* (Piscataway, NJ: Rutgers University Press, 2008), 5.

23. Kelsey Sheehy, "10 Colleges Where the Most Students Study Abroad," *U.S. News and World Report*, February, 26, 2013, http://www.usnews.com/education/best-colleges/the -short-list-college/articles/2013/02/26/10-colleges-where-the-most-students-study-abroad (accessed February 26, 2013); Judi Lerman et al., "Millennials' Attitudes toward Immigrants and Immigration Policies," *The Opportunity Agenda*, 2011, 13–14, http://opportu nityagenda.org/millennials_attitudes_immigrants (accessed March 14, 2013).

24. Emily Esfahani Smith and Jennifer L. Aaker, "Millenial Searchers," *New York Times*, December 1, 2013.

25. Ibid.

26. Ibid.

27. Kennon M. Sheldon and Holly A. McGregor, "Extrinsic Value Orientation and the Tragedy of the Commons," *Journal of Personality* 68(2) (2000): 383–411, http://web.missouri .edu/~sheldonk/pdfarticles/JP00trag.pdf (accessed June 16, 2013).

28. David Madland and Ruy Teixeira, "New Progressive America: The Millennial Generation," Center for American Progress, May 13, 2009, http://www.americanprogress.org /issues/progressive-movement/report/2009/05/13/6133/new-progressive-america-the-mil lennial-generation/ (accessed March 14, 2013).

29. Ibid.

30. Ronald Lee, "The Demographic Transition: Three Centuries of Fundamental Change," *Journal of Economic Perspectives* 17(4) (Fall 2003): 167–90.

31. "Kandeh K. Yumkella and Jeremy Rifkin Speaking about the Third Industrial Revolution," UNIDO video, 3:27, November 29, 2011, http://www.youtube.com/watch?v=wJYu MTKG8bc (accessed June 6, 2013).

32. Geoffrey Mohan, "Carbon Dioxide Levels in Atmosphere Pass 400 Milestone, Again," *Los Angeles Times*, May 20, 2013, http://www.latimes.com/news/science/sciencenow/la-sci -sn-carbon-dioxide-400-20130520,0,7130588.story (accessed May 21, 2013); "Why Are Humans Responsible for Global Warming?," Environmental Defense Fund, 2013, http:// www.edf.org/climate/human-activity-causes-warming (accessed May 21, 2013).

33. "Climate Change Indicators in the United States: Atmospheric Concentrations of Greenhouse Gases," U.S. Environmental Protection Agency, June 13, 2013, http://www.epa.gov /climatechange/science/indicators/ghg/ghg-concentrations.html (accessed June 27, 2013).

34. Susan Joy Hassol, "Emissions Reductions Needed to Stabilize Climate," *Climate Communication* (2011): 1, 4, http://www.climatecommunication.org/wp-content/uploads/2011/08 /presidentialaction.pdf (accessed June 28, 2013).

35. Ibid., 2.

36. Kevin E. Trenberth, "Changes in Precipitation with Climate Change," *Climate Research* 47 (March 2011): 123, http://nldr.library.ucar.edu/repository/assets/osgc/OSGC-000-000 -000-596.pdf (accessed June 27, 2013).

37. Julia Whitty, "Gone: Mass Extinction and the Hazards of Earth's Vanishing Biodiversity," *Mother Jones*, May/June 2007, http://www.motherjones.com/environment/2007/05/gone (accessed May 3, 2013).

38. James Hansen et al., "Target Atmospheric CO_2: Where Should Humanity Aim?," *Open Atmospheric Science Journal* 2 (2008): 217, http://pubs.giss.nasa.gov/docs/2008/2008_Han sen_etal.pdf (accessed June 25, 2013).

39. Bruce Campbell, "Serious About Climate Change? Talk About Agriculture," CNN, November 21, 2013, http://globalpublicsquare.blogs.cnn.com/2013/11/21/serious-about-climate-change-talk-about-agriculture/ (accessed November 25, 2013).

40. Erica Rex, "Catastrophic European Floods Raise Climate Concerns," *Environment & Energy Publishing*, June 10, 2013, http://www.eenews.net/stories/1059982544/ (accessed June 11, 2013).

41. Laura Stevens, "Flooded Europe Towns Brace for New Recovery," *Wall Street Journal*, June 9, 2013, http://online.wsj.com/article/SB10001424127887324904004578535492504355754.html (accessed June 11, 2013).

42. Erica Rex, "Catastrophic European Floods Raise Climate Concerns," Environment & Energy Publishing, June 10, 2013, http://www.eenews.net/stories/1059982544/ (accessed June 11, 2013).

43. Gary Paul Nabham, "Our Coming Food Crisis," *New York Times*, July 21, 2013, http://www.nytimes.com/2013/07/22/opinion/our-coming-food-crisis.html?_r=0 (accessed November 25, 2013).

44. Brad Plumer, "What We Know About Climate Change and Drought," *Washington Post*, July 24, 2012, http://www.washingtonpost.com/blogs/wonkblog/wp/2012/07/24/what-we-know-about-climate-change-and-drought/ (accessed November 25, 2013).

45. Justin Sheffield, Julio E. Herrera-Estrada, Kelly Caylor, and Eric F. Wood, "Drought, Climate Change and Potential Agricultural Productivity," NASA, http://www.nasa.gov/pdf/607932main_sheffield_et_al_drought_press_conf.pdf (accessed November 25, 2013).

46. "Impact of Climate Change on Agriculture—Fact Sheet on Asia," International Food Policy Research Institute, 2009, http://www.ifpri.org/publication/impact-climate-change-agriculture-factsheet-asia (accessed February 27, 2013); Lenny Bernstein, Peter Bosch, Osvaldo Canziani, et al., "Climate Change 2007: Synthesis Report," Intergovernmental Panel on Climate Change, November 12, 2007, 20–21, http://www.ipcc.ch/pdf/assessment-report/ar4/syr/ar4_syr_spm.pdf (accessed March 3, 2013).

47. "Impact of Climate Change on Agriculture—Fact Sheet on Sub-Saharan Africa," International Food Policy Research Institute, 2009, http://www.ifpri.org/publication/impact-climate-change-agriculture-factsheet-sub-saharan-africa (accessed February 27, 2013).

48. "Impact of Climate Change on Agriculture—Fact Sheet on Middle East and North Africa," International Food Policy Research Institute, 2009, http://www.ifpri.org/publication/impact-climate-change-agriculture-factsheet-middle-east-and-north-africa (accessed February 27, 2013).

49. "Impact of Climate Change on Agriculture—Fact Sheet on Latin America and the Caribbean," International Food Policy Research Institute, 2009, http://www.ifpri.org/publication/impact-climate-change-agriculture-factsheet-latin-america-and-caribbean (accessed February 27, 2013).

50. Wolfram Schlenker and Michael J. Roberts, "Nonlinear Temperature Effects Indicate Severe Damages to U.S. Crop Yields Under Climate Change," *Proceedings of the National Academy of Sciences of the United States of America* 106(37) (September 15, 2009), http://www.ncbi.nlm.nih.gov/pmc/articles/PMC2747166/ (accessed July 22, 2013).

51. Andy Newman, "Hurricane Sandy vs. Hurricane Katrina," *New York Times,* November 27, 2012, http://cityroom.blogs.nytimes.com/2012/11/27/hurricane-sandy-vs-hurricane-katrina/ (accessed June 11, 2013).

52. Ibid.

53. "Status of the Nuclear Reactors at the Fukushima Daiichi Power Plant," *New York Times,* April 29, 2011, http://www.nytimes.com/interactive/2011/03/16/world/asia/reactors-status.html (accessed June 22, 2013); Mitsuru Obe, "Japan Finds Radiation Spread over a Wide

Area," *Wall Street Journal,* August 31, 2011, http://online.wsj.com/article/SB1000142405
3111904332804576540131142824362.html (accessed June 22, 2013).

54. "Transport, Infrastructure, and Building Russia: Vulnerabilities—Pipelines," Centre for
Climate Adaption, http://www.climateadaptation.eu/russia/transport-infrastructure-and
-building/ (accessed May 23, 2013).

55. Dirk Rubbelke and Stefan Vogele, "Impacts of Climate Change on European Critical Infrastructures: The Case of the Power Sector," *Environmental Science and Policy* 14(1) (2011);
Anita Elash, "Heat Spells Trouble for France's Nuclear Reactors," NPR, August 21, 2007,
http://www.npr.org/templates/story/story.php?storyId=13818689 (accessed February 2,
2013).

56. "Six Sources of Energy—One Energy System," Vattenfall, 2013, http://www.vattenfall
.com/en/file/Nuclear_power-ENG.pdf_16469558.pdf (accessed November 14, 2013).

57. "New York Subway Repairs Border 'on the Edge of Magic,'" *New York Times,* November
8, 2012, http://www.nytimes.com/2012/11/09/nyregion/new-york-subways-find-magic-in
-speedy-hurricane-recovery.html?pagewanted=all (accessed June 11, 2013).

58. "Infrastructure, Engineering and Climate Change Adaptation—ensuring services in an un-
certain future," Engineering the Future (London: Royal Academy of Engineering, 2011),
21, https://www.gov.uk/government/publications/infrastructure-engineering-and-climate
-change-adaptation-ensuring-services-in-an-uncertain-future (accessed June 27, 2013).

59. James Neumann, "Adaptation to Climate Change: Revisiting Infrastructure Norms,"
Resources for the Future Issue Brief 09-15 (December 2009): 4, http://www.rff.org/RFF
/Documents/RFF-IB-09-15.pdf (accessed November 14, 2013).

60. Choe Sang-Hun, "Computer Networks in South Korea Are Paralyzed in Cyberattacks,"
New York Times, March 20, 2013, http://www.nytimes.com/2013/03/21/world/asia/so
uth-korea-computer-network-crashes.html (accessed March 21, 2013); Siobhan Gorman,
"Electricity Grid in U.S. Penetrated by Spies," *Wall Street Journal,* April 8, 2009, http://
online.wsj.com/article/SB123914805204099085.html (accessed March 21, 2013).

61. James A. Lewis, "Assessing the Risks of Cyber Terrorism, Cyber War, and Other Cyber
Threats," Center for Strategic and International Studies, 2002, 1, http://csis.org/files/media
/csis/pubs/021101_risks_of_cyberterror.pdf (June 15, 2013).

62. Nicole Perlroth and David E. Sanger, "Cyberattacks Seem Meant to Destroy, Not Just
Disrupt," *New York Times,* March 28, 2013, http://www.nytimes.com/2013/03/29/tech
nology/corporate-cyberattackers-possibly-state-backed-now-seek-to-destroy-data.html?pa
gewanted=all&_r=0 (accessed March 29, 2013).

63. Jamie Miyazaki, "Power Up on Smart Grid Cyber Security," *Wall Street Journal,* February 25, 2010, http://blogs.wsj.com/source/2010/02/25/power-up-on-smart-grid-cyber
-security/ (accessed July 16, 2013); "Global Cybersecurity Market to Reach $61 Billion
This Year," *Infosecurity,* January 30, 2012, http://www.infosecurity-magazine.com/view
/23548/ (accessed July 16, 2013).

64. "Report of the Commission to Assess the Threat to the United States from Electromagnetic
Pulse (EMP) Attack," EMP Commission, April 2008, vii, http://www.empcommission
.org/docs/A2473-EMP_Commission-7MB.pdf (accessed February 3, 2014).

65. Ibid.

66. Stew Magnuson, "Feds Fear Coordinated Physical, Cyber-Attacks on Electrical Grids," *National Defense,* September 2012, http://www.nationaldefensemagazine.org/archive/2012
/september/Pages/FedsFearCoordinatedPhysical,Cyber-AttacksonElectricalGrids.aspx
(accessed July 16, 2013).

67. "Cybersecurity," *Congressional Record* 158, no. 103 (July 11, 2012): 7, http://www.fas
.org/irp/congress/2012_cr/whitehouse-cyber2.html (accessed July 16, 2013).

68. Matthew L. Wald, "A Drill to Replace Crucial Transformers (Not the Hollywood Kind),"
New York Times, March 14, 2012, http://www.nytimes.com/2012/03/15/business/energy

-environment/electric-industry-runs-transformer-replacement-test.html (accessed July 16, 2013).

69. Matthew L. Wald, "Terrorist Attack on Power Grid Could Cause Broad Hardship, Report Says," *New York Times,* November 14, 2012, http://www.nytimes.com/2012/11/15/science /earth/electric-industry-is-urged-to-gird-against-terrorist-attacks.html?_r=0 (accessed July 16, 2013).

70. April Mara Major, "Norm Origin and Development in Cyberspace: Models of Cybernorm Evolution," *Washington University Law Review* 78(1) (2000):78–79; "Paul Baran and the Origins of the Internet," RAND Corporation, 2013, http://www.rand.org/about/history /baran.html (accessed November 14, 2013).

71. Diane Cardwell, "Solar Companies Seek Ways to Build an Oasis of Electricity," *New York Times,* November 19, 2012, http://www.nytimes.com/2012/11/20/business/energy -environment/solar-power-as-solution-for-storm-darkened-homes.html (accessed February 2, 2013).

72. "SPIDERS Microgrid Project Secures Military Installations," Sandia National Laboratories, February 22, 2012, https://share.sandia.gov/news/resources/news_releases/spiders/ (accessed May 29, 2013).

CHAPTER 16

1. Robin Dunbar, *Grooming, Gossip, and the Evolution of Language* (Cambridge, MA: Harvard University Press, 1998), 70.

2. Roger B. Beck et al., *World History: Patterns of Interaction* (Boston: McDougal Littell, 2006), 27, http://www.ltisdschools.org/cms/lib/TX21000349/Centricity/Domain/287/Cha pter2.pdf (accessed November 6, 2013).

3. Georg Wilhelm Friedrich Hegel, *Lectures on the Philosophy of World History* (Cambridge: Cambridge University Press, 1975), 79.

AFTERWORD

1. Adam Smith, *An Inquiry Into the Nature and Causes of the Wealth of Nations* (London: W. Strahan and T. Cadell, 1776).

2. Toby Elwin, "The Cost of Culture, a 50% Turnover of the Fortune 500," Toby Elwin, February 4, 2010, http://www.tobyelwin.com/the-cost-of-culture-a-50-turnover-of-the-fortu ne-500/ (accessed November 6, 2013).

BIBLIOGRAPHY

Adams, Richard Newbold. *Energy and Structure: A Theory of Social Power.* Austin: University of Texas Press, 1924.

Anderson, Benedict. *Imagined Communities: Reflections on the Origin and Spread of Nationalism.* London: Verso, 1983.

Anderson, Chris. *Free: How Today's Smartest Businesses Profit By Giving Something For Nothing.* New York: Hyperion, 2009.

——. *Makers.* London: Random House, 2012.

Anderson, Robert. *Fundamentals of the Petroleum Industry.* Norman: University of Oklahoma Press, 1984.

Anielski, Mark. *The Economics of Happiness.* Gabriola Island BC,CA: New Society Publishers, 2007.

Appleby, Joyce. *The Relentless Revolution.* New York: W.W. Norton, 2010.

Aries, Philippe. *The Hour of Our Death.* New York: Oxford University Press, 1981.

Axelrod, Robert. *The Evolution of Cooperation.* New York: Basic Books, 1984.

Ayres, Robert and Edward Ayres. *Crossing The Energy Divide.* Upper Saddle River, NJ: Wharton School Publishing, 2010.

Ayres, Robert and Benjamin Warr. *The Economic Growth Engine: How Energy and Work Drive Material Prosperity.* Laxenburg: The International Institute for Applied Systems Analysis,. Oct 31, 2010)

Bakan, Joel. *The Corporation: The Pathological Pursuit of Profit and Power.* New York: Free Press, 2004.

Banks, James A. and Cherry A. McGee Banks, eds. *Multicultural Education: Issues and Perspectives.* 6th ed. Hoboken, NJ: John Wiley & Sons, 2007.

Barlow, Maude and Clarke Tony. *Blue Gold.* New York: The New Press, 2002.

Barnes, Peter. *Who Owns The Sky?* Washington, DC: Island Press, 2001.

Belgin, Stephen and Bernard Lietaer. *New Money for a New World.* Boulder, CO: Qiterra Press, 2005.

Beniger, James R. *The Control Revolution: Technological and Economic Origins of the Information Society.* Cambridge, MA: Harvard University Press, 1986.

Benkler, Yochai. *The Wealth of Networks: How Social Production Transforms Markets and Freedom.* New Haven, CT: Yale University Press, 2006.

Bentham, Jeremy and Etienne Dumont. *Theory of Legislation.* London: K. Paul, Trench, Trubner & Company Limited, 1908.

Berle, Adolf A. and Gardiner C. Means. *The Modern Corporation & Private Property.* New Brunswick: Transaction Publishers, 2010.

Blanning, Tim. *The Romantic Revolution.* New York: Modern Library, 2011.

Bok, Derek. *The Politics of Happiness.* Princeton, NJ: Princeton University Press, 2010.

Bollier, David. *Silent Theft: The Private Plunder of Our Common Wealth*. New York: Rutledge, 2003.

————. *Viral Spiral*. New York: The New Press, 2008.

Bonpasse, Morrison. *The Single Global Currency*. Newcastle, ME: Single Global Currency Association, 2006.

Borbely, Anne-Marie and Jan F. Kreider. *Distributed Generation: The Power Paradigm for the New Millennium*. Washington DC: CRC Press, 2001.

Botsman, Rachel and Roo Rogers. *What's Mine Is Yours: The Rise of Collaborative Consumption*. New York: HarperCollins, 2010.

Boyle, James. *Cultural Environmentalism and Beyond*. San Francisco: Creative Commons, 2007.

Brewer, Richard. *Conservancy: The Land Trust Movement in America*. Hanover, NH: Dartmouth College Press, 2003.

Brock, Gerald W. *The Telecommunications Industry: The Dynamics of Market Structure*. Cambridge, MA: Harvard University Press, 1981.

Bryant, John. *Thermodynamics: A Thermodynamic Approach to Economics*. 2nd ed. Herts, UK: VOCAT International Ltd, 2011.

Brynjolfsson, Erik and Andrew MaAfee. *Race Against the Machine: How the Digital Revolution Is Accelerating Innovation, Driving Productivity, and Irreversibly Transforming Employment and the Economy*. Lexington, MA: Digital Frontier Press, 2011.

Burger, Christoph and Jens Weinmann. *The Decentralized Energy Revolution*. New York: Palgrave Macmillan, 2013.

Carr, Nicholas. *The Big Switch*. New York: W.W. Norton, 2009.

Chambers, Ann. *Distributed Generation*. Tulsa: PennWell Corporation, 2001.

Chandler Jr., Alfred D. *The Visible Hand: The Managerial Revolution in American Business*. Cambridge: The Belknap Press of Harvard University Press, 1977.

Chesbrough, Henry. *Open Innovation*. Boston: Harvard Business School Press, 2006.

Christman, John. *The Myth of Property: Toward an Egalitarian Theory of Ownership*. New York: Oxford University Press, 1994.

Daly, Herman. *Beyond Growth*. Boston: Beacon Press, 1996.

Daly, Hermen E. and John Cobb Jr. *For The Common Good*. Boston: Beacon Press, 1999.

Danielian, Noobar Retheos. *AT&T: The Story of Industrial Conquest*. New York: Vanguard Press, 1939.

Darwin, Charles. *The Variation of Animals and Plants Under Domestication*. Vol. 1. London: John Murray, 1899.

De Forest Sackett, Ross. *Time, Energy, and the Indolent Savage: A Quantitative Cross-Cultural Test of the Primitive Affluence Hypothesis*. Los Angeles: University of California, 1996.

De Grazia, Sebastian. *Of Time, Work, and Liesure*. Garden City, NJ: Anchor Books, 1964.

De Soto, Hernando. *The Mystery of Capital*. New York: Basic Books, 2011.

Dobb, Maurice. *Studies in the Development of Capitalism*. New York: International Publishers, 1947.

Doctorow, Cory. *Over Clocked: Stories of the Future Present*. New York: Thunder's Mouth Press, 2007.

Dugger, William and James Peach. *Economic Abundance: An Introduction*. New York: M.E. Sharpe, 2009.

Dunbar, Robin. *Grooming, Gossip, and the Evolution of Language*. Cambridge, MA: Harvard University Press, 1998.

Eisenstein, Charles. *Sacred Economics: Money, Gift and Society in the Age of Translation*. Berkeley, CA: Evolver Editions, 2011.

Eisenstein, Elizabeth L. *The Printing Revolution in Early Modern Europe*. Cambridge: Cambridge University Press, 1983.

Elkington, John. *The Zeronauts: Breaking the Sustainability Barriers*. Washington, DC: Earth-Scan, 2012.

Epstein, S. R. and Maarten Prak. *Guilds, Innovation and the European Economy, 1400–1800*. Cambridge: Cambridge University Press, 2008.

Faraone, Chris. *99 Nights With the 99 Percent*. United States: Write To Power, 2012.

Ford, Martin. *The Lights in the Future*. United States: Acculant Publishing, 2009.

Frey, Bruno S. *Happiness: A Revolution in Economics*. Cambridge, MA: MIT Press, 2010.

Frieden, Jeffry A. *Global Capitalism*. New York: W.W. Norton, 2006.

Frischmann, Brett M. *Infrastructure: The Social Value of Shared Resources*. USA: Oxford University Press, 2013.

Fyfe, Aileen. *Steam-Powered Knowledge: William Chambers and The Business of Publishing, 1820–1860*. Chicago: University of Chicago Press, 2012.

Ganksky, Lisa. *The Mesh*. New York: Penguin Portfolio, 2010.

Gershenfeld, Neil. *Fab*. New York: Basic Books, 2005.

Ghosh, Rishab. *Code*. Cambridge, MA: MIT Press, 2005.

Gimpel, Jean. *The Medieval Machine: The Industrial Revolution of the Middle Ages*. London: Penguin, 1977.

Graham, Carol. *The Pursuit of Happiness: An Economy of Well-Being*. Washington, DC: Brookings Institution, 2011.

Grazia, Sebastian de. *Of Time, Work, and Leisure*. New York: Anchor Books, 1964.

Greco Jr., Thomas H. *Money: Understanding and Creating Alternatives to Legal Tender*. White River Junction, VT: Chelsea Green, 2001.

Gupta, Shanti. *The Economic Philosophy of Mahatma Gandhi*. New Delhi: Concept Publishing Company, 1994.

Haber, Samuel. *Efficiency and Uplift: Scientific Management in the Progressive Era 1890–1920*. Chicago: University of Chicago Press, 1964.

Habermas, Jurgen. *The Structural Transformation of the Public Sphere*. Cambridge, MA: MIT Press, 1991.

Haidt, Jonathan. *The Happiness Hypothesis*. New York: Basic Books, 2006.

Hannesson, Rognvaldur. *The Privatization of the Oceans*. Cambridge, MA: MIT Press, 2004.

Hart, Sura and Victoria Kindle Hodson. *The Compassionate Classroom: Relationship Based Teaching and Learning*. Encinitas, CA: Puddle Dancer Press, 2004.

Havelock, Eric A. *Preface to Plato*. Cambridge, MA: Belknap Press, 1963.

Hawken, Paul, Amory Lovens, and L. Hunter Lovins. *Natural Capitalism*. New York: Little, Brown, 1999.

Hegel, Georg Wilhelm Friedrich. *Lectures on the Philosophy of World History*. Cambridge: Cambridge University Press, 1975.

Henderson, Hazel. *Ethical Markets*. White River Junction, VT: Chelsea Green, 2006.

Hess, Charlotte and Elinor Ostrom, eds. *Understanding Knowledge as a Commons: From Theory to Practice*. Cambridge, MA: MIT Press, 2007.

Hippel, Eric Von. *Democratizing Innovation*. Cambridge, MA: MIT Press, 2005.

Hobsbawm, E. J. *The Age of Capital 1848–1875*. London: Penguin, 1980.

Hobsbawm, E. J. *The Age of Empire 1875–1914*. New York: Vintage Books, 1987.

Hobsbawm, E. J. *The Age of Revolution 1789–1848*. New York: Mentor, 1962.

Hoeschele, Wolfgang. *The Economics of Abundance: A Political Economy of Freedom, Equity, and Sustainability*. Surrey, UK: Gower, 2010.

Hoyt, Robert S. *Europe in the Middle Ages*. 2nd ed. New York: Harcourt, Brace & World, 1966.

Hume, David. *An Enquiry Concerning the Principles of Morals*. London: Printed for A. Millar, 1751.

Jackson, Tim. *Prosperity Without Growth: Economics for a Finite Planet*. Washington, DC: Earthscan, 2009.

Jean-Claude Debeir, Jean-Paul Deleage, and Daniel Hemery, *In the Servitude of Power: Energy and Civilization Through the Ages*. London: Zed Books, 1992.

Kanigel, Robert. *The One Best Way: Frederick Winslow Taylor and the Enigma of Efficiency*. New York: Penguin, 1997.

Keen, Andrew. *The Cult of the Amateur*. New York: Doubleday, 2007.

Kellmereit, Daniel, and Daniel Obodovski. *The Silent Intelligence: The Internet of Things*. San Francisco: DND Ventures LLC, 2013.

Keynes, John Maynard. *The General Theory Of Employment, Interest, and Money*. San Diego: Harcourt Brace, 1964.

Kleindorfer, Paul R. and Wind Yorman with Robert E. Gunther. *The Network Challenge*. Upper Saddle River, NJ: Wharton School Publishing, 2009.

Klinenberg, Eric. *Going Solo*. New York: Penguin Press, 2012.

Kramer, Matthew H. *John Locke and the Origins of Private Property*. Cambridge: Cambridge University Press, 1997.

Kropotkin, Petr. *Mutual Aid: A Factor of Evolution*. Boston: Extending Horizons Books, 1914.

Kumar, C. Arvind. *Welcome to the 'Free' World: A Free Software Initiative*. Andhra Pradesh: Indian Universities Press, 2011.

Kurzweil, Ray. *The Singularity is Near*. New York: Viking, 2005.

Lane, Robert E. *The Loss of Happiness in Market Democracies*. New Haven, CT: Yale University Press, 2000.

Lanier, Jaron. *You Are not a Gadget*. New York: Vintage Books, 2011.

Layard, Richard. *Happiness: Lessons From a New Science*. New York: Penguin Press, 2005.

Le Goff, Jacques. *Time, Work, & Culture in the Middle Ages*. Chicago: University of Chicago Press, 1980.

Lefebvre, Georges, et al. *The Transition from Feudalism to Capitalism*. London: Versa, 1976.

Lessig, Lawrence. *The Future of Ideas*. New York: Random House, 2001.

Linebaugh, Peter. *The Magna Carta Manifesto*. Berkeley: University of California Press, 2008.

Locke, John. *Two Treatises of Government*. London: Printed for Whitmore and Fenn, Charing Cross; and C. Brown, Duke Street, Lincoln's-Inn-Fields, 1821.

Louv, Richard. *The Nature of Money*. Chapel Hill, NC: Algonquin Paperbacks, 2011.

Lovelock, James. *Gaia: A New Look at Life on Earth*. Oxford: Oxford University Press, 1995.

———. *The Ages of Gaia: A Biography of Our Living Earth*. Oxford: Oxford University Press, 1988.

Lovins, Amory and The Rocky Mountain Institute. *Reinventing Fire*. White River Junction, VT: Chelsea Green, 2011.

Lukacs, John. *Historical Consciousness: The Remembered Past*. New Brunswick, NJ: Transaction, 1994.

MacKinnon, Rebecca. *Consent of the Networked*. New York: Basic Books, 2012.

Macpherson, Crawford B. *Democratic Theory*. Oxford University Press, 1973.

Margulis, Lynn. *Symbiotic Planet*. New York: Basic Books, 1998.

Marsh, Peter. *The New Industrial Revolution*. London: Yale University Press, 2012.

Marvin, Carolyn. *When Old Technologies Were New: Thinking About Electric Communication in the Late Nineteenth Century*. New York: Oxford University Press, 1988.

Marx, Karl. *Capital*. Oxford, UK: Oxford University Press, 1995.

Mason, Paul. *Why It's Kicking Off Everywhere*. London: Verso, 2012.

May, Christopher. *A Global Political Economy of Intellectual Property Rights*. New York: Routledge, 2000.

McMahon, Darren M. *Happiness: A History*. New York: Grove Press, 2006.

More, Thomas. *Utopia*. Rockville, MD: Arc Manor, 2008.

Noble, David F. *Forces of Production: A Social History of Industrial Automation*. Oxford: Oxford University Press, 1984.

Nye, David E. *Electrifying America: Social Meanings of a New Technology, 1880–1940.* Cambridge, MA: MIT Press, 1991.

Ollman, Bertell. *Alienation: Marx's Conception of Man in Capitalist Society.* London: Cambridge University Press, 1971.

Ong, Walter J. *Orality and Literacy.* New York: Methuen, 2002.

Ostrom, Elinor, et al., eds. *The Drama of the Commons.* United States: National Academy of Sciences, 2002.

Ostrom, Elinor. *Governing the Commons: The Evolution of Institutions for Collective Action.* Cambridge: Cambridge University Press, 1990.

Packard, Vance. *The Hidden Persuaders.* Brooklyn: Pocket Books, 1980.

Petrini, Carlo. *Terra Madre.* White River Junction, VT: Chelsea Green, 2009.

Polanyi, Karl. *The Great Transformation: The Political and Economic Origins of Our Time.* Boston: Beacon Press, 1944.

Randall, John Herman Jr. *The Making of the Modern Mind: A Survey of the Intellectual Background of the Present Age.* Cambridge, MA: Riverside Press, 1940.

Raymond, Eric. *The Cathedral and the Bazaar: Musing on Linux and Open Source by an Accidental Revolutionary.* Sebastopol, CA: O'Reilly Media, 2001.

Rifkin, Jeremy. *Biosphere Politics.* New York: Crown, 1991.

Rifkin, Jeremy. *The Age of Access.* New York: Tarcher/Putnam, 2000.

Rifkin, Jeremy. *The Biotech Century.* New York: Tarcher/Putnam, 1998.

Rifkin, Jeremy. *The Empathic Civilization.* New York: Penguin, 2009.

Rifkin, Jeremy. *The End of Work.* New York: Penguin, 1995.

Rifkin, Jeremy. *The Third Industrial Revolution.* New York: Palgrave Macmillan, 2011.

Rowe, Jonathon. *Our Common Wealth.* San Francisco: Berret-Koehler, 2013.

Sahlins, Marshall. *Stone Age Economics.* New York: Aldine De Gruyter, 1972.

Sandel, Michael. *What Money Can't Buy.* New York: Farrar, Straus and Giroux, 2012.

Schewe, Phillip F. *The Grid.* Washington, DC: Joseph Henry Press, 2007.

Schlatter, Richard. *Private Property: The History of an Idea.* New Brunswick, NJ: Rutgers University Press, 1951.

Schor, Juliet B. *Born to Buy: The Commercialized Child and the New Consumer Culture.* New York: Scribner, 2004.

———. *Plenitude: The New Economics of True Wealth.* New York: Penguin Press, 2010.

Schuler, Douglas and Peter Day. *Shaping the Network Society.* Cambridge, MA: MIT Press, 2004.

Sedlacek, Thomas. *Economics of Good and Evil: The Quest for Economic Meaning from Gilgamesh to Wall Street.* Oxford: Oxford University Press, 2011.

Shiva, Vandana. *Water Wars: Privatization, Pollution, and Profit.* Cambridge, MA: South End Press, 2002.

Simmel, Georg. *The Philosophy of Money.* London: Routledge, 2004.

Slater, Gilbert. *The English Peasantry and the Enclosure of the Commons.* New York: A.M. Kelley, 1968.

Smith, Adam. *An Inquiry into the Nature and Causes of the Wealth of Nations.* Edinburgh: Thomas Nelson, 1843.

Sobel, Robert. *Panic on Wall Street: A History of America's Financial Disasters.* Washington, DC: Beard Books, 1999.

Solomon, Elinor Harris. *Virtual Money.* New York: Oxford University Press, 1997.

Spence, Michael. *The Next Convergence.* New York: Farrar, Straus and Giroux, 2011.

Spencer, Herbert. *The Principles of Biology.* Vol. 1. London: Williams and Norgate, 1864.

Sperber, Jonathan. *The European Revolutions, 1848–1851.* Cambridge: Cambridge University Press, 1994.

Stein, Janice Gross. *The Cult of Efficiency.* Toronto: Anansi, 2001.

Steinberg, Theodore. *Slide Mountain.* Berkeley: University of California Press, 1995.

Steiner, Christopher. *Automate This: How Algorithms Came to Rule Our World*. New York: Penguin Group, 2012.

Stover, John F. *American Railroads*. Chicago: University of Chicago Press, 1961.

Suárez-Orozco, Marcelo, ed. *Learning in the Global Era: International Perspectives on Globalization and Education*. Berkeley: University of California Press, 2007.

Surowiecki, James. *The Wisdom of Crowds*. New York: Doubleday, 2004.

Tapscott, Don and Anthony Williams. *MacroWikinomics: Rebooting Business and the World*. New York: Portfolio Penguin, 2010.

Tawney, R. H. *Religion and the Rise of Capitalism*. New Brunswick, NJ: Transaction, 2011.

———. *The Acquisitive Society*. New York: Harcourt, Brace & Co., 1920.

The Dalai Lama and Howard Cutler. *The Art of Happiness*. London: Hodder and Stoughton, 2009.

Thirsk, Joan. *Tudor Enclosures*. London: Historical Association, 1958.

Thompson, E. P. *The Making of the English Working Class*. New York: Vintage Books, 1966.

Tobey, Ronald C. *Technology as Freedom: The New Deal and the Electrical Modernization of the American Home*. Berkeley: University of California Press, 1996.

Turkle, Sherry. *Alone Together*. New York: Perseus Books, 2011.

Turner, Frederick Jackson. *The Frontier in American History*. Tucson: University of Arizona Press, 1994.

Useem, Micheal. *Investor Capitalism*. New York: Basic Books, 1996.

Vietor, Richard H. K. *Contrived Competition: Regulation and Deregulation in America*. Cambridge, MA: Harvard University Press, 1994.

Walljasper, Jay. *All That We Share*. New York: New Press, 2010.

Wann, David. *Simple Prosperity*. New York: St. Martin's Press, 2007.

Weber, Max. *Economy and Society: An Outline of Interpretive Sociology*. Berkeley: University of California Press, 1978.

———. *The Protestant Ethic and the Spirit of Capitalism*. New York: Charles Scribner's Sons, 1958.

Weber, Steven. *The Success of Open Source*. Cambridge, MA: Harvard University Press, 2004.

White, Leslie A. *Modern Capitalism Culture*. Walnut Creek, CA: Left Coast Press, 2008.

White, Lynn Jr. *Medieval Technology and Social Change*. London: Oxford University Press, 1962.

William, James. *The Principles of Psychology*. Vol. 1. New York: Henry Holt, 1890.

Wilson, Edward O. *The Social Conquest of Earth*. New York: Liveright, 2012.

Wu, Tim. *The Master Switch*. New York: Vintage Books, 2009.

Yergen, Daniel. *The Prize*. New York: Simon and Schuster, 1992.

INDEX